Fiscal Decentralization in Developing Countries

Recent years have seen a worldwide trend toward fiscal decentralization. In particular, many developing countries are turning to various forms of fiscal decentralization as an escape from inefficient and ineffective governance, macroeconomic instability, and inadequate growth.

Fiscal Decentralization in Developing Countries, edited by Professors Bird and Vaillancourt and featuring important, original, and up-to-date research from leading scholars, assesses the progress, problems, and potentials of fiscal decentralization in a variety of developing countries around the world. With rich and varied case-study material from countries as diverse as India, China, Colombia, Bosnia-Herzegovina and South Africa, this volume complements neatly the recent collection *Fiscal Aspects of Evolving Federations*, edited by David Wildasin and also published by Cambridge, which presented theoretical advances in the area of research.

Fiscal Decentralization in Developing Countries is the latest volume in the distinguished Cambridge series TRADE AND DEVELOPMENT.

RICHARD M. BIRD is Professor of Economics, University of Toronto and a consultant to the World Bank. He has previously taught at Harvard University and has worked at the Fiscal Affairs Department of the International Monetary Fund.

FRANÇOIS VAILLANCOURT is Professor of Economics, Université de Montréal and a consultant to the World Bank. He has previously been a Visiting Fellow at both the Federalism Research Centre, Australian National University and the Institut d'Etudes Européennes, Brussels, as well as a Visiting Lecturer at the Shastri Institute.

T0339985

TRADE AND DEVELOPMENT

A series of books on international economic relations and economic issues in development

Academic editor
Ron Duncan, *National Centre for Development Studies,*
  The Australian National University

Advisory editors
Ross Garnaut, *The Australian National University*
Reuven Glick, *Federal Reserve Bank of San Francisco*
Enzo R. Grilli, *The World Bank*
Mario B. Lamberte, *Philippine Institute for Development Studies*

Executive editor
Maree Tait, *National Centre for Development Studies,*
  The Australian National University

Other titles in the series
Helen Hughes (ed.), *Achieving Industrialization in East Asia*
Yun-Wing Sung, *The China–Hong Kong Connection: The Key to China's Open Door Policy*
Kym Anderson (ed.), *New Silk Roads: East Asia and World Textile Markets*
Rod Tyers and Kym Anderson, *Disarray in World Food Markets: A Quantitative Assessment*
Enzo R. Grilli, *The European Community and Developing Countries*
Peter Warr (ed.), *The Thai Economy in Transition*
Ross Garnaut, Enzo Grilli, and James Riedel (eds.), *Sustaining Export-Oriented Developments: Ideas from East Asia*
Donald O. Mitchell, Merlinda D. Ingco, and Ronald C. Duncan, *The World Food Outlook*
David C. Cole and Betty F. Slade, *Building a Modern Financial System: The Indonesian Experience*
Ross Garnaut, Guo Shutian, and Ma Guonan (eds.), *The Third Revolution in the Chinese Countryside*
David Robertson (ed.), *East Asian Trade After the Uruguay Round*
Yiping Huang, *Agricultural Reform in China: Getting Institutions Right*
Christopher Manning, *Indonesian Labour in Transition*

Fiscal Decentralization in Developing Countries

EDITED BY
RICHARD M. BIRD
AND
FRANÇOIS VAILLANCOURT

CAMBRIDGE
UNIVERSITY PRESS

CAMBRIDGE UNIVERSITY PRESS
Cambridge, New York, Melbourne, Madrid, Cape Town, Singapore, São Paulo, Delhi

Cambridge University Press
The Edinburgh Building, Cambridge CB2 8RU, UK

Published in the United States of America by Cambridge University Press, New York

www.cambridge.org
Information on this title: www.cambridge.org/9780521641432

First published 1998
This digitally printed version 2008

A catalogue record for this publication is available from the British Library

Library of Congress Cataloguing in Publication data

Fiscal decentralization in developing countries / edited by Richard M. Bird, François
Vaillancourt.
    p.   cm. – (Trade and development)
ISBN 0 521 64143 8 (hardbound)
1. Fiscal policy – Developing countries. 2. Intergovernmental fiscal relations –
Developing countries. 3. Decentralization in government – Developing countries. I. Bird,
Richard Miller, 1938–. II. Vaillancourt, François. III. Series: Trade and development
(Cambridge, England)
HJ1620.F538   1999
336.1′8′091724 – dc21   98-20491   CIP

ISBN 978-0-521-64143-2 hardback
ISBN 978-0-521-10158-5 paperback

Contents

Tables

Contributors

Junaid K. Ahmad, *World Bank*
Roy W. Bahl, *Georgia State University*
Richard M. Bird, *University of Toronto*
Ariel Fiszbein, *World Bank*
William Fox, *University of Tennessee*
M. Govinda Rao, *Australian National University*
Ernesto Rezk, *Universidad Nacional de Córdoba*
Anwar Shah, *World Bank*
François Vaillancourt, *Université de Montréal*
Christine Wallich, *World Bank*

Preface

Interest in fiscal decentralization has grown greatly all over the world in recent years. The public finances of many developed economies have to varying degrees become more decentralized as one way of attempting to accommodate the fiscal realities of the "post-welfare state" era. Throughout eastern and central Europe new systems of local and intergovernmental finance are being established as part of the evolution away from the old central planning system. Finally, an increasing number of developing countries are turning to various forms of fiscal decentralization as one possible way of escaping from the traps of ineffective and inefficient governance, macroeconomic instability, and inadequate economic growth in which so many of them have become mired in more recent years. Discussion of various aspects and issues of fiscal decentralization is thus in the air more or less everywhere these days. Economic theorists are theorizing about fiscal decentralization, applied economists are attempting to measure its potential effects in various dimensions, and policy economists are busily flying around the world dispensing advice about it.

In many developing countries, moreover, fiscal decentralization is not only in the air but also, to varying degrees, already on the ground. The studies in this book describe and analyze some of the many varieties of fiscal decentralization found throughout the developing world. Although what has happened in the ten very different countries covered here can in no sense be considered a representative sample, these case studies should prove of considerable interest to a wide variety of readers both in developing countries and in the increasingly wide circles of those throughout the world, whether in the private or public sectors, on whose activities and interests the manifold and changing dimensions of intergovernmental fiscal relations described here will impinge, whether they realize it yet or not.

The contributions to this volume were originally presented at the

PARADI/ICTS* Conference held in Montreal, Canada on September 19–20, 1996. They were subsequently revised and edited for inclusion in this volume, together with an initial overview chapter prepared by the editors. We thank André Martens, director of PARADI, who first suggested that this conference be organized. We are also most grateful not only to the various authors represented here, but also to the discussants and commentators whose inputs are reflected in the volume: Leonard Dudley, Nicolas Marceau, Louis Massicotte, David Sewell, France St-Hilaire, William Watson, and Stanley Winer. In addition, we are extremely grateful for the financial support provided by the International Development Research Centre (IDRC), the PARADI Program, and the Social Sciences and Humanities Research Council of Canada. Finally, we acknowledge the indispensable administrative support provided by Marie-Christine Thirion in Montreal and the substantial assistance provided by Duanjie Chen in Toronto. Coordinating nine papers on ten countries by ten authors currently living in five countries has not been the easiest task we have ever undertaken, but it has proved surprisingly pleasant, and we think that the results are worth it.

Richard M. Bird
François Vaillancourt

* The Programme d'analyses et de recherches économiques appliquées au développement international (PARADI) is funded by the Canadian International Development Agency (CIDA). The institutions affiliated with the PARADI program are the Centre de recherche et développement en économique (CRDE) of the Université de Montréal and the Centre de recherche en économie et finance appliquées (CREFA) of the Université Laval. The International Centre for Tax Studies (ICTS) is located at the Faculty of Management of the University of Toronto.

1

Fiscal decentralization in developing countries: an overview

RICHARD M. BIRD AND FRANÇOIS VAILLANCOURT

Recent years have seen worldwide interest in fiscal decentralization. Developed countries are reshaping their intergovernmental fiscal structure to be more in tune with the realities of the "post-welfare state" (Bennett, 1990; Wildasin, 1997a).[1] The countries in transition in eastern and central Europe are busily setting up new systems of local and intergovernmental finance (Bird, Ebel, and Wallich, 1995). Many developing countries are also turning to various forms of fiscal decentralization as one possible way of escaping from the traps of ineffective and inefficient governance, macroeconomic instability, and inadequate economic growth in which so many of them have become mired in recent years.[2] Each country does what it does for its own peculiar reasons, but when so many countries in so many different circumstances do somewhat similar things, there is likely to be more at work than meets the local eye. The principal purpose of this book is to take stock of the progress, problems, and potentials of fiscal decentralization in developing countries by bringing together a set of studies from a variety of countries around the world.

Decentralization in developing countries sometimes seems to be viewed as either a panacea or a plague – either a cure for all the ills of such countries or an addition to their already heavy burdens. Some argue for decentralization on grounds of improved economic efficiency, some on grounds of cost efficiency, some in terms of improved accountability, and some in terms of increased resource mobilization.[3] On the other hand, others argue that none of these virtuous outcomes is likely to be achieved in countries in which citizen preferences are unlikely to be reflected in budget outcomes and the institutional capacity of existing subnational (state and local) governments is close to nil.[4] From this perspective, decentralization seems likely to result in increased costs, lessened efficiency in service delivery, and probably greater inequity and macroeconomic instability (Prud'homme, 1995).

In general terms, it is not difficult to defend and elaborate either side of this controversy. With respect to efficiency, for example, the standard

1

economic view is that the existence of different tax-spending packages in different jurisdictions, coupled with individual mobility, is sufficient to ensure that there will be efficiency-producing interjurisdictional competition in service provision (Tiebout, 1956). Similarly, empirical evidence from a number of countries supports the proposition that locally controlled services are likely to be provided at lower costs than centrally provided ones (Campbell, Peterson, and Brakarz, 1991). On the other hand, reaping these benefits appears to require the prior existence of such rare conditions in developing countries as significant local administrative capacity and locally responsive and responsible officials with substantial discretionary financial control (Bahl and Linn, 1994).

Interesting as such generalities may be, they largely miss the mark. The essence of decentralization is that it does not occur *in general* but rather in a particular country – in a country with its own history and traditions and its own specific institutional, political, and economic context. Moreover, as the various case studies in this book demonstrate, decentralization has taken many different forms in different countries at different times, and even exactly the same variety of decentralization may have very different effects under different conditions – compare, for example, the decentralization in Morocco with that in Tunisia (Vaillancourt, this volume), two countries similar in language, religion, and colonial administrative legacy.

As the ten case studies that constitute the bulk of this book illustrate, economic theorists are theorizing about fiscal decentralization, applied economists are attempting to measure its effects in various dimensions, and policy economists are busily flying around the world dispensing advice about it. But just what is meant by fiscal decentralization? What advice does the academic literature suggest should be given? And how does this advice relate to what is actually taking place in the real world? In this first chapter we attempt both to answer these questions to provide some general background to the case studies that follow and also to draw some general conclusions relevant to these questions from those case studies.

In the next section, we discuss what fiscal decentralization is and why it is a matter of policy concern. We then provide a brief quantitative overview of the extent and nature of fiscal decentralization in the countries covered in this volume and, for comparison, in a few others as well. But numbers alone cannot depict adequately the complex institutional reality that constitutes fiscal decentralization in any country. The third section of this chapter therefore sketches briefly some of the important patterns of fiscal decentralization to be found in the world, referring to some of the key points developed in more detail in the country analyses that constitute the bulk of this book. Finally, in the concluding section of the chapter, we draw some general lessons from the very diverse experiences recounted here with respect to both the substance and the process of fiscal decentralization in developing countries.

Fiscal decentralization: what and why?

Four questions are addressed in this section. First, how do we define "fiscal decentralization" and assess its success? Second, what macroeconomic questions are associated with decentralization, and, in particular, how should subnational borrowing be managed? Third, how do local managerial capacity and local taxation impact on decentralization? Fourth, what do theory and experience suggest are necessary and sufficient conditions for "successful" fiscal decentralization?

Definition and assessment

Three varieties of fiscal decentralization may be distinguished, corresponding to the degree of independent decision-making exercised at the local level.[5] First, *deconcentration* means the dispersion of responsibilities within a central government to regional branch offices or local administrative units.[6] Second, *delegation* refers to a situation in which local governments act as agents for the central government, executing certain functions on its behalf. Third, *devolution* refers to a situation in which not only implementation but also the authority to decide what is done is in the hands of local governments.[7]

How one assesses decentralization clearly depends in part upon whether what has occurred is best characterized as deconcentration, delegation, or devolution. It also depends upon whether one views decentralization from the top down or from the bottom up (Bird, 1980). The approach to fiscal decentralization from the *bottom up* generally stresses political values – improved governance in the sense of local responsiveness and political participation, for example – as well as allocative efficiency in terms of improving welfare (as in the decentralization theorem of Oates, 1972). The political literature is replete with passages praising the virtues of decentralization. Not only will it produce more efficient and equitable service delivery through making better use of local knowledge, but it will also, so we are sometimes told, lead to greater participation and democracy and hence result in more popular support for government, and presumably in improved political stability. When to these good qualities are added such further ascribed virtues as increased resource mobilization and reduced strain on central finances, greater accountability, and more responsive and responsible government in general, it is not surprising that some have seen decentralization to be *intrinsically* valuable.

Whatever the precise outcomes of adopting a decentralized (in the sense of devolved) system of decision-making, such outcomes are presumed, from this perspective, to be satisfactory simply because the process itself is intrinsically desirable. Local people may make wrong decisions from the perspective of the central government or of an outside observer, but if *they* make them, the decisions must, by definition, be assumed to be right for them. From this perspective, then, decentralization is intrinsically good because it institutionalizes the participation of those affected by local decisions. The results of a good process must themselves be good.

But matters may not seem so clear if one looks at the process from the top down, rather than from the bottom up. From the *top down* (the central government) the rationale for decentralization may be, for example, to make the life of the central government easier by shifting deficits (or at least some of the political pressures resulting from deficits) downward.[8] Or it may be a desire on the part of the central government to achieve its allocative goals more efficiently by delegating or decentralizing authority to local governments, as appears to have been the case to some extent in Colombia (Bird and Fiszbein, this volume) and Indonesia (Shah, this volume). The goal of the central government may even be to increase the level of national welfare, as often assumed in theoretical discussion (for example, Boadway, Roberts, and Shah, 1993). Whatever the rationale, this top-down approach suggests that the main criterion for evaluating fiscal decentralization should be how well it serves the presumed national policy objectives.

An initial problem in analyzing fiscal decentralization in any specific setting is thus to determine whether a "good" fiscal decentralization is one which better achieves the goals of the central government (or improves national welfare as a whole, if one prefers) or one which frees local governments most from central dictates (or, if one prefers, improves local welfare most). Decentralization may have many virtues: it may, for instance, improve accessibility, local responsibility, and the effectiveness of government. But it is not likely to yield, for instance, precisely the same expenditure pattern the central government would choose to implement except in the extremely unlikely case that the goals of central and local government precisely coincide. In a geographically heterogeneous society, this is simply not possible. Conflicts between central and local governments as to what should be done are inevitable, even if each government tries faithfully to serve the interests of its (different mix of) constituents.

The choice of perspective is thus essential in approaching issues of fiscal decentralization. The bottom-up perspective may be particularly appropriate for countries like India (Rao, this volume), South Africa (Ahmad, this volume) or Bosnia-Herzegovina (Fox and Wallich, this volume) in which heterogeneity among different territorial units on various dimensions is high, and to a considerable extent reflects political decisions intended to make the national state at least potentially viable. In most of the other countries covered in this volume, however, as in developing countries more generally (Bird, 1993), the top-down perspective seems more likely to be appropriate. In China, for example, Bahl (this volume) suggests that the recent reforms of taxation and intergovernmental finance were intended (1) to reassert macroeconomic control and (2) to secure adequate resources for the central government to achieve such objectives as developing important interregional infrastructure.[9]

Macroeconomic aspects of decentralization

The stringent conditions for successful decentralization have recently been emphasized with respect to developing countries.[10] In particular, it has been argued that not only may decentralization fail to improve local service delivery, it may even risk national destabilization. This risk is greatest when revenues are decentralized without adequate steps being taken to ensure both that local revenue mobilization is maintained and that local authorities are capable of carrying out the corresponding expenditure responsibilities. Argentina in the 1980s is a commonly cited example,[11] but others are not hard to find in the transitional economies of eastern and central Europe (Bird, Ebel, and Wallich, 1995). As just noted, similar fears appear to have played an important role in the recent Chinese fiscal reforms (Bahl, this volume).

International experience indeed suggests that if countries decentralize more expenditure responsibilities than revenue resources, either service levels will likely fall or else local governments will press – successfully, it is usually assumed – for either more transfers, or more loans, or both. One of the clearest, and most analyzed, cases exhibiting this phenomenon is the Russian Federation (Wallich, 1994). On the other hand, if more revenues than expenditures are decentralized, it is often argued that local revenue mobilization may decline and again macroeconomic imbalances may emerge.[12] Countries such as Colombia, Argentina, and Brazil are frequently cited as bad examples in this respect.[13] Even if both sides of the budget are decentralized in a balanced fashion, it is often feared that local governments may not have adequate administrative or technical capacity to carry out their new functions in a satisfactory fashion.[14] Such problems may give rise to particular concern in developing countries where local governments are charged with important social and economic infrastructure investments (Bird, 1994a) – an aspect stressed in this volume in the chapter on Morocco and Tunisia.

In view of the apparent widespread concern about the destabilizing effects of fiscal decentralization, it may surprise some readers that some of the case studies in this book – see especially those on Colombia and South Africa – lend little support to the more dire predictions of macroeconomic disaster ensuing from fiscal decentralization. Nonetheless, such concerns continue to rank high in many countries, and care must clearly be taken to avoid unwanted outcomes in this respect. The key to unlocking this problem, we shall argue, is to ensure that decentralization is undertaken in such a fashion as to increase rather than decrease accountability.

Concern for macro imbalance lies behind the common recommendation that strict limits be imposed on the borrowing ability of subnational governments.[15] Some fear that, unchecked, subnational governments, particularly those highly dependent on national transfers, may increase current expenditures well above their capacity to finance them out of current revenues and then close the gap through borrowing. Others argue that since macroeconomic stabilization is properly a national government task, it is important that the national government have full control over all the instruments of policy it needs to carry out this task properly, including borrowing – and particularly borrowing abroad.

Such arguments (or variants of them) have been made in many countries, and the result has often been the imposition of a variety of restraints on provincial and local borrowing, for example, limiting such borrowing to financing capital expenditures, limiting debt service to a maximum percentage of current revenues, or requiring prior approval of central government for borrowing (Bird, Ebel, and Wallich, 1995).

In fact, however, a properly designed local finance system would not appear to require any specific controls on debt beyond those imposed by a well-functioning private capital market – something which may not, of course, be considered to exist yet in many developing countries. With respect to foreign borrowing by subnational governments, however, there may be a special problem owing to the apparent assumption by many lenders that all "public" debt is (implicitly) guaranteed by the central government. A possible (partial) solution to this problem might be through "semi-privatizing" subnational borrowing as much as possible, for example, through "revenue bonds" which are guaranteed explicitly and solely by specific (related) revenue sources. This approach would have the additional virtue of increasing one of the potential advantages of decentralizing public borrowing in the first place – namely, risk diversification – by increasing the (so to speak) portfolio of public debt on offer, assuming (as seems not implausible) that the revenue streams attributable to different components of the public sector are not highly correlated.[16]

Imposing debt limits to prevent local governments from making fiscal mistakes may produce more perverse results than the public insurance of savings deposits so often condemned by economists. Like deposit insurance, debt limits and similar controls may be perverse precisely because they prevent market discipline from being applied (see Ahmad, this volume). Potential lenders to governments, unlike ordinary citizens choosing a bank in which to place their savings, can reasonably be expected to be capable and motivated with respect to finding out what risks they are running with their money. From this perspective, much of the concern about irresponsible local governments getting themselves into trouble seems like another instance of inappropriate and misconceived paternalism – the "father knows best" attitude so common with central governments facing the uncomfortable prospect of losing control as a result of decentralization. In life, children seldom learn to save unless they suffer the consequences of not having done so. And local governments are as unlikely to be well managed if they are saved from the possibility of making mistakes by the imposition of arbitrary limits as they are if they know they will always be bailed out by the central government.

If a national government wants to avoid macro problems arising from subnational debt, it can do so by not subsidizing such borrowing and by letting subnational governments that borrow too much go bankrupt. This is exactly what was done in Morocco, where the government changed the subsidy scheme for local governments from one of budget-balancing grants, in which both capital and interest payments on loans increase transfer receipts, to a formula-based equalization transfer which takes no account of borrowing (Vaillancourt, this volume). In addition, lenders were explicitly told not to count on financial bail-outs.[17] The possible problems arising from misguided foreign borrowing, however, may require more careful national attention, for instance, requiring explicit prior approval from the central government before any such loans may be contracted.

Unless subnational governments are able, so to speak, to "save themselves" from fiscal crises by drawing on their taxing powers, however, their only options in practice in many countries may be bankruptcy or bailout. In the end, the only way to reduce the moral hazard implicit in this situation may be by imposing strict limits on subnational borrowing. What needs to be emphasized, however, is that the root of the problem lies in the very limited taxing powers available to subnational governments that are expected and required to carry out a much wider range of functions than they can finance on their own without extensive reliance on central support (either direct through transfers or indirect through bail-outs).[18] Unless local "ownership" of the tax base is extended considerably beyond the narrow limits existing in most developing countries (see later discussion) it may not be desirable to loosen borrowing rules.

The difficulty of envisioning, let alone carrying out, bankruptcy in the public sector provides good reason to require that there be fairly stringent conditions on all subnational borrowing – not for macro reasons, however, but in order to ensure local government accountability. Along the same lines, all local borrowing should be reported immediately and in a transparent fashion so that no one can shift hidden debts onto the next administration, and so that both local voters and the national government can have a better handle on what is going on. Moreover, since the only case for local borrowing – and it is a good one – is to finance capital investment, no borrowing should be permitted for other purposes, no matter how worthy.[19]

Finally, one matter that sometimes gives rise to concern appears to be largely a non-problem, namely, the ability of local governments to borrow on the basis of the increased cash flow as a result of transfers (or, for that matter, royalties). As long as the borrowing is not subsidized, why is this a problem? The portion of these transfers that is not specifically earmarked constitutes "own revenues" of local governments, and if some agency is willing to lend money based on this security it should be free both to do so and to bear the consequences if the loan goes bad. Of course, transfers make good security only if they are predictable, which has by no means always been the case in developing countries (Bird, 1990). Generally, transfers are more likely to be used for this purpose when they are enshrined in law (Tunisia) or, even better, in the constitution (Colombia, Argentina, South Africa), than when, as in Morocco, they are made by ministerial directive or, as in China, effectively negotiated on an *ad hoc* basis.

Local capacity and taxation

An essential ingredient in improving the life of the poor in many countries, both immediately and in terms of enhanced productivity in the long run, is the improvement of basic infrastructure – roads, water, sewerage, and electricity (World Bank, 1994). A number of countries have used intergovernmental transfers to guide and shape local investments in these areas, as emphasized, for example, in the chapter on Morocco and Tunisia.

Similarly, in Indonesia, specific grants are provided for provincial and district road improvement (Shah and Qureshi, 1994; Shah this volume). The program is designed to provide minimum standards of road service across the nation and to facilitate the development of an internal common market. The grant allocation formula is related positively to indicators of poor roads and low motor vehicle registrations (proxies for road expenditure needs). As in the case of other Indonesian transfers, local discretion in the use of this grant is restricted, which may limit its effectiveness. The use of the grant is confined to the repair and upgrading of existing roads: new roads have to be financed from other sources. Projects for the repair of roads have to be approved by districts and then forwarded to the central government.

Some have been concerned that local governments subject to less detailed guidance and control than in this case may not have the capacity to handle such critical functions. Colombia, for example, has a much less "guided" system, which nonetheless appears to have been moderately successful in directing infrastructure investment to the poor (World Bank, 1996c). Under the so-called "coparticipation" system, local communities provide labor and local materials, and municipal governments contribute a portion of the cost. This fund not only fosters community involvement in identifying needs and choosing projects but also promotes community participation in the execution, operation, and maintenance of the works. Municipalities have to prepare projects which are then appraised by the fund against technical and environmental criteria. The other important requirement is that the beneficiaries should be low-income rural families. Projects may be carried out by any of a number of types of contractor (private firms, non-government organizations, state agencies, or universities), who compete to supply the works and services.

Although partial and preliminary, the evidence so far concerning local capacity to carry out such functions in Colombia is surprisingly encouraging. A recent study of a sample of sixteen municipalities found numerous beneficial results of decentralization in terms of the enhancement of local capacity in the areas of labor, capital, and technology (World Bank, 1995a). Colombian municipalities are, for example, increasing the skills of local bureaucracies through such means as competitive hiring, sharing the services of professionals among municipalities, training municipal employees, and rotating personnel through different departments in the same municipality. Capacity in terms of capital has also been increased. One municipality has totally privatized road maintenance; another has put private developers in charge of the construction of urban roads.[20] Computers have been introduced to monitor water and sanitation services in other localities. Municipalities have started to share certain equipment. They have also improved their technological capability in terms of internal organization, planning, and monitoring to ensure better management of municipal projects.

Underlying these improvements is a more basic change: Colombian municipalities have been moving to a "demand-driven" (bottom-up) approach to public services as opposed to the previous "supply-driven" (top-down) one. Increasingly, reflecting both the new liveliness of local politics and (with substantial variations from area to area) more extensive community participation, people are getting what they want, rather than what someone in the capital thinks they should want. In practice, emphasis has been put on roads, education, and water projects: these are the needs people perceive, and these are the needs that the newly empowered and responsive local governments are attempting to satisfy. Opinion surveys suggest that the resulting sectoral allocation of resources is consistent with community preferences, with most respondents indicating that they trust the local government more than the national government to deliver goods and services (World Bank, 1995a).

All this is most encouraging for believers in the potential allocative and democratic virtues of decentralization. As in such well-known Asian cases as the Orangi project in Karachi, Pakistan (Bird, 1995), such popular participation both reveals strong preferences for the project being built and tends to keep costs down. Depending on the precise nature of the project, such community involvement may also enhance substantially the effectiveness of "targeting" in terms of poverty alleviation. Participants in such communal work projects are in effect "self-selected," being poor and willing enough to volunteer their major asset, their labor, without remuneration.

A recent review of experience with the social investment funds set up on roughly similar lines in a number of Latin American countries (Glaessner *et al.*, 1994) concluded that such funds have proved to be generally effective because

(1) they have been demand-driven, thus requiring a high degree of local involvement,
(2) their operations have been transparent and hence accountable,
(3) they have been carefully targeted to low-income groups, and
(4) they have been relatively autonomous in their operation, usually being run by private-sector managers and freed from much official red tape.

Most important is the direct involvement of the beneficiary groups in both the management of the fund, and in the selection, operation, and financing of projects. In particular, it appears to be critical to require cost-sharing from even the poorest communities – usually their contribution takes the form of land and labor – on the well-founded grounds that people take more interest in what they have to pay for and are hence more likely to be interested in ensuring that they get value for their contributions. On the whole, Latin American experience clearly shows that it is possible to deliver local public services relatively effectively and efficiently even in the face of adverse macroeconomic circumstances and, in some cases, very poorly functioning public administrations. Where there is a will, the way seems to have been shown.

As for local *taxes*, the "correct" revenue assignment in a multi-level government structure is by no means clear in principle, and is generally controversial in practice. The fundamental problems are twofold. First, the central government can inherently collect most taxes more efficiently than can local governments. Second, the potential tax bases that can be reached by the latter vary widely from region to region. The first of these problems gives rise to vertical imbalance; the second produces horizontal imbalance.[21]

Two basic principles of assigning revenues to subnational governments may be suggested. First, "own-source" revenues should ideally be sufficient to enable at least the richest subnational governments to finance from their own resources all locally provided services primarily benefitting local residents. Second, to the greatest extent possible, subnational revenues should be collected from local residents only, preferably in relation to the perceived benefits they receive from local services. More specifically, among the characteristics that might be sought in an "ideal" subnational tax are the following:

(1) the tax base should be relatively immobile, to allow local authorities some leeway in varying rates without losing most of their tax base;
(2) the tax yield should be adequate to meet local needs and sufficiently buoyant over time (that is, it should expand at least as fast as expenditures);
(3) the tax yield should be relatively stable and predictable over time;
(4) it should not be possible to export much, if any, of the tax burden to non-residents;
(5) the tax base should be visible, to ensure accountability;
(6) the tax should be perceived to be reasonably fair by taxpayers;
(7) the tax should be relatively easy to administer efficiently and effectively.

Not everyone would agree that all these characteristics are necessarily or equally desirable – for example, is it unequivocally good that local governments should be insulated from either the tax base consequences of their tax rate choices or from inflation? Moreover, it is by no means simple to draw from the array of (subjective) information any clear conclusions about different possible local taxes that may be included within this framework. But some candidates come to mind, as discussed to varying extents in the country studies included in this volume, notably property taxes, taxes on automobiles, and, perhaps most importantly if local governments are to have major expenditure responsibilities (for example, for education), some form of surcharge on national taxes. Most of the desired (and desirable) aims of decentralized revenue policy may be achieved solely by allowing variation of the rates of such surcharges, perhaps subject to a constraint on minimum rates to restrict competition for tax base. In addition, since "tax-exporting" breaks the critical link between local spending decisions and the taxes borne by local residents, care should also be taken to prevent provinces from exporting their tax burdens – for example, by limiting access to the taxation of business.

Conditions for success

Experience in a variety of settings suggests that two conditions seem particularly important for successful decentralization, whether success is defined in terms of macro balance or micro efficiency. First, the local decision process must be *democratic* in the sense that the costs and benefits of decisions are transparent and that all those affected have an opportunity to influence the decision. Given the inevitable imperfection of democratic institutions, and the ability of the rich and powerful to come out on top in most systems, this is obviously a counsel of perfection. Nevertheless, the implication is clearly that decentralization means something quite different in countries such as China, Indonesia, and others in this volume that are notably not democratic in this sense than in others such as Argentina and South Africa that, on the whole, are. In the terms used earlier, in the absence of meaningful local democracy, only the "top-down" delegation approach seems to make sense.

Second, and more amenable to policy design, the costs of local decisions must be fully borne by those who make the decisions. That is, there should be no significant "tax-exporting," and no funding at the margin from transfers from other levels of government.[22] This means that local governments need to control the rates (and perhaps bases) of at least some taxes. When these rather strict conditions are satisfied, *devolution* is sensible, whether viewed instrumentally or intrinsically. When they are not, it may not be.

Even when one or more of the conditions set out above does not hold, the *delegation* of implementation responsibilities to local bodies may still make *instrumental* sense provided that the incentives facing local decision-makers are properly structured, that is, structured to produce the results desired by the central government (in its capacity as representing the population as a whole). In the absence of the right incentive structure, the effects of either delegation or devolution on the efficiency and equity of resource allocation may be much less beneficial than often alleged. What is required for decentralization to produce efficient outcomes is what has been called a *hard budget constraint* with respect to devolved functions in order to ensure accountability, combined with incentive-compatible rules (prices, monitoring) with respect to delegated functions (Bird, 1993).

Accountability is a complex concept, with many dimensions. Political accountability requires political leaders at all levels to be responsive and responsible to their constituents, and those constituents to be fully informed about the consequences of their (and their leaders') decisions. Administrative accountability requires a clear legal framework with respect to who is responsible for what, what financial reports are to be made in what form, to whom, and when, and so on. Economic accountability requires that local residents are responsible for paying for local services, which in turn requires that local authorities can set some tax rates. The critical point in this respect is accountability *at the margin*. It is perfectly possible (in principle) for a local government to be 90 percent dependent on central transfers and still be fully accountable – to its citizens and/or the central government, depending on circumstances.[23] For this reason, the best form of intergovernmental transfer is one the amount of which is fixed in advance and will not be altered as a result of any (in-period) action by the recipient (Ahmad and Thomas, 1997). Such a lump-sum transfer by formula implies that, at the margin, local actions to raise or lower local revenues or expenditures will directly affect outcomes – which is what is needed to ensure accountability.[24]

If decentralization is to work, those charged with providing local infrastructure and services must be accountable both to those who pay for them and to those who benefit from them. Unfortunately, enforcing accountability at the local level is not easy. It requires not only clear incentives from above but also the provision of adequate information to local constituents as well as the opportunity for them to exercise some real influence or control over the service delivery system. "Informal" organizations must be structured like this almost by definition or they cannot exist. But it can be a challenge in the political and social circumstances of many developing countries to introduce a similar degree of responsiveness into formal governmental organizations.

Just as accountability is the key to improved public sector performance, information is the key to accountability. The systematic collection, analysis, and reporting of information that can be used to verify compliance with goals and to assist future decisions is a critical element in any decentralization program. Such information is essential both to informed public participation through the political process and to the monitoring of local activity by central agencies responsible for supervising and (usually) partially financing such activity. Unless local "publics" are made aware of what is done, how well it is done, how much it cost, and who paid for it, no local constituency for effective government can be created. Unless central agencies monitor and evaluate local performance, there can be no assurance that functions of national importance will be adequately performed once they have been decentralized.

An important accompaniment to any top-down decentralization program is thus an improvement in national evaluation capacity. Decentralization and evaluation (for example, using cost-benefit analysis) are not substitutes; they are complements. Another essential element of the "hard budget constraint" system needed to induce efficient local decisions is adequate central enforcement capacity in the shape of credible information-gathering and evaluation. The "carrot" of central financial support of local efforts must be accompanied by the "stick" of withdrawn support if performance is inadequate, which of course requires both some standard of adequacy and some way of knowing whether performance is satisfactory.

Various mechanisms for building such evaluative capacity into a decentralization program are conceivable. One might be to build "sunset" provisions into the program, that is, to provide that (say) the newly prominent role given to local institutions in the water supply area will be subject to renewal in a number of years, provided they pass some kind of independent evaluation of their performance. As noted in Bird and Fiszbein (this volume), such a sunset clause was incorporated in Colombia's 1991 constitutional reform. Another approach, as in India (Rao, this volume), may be to establish a Finance Commission to re-examine intergovernmental fiscal relations periodically and adjust them if necessary. South Africa has adopted a somewhat similar approach with its Financial and Fiscal Commission (Ahmad, this volume). A quite different approach might be to use the likely need for some centrally supported access to capital markets to finance local infrastructure not only as a screening device to reject obviously flawed projects but also as an evaluation system to build up "ratings" of local capacity.[25]

A quantitative overview of fiscal decentralization

The way in which any country organizes its public sector invariably reflects its history, its geography, its political balance, its policy objectives, and other characteristics that vary sharply from country to country. Nonetheless, since all countries, except perhaps the very smallest, have more than one level of government, they necessarily all have some kind of intergovernmental fiscal system. Four big questions must be answered with respect to intergovernmental finance in any country:

(1) Who does what? – the question of expenditure assignment.
(2) Who levies what taxes? – the question of revenue assignment.
(3) How is the (virtually inevitable) imbalance between the revenues and expenditures of subnational governments that results from the answers to the first two questions to be resolved? – the question of vertical imbalance.
(4) To what extent should fiscal institutions attempt to adjust for the differences in needs and capacities among different governmental units at the same level of government? – the question of horizontal imbalance, or equalization.

Ideally, these questions should be approached in the specific circumstances of each country in a manner that is consistent with achieving the relevant policy objectives – not only the normal public finance trio of efficiency (allocation), equity (distribution) and stabilization but also economic growth, as well as such nebulous (but politically resonant) goals as "regional balance." In many instances, of course, there will be conflicts not only between these objectives but also between local and central perceptions of the weights to be attached to them. Moreover, like all public policies, intergovernmental fiscal policies must be developed taking into account both political constraints (for example, the strength of different regions and groups in political decisions) and economic constraints (for example, the stage of development of financial markets) facing policymakers. Finally, all policy changes proposed must of course start from the given set of initial conditions: every country has a history, and the current state of its fiscal institutions in large part reflects the product of an accretionary process of policy change over time.

Any country's intergovernmental finance system inevitably reflects in many ways the complex reality of the country. Clearly, countries differ on many dimensions with respect to intergovernmental finance: how many local governments are there? What are their relative sizes in terms of population and economic activity? How different are they in terms of per capita income? Natural resource wealth? What are the historical origins of the move to fiscal decentralization: bottom-up or top-down, peaceful or violent? What is the geography of the country: compact or dispersed? How homogeneous is it: in terms of language, in its ethnic groups, and in its unifying cultural myths? To what extent do state boundaries coincide with heterogeneity in any of these dimensions? Are regional interests explicitly represented in the central political structure? How?

Moreover, large countries tend to have more complex and formal systems of intergovernmental finance, often explicitly "federal" in nature.[26] Developing countries tend to face different problems, and possibilities, than developed countries in this as in other areas, in part arising from political instability, in part reflecting their economic status, and in part from lesser technical capacity. And countries in the process of transition from a central-planning to a more "market-oriented" environment have still different problems – for example, with respect to privatization and the allocation of assets among governments.[27]

Given this enormous variety, the optimal (not to mention feasible) solutions to intergovernmental fiscal problems will be quite different from country to country, depending upon where they are starting and what they are trying to do.[28] Nonetheless, although comparative analysis is most unlikely to yield a clear prescription as to what should be done at one particular time in one particular country, it may be helpful in understanding just how and why certain institutional structures work (or do not work) in particular circumstances.[29] While subject to misinterpretation in the absence of complete knowledge of all relevant aspects of the institutions and settings being compared, reference to experience abroad is often the only guide available and, despite its obvious limitations, such experience may provide useful lessons in assessing the potential strengths and weaknesses of decentralization in any country.

In particular, the reasons for success or failure, so far as they can be discerned, may help focus attention on some key factors in the process and at best may highlight a feature that appears to require more emphasis if success is to be achieved. At the very least, a comparative approach may help correct the belief, sometimes held by otherwise well-informed people, to the effect that there must be a simple solution in existence somewhere that could replace the seemingly unending complexity and negotiation characterizing intergovernmental financial arrangements in their own country.

Some international comparisons

How important is subnational spending? Bahl and Linn (1992) found that between 6 percent and 50 percent of total government spending, with an average of 23 percent, was accounted for by local governments in the twenty-one developing countries for which they had data. For ten developed countries, OECD (1991) found the comparable range to be from 12 percent to 53 percent, with an average of 26 percent. On the other hand, using a different source, and sample, Bird (1995) found an average local expenditure share of 22 percent for 18 developed countries and only 9 percent for 16 developing countries.[30] Comparative data on the importance of local (and other subnational) spending are surprisingly hard to find, and to interpret. Nonetheless, it is probably safe to say that, on the whole, the degree of fiscal decentralization in terms of spending tends to be greater in richer than in poorer countries (Wasylenko, 1987), but that there is considerable variation within each of these groups, however defined.

An alternative, though clearly less satisfactory, way of indicating the relative importance of subnational governments is in terms of the proportion of central government expenditure that goes to subnational governments in the form of transfers. From this perspective, there appears to be no necessary relation between the level of a country's development, the size of its central government, and the importance of subnational fiscal transfers. For example, Bird (1995) found that on average local governments in the industrial countries in his sample financed only 62 percent of their expenditures from their own resources, compared to 88 percent for the developing countries. As usual, of course, there is substantial variation within each group. In Chile and Malaysia, for example, local governments financed more than 60 percent of their expenditures from own revenues in 1990, while Argentina, India, and Pakistan had lower levels of financial autonomy (38 percent to 50 percent), and in Indonesia, the proportion was only 21 percent in 1989 (UNDP, 1993). In most countries, fiscal decentralization in the form of increasing the importance of local expenditures is in practice likely to be accomplished only by simultaneously increasing the importance of national fiscal transfers. The level and design of such transfers is therefore invariably a central aspect of any decentralization process.

Two further broad characteristics of decentralization around the world emerge from reviewing the scarce comparative data available. First, however much local governments spend, and whatever they spend it on, the revenues under their direct control are almost invariably less than their expenditures (Bird, 1995). The only exceptions are a few countries – rich and poor – in which local governments are without any importance as spenders, and a very few rich countries (mostly in Scandinavia) in which local governments have substantial access to large and elastic tax bases usually by levying surcharges on national income taxes (Bird and Slack, 1991). Countries clearly have considerable discretion in arranging the structure of their public sectors regardless of their level of income.

A similar conclusion emerges from consideration of the second characteristic common to all countries: not all subnational governments are equal. Even in quite small and homogeneous countries, there are big cities and small towns, heavily urbanized areas and rural municipalities. The resulting unevenness in access to local public resources can be marked: in 1993, per capita revenues in low-income provinces of Vietnam were only 9 percent of those in high-income provinces. However, owing to central government transfers, expenditures in the poorest provinces of Vietnam were 59 percent of those in the richest provinces (Bird, Litvack, and Rao, 1995). Similarly, in Indonesia, Timor (one of the poorest provinces) has a per capita own-source revenue equivalent to 4 percent of Jakarta's. Again, however, owing to transfers from the central government, Timor's per capita expenditures are 40 percent of those in Jakarta (Shah and Qureshi, 1994). Transfers are especially important in determining the pattern and level of expenditures in the poorer regions of countries. In Argentina, for instance, although the per capita GDP in low-income provinces is only 39 percent of that in high-income provinces, per capita public spending in the low-income provinces is 130 percent of that in the wealthier provinces (Rezk, this volume).

In the remainder of this section, we present some key comparative information both for the countries included in this volume and for a few other countries that seem relevant for various reasons, namely, the United States, Germany, Russia, Brazil, Vietnam, Australia, Switzerland, and Canada. Russia, like China, is large and in "transition." Vietnam is a smaller representative of the same group (though not nearly as small as Bosnia-Herzegovina). Brazil, like India (and Pakistan), is a large developing country and also a formal federation. The United States, of course, is the largest federal developed country. Germany, Australia, Canada, and Switzerland are smaller (and more equalization-minded) examples of the same group – more comparable in size to South Africa or Argentina, the other formal federations included in this volume.

As shown in tables 1.1 and 1.2, there are, of course, wide variations in many respects among this set of countries. The data shown in these tables, even for the same country, are often from different sources or for different years, and in some instances are estimated in whole or in part. Many of the specific data for individual countries may no doubt be questioned.[31] Nonetheless, the broad comparative patterns shown in these tables seem unlikely to be much changed by most plausible corrections.

Table 1.1. *Fiscal decentralization: the case-study countries*

	Argentina	Bosnia-Herzegovina[a]	China	Colombia	India	Indonesia	Morocco	Pakistan	South Africa[b]	Tunisia
Demographic										
(1) Population (millions)	34	3.1	1191	36	914	190	26	126	40	9
(2) Density (no./sq.km.)	12	n.a.	124	32	278	10	59	159	33	54
(3) Population growth (%)	1.2	n.a.	1.2	1.9	1.8	1.6	2.0	2.9	2.2	1.9
(4) Urban (%)	88	n.a.	29	72	27	34	48	34	50	57
Economic										
(5) GNP per capita (US$)	8110	728	530	1670	320	880	1140	430	3040	1790
(6) GNP per capita growth (%)	2.0	n.a.	7.8	2.4	2.9	6.0	1.2	1.3	−1.3	2.1
(7) Inflation (%)	317.2	n.a.	8.4	25.6	9.7	8.9	5.0	8.8	14.3	6.3
(8) Income of the lowest 20% (%)	n.a.	n.a.	6.2	3.6	8.5	8.7	6.6	8.4	3.3	5.9
Public sector										
(9) Number of regions	23	10	30	33	25	27	65	4	9	23
(10) Size of government (%)	27	n.a.	23	32	25	19	24	24	40	32
(11) Subnational as % of total exp.	43	57	60	40	58	20	15	33	52	8
(12) Subnational as % of total rev.	40	57	60	21	41	7	9	9	14	5
(13) Subnational rev. as % of subnational exp.	82	100	106	55	49	33	61	12	7	63

Notes and sources:

[a] Data cover only the "Federation" (Bosniac-Croat section) and fiscal data refer to planned 1997 budget.

[b] Fiscal data are for pre-1994 period.

(1) Population in millions, mid-1994. World Bank, 1996d, table 1.

(2) Number of persons per square kilometre, mid-1994. Calculated from data in World Bank, 1996d, table 1.

(3) Average annual rate of population growth, 1990–94. World Bank, 1996d, table 4.

(4) Urban population as percentage of total population, 1994. World Bank, 1996d, table 9.

(5) GNP per capita in US dollars, 1994. World Bank, 1996d, table 1.

(6) Average annual growth of GNP per capita, 1985–94. World Bank, 1996d, table 1.

(7) Average annual GDP deflator, 1984–94. World Bank, 1996d, table 2.

(8) Percentage share of income received by the lowest 20 percent of households/population, various years. World Bank, 1996d, table 5.

(9) Number of major regional units (some special territories may be excluded). Various sources.

(10) Total government expenditures as percentages of GNP, estimated from data on central government expenditures as percentage of GNP, 1994. World Bank, 1996d, table 14; IMF, 1993; UNDP, 1993, tables 4.2 and 4.3, and other information from a variety of country sources that are not directly comparable.

(11)–(13) Estimated from data from same sources as (10).

Table 1.2. *Fiscal decentralization: other countries*

	Australia	Brazil	Canada	Germany	Russia	Switzerland	USA	Vietnam
Demographic								
(1) Population (millions)	18	159	29	82	148	7	261	72
(2) Density (no./sq.km.)	2	19	3	228	9	170	28	22
(3) Population growth (%)	1.1	1.7	1.3	0.6	0.0	1.0	1.0	2.1
(4) Urban (%)	85	77	77	86	73	61	76	21
Economic								
(5) GNP per capita (US$)	18 000	2970	19 510	25 580	2650	37 930	25 880	200
(6) GNP per capita growth (%)	1.2	−0.4	0.3	n.a.	−4.1	0.5	1.3	n.a.
(7) Inflation (%)	4.1	900.3	3.1	n.a.	124.3	3.7	3.3	102.6
(8) Income of the lowest 20% (%)	4.4	2.1	5.7	7.0	3.7	5.2	4.7	7.8
Public sector								
(9) Number of regions	6	26	10	16	89	26	50	53
(10) Size of government (%)	40	35	49	52	45	32	38.0	25
(11) Subnational as % of total exp.	43	34	56	41	48	52	44	33
(12) Subnational as % of total rev.	28	23	50	35	66	51	42	58
(13) Subnational rev as % sub. exp.	55	57	76	75	100	41	75	177

Notes and sources:

(1) Population in millions, mid-1994. World Bank, 1996d, table 1.
(2) Number of persons per square kilometre, mid-1994. Calculated from data in World Bank, 1996d, table 1.
(3) Average annual rate of population growth, 1990–94. World Bank, 1996d, table 4.
(4) Urban population as percentage of total population, 1994. World Bank, 1996d, table 9.
(5) GNP per capita in US dollars, 1994. World Bank, 1996d, table 1.
(6) Average annual growth of GNP per capita, 1985–94. World Bank, 1996d, table 1.
(7) Average annual GDP deflator, 1984–94. World Bank, 1996d, table 2.
(8) Percentage share of income received by the lowest 20 percent of households/population, various years. World Bank, 1996d, table 5.
(9) Number of major regional units (some special territories may be excluded). Various sources.
(10–13) Estimated from data on central government expenditures as percentage of GNP, 1994. World Bank, 1996d, table 14; IMF, 1993; UNDP, 1993, tables 4.2 and 4.3, and other information from a variety of country sources that are not directly comparable.

Broadly and with some overlapping of categories, five types of countries are included in these quantitative comparisons:

(1) developed-country federations, two large (the United States and Germany) and three small (Canada, Australia and Switzerland);
(2) developing-country federations, both large (India, Pakistan and Brazil) and small (Argentina, South Africa, and Bosnia-Herzegovina);
(3) unitary developing countries, both large (Indonesia and China) and small (Colombia, Morocco, and Tunisia);
(4) transitional countries, one large and "federal" (Russia), one small and federal (Bosnia-Herzegovina), one large and unitary (China), and one small and unitary (Vietnam); and
(5) "new" countries (South Africa and Bosnia-Herzegovina).

The tables depict both some basic demographic and income characteristics of the selected countries and some important features of their intergovernmental fiscal systems. An important characteristic which is not captured in these numbers is the degree of "homogeneity" of the country in both ethnic and economic terms. For example, Russia is clearly considerably less homogeneous than China in most relevant respects.[32] Experience suggests that countries with a small number of constituent units and with substantial ethnic and other differences between the units (such as Canada), may work quite differently from countries with a larger number of less heterogeneous units (such as the United States), but this question cannot be discussed in detail here.

To paraphrase Shakespeare, some countries may be "born" federations in the sense that a federal structure from the beginning played a real role in the political and fiscal structure (India), some may "become" federations in order to reconcile regional differences and preserve the nation (South Africa), and some may have federation "thrust upon them" in a desperate attempt to keep them alive (Bosnia-Herzegovina). Matters do not always stay the same, however. Australia, for example, was born a federation because, given its history as a set of widely separated and separate colonies, there was no other viable model at the time. As time went on, and distances and distinguishing factors shrank, the center became much stronger. In contrast, as Rezk (this volume) notes, the opposite may take place in another basically "non-natural" federation, Argentina. Germany had federation thrust upon it after the Second World War in a deliberate effort to weaken the central state, but the recent addition of the eastern *Länder*, with their very different history, has probably strengthened the political basis for federation. On the other hand, "natural" federations such as multilingual Switzerland, Canada, and India are composed of entities that were distinct at the foundation of the country and have largely remained distinct.[33]

An interesting point that emerges in tables 1.1 and 1.2 is that the transitional countries stand out as those in which the basic flow of resources is from below to above. Because most revenues are collected at the local level, in effect transfers appear to flow upward rather than downward as in every other country. To a considerable extent this is simply an illusion, particularly in China and Vietnam. Since the central government in these countries in principle controls all revenue, by allowing different localities to retain different proportions of collections, it is in effect behaving as central governments in other countries that first collect the revenues and then distribute some part of them to lower levels of government.[34] Many of the recent intergovernmental fiscal problems in Russia reflect the inappropriate combination of this sort of "bottom-up" revenue collection system with a federal structure which has made it increasingly difficult for the central government to control local governments. As the chapter on Bosnia-Herzegovina discusses, this problem is likely to prove even more critical in that country. Moreover, it was at least in part to avoid similar problems in the face of growing local *de facto* economic independence that China's recent reform centralized the collection of the major taxes, thus creating the need to establish, for the first time in that country, a formal system of general intergovernmental fiscal transfers.

Patterns of fiscal decentralization

As the brief comparisons in the previous section suggest, as wide a range of institutional structures and relations is found within nominally federal as within nominally unitary countries (Norregaard, 1995). Indeed, the difference between a tight federation such as Malaysia or Germany and most unitary countries is probably less than that between such federations and looser federations such as India and Canada, in which state governments have more power to act independently with respect to expenditure and taxing patterns. The constitutional label matters less than the reality of how intergovernmental relations work in practice. Broadly, however, we suggest that two "models" of intergovernmental fiscal relations can be discerned in the literature. In addition, three broad patterns of intergovernmental fiscal relations may be discerned in the world, as shown in the matrix set out in table 1.3. The entries in the cells in this table are intended as illustrations only: they include both the countries listed in the earlier tables and a few others.

Table 1.3. *A taxonomy of fiscal decentralization*

	Fiscal federalism	Federal finance
Developed countries	France, Japan	USA, Canada
Developing countries	Indonesia, Colombia, Morocco, Tunisia	India, Brazil, Argentina, Pakistan, South Africa
Transitional countries	China, Vietnam	Russia, Bosnia-Herzegovina

Fiscal federalism and federal finance

The dominant economic literature on "fiscal federalism" sets out a normative model under which, in effect, the central government, acting as the benevolent interpreter of the will of the people, is given guidance as to how to structure the institutional rules of the intergovernmental system in order to ensure that local government agents act as the central government (and presumably the people as a whole) would wish. Even if the central government in many countries is not all that benevolent, these rules may still provide useful guidelines with respect to intergovernmental fiscal relations (Bird, 1993).

In this approach, local governments may for most purposes be considered to be agents of the central government – or, in some federal countries, of state governments – rather than independent actors.[35] France and Britain illustrate this pattern among developed countries (Bennett, 1990), while Indonesia, Morocco and Tunisia offer examples among the developing countries covered in this volume, as does Vietnam among the transitional countries (World Bank, 1996a). Among the transitional countries, China seems intermediate between Russia and Vietnam in this respect, although clearly closer to the latter. From this perspective, the appropriate framework for assessing decentralization is, in the terms used earlier, clearly "top-down" and takes the form of deconcentration or at most delegation, and the appropriate analytical framework is that of agency theory.[36]

A good example of where the fiscal federalism model clearly applies is with respect to intergovernmental fiscal transfers in Indonesia. Indonesia has had the same government since 1965. Authority is highly concentrated in the central government, which confirms the appointments of the governors of the twenty-seven provinces and which has officials dispersed throughout the country. On the other hand, the government has consistently emphasized both economic growth and regional development, including a marked degree of centrally directed decentralization.

Although financial autonomy – the share of local expenditures financed by local revenues – varies widely across provinces (from 0.08 to 0.70), on average local governments currently raise less than one-quarter of their own resources (Shah and Qureshi, 1994), with their major revenue source being a local property tax that is actually collected by the central government.[37] Funds to provinces or localities are intended to promote regional autonomy and improve local infrastructure, but they may only be spent subject both to the central government's general guidelines and to the requirement that they be spent in specific sectors. Among the stated rationales for transfers in Indonesia are two that require explicit conditionality to be effective: (1) to alleviate inefficiencies that arise from interjurisdictional spillovers and (2) the equal provision of minimum standards in services.

As one might expect in view of these objectives, most intergovernmental fiscal transfers in Indonesia allocate funds by formula, but require the funds to be spent on specified objectives. Grants for health, for example, are determined on a per capita basis. These grants include allowances for medicine, standardized expenditures for health centers, estimated expenditures on rehabilitation and renovation of health centers, and the costs of doctors and paramedics. Some components of the grant take the form of transfers in kind (for example, medicine). There is a small matching element in health grants in the sense that local governments must finance the cost of acquisition of land for health centers. The central government is directly involved in the provision of health through the appointment of medical personnel, the provision of medicine and other supplies, and the construction of health centers.

In contrast to the fiscal federalism model illustrated by the Indonesian case, what has been called a "federal finance" model seems more appropriate for some countries, particularly those in which there are important geographic or ethnic differences.[38] In such countries, a certain degree of local autonomy often emerges in practice as a means of achieving and retaining political stability even if the constitutional structure is formally unitary. In the traditional world of fiscal federalism (or multi-level finance), as set out by Oates (1972), in principle everything – boundaries, assignments, the level and nature of transfers, etc. – is subject to revision by the central government in its search for efficiency and, perhaps, equity. In the federal finance model, however, jurisdictional boundaries and the assignment of functions and finances must generally be considered as fixed at some earlier (constitutional) stage and not open to further discussion in normal circumstances. More importantly, where a federal structure is politically required to hold a country together – contrast Canada to Australia or the

United States (at least in this century) or Switzerland to Germany (Bird, 1986a) – the central concern in designing intergovernmental fiscal relations is invariably the extent to which they contribute (or not) to political stability (Breton, 1996).[39]

In the fiscal federalism model, the central government's policy preferences are clearly dominant. In the federal finance model, however, rather than simply assuming consensus on, for example, the degree of fiscal and regulatory harmonization to be attained, or even for that matter the degree to which an internal common market should be sought, such matters should ideally be determined jointly by both levels of government in some appropriate political (constitutional) forum.[40] In addition, both levels of government may properly pursue their own distributive policies (Tresch, 1981), again with no presumption of central dominance. In such a federal setting, intergovernmental transfers are appropriately often both equalizing and unconditional, as, for example, Shah (1994) and Ahmad (1997) emphasize.

The federal finance setting is in principle one of bargaining between principals (who are not necessarily equal) – what one Canadian author (Simeon, 1972) has called, in a useful analogy to the world of international relations, "federal–provincial diplomacy." The appropriate analytical framework is not that of principal–agent relations but rather one of negotiation among equals – in the words of Wheare's (1969: 10) classical political treatment of federalism among federal and state governments that are ". . . each, within a sphere, co-ordinate and independent." In some countries – for example, Canada and Switzerland – this may not be a bad description of federal–state relations (Dafflon, 1977, 1991; Bird, 1986a). With caution, a similar framework can clearly be applied to India, as shown by Rao (this volume) and a similar pattern may be emerging in Argentina, which has long been a "formal" federation but has only recently begun to act in what is called here a "federal finance" way (World Bank, 1996b; Rezk, this volume) as well as, perhaps, South Africa (Ahmad, this volume). In the extreme case of Bosnia-Herzegovina, the model is in a sense the reverse, with the subnational governments being the principals and the central government their agent with respect to relations to the outside (financial) world (Fox and Wallich, this volume).

In a fiscal federalism setting, however – which seems to be the best way to characterize cases as diverse as the Colombian, Moroccan, and Chinese ones considered here – the appropriate analytical framework is clearly a principal–agent model in which the principal (the central government) may unilaterally alter both local government revenue and expenditure responsibilities and intergovernmental fiscal arrangements in its attempt to overcome the familiar agency problems of information asymmetry and differing objectives between principal and agent – as indeed China has just done. In this setting, the case for both equalization transfers and for unconditional transfers is by no means as clear as is commonly assumed.[41] The accepted rationale for equalization transfers in the fiscal federalism literature is essentially to ensure that comparable bundles of public services may be provided throughout the country at comparable tax rates (Boadway and Flatters, 1982). Such arguments may be appealing to many, but there is clearly no agreement on either the desirability or effects of equalizing general intergovernmental transfers – as illustrated by the absence of such transfers in the United States.[42]

The two "models" of fiscal decentralization sketched above may apply in developed, developing, and transitional countries. We shall discuss only the developing countries here. As noted above, with the exception of a few large countries (such as India and Brazil), the appropriate normative framework for institutional design in most such countries is almost certainly the traditional fiscal federalism approach (Bird, 1993). In a few other countries – for example, Pakistan, Argentina and South Africa – the theory might be "federal finance" but the practice to date has been essentially "fiscal federalism." As the World Bank (1995b) emphasizes, however, the observed reality of intergovernmental fiscal relations in most developing countries may perhaps better be characterized as "overcontrolled," "undercontrolled," or "perversely controlled."

Local governments are frequently overcontrolled in the sense that they are subject to so many conflicting and unattainable rules that they are, as it were, prevented from behaving efficiently even if they wanted to do so. Similarly, localities may be subject to incentives that lead them to behave perversely. Moreover, the rules may change from place to place and time to time, depending upon the shifting winds of political favor. Finally, central capacity to monitor behavior may be so limited that local governments are in effect subject to no effective controls at all – an approach which seems equally flawed from the point of view of attaining the objectives of the central government efficiently and effectively. All in all, the picture in many developing countries is one of *ad hoc* negotiation between governments and regions, of considerable instability in intergovernmental relations, and of substantial difficulty in knowing exactly what is going on.

The situation may be somewhat different in developing transitional countries such as China and Vietnam. As Bird, Ebel, and Wallich (1995) emphasize, the task facing would-be designers of intergovernmental fiscal institutions in such countries is difficult for at least three additional reasons. First, government is almost invariably being downsized in such countries. Not only is it difficult to restructure incentives constructively when budgets are being cut, but it is virtually inevitable that establishing effective local governments will come very low on the priority list of hard-pressed central governments. Second, a critical part of the "transition" process is to develop not just an effective private market economy but also an effective public sector, to work with and guide such an economy. Again, it is hard enough to create a public sector in this sense at one level of government; to do so at more than one level is doubly difficult. Where political liberalization is part of the transitional process, this effort may have to be made in any case in order to prevent the development of separatist movements, particularly in the more prosperous parts of the country.[43] But when the political system remains centrally controlled, as in China, such concerns are again likely to fall to the end of the queue. Finally, both downsizing and disentanglement require the clear separation of "business" from "government" – something which has definitely not occurred in China to any significant extent to date.

Matters may also be quite different in essentially "new" countries. The studies of South Africa and Bosnia-Herzegovina in this volume are particularly interesting because they illustrate clearly the essentially political rather than economic nature of fiscal decentralization. South Africa is a country which, so to speak, had to become federal in structure – and perhaps will soon become federal in reality – as a necessary condition for its peaceful creation. In contrast, Bosnia-Herzegovina is a country which has, so to speak, been created in a federal form in the perhaps forlorn hope that this structure may enable it to exist at all.

These examples illustrate one extreme of a broader question that arises in many other countries, namely, the difficulty or even impossibility of assessing the economic aspects of fiscal decentralization in abstraction from the political goals that may be the primary rationale for decentralization. In many countries, particularly those encompassing territorially based ethnic minorities, decentralization is inevitably as much about issues of political power as it is about economic efficiency or equity. Even when there are no ethnic differences, but some regions are much richer than others or there is a marked regional divergence in growth patterns, political strains may make the potential role of intergovernmental finance as a means of maintaining national harmony critical.[44] When the center loses its grip, to them that have shall more be given, whether what they have is oil, a credible separation threat, or a strategically important border area.

A recent analysis of intergovernmental finance in the Russian Federation, for example, found that transfers have for the most part gone to those regions least satisfied with the central government – and, indeed, argued that this bias is probably one important reason why Russia has (with the minor exception of Chechnya) remained united while Yugoslavia, Czechoslovakia, and the Soviet Union all collapsed (Treisman, forthcoming). Students of federal finance in other countries would be surprised to see any other result (Bird, 1986a).[45] An important question for China is whether the political tensions created by the unbalanced nature of its growth process will require it either to rein back decentralization (and hence perhaps growth)[46] or to mute growth to some extent by redirecting more of the proceeds to the less favored regions on political grounds – that is, to move closer to a "federal finance" model by employing regional fiscal transfers as one means of maintaining political balance among disparate regions. It is quite unclear, however, whether it would do so in a formal, transparent grant system[47] or, as in the case of Russia (Treisman, forthcoming), by continuing the discretionary way in which intergovernmental relations have traditionally been resolved.[48] While most dramatically posed in Bosnia-Herzegovina, this question is also important in countries as diverse as Pakistan and South Africa.

The role and design of transfers

No matter how revenues and expenditures are reassigned a problem of vertical imbalance will almost certainly remain, or so worldwide experience suggests. Even if the tax base of the richest province enabled it to balance "own" revenues and expenditures, imbalances would remain for all the rest. Moreover, history and international experience both suggest strongly that the differential elasticity of expenditures and revenues assigned to different government levels would in any case soon lead to a re-emergence of a vertical imbalance problem even for the richest province. One way or another, structural "gaps" will emerge and will have to be dealt with.

In principle, there are at least four ways in which any revenue–expenditure gap might be closed.

(1) Revenues could be increased at the provincial level. But this is unlikely to be either feasible to any great extent or (if the system has been properly set up in the first place) desirable.

(2) Provincial expenditures could be reduced. While always popular (with central governments), and perhaps sometimes necessary, this approach is also unlikely to be advisable if the system has been properly set up at the outset.

(3) Expenditure functions could be transferred up to the level with more revenue (or revenue-raising power) or down to the level with more expenditures – though this is again both unnecessary and unwise if the basic structure of the system is correct.

(4) Finally, some centrally collected revenues could be transferred to provincial governments. In the end, in every country, it is this alternative that almost always prevails.

Intergovernmental fiscal transfers may of course have many objectives in addition to simply closing the fiscal gap. Transfers may, for example, be designed to equalize revenue effort, or expenditure levels, or outcomes in terms of services provided. Such equalization may be desired for purposes of income redistribution, or to ensure that for the same revenue effort, citizens obtain the same expenditures (or outcomes) regardless of where they live, or to provide at least minimum standards of key public services to everyone, or to provide everyone with an equal opportunity to access public services. Transfers may also be intended to achieve objectives more directly related to growth and efficiency in resource allocation such as encouraging local governments to build critical public works or to provide more services that provide "spillover" benefits to residents of other areas. They may also be one way in which to recognize that certain areas in a sense may have some "right" to certain incomes, for example, because the natural resources that give rise to those incomes are physically located there. Finally, as emphasized earlier, transfers may have more explicitly political objectives, such as making it possible for even the poorest areas to sustain a certain level of public sector activity or increasing the acceptability of other policies that may affect certain regions adversely.

The extent of equalization in federal countries varies widely from country to country, and appears to reflect differences in national history (preferences) as much or more than any theoretical consideration (Ahmad, 1997). Moreover, there appears to be little, if any, relation between the existence of formal equalization systems and the extent of regional equalization actually effected through the fiscal system (Bird, 1986a). Each country must find its own solution, in accordance with its own imperatives. What any country does with respect to regional "rebalancing," and how it does it, should be decided in light of the real objectives of policy, not in terms of someone else's theory or practice.

Nonetheless, international experience suggests that even general purpose transfers can probably be expected to deviate in practice from the rigid lines of an equalization formula, in response to the overriding need to maintain political stability in the face of rapid economic change. This need may manifest itself in two ways, both of which may reduce the amount of equalization attainable through a formal transfer system. First, to keep the richer regions on side, it may be necessary to direct some transfers to them even if they do not "deserve" them in equity terms.[49] Second, not all the equally poor may be considered to be equally deserving in political terms, so some may do better than others. In Indonesia, for instance, the frontier province of Irian Jaya receives more than three times the average provincial per capita transfer. Frontier regions also receive special attention from central governments in countries such as Argentina and Chile. Such developments may be deplored by those who view equity as the only appropriate objective of fiscal policy. This focus is not only naive but unduly limited in any real-world country. The design of intergovernmental transfers is always and everywhere an exercise not solely in normative economics but also in political economy.[50]

Transfers thus constitute the heart of subnational finance. In themselves, transfers are neither good nor bad: what matters are their effects on such policy outcomes as allocative efficiency, distributional equity, and macroeconomic stability. There are only three basic ways to determine how much is to be distributed through intergovernmental fiscal transfers:

(1) as a fixed proportion of central government revenues;
(2) on an *ad hoc* basis, that is, in the same way as any other budgetary expenditure;
(3) on a "formula-driven" basis, that is, as a proportion of specific local expenditures to be reimbursed by the central government or in relation to some general characteristics of the recipient jurisdictions.

Variants of all three methods are found around the world.

Examples of transfer systems that determine transfers as a proportion of national current revenues may be found in the Philippines, where 20 percent of national internal revenue collections are distributed among local governments (on the basis of population and land area), and in Colombia, where approximately 25 percent of (non-earmarked) national current revenues are distributed to the departmental (intermediate-level) governments (in part in equal portions and in part on the basis of population). Similar systems operate with respect to most major taxes in some developed countries: for example in Austria, where local governments receive about 12 percent of income and value-added taxes; and in Japan, where local governments receive 32 percent of income and alcohol taxes. In both these examples, the resulting total is distributed in accordance with a formula taking into account such factors as population and community size. Large federal countries such as India, Brazil, and Nigeria also tend to use such systems.

Many other countries (including most of the transitional countries) have "tax-sharing" systems that distribute a fixed share of certain national taxes – for example, the income tax or the value-added tax – among local governments. Although many of these systems of "sharing" particular central taxes attempt to allocate all or part of the total thus determined in accordance with the origin (or "derivation") of the tax revenues being shared, others (such as those in Germany, Hungary, and Morocco) allocate the total set by the shared tax amount in accordance with a formula that attempts to take into account both needs and capacity. On the whole, despite its popularity, sharing specific national taxes is less desirable than sharing all national taxes because it leads central governments over time to tend to increase those taxes which they do not have to share.

An alternative system is used in Canada with respect to the largest federal transfer to the provinces (the Canada Health and Social Transfer), which was initially set in per capita terms to be equal in amount to certain (matching) transfers it replaced, and has since been increased as a function of a three-year moving average of nominal GDP growth. Something similar has recently been suggested for Argentina (World Bank, 1996b), although it should perhaps be noted that under increasing budgetary pressure, the Canadian federal government has, over time, both weakened the link to GDP growth (the adjustment factor is now GDP growth less 3 percent) and imposed a "cap" on the absolute amount of transfers going to the richest provinces. Such measures may relieve federal finances, but they obviously vitiate to some extent the stability of revenue flow accruing to the provinces (Smart and Bird, 1997). Another approach might be to have a "horizontal equalization" transfer, as in Germany and Denmark, under which, in effect, rich local governments directly transfer resources to poor localities without directly affecting central revenues (Lotz, 1997). Among developing countries, only Chile appears to have such a system in operation (World Bank, 1993), although the new Moroccan law creating sixteen regional entities provides for an equalization scheme funded in part by contributions from the richer regions.

Once the total to be distributed in transfers to provinces is determined, how should it be distributed? Most experts agree that a formula incorporating both local "needs" for expenditures and local "capacities" to finance such expenditures out of their own resources should be used for this purpose. Such a formula, if properly designed, has the additional virtues of stimulating local governments to make at least an average level of "effort" to finance the expenditures they carry out and ensuring that they remain accountable to local residents at the margin.

If horizontal fiscal balance (another name for equalization) is interpreted in the same gap-filling sense as vertical fiscal balance, an equalization transfer might seem to imply that sufficient transfers are needed to equalize revenues (including transfers) and the *actual* expenditures of each local government. Such "fiscal dentistry" makes no sense, however. Closing all gaps between actual outlays and actual own-source revenues for all local governments ignores differences in local preferences for public and private goods and thus vitiates the basic economic rationale for local government in the first place. Moreover, this approach to equalization ignores local differences in needs, in costs, and in own revenue-raising capacity. Finally, equalizing actual outlays clearly discourages both local revenue-raising effort and local expenditure restraint, since under this system those with the highest expenditures and the lowest taxes would get the largest transfers.

For these reasons, in all countries with formal systems of equalization transfers, the aim is either to equalize the *capacity* of local governments to provide a certain level of public services or the actual *performance* of this level of service by local governments.[51] The performance criterion, which adjusts the transfer received in accordance with the need for the aided service (and which may also allow for cost differentials) is in principle more attractive to central governments – or those concerned primarily with the provision of certain services such as education or social assistance – since the level of service to be funded is determined centrally and the transfer can be made conditional on the provision of that level of service. Unfortunately, this approach may suffer from the same disincentive effect on the revenue side as equalizing actual outlays, for unless adjustment is made for differential fiscal capacity, the government which tries least again gains most.

In principle, then, any sound design for general fiscal transfers to provinces should pivot on some notion of *revenue capacity*. At one extreme, the aim might be to provide each local government with sufficient funds (own-source revenues plus transfers) to deliver a (centrally) predetermined level of services. Because such capacity-based transfers are generally based on measures of *potential* revenue-raising capacity and not on actual revenues, no disincentive to fiscal effort is created by this approach. Differentials in the cost of providing services may or may not be taken into account. Ensuring that the recipient governments will in fact use the funds they receive as the central government might wish, requires that receipt be conditioned in some way on performance (and compliance be monitored in some way).

A number of developing countries use some variety of formula intended both to equalize public expenditures in localities with differing needs and capacities, and to stimulate local fiscal efforts, although severe data problems often constrain the parameters employed in such formulas.[52] Brazil and India, for example, allocate some proportion of transfers in accordance with per capita income levels in the different states, but few other developing countries do so owing to data difficulties. Argentina had some experience with a transfer formula along these lines with the 1973 coparticipation law, which distributed 65 percent in accordance with population, 10 percent in accordance with the inverse of population density, and 25 percent in accordance with an index of the "developmental gap," which in turn was based on measures of the quality of housing, the number of vehicles per inhabitant, and the level of education.

Sometimes, cruder adjustments are made simply by reserving a larger share of the transfer for parts of the country considered to be especially poor or needy, for example, mountainous regions (as in Switzerland) or remote regions (in the systems of municipal transfers of some Canadian provinces), or those with large concentrations of particularly poor groups (India). Perhaps the most common formula elements found in developing countries are population and land area, perhaps with some adjustment for some of the factors just mentioned (for example, remoteness from central markets) or for the size of the municipality (as in some proposed systems in Colombia – Bird, 1984).

Transfers intended to finance particular types of service, for example, road maintenance or education, are often linked to particular measures of need – or existing capacity – such as length of roads or number of students. At one extreme, this approach leads to the sort of "norms" found in Vietnam and a number of other transitional countries (such as Hungary), and may give rise to problems, including allocating funds on the basis of installed capacity, which may reflect past political decisions, rather than need. More careful determination of expenditure needs may have some role with respect to conditional grants – for example, for basic education[53] – but it is not likely to prove useful with respect to grants intended to finance general local expenditures. Experience in countries such as Australia and Canada suggests that a high level of reliable disaggregated data is required before the detailed "norm" approach makes sense. In the absence of such data, simpler approaches, based on, for example, population and a simple "categorization" of localities (by size, by type, or perhaps by region), seem more likely as a rule to prove useful in measuring general expenditure needs.

Despite the strong theoretical reasons for doing so, however, few developing countries appear to include explicit measures of *fiscal capacity* in their formulas. Examples of where this is done are India and Nigeria, where some measure of tax effort is included in the basic distributional formula to states, and Korea, which assumes that a standard tax rate is applied by cities and lowers the transfer if the actual rate is lower (Ahmad, 1997). Colombia also has such an element in one of its transfer programs. Chile goes further and, as noted above, actually "taxes" richer localities to some extent by reducing their transfers and raising those granted to poorer localities. Capacity measures of various sorts are more common in transfer formulas in developed countries. In Spain, for example, 25 percent of local transfers are allocated in accordance with local tax collections (and 70 percent on population). Denmark and Sweden, like Canada and Australia, explicitly calculate local transfers on the assumption that the average "national" local tax rate is applied. The result is that those localities that levy above average local taxes are not penalized by having their grant reduced while those that levy below average taxes are not rewarded by having their grant increased. Of course, this approach makes sense only if local governments have the ability to vary local tax rates. The absence of significant local autonomy with respect to local taxes combined with data difficulties probably explains the relatively few examples of transfer programs incorporating explicit capacity measures in developing countries. Often, as with the Planning Commission grants in India (Rao, this volume), transfers vary by type of project and are essentially means of implementing national planning goals.

Compliance with conditions imposed on transfers can be monitored in part through requirements for uniform and timely local financial reporting and through periodic national inspections and audits of local facilities, although no developing country currently seems to do much on either of these lines. At the very least, the central government should make every reasonable effort to improve local financial reporting – for example, making the provision of such reports a condition for receiving grants – as well as attempting to improve its information base on what is happening with respect to the provision of local public services. Unfortunately, few developing countries appear as yet to have progressed very far along these lines.

What have we learned about fiscal decentralization?

Two general lessons emerge from the brief consideration of intergovernmental arrangements around the world in this chapter and the more detailed case studies that follow. The first lesson is that since every country both is unique and in some sense constitutes an organic unity, the significance of any particular component of its federal finance system – for example, the assignment of taxes or the design of intergovernmental transfers – may be understood only in the context of the system as a whole. One cannot pick an institution from a specific setting, plant it in the alien soil of another environment, and expect to obtain the same results. Policy recommendations in the area of intergovernmental finance must be firmly rooted in understanding the rationale of the existing intergovernmental system and its capacity for change if they are to be acceptable and, if accepted, successfully implemented.

What is feasible and desirable in any particular setting depends very much upon what that setting is, and why it is that way. In the world of intergovernmental finance, one size does not fit all: simple general pronouncements – for example, that unconditional transfers are better (or worse) than conditional ones or that income taxes should always be assigned to central governments – are worse than useless as a guide to policy: they may be positively dangerous. Thus good policy recommendations with respect to matters of intergovernmental finance must, in a sense, be *tailor-made* for each country.

The second lesson suggested by experience is that in the end what may matter more than the precise nature of the technical solutions found in the different countries is the *process* through which such solutions are reached. In federal countries, for instance, the continued viability of the component units – the states – is generally considered an important and explicit objective of policy. The form that regional policy takes often provides a good indication of the extent to which the federal system reflects underlying sociopolitical realities. The greater the value placed, for political or social reasons, on regional survival, the more emphasis is likely to be placed on relatively unfettered regional tax powers supplemented by equalization (as in Switzerland) or large unconditional regional transfers (as in Canada and India). Such factors, together with the institutional structure of decision-making, play a larger role in all federations than efficiency concerns in determining the assignment of taxing powers, the degree of vertical and horizontal fiscal coordination, and the size and nature of intergovernmental fiscal transfers.

Fiscal arrangements invariably constitute perhaps the most important component of the intergovernmental system in any country. Changes in such arrangements reflect, and may sometimes also induce, changes in that system, and the design of such changes is of course a proper subject for economic analysis. In the end, however, any governmental system is invariably a political creation with primarily political ends. The fiscal system existing in any country must therefore be understood and assessed within a political as well as an economic framework. What matters most in intergovernmental finance is thus who determines the rules of the game and how those rules are changed.

Analysis of technical issues is interesting and important, but if such analysis is to play a meaningful role in the essentially political process of intergovernmental bargaining, the institutional framework must be one that accommodates the analysis in the process of achieving sufficient consensus for decision-making purposes in a society which is complex and divided. Those who would improve the economic outcomes of the intergovernmental finance system in any country would be well advised to develop and publicize accurate and relevant information in order to influence the outcome of the inevitably political processes that shape that system.

Lessons for policy in any one country may be drawn only with caution from the welter of confusing details and often contradictory evidence that constitutes the experience of other countries that have utilized somewhat similar policies in inevitably rather different circumstances. Nonetheless, several possibly useful guidelines for decentralization policy seem to emerge, with varying degrees of support, from the international experiences reviewed in this book. Some obvious potential conflicts between these guidelines may perhaps be averted by clever policy design and implementation. But one big conflict cannot be dodged: the greater the weight that the central government places upon specific policy goals, such as the equitable delivery of essential services to specific groups of poor citizens, the less the weight that can be given to the autonomy of local governments in the sense of leaving them free to spend as they see fit. As noted earlier in this chapter, decentralization, properly carried out, may have many virtues; but doing exactly what the central government wants is not likely to be one of them.

Would-be decentralizers should not be in too much of a hurry. Building viable, efficient, and equitable local governance structures is the work of decades, not years. Rome was not built in a day; nor is a village water supply agency or a functioning regional health center, or an efficient municipal council. Any central government that is serious about decentralizing needs not only the will and the resources to do so but also, and critically, a clear and sustained strategy and an adequate (central) institutional structure to support the decentralization effort.

Whenever possible, new institutions should be built on existing foundations. Decentralization will work better if it relates more closely to existing community structures and organizations. "Small" may not always be beautiful, but it is more likely to reflect and yield what local people really want. How, and how far to follow this principle in large and diverse urban areas is one of the central problems facing any decentralization policy; it is difficult, but not impossible (Bird and Jenkins, 1993).

As emphasized above, what local people want may not be what the central government wants. The political aspect of decentralization in the sense of better reflecting local preferences is the key to achieving its efficiency advantages, but to the extent local policy choices are driven by local demand they are less likely to reflect central policy preferences. Decentralization policy must therefore set out clearly in which, if any, areas local differences are not to be permitted to develop – for example, in providing services to the poor – and then to develop institutions that will achieve the desired results.

Local autonomy should not include the right to spend "other people's money" freely. To ensure accountability at the margin (which is where it matters) in principle, local spending decisions should relate to locally raised (and locally borne, not exported) revenues. However, since under almost any conceivable assignment of expenditure and revenue responsibilities some localities will inevitably be dependent upon fiscal transfers – and under some assignments, all will be – the appropriate design and monitoring of transfers is invariably a critical element in effective decentralization policy. What design is best depends upon whether the central government views local governments as its agents in implementing national policy (in which case transfers should, for example, be conditioned on the delivery of basic health and education services) or as independent actors who can do what they (local citizens) want.

Money should follow functions, not precede them. Perhaps the worst of all decentralization policies is to dump a lot of money on an ill-prepared (and often ill-conceived) local government structure without first considering carefully:

- the appropriate expenditure tasks for local government;
- what interest the central government has in how well, or how ill, these tasks are carried out;
- if it has such an interest, how it can best be achieved in the new system of intergovernmental finance.

Good transfer design can assist in implementing a well-thought-out policy in this regard, but it cannot replace it.

Many local governments may need help to do their jobs properly. Local governments can and should carry out a variety of local public services (such as infrastructure development) with little central control or direction. If they are to do so effectively, however, careful attention has

to be paid to three critical and too often neglected aspects of decentralization:

- developing a viable staffing policy – including the often troublesome
  problem of incorporating officials from other levels of government
  without unduly inflating wage bills or unduly lowering service quality;
- implementing a sound information system for accounting and financial
  reporting – to ensure accountability to local residents and to enable the
  central government to monitor and evaluate the decentralization
  process;
- providing adequate technical support – both for the previous two points
  and for such matters as project development and contracting and pro-
  curement.[54]

The focus should be on local services, not local governments. Local
governments need not – indeed, often should not – themselves produce
most local services. Instead, particularly in smaller localities, private and
other providers should be used as extensively as possible to provide local
public services efficiently. The path to the decentralized twenty-first
century for most developing countries seems unlikely to be via the
twentieth-century "big government" model, but via more eclectic and
imaginative modes of service provision.[55] To make such "decentralized"
decentralization work, however, will require very close attention by the
centre to issues of technical assistance and support. Such matters are not
minor "add-ons" to the big decisions on, for example, tax and expenditure
assignment. Developing an adequate institutional framework for decentralization is essential for success no matter what the big decisions may be.

Above all, intergovernmental finance should not be unnecessarily complicated. In all countries, fiscal relations between governments are
inevitably complex and usually unsatisfactory in some respects to all
parties concerned. If what the central government wants to do is accomplish a specific goal such as delivering specific services to specific (poor)
households, it should, whenever possible, do so without further complicating intergovernmental finance. Many of the complications, and complaints, characterizing intergovernmental fiscal issues in most countries
result from overloading the system with tasks for which it is ill-equipped,
such as targeted poverty alleviation. Whenever feasible, direct transfers to
the poor are better than indirect transfers to localities – even poor localities – that are intended primarily to help poor households. In short, if the
provision of a nationwide basic uniform level of health or educational services is an important objective of national policy, the national government
should either provide such services itself or directly (such as through

some variant of vouchers) transfer the needed resources to the target population.

When local governments are expected to play a major role in delivering social services, they must inevitably depend in large part upon central fiscal transfers for the funds needed to do so. Two quite different approaches may be taken to the design of such transfers. On one hand, to the extent that their primary objective is to ensure that all regions of the country that are expected to provide such services at acceptable minimum standards have adequate resources to do so, simple "lump-sum" transfers, with no conditions other than the usual requirements for financial auditing, are called for (Shah, 1994). In this "federalist" approach, it is essentially assumed that the fact that the funds flow to locally responsible political bodies will ensure sufficient accountability and that it is neither necessary nor desirable for the central government to attempt to interfere with, or influence, local expenditure choices. On the other hand, if the central government is, in effect, using local governments as agents in executing national policies – for example, to provide primary education at a specified level throughout the country – then it would seem to make sense to make the transfer conditional upon the funds actually being spent on education or on the attainment of some level of educational performance (Bird, 1993).

If key services are to be provided through decentralized governments, careful attention has to be paid to:

- getting the prices facing service providers right (for example, by means of a well-designed system of matching grants);
- setting up an information and inspection system sufficient to ensure that the desired services are in fact delivered to the target groups;
- devising some system (such as a nationally organized "fail-safe" provision) for dealing with the non-compliant without punishing the innocent.

None of these tasks is easy. None is costless. And the results are not likely to be very satisfactory. The moral is simply that if it is really important to the central government that something should be done in a particular way, it should, if at all possible, do it itself.

Decentralization is often, but not always, a good policy, but it must be done correctly. Decentralization is not a panacea; it cannot and will not solve all problems. Indeed, it may sometimes create new ones (or at least make them more obvious), and, inappropriately implemented, it may sometimes make matters worse (for example, for the poor). However, decentralization has many virtues – not least letting people take more control over their own lives, better satisfying local preferences, and, often, lowering the costs of service provision. Careful planning, carefully monitored and supported implementation, and, above all, careful and continuous efforts both to involve local people in the process and to make them face the opportunity costs of their decisions are essential to success, which even in the best conditions is unlikely to come quickly or easily. As several of the countries discussed in this volume have demonstrated, however, these obstacles can be overcome and at least some of the virtues of decentralization realized without undue sacrifice of either efficiency or equity – indeed, on the contrary, with improvements in both dimensions. A good decentralization policy is not easy to design, and is even harder to implement. But it can be done, and it is worth doing.

Notes

1 For other recent collections of papers on this topic, see Prud'homme (1991) and Owens and Panella (1991).
2 See Bahl and Linn (1992), Shah (1994), Ahmad (1997), and CEPAL/GTZ (1996) for numerous examples.
3 For empirical examples from a number of countries, see Campbell, Peterson, and Brakarz (1991).
4 As Bahl and Linn (1994: 5) say,

> the situation in a developing country that could provide maximum gains from a more decentralized local government structure would include: (1) enough skilled labor, access to materials, and capital plant to expand public service delivery when desired; (2) an efficient tax administration; (3) a taxing power able to capture significant portions of community income incrementally; (4) an income-elastic demand for public services; (5) popularly elected local officials; and (6) some local discretion in shaping the budget and setting the tax rate.

They might have added: (7) a tradition of local decision-making.
5 Of course, fiscal decentralization is only one aspect, and not necessarily the most meaningful one, of decentralization, and measuring the degree of even fiscal decentralization, however defined, is itself a complex and often treacherous exercise (Bird, 1986b), but neither of these points can be further discussed here.
6 Deconcentration may take the form of "field administration," under which local administrative units (or branches of central ministries) have responsibility for service delivery but the staff remains under the direction and control of the center, or "local administration," under which local units have more responsibility for policy and program implementation but are still under the technical supervision of central ministries. For further discussion of this and other forms of decentralization, see World Bank (1996a).

7 With delegation, local governments basically have the responsibility for the function, but remain accountable to the central government with respect to how well they perform it. With devolution, local governments are fundamentally accountable to local residents.

8 Wallich (1994) suggests that this motive has been important in Russia, for example.

9 See also Qiang (1995) who explicitly cites these two rationales for reform.

10 In particular, Prud'homme (1995) at times seems to suggest that all versions of decentralization are necessarily defective. In reality, viewed from any reasonable perspective there may be "good" or "bad" decentralization in any country: it depends upon what is done, and how. See McLure (1995) and Sewell (1996) for persuasive critiques of Prud'homme's extreme position. A more balanced, though still basically negative, approach may be found in Tanzi (1996).

11 See World Bank (1990); for a more skeptical view of the extent to which decentralization *per se* was the destabilizing villain even in the Argentine case, see World Bank (1996b).

12 In countries such as China, Russia, and Vietnam in which most central government revenues have traditionally been collected at the local level, there is perhaps more danger of discouraging collection effort by equalizing transfers, which from the perspective of local governments amount to implicit progressive taxes (Yu, 1996). Ma (1996), for example, argues that the constantly changing nature of revenue-sharing arrangements in China – in effect, the lack of pre-commitment – has discouraged local collection efforts.

13 But see Bird and Fiszbein (this volume) on Colombia and World Bank (1996b) on Argentina for counter-arguments.

14 As Lewis (1966) said long ago, however, giving more responsibility to local governments can often utilize previously unused entrepreneurial and managerial resources and hence strengthen rather than weaken the overall level of public administration in a country. As noted in the chapters on Colombia (see also World Bank, 1995a) and South Africa in this volume, there appears to be some merit in this argument.

15 For a balanced assessment of this issue, see Ter-Minassian (1996). A useful theoretical framework for considering the interaction of local accountability and access to capital markets is presented in Wildasin (1997b).

16 For an argument along these lines, see Brean and Bird (1986).

17 Given the impossibility of bankruptcy proceedings against local governments, reducing this moral hazard will have to depend upon the institution of a credible review/control system for debt work-outs. See the chapter on South Africa (Ahmad, this volume) for further discussion of how to make the "no bail-out" option credible; also World Bank (1996b) for a similar proposal for Argentina.

18 This is the nub of the analysis in Eichengreen and Von Hagen (1995): there is an inverse correlation between local taxing powers and central controls over local borrowing.

19 Some arrangements may have to be made for smoothing out cash flows, but this should not be a concern in most muncipalities which are, and will remain, transfer-dependent, that is, will largely get their funds in monthly cheques from the central government.

20 Similar innovative local methods of dealing with roads in Indonesia are described in Bird (1995).

21 For a more precise discussion of these concepts see the chapters in this volume on India and Argentina.

22 Although this point cannot be further discussed here (but see the chapter on South Africa), there should also be no "bail-outs" of improvident local authorities (World Bank, 1996b).

23 No one has ever argued, for instance, that the province of Prince Edward Island in Canada, which is 80 percent dependent on federal transfers, is less accountable to its citizens than the province of Ontario, which is less than 20 percent transfer-dependent.

24 Two exceptions to this rule are when transfers are explicitly intended either to ensure the provision of specific services at specific levels (that is, the transfers are essentially payments to provinces acting as agents) or to induce provinces to provide more of certain services than they would otherwise do.

25 Note, however, that this approach may not be entirely compatible with the idea of using capital markets as an independent source of "fiscal discipline" or accountability.

26 See Bird and Chen (1996) for the argument that in most such countries the system may more properly be described as one of "federal finance" than "fiscal federalism."

27 These problems are discussed extensively with respect to the former socialist countries of Europe in Bird, Ebel, and Wallich (1995).

28 Compare, for example, the very different intergovernmental systems in neighboring countries that are similar in many respects – for example, Canada and the United States, Switzerland and Germany, India and Pakistan, or Argentina and Brazil (all of which countries have formally federal structures).

29 This argument is developed in Bird (1986a, 1994b).

30 These figures exclude the important regional-level governments in some federal countries.

31 Those who have not looked into the question seldom believe how difficult it is to obtain such figures in most countries. Take the case of Brazil, for example. Table 1.2 presents data based largely on the IMF's *Government Finance Statistics*. In contrast, although Afonso and Lobo (1996) indicate that the size of the public sector in 1995 is roughly comparable (35 percent) to that shown in table 1.2, their breakdown between the central and subnational sectors is completely different, with the latter accounting for about 44 percent of the total with respect to both revenues and expenditures. Without further detailed examination of the underlying data used by Afonso and Lobo (1996), it is not possible to reconcile these figures for Brazil with those in table 1.2. Similar stories could be told about a number of the other countries included in these tables.

32 Contrast, for example, Zhu (1995) with Litvack (1994).

33 The case of Canada is particularly interesting in the sense that it is both a "natural" (linguistic) federation in the case of Quebec and a "non-natural" federation like Australia with respect to most of the rest of the country, which is perhaps one reason Canadian federation is uneasy these days.

34 The mechanism used for the interregional allocation in both (pre-1994) China and Vietnam is (1) to allow the provinces that collect the revenues a (variable) share of what they collect and (2) to provide, in addition, a variety of explicit central government grants for specific purposes (see the chapter on China in this volume and World Bank, 1996a).

35 This is broadly the normative perspective taken in Bird (1993).

36 Bird (1993) argues that this is the appropriate framework in most developing countries. It is also that employed by Ma (1996) to analyze the Chinese case.

37 For further discussion of the Indonesian case, see Shah (this volume), Bagchi (1995), and Qureshi (1997).

38 Such a model is sketched in Bird (1994b) and Bird and Chen (1996).

39 Both models may apply within one country at different levels. In Canada, for example, Bird and Chen (1996) suggest that the federal finance model characterizes federal–provincial fiscal relations and the fiscal federalism model characterizes provincial–municipal fiscal relations.

40 Contrast Ahmad (1997: 4), which simply assumes that a unified market is a *sine qua non* of any federal system, with Bird (1989), which argues that Canada is in some respects less unified than the European Union – and probably correctly so.

41 See, for example, the various studies in Ahmad (1997).

42 On this, see the recent debate between Oakland (1994) and Ladd and Yinger (1994).

43 In most countries of eastern and central Europe, the fall of communist regimes brought with it the rejection of all central-planning institutions, including the previously centralized control of local budgets. If such countries were to remain functioning wholes, they had to develop more autonomous and effective subnational governments (Bird, Ebel, and Wallich, 1995). All have found this task difficult in the face of all the other changes taking place, and some have found it impossible – the former Yugoslavia, the former Czechoslovakia, and the former Soviet Union – and perhaps in future also Bosnia-Herzegovina?

44 Consider, for instance, the recent discussion about adopting a more federal structure in Italy in response to the secessionist movement ("Padania") in the north; or, again, the extensive and expanding form of federalism being implemented in Spain, particularly in Catalonia and the Basque Country (Vizcaya); while both Spanish cases have ethnic components, Catalan separatism has a clear economic motive as well.

45 For a theoretical rationale along related lines, see Breton (1996: 9).

46 For divergent views on the direction of the relationship between decentralization and growth in China, see Zhang and Zou (1996) and Qiang (1995).

47 As has been urged by many authors, for example, Lou (1997).

48 See, for example, Qiang (1995).

49 Bird (1993) calls this the "social security" argument, by analogy with the relatively greater success achieved in many countries in delivering income to the poor through a general transfer system such as social security as opposed to a more targeted scheme of poverty assistance.

50 See, for example, the discussion in Bird (1986a) of the constant revision, largely

on political grounds, of equalization schemes, even in such strongly federal countries as Canada and Switzerland.

51 The original formulation of many of these arguments was done by Musgrave (1961). For a recent full treatment of most of these design issues, see Ahmad (1997).

52 Most of what follows is based in part on Shah (1994) and Ahmad (1997).

53 A strong case might perhaps be made for tying equalization transfers to the provision of particularly important public services, for example, education and perhaps basic health care, as is argued in the chapter on Colombia in this volume.

54 Note that this does not mean this support must necessarily, or even desirably, come from the central government.

55 For examples, see Roth (1987) and Jenkins and Sisk (1993).

References

Afonso, José Roberto Rodrigues, and Lobo, Thereza (1996), "Fiscal decentralization and participation in delayed democratic experiences," paper for Tinker Forum on the Role of the State in Latin America and the Caribbean, Cancún, Mexico (October).

Ahmad, Ehtisham, ed. (1997), *Financing Decentralized Expenditures: An International Comparison of Grants*, Cheltenham: Edward Elgar.

Ahmad, Ehtisham, and Thomas, Ravi (1997), "Types of transfers – a general framework," in Ahmad (1997).

Ahmad, Ehtisham, Qiang, Gao, and Tanzi, Vito, eds. (1995), *Reforming China's Public Finances*, Washington, DC: International Monetary Fund.

Bagchi, Amaresh (1995). "Intergovernmental fiscal relations: the cases of India and Indonesia," in Jayanta Roy, ed., *Macroeconomic Management and Fiscal Decentralization*, Washington, DC: World Bank.

Bahl, Roy, and Linn, Johannes (1992), *Urban Public Finance in Developing Countries*, New York: Oxford University Press.

(1994), "Fiscal decentralization and intergovernmental transfers in less developed countries," *Publius: The Journal of Federalism*, 24: 1–19.

Bennett, Robert J., ed. (1990), *Decentralisation, Local Governments and Markets*, Oxford: Clarendon Press.

Bird, Richard M. (1980), *Central–Local Fiscal Relations and the Provision of Urban Public Services*, Canberra: Centre for Research on Federal Financial Relations, Australian National University.

(1984), *Intergovernmental Finance in Colombia*, Cambridge, MA: Harvard Law School International Tax Program.

(1986a), *Federal Finance in Comparative Perspective*, Toronto: Canadian Tax Foundation.

(1986b), "On measuring fiscal centralization and fiscal balance in federal states," *Environment and Planning C: Government and Policy*, 4: 389–404.

(1989), "Tax harmonization in federations and common markets," in Manfred

Neumann and Karl W. Roskamp, eds., *Public Finance and Performance of Enterprises*, Detroit: Wayne State University Press.

(1990), "Intergovernmental finance and local taxation in developing countries: some basic considerations for reformers," *Public Administration and Development*, 10: 277–88.

(1993), "Threading the fiscal labyrinth: some issues in fiscal decentralization," *National Tax Journal*, 46: 207–27.

(1994a), "Decentralizing infrastructure: for good or for ill?" Policy Research Working Paper 1258, World Bank, Washington, DC (February).

(1994b), "A comparative perspective on federal finance," in K. G. Banting, D. M. Brown, and T. J. Courchene, eds., *The Future of Fiscal Federalism*, Kingston, Ont.: Queen's University School of Public Policy.

(1995), *Financing Local Services: Patterns, Problems, and Possibilities*, Toronto: Centre for Urban and Community Studies, University of Toronto.

Bird, Richard M. and Chen, Duanjie (1996), "Federal finance and fiscal federalism: the two worlds of Canadian public finance," Discussion Paper No. 6, International Centre for Tax Studies, University of Toronto (July).

(forthcoming) "Intergovernmental finance in China in international perspective," in Donald J. S. Brean, ed., *Taxation in Modern China*.

Bird, Richard M. and Gendron, Pierre-Pascal (1998), "Dual VATs and cross-border trade: two problems, one solution?," *International Tax and Public Finance*, 5: 429–42.

Bird, Richard M. and Jenkins, Jerry (1993), "Expanding consent in the finance and delivery of urban services," in Jenkins and Sisk (1993).

Bird, Richard M. and Slack, Enid (1991), "Financing local governments in OECD countries: the role of local taxes and user charges," in Owens and Panella (1991).

Bird, Richard M., Ebel, Robert, and Wallich, Christine, eds. (1995), *Decentralization of the Socialist State: Intergovernmental Finance in Transition Economies*, Washington, DC: World Bank.

Bird, Richard M., Litvack, Jennie, and Rao, M. Govinda, (1995) "Intergovernmental fiscal relations and poverty alleviation in Vietnam," Policy Research Working Paper 1430, World Bank, Washington, DC (March).

Boadway, Robin W. and Flatters, Frank (1982), "Efficiency and equalization payments in a federal system of government: a synthesis and extension of recent results," *Canadian Journal of Economics*, 15: 613–33.

Boadway, Robin W., Roberts, Sandra, and Shah, Anwar (1993), "The reform of fiscal systems in developing countries: a federalism perspective," paper for Conference on Fiscal Reform and Structural Change, International Development Research Centre, New Delhi (August).

Brean, Donald J. S. and Bird, Richard M. (1986), "Fiscal risk of state-owned enterprise," in Bernard F. Herber, ed., *Public Finance and Public Debt*, Detroit: Wayne State University Press.

Breton, Albert (1996), *Competitive Governments: An Economic Theory of Politics and Public Finance*, Cambridge: Cambridge University Press.

Bruce, Neil (1995), "A fiscal federalism analysis of debt policies by sovereign regional governments," *Canadian Journal of Economics*, 28: S195–S206.

Campbell, Tim, Peterson, George, and Brakarz, J. (1991), *Decentralization to Local Government in LAC*, Washington DC: World Bank.

CEPAL/GTZ (1996), *Descentralización Fiscal en América Latina: Balance, Principales, Desafíos*, Proyecto Regional de Descentralización Fiscal CEPAL/GTZ, Santiago, Chile.

Dafflon, Bernard (1977), *Federal Finance in Theory and Practice with Special Reference to Switzerland*, Bern: Verlag Paul Haupt.

(1991), "Assigning taxes in a federal context: the experience of Switzerland," paper for seminar on Fiscal Federalism in Economies in Transition, OECD, Paris (April).

Eichengreen, Barry, and von Hagen, Jurgen (1995), "Fiscal policy and monetary union: federalism, fiscal restrictions and the no-bailout rule," Working Paper C95–056, Center for International and Development Economics, University of California, Berkeley (September).

Glaessner, Philip, *et al.* (1994), "Poverty alleviation and social development funds: the Latin American experience," Discussion Paper 261, World Bank, Washington, DC.

IMF (International Monetary Fund) 1993, *Government Finance Statistics 1993*, Washington DC.

Jenkins, Jerry, and Sisk, David E., eds. (1993), *Development by Consent: The Voluntary Supply of Public Goods and Services*, San Francisco: ICS Press.

Ladd, Helen, and Yinger, John (1994), "The case for equalizing aid," *National Tax Journal*, 47: 211–24.

Lewis, W. Arthur (1966), *Development Planning*, London: George Allen & Unwin.

Litvack, Jennie I. (1994), "Regional demands and fiscal federalism," in Wallich (1994).

Lotz, Jorgen (1997), "Denmark and other Scandinavian countries: equalization and grants," in Ahmad (1997).

Lou, Jiwei, (1997), "Constraints in reforming the transfer system in China," in Ahmad (1997).

Ma, Jun (1996), *Intergovernmental Relations and Macroeconomic Management in China*, New York: St. Martin's Press.

McLure, Charles E., Jr. (1993a), "The Brazilian tax assignment problems: ends, means, and constraints," in *A Reforma Fiscal no Brasil*, São Paulo: Fundação Instituto de Pesquisas Econômicas.

(1993b), "A North American view of vertical fiscal imbalance and the assignment of taxing powers," in D. J. Collins, ed., *Vertical Fiscal Imbalance and the Allocation of Taxing Powers*, Sydney: Australian Tax Research Foundation.

(1995), "Comment on Prud'homme," *World Bank Research Observer*, 10: 221–26.

(1997) "Topics in the theory of revenue assignment: gaps, traps,and nuances," in Mario I. Blejer and Teresa Ter-Minassian, eds., *Macroeconomics and Public Finance*, London: Routledge.

Musgrave, Richard A. (1961), "Approaches to a fiscal theory of political federalism," in *Public Finances: Needs, Sources, and Utilization* (National Bureau of Economic Research Special Conference Series), Princeton: Princeton University Press.

(1983), "Who should tax, where, and what?" in Charles E. McLure, Jr., ed., *Tax*

Assignment in Federal Countries, Canberra: Australian National University Press.

Norregaard, John (1995), "Intergovernmental fiscal relations," in P. Shome, ed., *Tax Policy Handbook*, Washington, DC: International Monetary Fund.

Oakland, William (1994), "Fiscal equalization: an empty box?," *National Tax Journal*, 47: 199–209.

Oates, Wallace E. (1972), *Fiscal Federalism*, New York: Harcourt, Brace, Jovanovich.

OECD (Organisation for Economic Co-operation and Development) (1991), "The role of intermediate and local levels of government: the experience of selected OECD countries," background document for Seminar on Fiscal Federalism in Economies in Transition, Paris.

Owens, J. and Panella G., eds. (1991), *Local Government: An International Perspective*, Amsterdam: North-Holland.

Prud'homme, Remy, ed. (1991), *Public Finance with several Levels of Government*, The Hague/Königstern: Foundation of Public Finance Journal.

(1995) "The dangers of decentralization," *World Bank Research Observer*, 10: 201–20.

Qiang, Gao (1995), "Problems in Chinese intragovernmental fiscal relations, tax-sharing system, and future reform," in Ahmad, Qiang, and Tanzi (1995).

Qureshi, Zia (1997), "Fiscal transfers in Indonesia," in Ahmad (1997).

Roth, Gabriel (1987), *The Private Provision of Public Services in Developing Countries*, New York: Oxford University Press.

Sewell, David (1996), "The dangers of decentralization according to Prud'homme: some further aspects," *World Bank Research Observer*, 11: 143–50.

Shah, Anwar (1994), *The Reform of Intergovernmental Fiscal Relations in Developing Countries and Emerging Market Economies* (Policy and Research Series No. 23), Washington, DC: World Bank.

Shah, Anwar, and Qureshi, Zia (1994), "Intergovernment fiscal relations in Indonesia," Discussion Paper No. 239, World Bank, Washington, DC.

Simeon, Richard (1972), *Federal–Provincial Diplomacy*, Toronto: University of Toronto Press.

Smart, Michael, and Bird, Richard (1997), "Federal fiscal arrangements in Canada: an analysis of incentives," in National Tax Association, *Proceedings of the Annual Tax Conference*, Washington, DC.

Tanzi, Vito (1996), "Fiscal federalism and decentralization: a review of some efficiency and macroeconomic aspects," in Michael Bruno and Boris Pleskovic, eds., *Annual World Bank Conference on Development Economics 1995*, Washington, DC: World Bank.

Ter-Minassian, Teresa (1996), "Borrowing by subnational governments: issues and selected international experiences," IMF Papers on Policy Analysis and Assessment PPAA/96/4, International Monetary Fund, Washington, DC (April).

Tiebout, Charles M. (1956), "A pure theory of local government expenditure," *Journal of Political Economy*, 64: 416–24.

Treisman, Daniel (forthcoming) *After the Deluge: The Politics of Regional Crisis in Post-Soviet Russia*, Ann Arbor, MI: University of Michigan Press.

Tresch, Richard (1981), *Public Finance*, Plano, TX: Business Publications.

UNDP (United Nations Development Program) (1993), *Human Development Report 1993*, New York: Oxford University Press.

Wallich, Christine, (ed.) (1994), *Russia and the Challenge of Fiscal Federalism*, Washington, DC: World Bank.

Wasylenko, Michael (1987), "Fiscal decentralization and economic development," *Public Budgeting and Finance*, 7: 57–71

Wheare, Kenneth (1969), *Federal Government*, 4th edn., Oxford: Clarendon Press.

Wildasin, David, ed. (1997a), *Fiscal Aspects of Evolving Federations*, Cambridge: Cambridge University Press.

(1997b) "Externalities and bailouts: hard and soft budget constraints in inter-governmental fiscal relations," paper presented to IIPF Congress, Kyoto.

World Bank (1990), *Argentina: Provincial Government Finances*, Washington, DC.

(1993), *Subnational Finance in Chile*, Washington, DC.

(1994), *World Development Report 1994*, New York: Oxford University Press.

(1995a), *Colombia: Local Government Capacity – Beyond Technical Assistance*, Washington, DC.

(1995b), *Better Urban Services*, Washington, DC.

(1996a), "Vietnam: fiscal decentralization and the delivery of rural services," Report No. 15745-VN, Washington, DC (October).

(1996b), "Argentina: Provincial Finances Study," Report No. 15487-AR, Washington, DC (July).

(1996c), "Colombia: reforming the decentralization law," Report No. 15298-CO, Washington, DC.

(1996d), *World Development Report 1996*, New York: Oxford University Press.

Yu, Xiaoping (1996), "Intergovernmental transfer system in China," paper for workshop on International Experience on Intergovernmental Fiscal Transfer, Hanoi, Vietnam (March).

Zhang, Tao, and Zou, Heng-fu (1996), "Fiscal decentralization, public spending, and economic growth in China," Policy Research Department, World Bank.

Zhu, M. Zhenjun (1995), "China's financial policies for minority nationalities and poor areas," in Ahmad, Qiang, and Tanzi (1995).

2

China: evaluating the impact of intergovernmental fiscal reform

ROY W. BAHL

In China's fiscal system, the distinction blurs as among tax policy reform, tax administration reform, and intergovernmental fiscal reform. So linked are they that changes in any one of the three legs of the public financing structure will automatically affect the other two:

- all tax rates and bases are centrally determined, so structural changes have direct impacts on local as well as central government revenues;
- revenues from these centrally determined taxes are shared between the central and local governments, partly on a derivation basis with the retention rates varying by tax, and partly in the form of an *ad hoc* grant;
- the tax administration system is decentralized enough that local governments have derived some fiscal autonomy from a creative implementation of the tax assessment and collection system.

The comprehensive fiscal reform in China in 1994 altered the structure of the major taxes, changed the responsibilities for tax administration, and modified the revenue-sharing arrangements. It also curtailed the ability of local governments to use "back-door" approaches to revenue mobilization. As a result, the entire intergovernmental system was redefined. This chapter is an attempt to evaluate the impact of these changes.[1]

In the next sections, the Chinese intergovernmental fiscal system before and after the 1994 reform is described and the underlying revenue concerns that drove the reform are considered. Most of the remainder of the chapter is an evaluation of the impacts of the 1994 reform on the intergovernmental fiscal system.[2] A concluding section presents a summary comparison of Chinese fiscal decentralization with the world practice.

Revenue structure

The Chinese tax structure is highly centralized, with the rates and bases of all taxes in the system set by the central government. However, the enterprise income tax and sales taxes together account for about 90 percent of

Table 2.1. *China: distribution of budgetary revenues, 1992 and 1995 (percentages)*

	1992	1995
Industrial and commercial taxes[a]	68.1	76.0
Tariffs	6.5	4.8
SOE income tax	19.0	12.6
Collective income tax	2.9	2.0
Other	3.6	4.6

Note: [a] Primarily sales taxes.
Source: Statistical Yearbook of China, 1996.

total budgetary revenue (table 2.1). The other thirteen taxes in the system give considerably less than 10 percent of total revenues, with the balance coming from miscellaneous non-tax revenues.[3] With the enterprise income tax in decline, and the individual income tax very narrowly based, China has moved to heavier reliance on sales taxes. By 1992, indirect taxes accounted for more than 70 percent of total collections.

Enterprise income tax

Before the 1994 reform, income tax on enterprises comprised a family of taxes. There were separate tax treatments for large state-owned enterprises, small state-owned companies, collectives, individual household enterprises, joint ventures, and foreign enterprises. There were five different rate structures, and differences in the definition of the tax bases for the several surtaxes applied. Taxable profit was defined as the difference between gross sales and allowable costs, but there were some notable departures from the conventional practice; for example, repayment of loan principal was an allowable deduction, the depreciation deduction was an actual cash expense, and bonuses and some fringe benefit payments were not allowable labor cost deductions.

A combination of this complex tax structure, the uneven quality of record-keeping by enterprises, and the manually operated collection, assessment, and audit system made this an especially difficult tax to administer. To complicate matters further, most state-owned enterprises did not pay according to the legal rate schedule, but according to a contractual arrangement with the local government.[4] This "contract," agreed to by the local government administration and the enterprise (but not by the central government), usually required the enterprise to pay a quota amount of tax or to guarantee a quota level of taxable profit. In effect, contracting was a step backward to the time when enterprises were not taxed but paid their profits to the government sector.

Not only did these practices affect the efficiency with which the economy operated, but also they had built-in biases against some provinces and in favor of others, depending on the structure of their economy. Those provinces with profitable enterprises of course did better, and those with a greater concentration of state-owned enterprises were favored because the tax system did not fully reach the collective and private enterprise sectors. Moreover, provinces with more profitable, state-owned enterprises were in a position to use preferential tax treatment in effect to transfer enterprise profits from (shared) general taxes to local extrabudgetary accounts.

The 1994 reform dramatically changed the enterprise income tax and the intergovernmental fiscal system. The surtaxes were eliminated, all domestic enterprises were brought under the same regime regardless of ownership, and there was a reduction in the top rate from 55 percent to 33 percent. Tax-contracting between enterprises and government was prohibited, and the system of deductions was restructured to move closer to international practice. Central–local sharing of enterprise income tax revenues was dropped in favor of assignment of all enterprise income tax revenues to provincial governments.[5] The new system was meant to be revenue-neutral in total, but it is not revenue-neutral for every province individually.

Indirect taxes

Before the 1994 reform, there were three sales taxes in China: product tax, business tax and value-added tax (VAT).[6] The product tax was levied on the total sales value of specified manufactured and imported goods. The base of the tax was the price paid by the buyer, with rates ranging from 3 percent to 60 percent. Over the last few years, the VAT has gradually replaced the product tax as the standard levy on manufactured and imported goods. The pre-reform VAT had twelve different rates. The base of the Chinese VAT is similar to international practice in that exports are zero-rated, and exemptions include agriculture and most services. But it is different in that exemptions include the construction, transport, communications, wholesale, and retail sectors. Credit is not allowed for tax paid on capital inputs. The method of calculating the base is a major departure from international practice. Taxes paid on intermediate goods were credited, but, until recently, according to presumptive methods rather than invoices. The service sector was taxed through a turnover tax referred to as the business tax. It was levied on gross receipts, with rates ranging from 3 to 10 percent.

The sales tax was overdue for reform. It was terribly complicated and costly to administer. Earlier the sales tax had been used as a device to regulate profits and prices, and by the late 1980s, there were over 250 different sales tax rates. But, with most prices decontrolled, this was no longer necessary and created significant distortions in the economy (World Bank, 1990). Evasion seemed to be a problem, and the revenue income elasticity was less than unity. Finally, the structure and administration of the VAT departed too much from good practice and did not give China the revenue productivity and self-policing advantages that it has given other countries.

The structure of the pre-reform indirect tax system also raises issues of intergovernmental fiscal relations, because some provinces fared better than others under the taxing and revenue-sharing rules that governed the indirect taxes. First, the indirect taxes were part of the sharing pool, so a larger sales tax base meant greater revenues under China's derivation-based sharing system. The VAT was a counter-equalizing form of revenue-sharing. Second, some of the structural features of the indirect taxes had implications for the relative fiscal capacity of provinces: the failure to credit capital expenses both raised more revenues from capital-intensive enterprises and discouraged capital investment; export credits were paid by the central government thereby advantaging exporting provinces; state-owned enterprises were taxed more heavily than collectives or private enterprises; and the complicated rate structure made the revenue yield a function of provincial economic structure rather than total output.

The 1994 reform program substantially restructured the sales tax system. The VAT was expanded to absorb most sectors covered under the product tax, and the latter will eventually be phased out. The wholesale and retail sectors are taxed under VAT rather than under the business tax. A two-rate VAT system was adopted (17 percent and 13 percent), and presumptive crediting was eliminated in favor of an invoice method. Because of the potential revenue cost, there was no proposal to permit a credit for taxes paid on capital goods.

From the point of view of intergovernmental relations, the 1994 reform was a major change. The VAT was made a central government levy, not subject to sharing, though a transitional sharing arrangement was put in place. Administrative arrangements were also changed, and beginning in 1994, the VAT was fully administered by the central government without local involvement.

Tax administration

The 1994 reform established separate national and local tax administration services. This was a major national policy change with far-reaching implications. Economists have long written about the folly of separating tax structure reform from tax administration considerations (Bird, 1989), but in China it is also true that intergovernmental reform cannot be divorced from tax administration reform. Reform of the revenue-sharing and taxation systems in 1994 could not have achieved its objectives unless the administrative system was also changed.

The responsibility of the National Tax Service (NTS) is to collect central and shared taxes. The NTS has about 500,000 employees and operates down to the county level. Prior to the 1994 reform, two-thirds of these employees operated at the lowest level of government, with relatively little central supervision. Consequently, they developed close ties with the local finance offices, and with the locally owned enterprises (IMF, 1994). This led to a kind of collusion that was thought to weaken the position of the central government in revenue-sharing (World Bank, 1990).

Under the reformed system, a separate local tax service operates in each province with responsibility for collection of "local taxes," including the enterprise income tax on locally owned enterprises, collectives, and private businesses.[7] The local tax service is now part of the local finance departments, and its operations are funded from local resources. The central tax service is responsible for collecting the VAT and all other central or shared taxes. The NTS still operates on a regional basis, but is independent from the local tax service.

This reform is an attempt to solve a longstanding problem of divided loyalties among the local officers in the former State Tax Bureau. There no longer will be a question about the objectives of the tax administration office as regards the choice between full taxation under the law and maximization of retained local revenue. The NTS now has every incentive to collect fully the indirect taxes due, since these are the mainstay of the central government revenue structure. The local tax service must decide how it will treat local enterprises under the income tax, but if it chooses to grant preferential treatment it must absorb whatever revenue costs occur.

Revenue-sharing

China's revenue-sharing system is primarily a division of national sales and profit taxes among the central, provincial, and local governments. Whereas in most countries taxes are collected by the central government and then allocated to the subnational governments, in China they have been collected by the local governments and "shared-up" to the higher levels. The amount of shared tax revenue that finally shows up in the local government budget depends on the centrally determined tax base and tax rates, the tax administration, the assignment of revenues to the local government, and the sharing formulas. These formulas, in turn, have two elements: the proportion of revenues from any given tax that is to be shared with the province, and the method by which this amount is distributed amongst local governments within the province. In addition, there are earmarked grants which are given to provincial governments by the center. To understand the revenue-sharing system in China, and to understand the implications of the 1994 reform, one must understand all of these dimensions. It is a very complicated matter.

In the following subsections, the three major issues surrounding revenue sharing are taken up: the actual distribution formulas for shared taxes, the distribution of earmarked grants, and the pattern of extrabudgetary revenues of local governments. The last of these is properly part of the discussion of intergovernmental fiscal relations in China, because extrabudgetary funds reflect the success of Chinese local governments in mobilizing resources outside the sharing pool.

Shared taxes

The revenue-sharing formulas have been regularly adjusted since the fiscal reform began in 1983. The 1994 reform can be best understood as another step in this transition. The formula has changed over time and was not always strictly applied, but the government has held to a basic philosophy: that local governments should retain enough revenue to cover a "basic" level of services and should turn the remainder over to the center. The debate and negotiation usually centered around what should be the "approved level" of expenditure and by how much the approved level should grow each year.[8]

The revenue-sharing formula in operation from 1985–88 provided for three categories of provinces: those which retain a fixed percentage of what they collect (fifteen provinces), those which keep all they collect and receive a subsidy, and those which retain all they collect and pay a fixed subsidy to the center (Guangdong Province).

There was dissatisfaction with this system of tax-sharing. The subnational governments felt that their shares were too low, and both sides felt that the system was too arbitrary. The ability of the central government to use fiscal policy as an instrument of macroeconomic policy and regional equalization was limited, local government incentives for increased revenue mobilization were weak, and local government incentives to move revenues to the extrabudgetary sector were strong. Some *ad hoc* adjustments were made in 1987 to address the incentives issue (an incremental sharing rate on revenues above a target level was introduced in Jiangsu, Zhejiang, Hebei, Beijing, and Tianjin) but this did not quiet the calls for a complete reform.

Beginning in 1988, the system was changed to an even more negotiated approach. The idea was still to allow the local governments to retain an amount of revenue that would enable them to cover a basic level of expenditure needs. The base year chosen to define the expenditure amount was 1987. Local governments retained the base amount plus a share of any increase in revenues, as negotiated in advance. This agreement, originally planned to be in force for three years, led to six different arrangements for tax-sharing.[9]

The fundamental problem, however, remained. The system was negotiated and not transparent. This led to criticisms that it was unfair. The local governments continued to have an incentive to channel tax money to their own treasuries, outside the formal revenue-sharing system. And, though neither the central nor the local governments felt that the division of the revenues was correct, the flow of resources to the central government and the overall level of revenue mobilization declined.

The 1994 reform also directly addressed the revenue-sharing system. The most important element of the revenue-sharing reform was the designation of the value-added tax as a central tax which would be shared 75/25 between the center and the provinces.[10] The enterprise income tax (other than that collected from centrally owned enterprises) and the individual income tax would be assigned fully to the local governments. Local governments would also have responsibility for income tax collection. This would seem to be a first step toward an assignment system – though as noted above, the local governments have no authority to set the rate and base of the tax.

Earmarked grants

In addition to shared taxes, local governments receive earmarked grants from the central government. The purposes of this subsidy include appropriations for capital construction projects, price subsidies for urban grain consumption, social relief funds, and special subsidies for health and education of the poor, of ethnic minorities, and in border provinces.[11] There is no set formula to determine the amount of earmarked grants for distribution in any given year, and the distribution among the provinces appears to be *ad hoc* rather than formula-based. Earmarked grants have grown significantly, and were greater in magnitude than tax-sharing transfers to the central government in 1992.[12] In 1990, earmarked grants were equivalent in amount to 14.4 percent of local government budgetary expenditures, slightly less than in 1985.

Some would argue that a primary purpose of earmarked grants is equalization. In fact, China has no equalization grant program. Simple correlations show that per capita earmarked grants are distributed in significantly larger amounts to higher income provinces.[13] These are project rather than entitlement grants, and it is not unusual for more developed regions to absorb more of such grants because of their greater capability at project preparation and their greater ability to "buy in" on a matching basis.

Extrabudgetary revenue

The 1980s and early 1990s saw a rapid growth in revenue outside the budgetary accounts. Local governments in particular had found a way to siphon revenues away from the normal budgetary accounts – and the sharing pool – to special purpose spending. The declining ratio of taxes to GNP over the past decade reflects this transfer of funds.

There are two types of extrabudgetary revenue in China. The first is the "fiscal extrabudgetary funds" of the government. These are earmarked for capital purposes and include a set of taxes and charges that are controlled by the local government finance department. The most important is the public utility surcharge – a 10 percent tax on the utility bills of consumers – and the urban construction and maintenance tax. There are also some minor taxes and charges in this category, including the surcharge on the agricultural tax, revenues received from public housing and public property, and some institutional income that accrues to the various city enterprises. The latter include such items as fees and charges from hospitals, road maintenance charges, advertisement fees, etc. The World Bank (1994: 31) estimates that fiscal extrabudgetary revenues grew from 2.6 percent of GDP in 1978 to 4.2 percent in 1993, and now are equivalent to about one-fourth of total budgetary revenues.

The other type of extrabudgetary revenue is the retained earnings and depreciation funds of locally owned enterprises. Extrabudgetary funds of this type expanded very rapidly in the 1980s, and in 1993 were equivalent in amount to about 12 percent of GDP. In principle, these funds should not be classified as part of the government budget because they are not resources over which the local governments have direct control. Nor is their rapid growth necessarily a cause for alarm. It could reflect increased profitability, increased enterprise savings, and government policy to allow enterprises more flexibility in managing their resources (World Bank, 1993: 17–19). However, the flagging level of enterprise income tax collections suggests that the increase in extrabudgetary funds was at least partly a result of the contracting system between local governments and enterprises that led to a channeling of resources from the budgetary to the extrabudgetary side. Some of these revenues were used for social purposes and to support the economic development goals of the local government administration, and their growth was heavily influenced by local taxing and contracting practices.[14]

Extrabudgetary funds are by their very nature sensitive to the business cycle. In 1992, total extrabudgetary revenues of local governments were equivalent to about 89 percent of local government budgetary collections. This share increased after 1986 when enterprise contracting began to grow significantly. The responsiveness of extrabudgetary revenues to GNP would appear to be greater than the responsiveness of budgetary revenues – there is a positive and significant relationship between the ratio of local government extrabudgetary revenues to budgetary collections, and to GNP, over the 1983–92 period.[15]

Objective of the reform

The 1994 reform of the fiscal system was prompted by the slow growth in central government revenues. The primary contributing factors were a long-term decline in tax revenue collections as a share of GNP and a reduced share of total revenue going to the central government. The 1994 reform was an attempt both to increase the revenue income elasticity of the system and to recentralize. It also reflected an attempt by the center to regain control over fiscal policy.

The declining tax ratio

The revenue trend over the period 1985–95 is described in table 2.2. The national tax ratio (collections as a share of GNP) had fallen to less than half of its level of about 23 percent at the time the enterprise income tax was introduced.[16] By 1995, government revenue mobilization was about 11 percent of GNP, a low share by international standards.[17] A declining government share of GNP in China is not a problem *per se* because it reflects the narrowing of the scope of government responsibility.[18] However, this decline was greater than was planned and fiscal deficits arose.[19] Between 1985 and 1993, the revenue income elasticity of the

Table 2.2. *Tax revenue performance, 1985–95*

	Total tax revenue (billions of yuan)	Total tax revenue as a percentage of GNP	Enterprise income tax revenues as a percentage of GNP[a]
1985	208.5	23.18	8.23
1986	213.3	20.90	7.20
1987	218.3	18.26	5.91
1988	244.2	16.36	4.87
1989	279.1	16.49	4.51
1990	290.0	15.59	4.27
1991	306.5	14.14	3.72
1992	335.7	12.59	2.93
1993	430.5	12.45	2.11
1994	512.7	11.01	1.52
1995	603.8	10.54	1.53

Note: [a] Includes direct remittances by enterprises.
Source: Statistical Yearbook of China, 1996.

Chinese tax system was only 0.60, that is, the rate of revenue growth was a little more than half the rate of growth in GNP.[20] Such a slow growth in revenue will almost certainly create budgetary balance problems and restrain expenditure growth. Government policy is to increase the income elasticity of the revenue system, and reduce the size of the deficit (Zhongli, 1996).

The decline in the revenue share of GNP is largely due to the declining budgetary contributions of the enterprise income tax. On the one hand, this is neither unexpected nor undesirable. The enterprise reform in China was meant to reduce payments to the government and to give enterprises more control over their resources (World Bank, 1994). On the other hand, this industrial policy alone would not seem to have dictated so great a reduction in enterprise tax payments. There are several explanations for the large reduction: the offloading of some enterprises from the government sector, the granting of tax incentives by local governments, and enterprise losses. Another reason for the weak revenue performance of the enterprise income tax is the failure to expand the tax base adequately to include the private and collective enterprise sector. In the early 1990s, about 60 percent of GNP was accounted for by the non-state sector, but almost 80 percent of tax revenues were derived from the state-owned enterprises (IMF, 1994: 28). Whatever the reason, at a 1.5 percent share of GNP, the enterprise income tax has become much less a force in economic policy than it was at over 8 percent of GNP in its early years (see table 2.2).

Division of revenues

The revenue–expenditure balance between central and local governments changed markedly in the 1980s and early 1990s. At the time of the income tax reform in 1983, the local government sector was spending an amount equivalent to 74 percent of what it collected and turning a net 26 percent over to the central government for national purposes. By 1992, the local government sector was spending all of its collections and receiving an additional subsidy from the center equivalent in amount to about 2 percent of expenditures (table 2.3). Historically (through the mid-1980s) central fixed revenues were considerably less than central government expenditures, and the difference was made up with net transfers from the local government sector. For example, in 1984, the local governments ran a "collections surplus" of about 17 billion yuan while the central government ran a "collections deficit" of about 23 billion yuan (table 2.3). The net transfer was from local to center. However, by 1988, the local government sector was regularly running a collection deficit. In fact, in 1992, there was a net transfer from the center to the subnational sector (excluding any earmarked grants) equivalent to about 19 percent of central collections. It is this change in the division of revenues that prompted the 1994 reform of the revenue-sharing system.

Central government macroeconomic policy

Prior to the 1994 reform, central officials complained that the intergovernmental system compromised the effectiveness of macroeconomic policy. Because subnational governments retained too large a share of the pie, the central government did not have the resources to invest adequately in national projects, to compensate poor regions for inadequate taxable capacity, or to control the aggregate level of expenditure and investment in the country. Moreover, during periods of expansion, enterprises were prone to increase their rate of investment because of the availability of funds and because the automatic stabilizer built into the enterprise income tax was nullified by the practice of contracting. The result was that aggregate demand grew, the government revenue share of GNP fell, and a fiscal deficit resulted. There is an analogous procyclical effect in times of recession. Under the contract system, the central government could do very little to control this situation.

It was also the case in the pre-reform period that the ability of the central government to pursue discretionary fiscal policy was limited because of the possibility of offsetting policy reactions by the local governments. For

Table 2.3. *Tax collection and expenditure of central and local governments, 1980–95 (billions of yuan)*[a]

	1980	1981	1982	1983	1984	1985	1986	1987	1988	1989	1990	1991	1992	1993	1994	1995
Central government																
Collection[b]	28.4	31.1	34.7	49.0	66.5	77.0	77.8	73.6	77.5	82.3	99.2	98.8	98.0	95.8	290.7	325.7
Expenditure	66.7	62.6	65.2	76.0	89.3	79.5	83.6	84.6	84.5	88.9	100.4	109.1	117.0	131.2	175.4	199.5
Collection surplus/ deficit	−38.2	−31.5	−30.5	−27.0	−22.8	−2.6	−5.8	−10.9	−7.0	−6.6	−1.2	−10.3	−19.1	−35.5	115.2	126.1
Local government																
Collection[b]	87.5	86.5	86.5	87.7	97.7	123.5	134.4	146.3	158.2	184.2	194.5	221.1	250.4	339.1	231.2	298.6
Expenditure	56.2	51.3	57.8	65.0	80.8	120.9	136.9	141.7	164.6	193.5	207.9	229.6	257.2	333.0	403.8	482.8
Collection surplus/ deficit	31.3	35.2	28.7	22.7	17.0	2.6	−2.5	4.7	−6.4	−9.3	−13.4	−8.5	−6.8	6.1	−172.7	−184.3

Notes:

[a] The difference between the local government's surplus and the central government's deficit is the central government's foreign borrowing and domestic budget deficit.

[b] Central and local government collections are before transfer from local governments to the central government, and before earmarked grant distribution to the local governments.

Source: Statistical Yearbook of China, 1996.

example, the central government might levy an extra tax to cool down an overheated economy, but local governments could react to this by renegotiating their contracts with enterprises to stimulate investment, or they could give preferential tax treatments to avoid the consequences of the central tax.

Another problem with the revenue-sharing system was that it compromised the implementation of the government's industrial policy. Qiang (1995) makes the point that the sharing of income taxes from local enterprises and the sharing of indirect taxes collected in local areas encourages local governments to favor development of projects that show high profits and sales. It is a problem in all countries that local officials, facing a relatively short political life, favor investment projects that have a high visibility and offer a substantial short-term return. It is an especially acute problem for China because of the substantial amount of resources in the hands of local governments and locally owned enterprises (Chinese People's Bank of Construction, 1993).

This leads to a number of problems. First, it diverts resources away from the more productive social investments that the central government would prefer. In effect, it dramatically limits the ability of the central government to control the direction of investment in the economy. Second, it has encouraged some governments to erect barriers to trade in order to protect local investments (and implicitly to protect the local tax base). Third, it is not clear that decentralization in the budgetary and extrabudgetary accounts has led to a more rapid economic growth rate (Zhang and Zou, 1996).

The validity of the argument that the center was losing its ability to control effectively the fiscal sector rests on the argument that an increasing share of total revenues was accruing to the local government sector.[21] This concern is borne out by the evidence presented in table 2.3. Moreover, the situation worsened through the early 1990s. The elasticity of central government revenue collections with respect to GNP during the 1985–93 period was 0.24, which is less than the 0.72 GNP elasticity of subnational government collections.[22] The collections' disparity in favor of local governments accelerated with the growth of the contracting system from 1988. During the 1985–87 period, the ratio of local government to total government budgetary collections averaged 54.2 percent. During the 1988–92 period, the average was 59.5 percent. The nexus of collections had clearly shifted toward the local governments.

The bigger issue is that the subnational governments' proportion of revenues, *after sharing*, was increasing. There was a net transfer of resources from the center to local governments after 1986 ("net transfer" is measured here as the sum of local government budgetary collections and earmarked transfers from the center to the local governments, less shared tax transfers from the local governments to the center). By 1990, the net transfer was about 2 billion yuan from the center to the local governments. As recently as 1985, there had been a significant net transfer to the center.

There are a number of reasons why this happened. First, the sharing formulas implemented in 1988 were negotiated to favor the local governments. Second, poor economic performance and natural disasters prevented local governments from reaching their negotiated amounts and forced the central government to forgive part of the planned transfer, and to increase earmarked grants. Third, local governments used their authority to grant tax concessions and favorable contracts, and this reduced the flow of revenue to the central government (Cullen and Fu, 1996: 7).

For whatever reasons, the central government's ability to use the fiscal system for macroeconomic policy purposes was quite limited by 1992. The center collected only 28 percent of total revenues in the country, and paid out more in transfers to the local government sector than it received back (table 2.3). The enterprise income tax had become a much less important fiscal instrument, largely because the local governments had more or less replaced it with negotiated contracts.

Evaluation of the 1994 reform

An evaluation of the success of the 1994 reform in improving intergovernmental fiscal relations is problematic, for two reasons. The first is that the objectives of the Chinese government were different from those pursued in most reforms of the system of central–local finances. The central government of China was attempting to wrestle control of fiscal and macroeconomic policy back from the local government sector. The evaluation of the reform must begin with an assessment of how well they did this. While it is also appropriate to consider the more usual issues that arise when one evaluates an intergovernmental reform – equalization and local autonomy, for example – it is necessary to recognize that these were not the driving forces behind the Chinese reform.

The second problem is that data are not yet available to carry out a quantitative analysis of the new system of revenue-sharing. In part, this is because the Chinese government has not yet made available the detailed data on the outcomes in the post-reform period. The data now available for 1994 and 1995 may show only muted effects of the reform on the intergovernmental fiscal system because of the provisions to maintain previous levels during a "transition" period.

Central control

Will the 1994 reform recentralize the fiscal system? The shift of the VAT to a central revenue source and the elimination of contracting would seem to guarantee this result. Note from table 2.3 that in 1994 and 1995, the central government collected 52 and 56 percent of total revenues, and was in a surplus position.[23] The local governments, on the other hand, were in a deficit position and forced to rely on grant distributions from the center. China has moved to the top-down revenue-sharing approach which is used by most countries in the world.

In fact the central government's gain of control over the aggregate budget is understated here because of a transitional revenue-sharing arrangement. In the longer term, fiscal recentralization will be occurring in three important ways:

- The VAT is the most productive tax in the system, is fully administered by the central government, and is no longer a shared tax.
- Revenue-sharing in China is now top-down rather than bottom-up, and the central government can more easily control the allocation of funds.
- There is no longer a contracting mechanism that will allow local governments and enterprises to negotiate tax liabilities. This means that the tax measures undertaken for stabilization purposes now have a better chance to achieve their desired objectives.

The move to an assignment system for local government revenues raises two issues. First, the assignment of the enterprise income taxes to local governments may present difficulties in the future. As and when Chinese enterprises begin to operate in multiple provinces, the problem of allocating profits will arise and will bring complication and possibly undesirable competition. The US experience is a case in point (McLure, 1981). It is unlikely that the provinces can build their long-run fiscal health on an enterprise income tax. The assignment of the VAT to the central government is appropriate, because the VAT is best administered centrally. But sharing the VAT on a derivation basis, as is still done, encourages protectionist-type activities by provinces to preserve their tax base. A formula-based system for sharing VAT revenues with the provinces would avoid this problem.

Resources available to local governments

The resources available to local government under the reformed system will depend on whether the overall rate of revenue mobilization is increased, and on the willingness of the central government to make transfers to local government from its new-found wealth.

With respect to total revenues available, the government expects the net effect of the reform to be revenue-neutral in the short run. On the one hand, there are expected negative revenue effects, *ceteris paribus* from lowering the top enterprise income tax rate from 55 percent to 33 percent; from eliminating the surtaxes; and from correcting part of the understatement of labor and capital costs in calculating enterprise profits. A potential short-run revenue loss could be anticipated from the switch to the credit invoice method under the VAT. This is a completely different approach to VAT administration, and some transition costs could be incurred in the first years of operation.[24]

Other elements of the reform are expected to produce revenue increases. The elimination of contracting could increase revenues significantly. Revenues from the enterprise income tax will also increase as a result of the elimination of the loan repayment deduction that will broaden the base. The World Bank (1990) estimated the revenue cost of the loan repayment deduction to be equivalent to about 3 percent of total revenue in 1986. If enterprise income tax revenues were to be restored to 1985 levels, relative to GNP, total government tax revenues would be higher by about 6 percent of GNP.

Short-run revenue-neutrality has not yet been achieved. Total revenue collections continued to fall in 1994 and 1995 relative to GNP (table 2.2).[25] The long-run revenue consequences of the reform, however, are likely to be more significant. The value-added tax is a more efficient revenue-raising instrument than the product tax, in that it reaches a much greater number of transactions and it has a self-policing component. If the administration of the Chinese sales tax was deficient, the shift to a credit-invoice VAT could bring significantly greater long-run revenue growth than the present system. Wong, Heady, and Woo (1995: 52), point out that the buoyancy of the Chinese VAT in the pre-reform period was low relative to that in other countries. The elasticity of the income tax could also increase because the incentives for locals to offer preferential income tax relief have been reduced. Moreover, the local governments have an intimate familiarity with local enterprises and can enhance the efficiency of local collections.

There are aspects of this reform that suggest diminished local government revenues. The more income-elastic VAT was assigned fully to the central government. Revenues from the VAT are now shared with local governments, but this seems to be a transition measure, and in the long run, derivation-based VAT-sharing may be phased out. The reform assigns all income taxes to the local governments. If the long-run elasticity of the income taxes is less than that of the VAT, and surely it will be, then the relative growth potential of local government taxes will be less. Moreover, the enterprise income tax is less stable over the business cycle, hence local government revenue streams will become less certain.

The longer-run revenue position of local governments would appear to depend on the central government assigning another significant source of taxation to the local governments or establishing a buoyant intergovernmental grant program. The individual income tax, with an expanded base and piggybacked on to the central tax, would seem the ideal revenue source for Chinese provincial governments. As to increased transfers, a more productive VAT would increase the central pool available for tax-sharing and for earmarked grants. Whether local governments would actually benefit from an increased revenue pool depends on the willingness of the central government to allocate more resources to the subnational level.

Local government autonomy

The 1994 reform did not increase the autonomy of local governments in taxation. The power to set rates and define bases, for all taxes, remained with the central government. In the past, local governments had taken some autonomy using "back-door" approaches such as providing preferential tax treatments in return for infrastructure investment, or to pursue industrial policy. The 1994 reform eliminated the practice of enterprise tax contracts with local governments. This was unquestionably good tax policy. The elimination of contracting substituted a transparent tax system for a negotiated one, and placed all enterprises on a more equal footing.

However much this measure improved the functioning of the economy, it did reduce the fiscal discretion of local governments. Local governments in China had made the granting of tax incentives an integral part of their industrial policy. Moreover, they had used a combination of tax incentives and discretion in matters of tax administration to leverage more social overhead investment by enterprises. The elimination of these preferential, discretionary tax treatments was necessary for macroeconomic purposes, but it clearly weakened fiscal decentralization.

The changes in the tax administration system may also be having a centralizing effect. Local governments now collect only income taxes and the smaller "local taxes" and no longer exert control over the assessment, collection, and audit of the VAT. An important component of local government discretion in tax administration was thus eliminated.

Fiscal disparities

Evaluation of the equalization features of the revenue-sharing system is not straightforward, since the government's objectives are not clear on this matter. We can, however, address the question of whether the reform will increase or reduce fiscal disparities. Four questions could be answered on an *a priori* basis, and supporting empirical evidence might be provided:

- Has the spread in the revenue collection rate between rich and poor provinces changed?
- Have expenditure differences between provinces changed?
- Is there evidence of greater equalization than in the pre-reform period?
- Do provinces still exert the same pattern of tax effort as in the pre-reform period?

Revenue capacity

Revenue collections are determined by income level and tax effort. One would expect wealthier provinces to have a significant advantage, and the data seem to bear this out in the pre-reform period. In 1992, the five wealthiest provinces accounted for 23 percent of GDP and 13 percent of the national population but about one-fourth of all revenue collections. In 1995, with local revenue collections now primarily income taxes, the revenue share rose to 30 percent (table 2.4). The five poorest provinces accounted for about 13 percent of national income but 19 percent of the population. The provinces collected about 12 percent of total revenue and the share fell between 1992 and 1995. The disparity in per capita revenue collections among the provinces in 1995 ranged from 1,551 yuan in Shanghai to 139 yuan in Anhui.

The relationship between income level and collection rate can be tested in a more systematic way to determine if it generally explains the pattern of variation in per capita collections across the twenty-eight provinces.[26] We have estimated a linear regression of per capita collections by local governments in 1990 and 1995 on per capita GDP and population size. Per capita GDP is included to measure the taxing power of the province, and population gives the impact of a size effect on local collections.

The results presented in table 2.5 show a strong significant relationship between per capita revenue collections and per capita income in both years. The cross-sectional income elasticities are about unity: in 1995, a 10 percent difference in per capita income tended to be associated with about a 10 percent difference in per capita revenue collections. Population size did show the expected negative relationship with revenues.[27]

Table 2.4. *Fiscal and economic concentration in rich and poor provinces*

	1990	1995
Five richest provinces[a]		
Percentage of GDP	22.8	23.9
Percentage of population	12.7	12.4
Percentage of revenue collections	26.0	30.3
Percentage of local government expenditures	19.8	25.5
Five poorest provinces[b]		
Percentage of GDP	12.7	10.6
Percentage of population	18.9	19.0
Percentage of revenue collections	12.3	10.5
Percentage of local government expenditures	14.0	12.4

Notes:
[a] Shanghai, Beijing, Tianjin, Guangdong, and Zhejiang.
[b] Guizhou, Gansu, Sha'anxi, Jiangxi, and Henan. Tibet and Hainan are excluded because of special circumstances and data availability.
Sources: Computed from data provided in the *Statistical Yearbook of China* and data provided by the Chinese Ministry of Finance.

Table 2.5. *Regressions of per capita local government revenues and expenditures on selected variables[a]*

	Per capita revenues		Per capita expenditures	
	1990	1995	1990	1995
Constant	−2.7636	−2.9755	2.4332	1.1178
	(3.64)	(4.32)	(4.10)	(1.63)
Population	1.1207	1.0736	0.5600	0.7235
	(12.25)	(14.01)	(7.84)	(9.46)
Per capita GDP	−0.0828	−0.1037	−0.3442	−0.2865
	(1.58)	(2.06)	(8.40)	(5.71)
R^2	0.88	0.95	0.89	0.86
N^b	28	28	28	28

Notes:
[a] All variables expressed in logarithms with *t*-statistics shown in parentheses below the regression coefficients.
[b] Tibet and Hainan are not included.

There has been some weakening in the relationship between collections and income. Virtually all of the higher income provinces had growth rates in budgetary collections that were below the 1987–92 national average (Bahl, 1994). The regression estimates presented in table 2.5 show that the cross-sectional income elasticity of collections fell from 1.12 in 1990 to 1.07 in 1995.

Expenditure variations

Disparities are much less pronounced on the expenditure side of local budgets, because of the equalizing effects of the transfer system. In 1995, per capita expenditures varied from highs of 1,837 yuan in Shanghai and 1,234 yuan in Beijing to 228 yuan in Henan and 225 yuan in Anhui.[28] The five highest-income provinces, with 13 percent of the population, account for 25 percent of the expenditures, whereas the five lowest-income ones, with 19 percent of the population account for 12 percent of expenditures. We can conclude that per capita expenditure variations in China are very great indeed, even though less than those for collections.

What are the determinants of the variations? Higher-income provinces spend significantly more on a per capita basis because of the greater demand for public services by their citizens and their enterprises, their ability to raise more "local fixed" revenues, their ability to attract more grants, and very importantly, their ability to slow the flow of revenues to the center. More heavily populated provinces spend less on a per capita basis, because the fixed component of their cost is spread over a larger population base. The expenditure regression results presented in table 2.5 confirm these expectations. About three-quarters of the interprovince variations in per capita expenditures can be explained by variations in per capita income and population size. Both variables are significant and have the expected sign. The expenditure income elasticity is smaller than the revenue elasticity in both years, suggesting some degree of equalization in the system. In 1995, a 10 percent higher level of per capita income was, on average, associated with about a 1 percent higher level of per capita expenditures and a 1 percent higher level of per capita collection. The equalization of the system appeared to lessen between 1990 and 1995.

Redistribution and the 1994 reform

One could make the case that the 1994 fiscal reform will not reduce disparities in per capita expenditures, nor will it compensate for uneven taxable capacity among the provinces. An unintended effect of the fiscal reform of 1994 is a possible widening of the fiscal disparities among provinces. By giving the local governments all revenues raised from income taxes, on a derivation basis, the central government has given an advantage to the higher-income provinces with more profitable enterprises. And by giving local governments responsibility for collecting these taxes, advantage has been given to the provinces that have the means to mount better administrative efforts. Again these are likely to be the better-off provinces.

The empirical analysis presented above shows that per capita expenditure disparities are less pronounced than per capita revenue collection disparities, suggesting some degree of equalization in the system. However, this pattern is less true in 1995 than it was in 1990, suggesting that the reformed system may be less equalizing.[29]

Tax effort
A criticism of the present intergovernmental fiscal system is that there is insufficient incentive for revenue mobilization, and therefore tax effort on the part of the local governments is lower than it should be. This should have been expected in the pre-reform system. The tax-sharing formula was based on a retention rate where a percentage of collections was paid to the central government. This provided a significant incentive to move funds from the budgetary accounts to the extrabudgetary ones. Moreover, the local administration still saw itself partly as tax collector from the state-owned enterprises, and partly as owner. Jun Ma (1996) shows that the central government's failure to commit to pre-announced revenue-sharing formulas tempted local governments to reduce their tax collection efforts.

Can local governments influence tax effort? In the pre-reform system, the answer was that they could, in many ways. The local administration could negotiate "revenue-losing" contracts with local enterprises, could give tax incentives to them, and could urge the local tax collection service to be less vigorous in their efforts. As Casanegra (1987: 25) has pointed out, ". . . tax administration *is* tax policy." Even in the reformed system, there may be inducements to lower levels of tax effort. Though they may no longer write tax contracts, local governments now control the administration of all income taxes. Though the giving of tax incentives now imposes a dollar-for-dollar loss to local budgets, relief from the enterprise income tax still may be provided for industrial policy purposes. The revenue cost may be made up with a central grant, which, without conditions, might be seen locally as a substitute for higher income tax collections.

We have carried out a tax effort analysis, following the approach described in Bahl and Wallich (1992) and updated in World Bank (1993). The first step is to estimate an OLS regression of per capita local government revenue collections on per capita income and population size. The

Table 2.6. *Tax effort indices and rankings: 1990 and 1995*

Province	1990			1995		
	Tax effort indices	Tax effort rankings	Per capita GDP ranking	Tax effort indices	Tax effort rankings	Per capita GDP ranking
Beijing	1.00	15	2	1.16	5	2
Tianjin	1.03	13	3	1.03	12	3
Hebei	0.92	20	13	0.92	21	14
Shanxi	1.14	5	15	1.30	3	18
Inner Mongolia	0.99	16	16	0.96	18	16
Liaoning	1.12	6	4	1.12	7	6
Jilin	1.07	7	19	0.99	16	13
Heilongjing	1.02	14	8	0.95	19	11
Shanghai	1.40	2	1	1.30	4	1
Jiangsu	0.93	19	7	0.68	27	7
Zhejiang	1.07	8	6	0.67	28	5
Anhui	0.84	23	24	0.93	20	22
Fujian	1.03	12	11	1.01	14	8
Jiangxi	0.88	21	22	1.08	9	26
Shandong	0.77	26	9	0.77	26	10
Henan	0.94	18	26	0.97	17	25
Hubei	0.87	22	12	0.85	23	15
Hunan	0.97	17	18	1.06	10	20
Guangdong	0.75	27	5	1.39	2	4
Guangxi	1.06	9	28	1.03	13	19
Sichuan	1.05	10	25	1.05	11	23
Guizhou	1.32	3	29	1.11	8	30
Yunan	1.78	1	21	1.60	1	24
Sha'anxi	1.05	11	20	1.00	15	27
Gansu	1.27	4	23	1.13	6	29
Qinghai	0.81	25	14	0.79	25	17
Ningxia	0.82	24	17	0.88	22	21
Xingjiang	0.68	28	10	0.83	24	12

results of this analysis are presented in table 2.5. This equation is then used to obtain an "estimated" value of per capita collections for each province. This might be interpreted as a measure of taxable capacity, that is, it is the amount that a province would raise if it used its tax base to the same extent as other provinces. For example, in 1995 Hebei is estimated to have a capacity to raise taxes of 203 yuan per capita (predicted by the equation), but actually raises only 186 yuan per capita. Hebei, then, has a tax effort index of 0.92, which is 8 percent below the average and ranks Hebei twenty-first among the provinces in tax effort in 1995.

The estimated indices of tax effort are presented for each province for 1990 and 1995 in table 2.6. There seems to be no clear pattern to the distribution of tax effort indices. There is no significant correlation with either per capita income, the ratio of expenditures to collections, or the rate of urbanization. The results do not support the hypothesis that the present revenue-sharing system reduces the rate of revenue mobilization.

Summary appraisal of the reform

China's 1994 reform was not promoted primarily as one to encourage fiscal decentralization – in fact, the announced objective was precisely the opposite. But the reform program has had profound effects on the balance of powers between central and local governments in one of the most important countries in the world. Though data are not yet available to do a full quantitative evaluation of the outcome, the following are some stylized conclusions that might be drawn.

First, China is not a federal country, but its public finance system has features of fiscal federalism. Using the Western model for evaluating reforms of fiscal federalism, we might conclude that the Chinese reforms were neither efficiency-enhancing nor equalizing. However, they were aimed primarily at redressing what was perceived as too great a revenue distribution to the local governments, and at regaining control over industrial policy.

Second, one cannot separate tax policy, tax administration, and intergovernmental fiscal structure in evaluating fiscal decentralization in China. The 1994 tax structure reform was good tax policy. But in assigning enterprise income taxes to local governments, and continuing a derivation-based VAT, the reform was not good intergovernmental policy. The division of tax administration powers between local and central governments was good policy in that it overcame the problem of divided loyalties on the part of local tax administrators, but local governments are left with full responsibility for a tax whose rate and base they cannot influence.

Third, there is little in the 1994 reform that will increase the fiscal autonomy of subnational governments in China. The new budget law does give some discretion over spending composition, but the revenue constraint is still imposed by the center. Moreover, anticipated future tax structure changes in the enterprise income tax may further tighten this constraint. Yet by moving the structure away from a negotiated model toward a more objective system, the center has put in place the basis for a future fiscal decentralization. The former negotiated system with divided tax administration responsibilities would never support a Western-type fiscal decentralization.

Fourth, the long-term impact of the new revenue-sharing system and the new tax structure is a recentralization of revenues. The local share will diminish in future years if the present arrangement is maintained. Either a new source of local government tax revenue must emerge, expenditure reassignment to the central government must take place, or the grant system must be expanded.

Fifth, the new revenue-sharing formula is more transparent than the previous negotiated system, and this is a major improvement. However, it is not equalizing, it does not provide incentives for increased revenue mobilization, and, in the transition period, it retains some bad features: the VAT continues to be shared on a derivation basis and the earmarked grants are still distributed on an *ad hoc* basis. As Bird (1984: 217) so correctly noted in the context of the Colombian reform, "more good ideas have probably come to naught because of transitional difficulties than for any other reason except the political opposition of those who would lose as a result of the change." The final test of the success of the revenue-sharing reform in China – at least from a Western perspective about what is good decentralization – is whether the transitional arrangements can be abandoned in favor of a fully objective system.

Grading China's decentralization

Large countries tend to decentralize their government because the diseconomies of central management are great, because large countries tend to be ethnically diverse, and because large countries have wide variations among their provinces in the demand for government services. China is something of a paradox in that it is the largest country in the world but continues with a highly centralized fiscal structure. Predictably, however, local governments, sometimes acting independently and sometimes acting with the consent of the central government, have taken "back-door" approaches to fiscal autonomy. The 1994 reform eliminated some of these surreptitious routes to local autonomy, and took the first steps toward establishing a modern, assignment-based intergovernmental fiscal system.

Because the 1994 reform represented such an important policy crossroads, it would seem a good time to take stock of the Chinese version of decentralization. The criteria for effective decentralization shown in the left column of table 2.7 provide a checklist. The conclusion from this evaluation is that China is in the very early stages of decentralization, and many of the features required for successful local governance are not yet in place.

The biggest difference between China and the decentralized systems in the West is the absence of popular representation. Local councils must be popularly elected and local chief officials must be locally appointed for the efficiency gains from decentralization to occur (Bahl and Linn, 1992: ch. 3). The other major difference from international practice in decentralized

Table 2.7. *Requirements for effective decentralization*

Benchmark	Situation in China
Elected local council	Elections, but not popular elections.
Locally appointed chief officials	Chief provincial and local government officials are appointed by the next highest level of government.
Locally approved budget	Local authority budgets do not require approval, but total revenues are fixed by the center.
Absence of mandates as regards local government employment and salaries	Guidelines provided by the central government.
Local governments may exert control on the level of some revenue sources	Local governments may choose whether or not to levy certain taxes or charges. The rates and bases of nearly all taxes, however, are beyond their reach.
Local governments have some powers to borrow	Local governments may not borrow directly.
The grant system is transparent and local governments understand their entitlements	The grant system is *ad hoc*. The central government decides on the retention rates under the sharing system, and on the distribution of earmarked grants.
Expenditure assignment is clear	Expenditure assignment is relatively clear to local government officials.
Local governments have the capacity to collect taxes and deliver services efficiently	Local governments vary widely in their capacity to deliver services effectively. Problems arise mostly because of limited revenues and shortage of capital and skilled employees.
Local governments keep adequate books of account	The professional and technical ability of staff in many local authorities is below the level needed to produce accurate and meaningful accounts. In some provinces the capacity is quite strong.
The central government has the ability to monitor the progress of effective fiscal decentralization	There is a fiscal planning unit that deals with intergovernmental fiscal relations in the Ministry of Finance, but there is no strong underlying data system to support the work of the staff.

countries is on the financing side: local governments in China may not set tax rates or borrow for capital projects. Again, determination of the size of local government is largely a matter of central decision. These are the major structural impediments to an effective system of local government financing.

There are also capacity problems to be overcome. There is a wide variation in the ability of local governments to absorb more fiscal responsibility.

Some provincial and municipal governments in China have well-developed systems of fiscal administration, while others (especially in the rural areas) have very weak ones. It is also a problem that the central government presently has only a limited ability to monitor local government fiscal behavior.

On the other hand, some significant recent changes in the fiscal system could set the stage for fiscal decentralization. The 1994 reform systematized the situation by eliminating the practice of "every province for itself" autonomy. The first steps toward decentralization have been taken on the expenditure side, which is the right place to begin. Local governments have some budget autonomy and are subject to relaxed guidelines as regards public expenditure mandates, and expenditure assignment seems relatively clear.

Looking forward, one could take two differing views about the future of decentralization in China. One is that the 1994 reform clearly was a recentralization of the fiscal system and weakened the hand of the local governments. The other view is that the reform replaced a negotiated system with a structure on which a decentralized system could be built. If decentralization were a goal of the Chinese government, and it is not clear that this is the case, then the following reforms are now more within reach than in the period before 1994: a transparent grant system, based on formula rather than *ad hoc* distributions and derivation; taxation by an assignment system and possibly with some local discretion to add surtaxes to national bases; an individual income tax as an important source of local government revenue; and local borrowing powers, at least for the largest and most prosperous provinces. If such measures are to be part of the next steps in Chinese fiscal reform, the central government would do well to begin by strengthening its capacity to provide technical leadership and to monitor local government fiscal behavior.

Notes

1 Throughout this chapter we use the term "local government" to refer to all subnational governments.

2 An evaluation of the tax structure implications of the reform is in Bahl (forthcoming). In the tax and revenue sections of this chapter, I draw liberally on that earlier analysis. Baoyun Qioa provided excellent research assistance for both this chapter and the earlier paper.

3 The *Statistical Yearbook of China*, which is the data source used for most of this analysis, does not disaggregate indirect tax revenues by type, nor does it present detail on the smaller local levies. It does, however, provide official statistics on Chinese public finance. Other studies, however, have provided more

detail relying on unpublished data provided by the Ministry of Finance and the State Tax Bureau. These reports have shown the VAT, product tax, and business tax to account for about equal shares of indirect tax revenue in 1992 (Bahl, 1994).

4 The tax contracts varied widely, from lump-sum payments to marginal rates that varied with the level of profits. For a description, see World Bank (1990: annex 2).

5 All income tax revenues collected from centrally owned enterprises belong to the central government. All other enterprise income tax revenues, regardless of ownership, revert to the provincial government.

6 For a good description of sales taxes in China, see World Bank (1990: 28–34).

7 In total, the local tax service collects fifteen different taxes.

8 The evolution of the tax-sharing formulas is discussed in Bahl and Wallich (1992).

9 This description is elaborated in Qiang (1995).

10 In fact, in the initial years the revenue-sharing may be different from the 75/25 target because local governments were promised their revenues would be kept at least at 1993 levels in the first years of the reform.

11 World Bank (1993: 80–81) and Bahl (1994).

12 Data are not available for more recent years.

13 The simple correlation between per capita earmarked grants and per capita income is 0.425, and between per capita earmarked grants and population is −0.662 (Bahl, 1994).

14 For a discussion of the long-term growth of extrabudgetary revenues, and the composition of this growth, see Wong, Heady, and Woo (1995: appendix I).

15 The ratio of extrabudgetary to budgetary revenue increased with GNP over the 1983–92 period, as indicated by the following regression results:

$$\text{EXB/B} = 69.8 + 0.00093 \text{ GNP} \qquad R^2 = 0.43$$
$$(2.45)$$

where EXB = extrabudgetary revenue, B = budgetary revenue, and the figure in parentheses is the t-statistic.

16 The decline in the revenue share is exaggerated by the Chinese definition of revenues and expenditures, notably the treatment of debt issued as a revenue, debt repaid as an expenditure, subsidies to cover enterprise losses as a negative revenue, and the exclusion of government "departmental" revenues from the budgetary accounts. When adjustments are made to conform these data to standard international classifications, the results show that the Chinese revenue share of GNP still declined substantially, but less than is reported in table 2.2 (World Bank, 1994).

17 Various analysts estimate the tax ratio to be higher by 1 to 2 percent of GNP, depending on the data source used and the definition of revenues (Xu, 1995; World Bank, 1994; IMF, 1994). Data from the *Statistical Yearbook of China*, used in this chapter, give consistently lower estimates. All analyses, however, show much the same declining trend.

18 Neither is a comparatively low tax ratio an indicator of "bad" fiscal performance. Many of China's social services, for example, are provided as tax expenditures rather than through tax financing.

19 The consolidated fiscal deficit in China is not large by international standards (about 6 percent of GDP) but it has grown significantly since the late 1980s (World Bank, 1994).

20 Estimated from a linear regression of tax revenues on GNP with both variables expressed in logarithms. Technically, this is a buoyancy rather than an elasticity coefficient because no adjustments have been made for discretionary changes.

21 This argument was also made by Xu (1995: 1–25).

22 The elasticities were estimated from linear regression of tax collections on GNP with both variables expressed in logarithms, but no adjustments were made for discretionary changes.

23 The data in table 2.3 also indicate a local surplus in 1993, but this is an "announcement effect." In anticipation of the 1994 reform, local governments increased revenues in 1993 to establish a larger base for the new revenue-sharing system (Xu, 1995: 18).

24 Xu (1995, tables 2 and 3) estimates a reduction in both direct and indirect taxes as a result of the reform.

25 In fact, a decline in the tax share of GDP may not be inconsistent with revenue-neutrality, because the pre-reform system was already showing a declining trend relative to GDP.

26 Tibet and Hainan have been dropped from this analysis as special cases.

27 These relationships also held for the period 1985–90 in work reported by Bahl and Wallich (1992), Bahl (1994), and a study by Hofman reported in World Bank (1993). Hofman shows that virtually all of the variation in per capita collections can be explained by a *squared* per capita income term.

28 The range in 1991 per capita state and local government expenditures in the United States (excluding Alaska) was from $6,525 in New York to $2,715 in Arkansas. The range in China was more than three times that in the United States.

29 It is not entirely correct to draw conclusions about the new system based on 1995 results, because it was still in a transition period where part of the VAT was shared with local governments. Moreover, the sharing arrangements were irregular because of a provision whereby provinces were guaranteed support for their basic level of expenditures in 1993.

References

Bahl, Roy (1994), "China: tax structure and intergovernmental fiscal relations," paper prepared for the World Bank, Washington, DC (March).

(forthcoming) "Central-provincial-local relations: the revenue side," in Donald J. S. Brean, ed., *Taxation in Modern China*, London: Routledge.

Bahl, Roy W. and Linn, Johannes F. (1992), *Urban Public Finance in Developing Countries*, New York: Oxford University Press.

Bahl, Roy, and Wallich, Christine (1992), "Intergovernmental fiscal relations in China," Working Paper No. 863, Country Economics Department, The World Bank, Washington, DC (February).

Bird, Richard (1984), *Intergovernmental Finance in Colombia*, Cambridge, MA: Harvard Law School.

(1989), "The administrative dimension of tax reform in developing countries," in Malcolm Gillis (ed.), *Tax Reform in Developing Countries*, Durham, NC: Duke University Press.

Casanegra, Milka (1987), "Problems in administering a value-added tax in developing countries: an overview," Report No. DRD246, Development Research Department, World Bank, Washington, DC.

Chinese People's Bank of Construction (1993), "Investment-related background materials," unpublished paper, Planning Department (July 3).

Cullen, Richard, and Fu, H. L. (1996), "China's ambitious intergovernmental fiscal reform agenda," unpublished paper, City University of Hong Kong

IMF (International Monetary Fund) (1994), *Economic Reform in China: A New Phase* (Occasional Paper 114), Washington, DC: World Bank.

Ma, Jun (1996), *Intergovernmental Relations and Macroeconomic Management in China*, New York: St. Martin's Press.

McLure, Charles E., Jr. (1981), "The elusive incidence of the corporate income tax: the state case," *Public Finance Quarterly* 9: 395–413.

Qiang, Gao (1995), "Problems in Chinese inter-governmental fiscal relations and the main difficulties in future reform," in Ehtishem Ahmad, Gao Qiang, and Vito Tanzi, eds., *Reforming China's Public Finances*, Washington, DC: International Monetary Fund.

Wong, Christine, Heady, Christopher, and Woo, Wing T. (1995), *Fiscal Management and Economic Reform in the People's Republic of China*, Manila: Asian Development Bank.

World Bank (1990), China: *Revenue Mobilization and Tax Policy*, Washington, DC.

(1993), *Budgetary Policies and Intergovernmental Fiscal Relations*, Washington, DC.

(1994), *China: Country Economic Memorandum, Macroeconomic Stability in a Decentralized Economy*, Washington, DC.

Xu, Shanda (1995), "Recent fiscal and tax reform in the People's Republic of China," Fifth Symposium on Tax Policy and Reforms in the Asian and Pacific Region (October 24–26).

Zhang, Tao, and Zou, Heng-Fu (1996), "Fiscal decentralization, public spending, and economic growth in China," Policy Research Department, World Bank.

Zhongli, Liu (1996), "Report on the implementation of the central and local budgets for 1995 and on the draft central and local budgets for 1996," paper delivered at the Eighth National Peoples' Congress (March 5).

3

India: intergovernmental fiscal relations in a planned economy

M. GOVINDA RAO

There has been a resurgence of interest in fiscal decentralization in virtually every part of the world in the last three decades. Interest has not merely been confined to constitutionally declared federations but has also been seen in unitary countries; it spans both the ideological spectrum and levels of development across countries. While the emergence of the European Union as an economic entity has underlined the advantages of having an enlarged common market with a distinct regional identity, the economic collapse of the former Soviet Union has demonstrated the dangers of economic and administrative centralization. In general, administrative and fiscal decentralization has been prompted by the emphasis placed on providing efficient and responsive public services. However, fiscal decentralization has often been warranted by market decentralization arising from economic liberalization. In India too, in keeping with the general trend, decentralization has been a much debated issue.

India represents a classic case of a federation with constitutional demarcation of functions and finances between the center and the states.[1] The 920 million people in the federation are spread over twenty-five states and seven centrally administered territories (two with their own elected governments). Separate legislative, executive, and judicial arms of government are constituted at both central and state levels. The upper house, or *Rajya Sabha*, in the federal parliament is the House of States, to which members are elected by an electoral college from each of the states. The Seventh Schedule to the Constitution specifies the legislative domains of the central and state governments in terms of union, state, and concurrent lists. The Constitution also requires the president of India to appoint a Finance Commission every five years (or earlier) to review the finances of

I am grateful to Richard Bird, K. P. Kalirajan, Rohinton Medhora, Ric Shand, Nirvikar Singh, and François Vaillancourt for useful discussions and comments on an earlier draft of this chapter. Thanks are also due to other participants in the conference on "Fiscal decentralization in developing countries" and particularly to Ms. France St-Hilaire for extremely useful comments.

the center and the states and recommend devolution of taxes and grants-in-aid for the ensuing five years.

Historical factors played an important part in the adoption in India of a federal constitution with strong unitary features. During British rule, administrative and fiscal centralization was a colonial necessity. At the same time, the difficulty of administering a large country with a number of principalities with divergent languages, cultures, and traditions did call for some degree of decentralization. Indeed, for a period of about two decades in British India, prior to the enactment of the Government of India Act 1935, the system required the provinces to make a contribution to the center. Although there were strong arguments for decentralization at the time of independence in 1947 and even though the United Kingdom Cabinet Mission Plan envisaged limited powers for the center in a three-tiered federal structure, the constitution that was eventually adopted by the Indian Republic closely followed the Government of India Act 1935, with pronounced "quasi-federal" features. The shift probably occurred for two reasons: first, once the Muslim majority areas opted out of India to form Pakistan, the major reason for a loose federal structure had vanished; second, a strong center was found desirable to safeguard against fissiparous tendencies within some of the constituent units (Chelliah, 1991).

The centralization inherent in the constitutional assignment was accentuated by the adoption of a planned development strategy. Centralized decision-making in relation to production and distribution activities and the disposal of resources in the "national interest" implicit in central planning are the negation of the very principle of federalism. Although in India economic planning has been implemented in a mixed-economy framework, the strategy of a public-sector-dominated, heavy-industry-based, import-substituting industrialization required the Planning Commission to allocate resources according to the envisaged priorities. The central government had to issue industrial licenses, allocate credit by controlling the financial institutions, and ration the scarce foreign exchange available among the different industries to conform to the envisaged priorities. It also had to introduce a host of measures to control and regulate the private sector to ensure that those who were given the license to produce and import did not exercise their oligopoly powers. This automatically concentrated economic as well as administrative powers (Chelliah, 1991).

Recent events, however, have called for a greater degree of decentralization to make the administrative and fiscal regimes compatible with political and economic changes. On the political front, the decline in the influence of the Indian National Congress, the political party which ruled the country for over four decades, and the emergence of a number of regional political parties in the ruling coalition at the center have shifted the balance of political power to the regions from the center. In the economic sphere, a compelling reason for a greater degree of fiscal decentralization has been the reassessment of the role of the state in resource allocation. The economic crisis of 1991 highlighted the inherent weaknesses in the dominant development strategy. The fiscal arrangements and institutions developed in the context of interventionist strategy need to be reoriented to provide public services according to the diversified demands of different regions.

This chapter reviews the federal fiscal arrangements in India with a view to identifying the areas for reform in the emerging economic environment. The starting point for such a review is the assignment of fiscal responsibilities. The assignment of taxes and expenditures between the center and individual states should not only be in accordance with the principle of comparative advantage but also ensure a clear linkage between revenue-raising and expenditure decisions at the margin. However, even the most efficient system of assignments cannot clearly match the revenue and expenditure powers of individual governmental units. When the fiscal powers of different governmental units overlap, free-riding behavior among them causes center–state and interstate fiscal disharmonies. The discussion on assignments and fiscal overlapping in the Indian federation leads us to the analysis of vertical and horizontal mismatches between revenue and expenditure powers, or what are known as fiscal imbalances. These imbalances can be a source of inequity and inefficiency and, therefore, intergovernmental transfer mechanisms must be designed to resolve them. The analysis of federal fiscal arrangements in India should lead us to identify critical areas for reform.

The assignment question

Tax and expenditure assignments – principles and practices

Assignment of functions and sources of finances among different layers of government is an important step in the efficient organization of federal fiscal systems. For analytical convenience, the layer-cake perspective on federalism in the Musgravian tripartite division of governmental functions assigns stabilization and redistribution mainly to the central government and the allocation function is shared among the hierarchical layers depending upon their comparative advantage in carrying out different functions.[2] The "decentralization theorem" (Oates, 1972) suggests that, so long as there are no scale economies, the subcentral provision of public services results in welfare gains. The gains will be greater, the larger the variation in the preferences for public services (Oates, 1977b). The above principle implies that progressive and mobile tax bases should be assigned primarily to the central government, and the subcentral units should raise revenues mainly through user charges, benefit taxes, and taxes on relatively less mobile bases (Musgrave, 1983). At the same time, to reap welfare gains, the lower-level jurisdictions would have to provide all non-national public services, and this would create a serious asymmetry between revenue sources and expenditure functions, or what is termed "vertical fiscal imbalance" (Hunter, 1977).

The above problem can be alternatively stated in terms of the literature on "competitive federalism."[3] Successful interjurisdictional competition requires that the assignment of functions should be done according to comparative advantage. Given that many tax bases are mobile across jurisdictions, the more senior governments have a comparative advantage in levying taxes since they can more effectively control "free-riding" (or enjoying the benefits of public services without making commensurate payments). Free-riding can take the form of tax avoidance and evasion, interstate tax exportation, or benefit spillovers. The lower-level governments, on the other hand, have a comparative advantage in reducing the welfare costs of providing public services. For, at lower levels, the mismatch between goods supplied and demanded would be smaller and the bundling of public services more flexible.[4] Welfare costs can be reduced either by moving to the jurisdictions providing the preferred bundle of public services ("exit") or by consumers influencing policies in order to obtain the preferred pattern of public services ("voice"). Thus, assignments made according to comparative advantage would result in revenue concentration and expenditure decentralization. Intergovernmental transfers are necessary to resolve this problem of vertical imbalance (Breton and Fraschini, 1992).

Analysis of the actual fiscal assignments in different federations, however, brings out three important features. First, vertical fiscal imbalance is a feature in all federations.[5] This has occurred because the actual assignments of tax and expenditure powers are made broadly according to the principle of comparative advantage. Of course, we cannot conclude from this that greater vertical fiscal imbalance necessarily denotes greater efficiency in assignments. Second, an assignment of powers which minimizes concurrence or overlap can only be made in a *de jure* sense. *De facto* overlapping of tax and expenditure powers between different jurisdictions is unavoidable. Third, concurrency in tax and expenditure powers is not necessarily undesirable if there are mechanisms to coordinate the policy actions of different governmental units, and the benefit of coordination exceeds its cost.

Tax and expenditure assignments in India

The tax and expenditure powers of the central and the state governments are specified in the Seventh Schedule to the Constitution. The functions required to maintain macroeconomic stability, international relations, and activities having significant scale economies have been assigned exclusively to the center or have to be carried out concurrently with the states. The functions which have a statewide jurisdiction are assigned to the states. Most broad-based and progressive tax bases have been assigned to the center. The center also has residual tax powers. A number of taxes have been assigned to the states as well, but from the point of view of revenue productivity, only the tax on the sale and purchase of goods is important. The states can borrow from the central government. They have the powers to borrow from the market as well, but if a state is indebted to the central government, the borrowing has to be approved by the center.

Notably, the tax powers are assigned on the basis of the principle of separation and the tax bases are assigned exclusively either to the center or to the states. However, the separation is only in the legal sense, not in the economic one, and this gives rise to anomalous situations. Thus, taxes on production (excise duty) can be levied by the center, whereas the tax on the sale of goods is leviable by the states. Similarly, the taxes on agricultural incomes and wealth are leviable by the states, whereas those on non-agricultural incomes and wealth are leviable by the center. The states have found taxing agricultural incomes politically infeasible besides being administratively difficult. At the same time, the separation of the tax base has opened up a floodgate for both avoidance and evasion of the personal income tax.[6]

The Constitution also recognizes that the states' tax powers are inadequate to meet their expenditure needs and, therefore, provides for the sharing of revenues from personal income tax (Article 270) and Union excise duty (Article 272). States in need of additional assistance can be also be given grants-in-aid (Article 275). The tax devolution and grants-in-aid are to be determined by the Finance Commission, an independent body appointed by the President every five years (Article 280).

The shares of the central and state governments in revenues and expenditures, summarized in tables 3.1 and 3.2, bring out their relative roles. It

Table 3.1. *India: revenue receipts of the central and state governments (percentages)*

Item of revenue	Revenue share 1985–86 Center	States	Revenue share 1990–91 Center	States	Revenue share 1994–95[a] Center	States	Percentage of total
Tax revenue	49.0	51.0	49.1	50.9	45.5	54.5	82.7
Exclusive central taxes	100.0	—	100.0	—	100.0	—	24.0
Corporation tax	100.0	—	100.0	—	100.0	—	7.6
Custom duties	100.0	—	100.0	—	100.0	—	15.2
Other	100.0	—	100.0	—	100.0	—	1.3
Exclusive state taxes	—	100.0	—	100.0	—	100.0	31.2
State excise duties	—	100.0	—	100.0	—	100.0	4.4
Sales taxes	—	100.0	—	100.0	—	100.0	16.4
Taxes on transport	—	100.0	—	100.0	—	100.0	2.6
Other	—	100.0	—	100.0	—	100.0	7.8
Shared taxes	51.6	48.4	51.4	48.6	49.1	51.9	27.4
Personal income tax	26.5	73.5	23.4	76.6	22.2	77.8	6.3
Union excise duty	56.6	43.4	57.5	42.5	55.9	44.1	21.1
Non-tax revenue	62.1	37.9	54.3	45.7	80.8	19.2	17.3
Net contribution from public enterprises	−875.9	975.9	−288.1	388.1	119.2	−19.2	2.0
Administrative receipts	47.1	79.2	33.8	66.2	18.8	81.2	8.9
Interest receipts[b]	66.6	33.4	59.6	40.4	161.2	−61.2	5.8
External grants	100.0	—	100.0	—	100.0	—	0.7
Grants to states	—	100.0	—	100.0	—	100.0	—
Total revenue accrual	38.2	61.8	37.7	62.3	38.4	61.6	100.0
Total revenue collections	65.6	34.4	63.9	36.1	65.5	34.5	100.0

Notes:
[a] Revised estimates.
[b] Netted for the interest paid to the central government.
Source: Based on data from Ministry of Finance, India.

is seen that the states on average raise about 35 percent of current revenues and disburse about 57 percent of expenditures. The revenues derived from exclusive central taxes constitute about 24 percent of total revenue; those from exclusive state taxes 31 percent, the sharable sources constitute 27 percent, and the remaining 17 percent is from non-tax revenues. The major taxes levied exclusively by the center are customs duty (15 percent of total revenue) and corporation tax (8 percent). Among the state taxes, the revenue from sales tax constitutes about 16 percent. Other state taxes individually contribute less than 6 percent of the total revenue.

On the other hand, the share of the states in spending is about 57 percent,

Table 3.2. *Share of state governments in total expenditures (percentages)*

Item of expenditure	1985–86			1990–91			1994–95[a]			Percentage of total expenditure
	Current	Capital	Total	Current	Capital	Total	Current	Capital	Total	
Interest payment	34.6	0.0	34.6	35.5	0.0	35.5	37.2	0.0	37.2	20.1
Defense	0.0	0.0	0.0	0.0	0.0	0.0	0.0	0.0	0.0	9.1
Administrative service	85.2	0.8	78.0	76.4	1.8	73.4	66.2	14.7	65.8	13.7
Social and community services, *of which*	94.8	67.0	92.7	78.9	74.1	78.7	86.4	71.2	85.4	21.5
Education	84.8	79.5	84.7	84.5	61.7	83.9	86.1	43.4	84.9	11.8
Medical and health	92.5	94.8	92.8	90.3	95.3	90.7	91.4	96.1	92.0	4.3
Family welfare	93.4	90.4	93.1	92.2	100.0	92.7	93.5	100.0	93.8	0.6
Others	98.1	40.7	88.2	61.1	64.0	61.4	81.6	65.2	79.9	4.8
Economic services, *of which*	78.1	46.3	62.9	50.2	53.1	51.1	56.8	66.0	59.5	27.4
Agriculture and allied services[b]	99.9	82.1	96.7	77.8	94.8	78.6	45.8	72.4	46.7	12.3
Industry and minerals	36.7	9.8	18.1	40.7	44.1	41.9	50.7	47.4	49.7	1.9
Power, irrigation and flood control	94.7	65.4	73.9	86.2	62.9	69.1	91.2	77.9	83.7	7.2
Transport and communication	68.3	68.3	68.3	70.4	32.1	47.3	67.6	52.7	60.1	3.8
Others	24.9	18.0	23.9	16.6	51.3	19.7	66.1	49.2	58.9	2.2
Other	80.0	14.7	33.2	57.2	0.0	57.2	85.9	0.0	85.8	5.1
Loans and advances	0.0	51.7	51.7	0.0	51.1	51.1	0.0	62.9	62.9	3.1
Total[c]	55.2	43.0	52.1	55.0	44.5	52.9	58.1	53.7	57.4	100.0

Notes:
[a] Revised estimates.
[b] Includes food and fertilizer subsidies.
[c] Excludes appropriation for reduction and avoidance of debt.
Source: Based on data from Ministry of Finance, India.

and in current expenditure, 58 percent. However, state control over spending is lower than indicated by these figures because about 15 percent of total expenditure is incurred on central sector and centrally sponsored schemes, which are the specific-purpose transfer schemes. State expenditures on these items actually increased from about 7 percent of the total in 1985–86 to about 13 percent in 1994–95.

The pattern of expenditures shown in table 3.2 indicates that the central government plays a major role in defense and industrial promotion. On the other hand, the states have a high share of expenditures on internal security, law and order, all social services, and economic services like agriculture, animal husbandry, forestry, fisheries, irrigation and power, and public works. The states' share in expenditure on administrative services is about two-thirds; on social services they spend over 85 percent and on economic services almost 60 percent.

Over the last decade, while the share of the states in raising revenues has remained stable, their expenditure share has increased by about five percentage points, particularly since 1990–91. This has occurred because fiscal reforms initiated in 1991 have led to deceleration in central government expenditures, but have not reduced central transfers to states; consequently, state expenditures have continued to grow as in the past to increase their share in the total. Interestingly, the expenditure share has increased for both current and capital expenditures.

This analysis of constitutional assignment in India brings out the following:

(1)   The Constitution exhibits a clear centripetal bias in the distribution of tax and regulatory powers. In addition to the expenditure functions assigned, the center can also influence the expenditure decisions of the states. The assignment of most of the broad-based taxes and residuary tax powers to the center, its overriding powers in regard to the functions in the concurrent list, and domination through economic planning and control of virtually the entire financial sector are only some instances of the center's dominance in the economic sphere.

(2)   The assignment of tax powers follows the principle of "separation," in contrast to that of "concurrence" followed in federations like the United States and Canada. This, however, cannot avoid *de facto* overlapping. The problem is particularly severe in the case of indirect taxes.

(3)   The Constitution allows the levy of certain taxes which create severe impediments to the interstate movement of goods. The levy of tax on interstate sale of goods by the exporting state (subject to a ceiling rate of

4 percent), besides creating resource distortions, has caused perverse transfer of resources from the poorer consuming states to the more affluent producing states. Similarly, the states can levy a tax on the entry of goods into a local area for consumption, use, or sale (*octroi*). This has created impediments to the free movement of goods and also erected a number of tariff zones coinciding with the localities in the country (Rao, 1993).

Tax and expenditure overlapping

Intergovernmental competition and fiscal disharmony

The pursuit of common objectives by different levels of government and the spillover effect of policies at one level on another can create conflict in jurisdictions. Often, the fiscal policies of subnational governments may conflict with that of the central government (Perloff, 1985). The subcentral governments may have their own ideas on redistributive and employment policies which the central fiscal action has to take into account. Besides, policies implemented at one level may spill over to affect the effectiveness of those at another level. An expansionary fiscal policy by the central government can enhance the unit cost and thus constrain the states' abilities to deliver public services. An increase in salary levels by the central government may itself have a demonstration effect on the states. Similarly, the central government may compress its own expenditures simply by reducing transfers to the states. Increases in the administered prices of central public enterprises could enhance the unit cost at the state level and vice-versa. A reduction in central subsidies may force the states to introduce them for electoral reasons. Similarly, increases in the excise duty by the center may cause the states to reduce taxes on these items.[7] These are just a few examples of the vertical interdependence of policies.

The most glaring instance of vertical fiscal overlapping is seen in the taxation of the same base by different levels of government. The Constitution assigns separate tax powers to the central and state governments, but, as mentioned earlier, the separation is done in the legal (administrative), not the economic, sense. Thus, while the center can levy tax on the production of goods (excise duty), the states can levy sales taxes on the sale of these goods. The states can also allow an urban local body to levy *octroi* on the same goods if they are transported into its jurisdiction.

The adverse allocative implications of the prevailing system of tax assignments are notable. First, the splitting of the power to levy taxes on income and capital between the central and the state governments on the basis of whether they are derived from agricultural or non-agricultural sources has led to distortions, tax avoidance, and tax evasion, besides violating the principle of horizontal equity (Chelliah, 1993). Second, although in a legal sense, the central excises and state sales taxes and *octroi* are separate levies, these fall virtually on the same base causing serious vertical tax overlapping. The levy of tax on tax and margins on taxes have created a divergence between producer and consumer prices greater than the tax element.

The Indian experience brings out three important lessons. First, tax assignment should not be done merely on legal considerations; economic consequences of such assignments must be taken into account. Second, avoidance of concurrency in a *de jure* sense does not prevent *de facto* overlapping. Third, overlapping by itself cannot be considered undesirable. What is important is that the tax policies of different levels should be properly coordinated and harmonized to minimize distortions. In the United States and Canada, even when the federal and state (provincial) governments enjoy concurrent tax powers, they have been able to achieve a greater degree of coordination and harmonization than India (Rao and Vaillancourt, 1994).

Interstate competition and fiscal disharmony

It is argued that efficiency under fiscal decentralization is enhanced because of the matching of the supply of public services with demand. The decentralization model, however, does not say much about production efficiency. Nevertheless, efficient and stable interstate competition in providing public services can help the governments to operate on the production frontier and even help them shift the frontier to the right.[8] However, the two important preconditions for efficient intergovernmental competition are "competitive equality" and "cost-benefit appropriability" (Breton, 1987). Competitive equality ensures that the larger/stronger units do not dominate or coerce smaller/weaker units, and this has to be enforced through either regional policies or intergovernmental grants. Cost-benefit appropriability ensures that the residents of a state are not able to consume public services without making commensurate payments.

Thus, in ensuring fair and efficient competition among the states, the central government has an important monitoring role. First, it should activate the process of competition by ensuring the free flow of factors and products across the country. Second, it should ensure "competitive equality" among the states through regional policies and by giving intergovernmental transfers to offset the fiscal disabilities of the poorer states. Third, it should initiate the process of harmonization in tax policies among the states to minimize interstate tax exportation and tax competition. Finally, it should, through cost-sharing programs, ensure optimal standards of services having a high degree of interstate spillovers.

A number of studies have examined the welfare implications of interjurisdictional tax competition but consensus on its desirability has yet to emerge. The conventional view is that interjurisdictional competition is a source of distortion. According to this view, cut-throat competition by states to attract trade and industry into their jurisdictions at the cost of other states can distort the allocation of resources (Netzer, 1991) and the race to the bottom in reducing tax rates would result in the less than optimal provision of public services. The alternative view is that interjurisdictional competition is a beneficent force. This view has found particular favor among the "leviathan" theorists who argue that such a competition can work as an effective constraint on the government's monopoly power to maximize revenue (Brennan and Buchanan, 1980). Oates and Schwab (1988) also show that when communities are homogeneous, where the costs and benefits are clearly perceived, and where public decision reflects the preferences of the residents of respective jurisdictions, interjurisdictional competition is efficiency-enhancing. However, even in this model, if the jurisdictions are constrained to tax capital for want of more efficient tax instruments and if public decisions deviate from the will of the electorate, tax competition may not lead to efficient outcomes.

It is difficult to find a situation where the assumptions of the model of benign competition will be satisfied in a developing country. Acute interstate inequalities in the level of development endow different states with differing degrees of competitive strength. The delinking of tax and expenditure decisions prevents the costs and the benefits of public decisions from being clearly perceived. Free-riding by the states can cause significant interstate tax spillovers.

When sales taxes predominate in state tax systems and when the states levy origin-based taxes, additional problems are created. First, the strategy of imposing different tax rates on items consumed by residents and on those exported to non-residents increases rate differentiation within each of the states. Second, tax competition can cause wide differences between the states' tax systems, depending on the structure of production and consumption and the type of strategy followed to maximize revenue and to attract capital. Third, origin-based consumption taxes which tax inputs and capital goods can result in cascading and may cause significant interstate tax exportation with adverse effects on both equity and efficiency. In particular, the levying of tax on interstate sales enables interstate tax exportation. Besides creating impediments to the free movement of goods across the country, the interstate sales tax causes significant resource transfers from the poorer to the richer states (Rao and Vaillancourt, 1994).

Thus, interstate tax competition results from attempts to indulge in free-riding behavior. The competition may take various forms:

- reducing nominal tax rates to maximize revenue by attracting cross-border purchases;
- levying selectively lower nominal tax rates and giving incentives to new industries to attract capital into their jurisdictions;
- adopting strategies to export the tax burden to non-residents by choosing appropriate tax systems and tax rates on both factors and products.

The strategy adopted by the states to divert trade into their jurisdictions and to export the tax burden to non-residents has been one of the causes of excessive differentiation in tax rates. The prevailing sales tax systems have a mix of first point (manufacturers), last point (retail), and multi-point (cumulative) taxes. In addition, to raise more revenue, the states have resorted to levying surcharges, turnover taxes, and additional sales taxes, resulting in acute differentiation in effective tax rates and making the tax system both complex and irrational. The attempt to attract capital through liberal tax concessions to new industries has further added to the complexity. The taxation of inputs and capital goods, in addition, has resulted in cascading.

Fiscal imbalances: trends and issues

Fiscal imbalance refers to the mismatch between the revenue-raising capacity and the expenditure need of different governmental units. Such imbalances can arise vertically, between different levels of government, or horizontally, between different jurisdictions. In most federations, given that the central government has a comparative advantage in raising revenues and the states are relatively better placed to deliver public services, vertical imbalance is implicit in the assignment itself. The interjurisdictional differences in income due to various historical and institutional factors as well as variations in resource endowments create horizontal imbalances.

Vertical fiscal imbalance

In India, the consequence of constitutional assignment as well as developments over the years has been to create a high degree of fiscal centralization and vertical fiscal imbalance. As shown in table 3.3, the state

Table 3.3. *Trends in vertical fiscal imbalance*

Period (1)	States' own current revenues as percentage of total current revenues (2)	States' current expenditure as percentage of total current expenditure (3)	States' own current revenues as percentage of states' current expenditure (4)	States expenditure[a] as percentage of total expenditure[a] (5)	States' own revenue as percentage of states' total expenditure[a] (6)
1955–56	41.2	59.0	68.9	61.7	48.5
1960–61	36.6	59.9	63.9	56.8	45.4
1965–66	32.6	55.6	63.5	53.3	42.7
1970–71	35.5	60.2	60.6	53.9	50.3
1975–76	33.5	55.1	70.4	47.6	54.2
1980–81	35.6	59.6	60.1	56.0	43.7
1985–86	35.5	56.0	57.7	52.6	45.5
1990–91	36.6	55.2	53.5	53.1	44.8
1991–92	37.6	58.3	54.8	56.2	47.5
1992–93	36.6	57.9	53.7	55.1	45.8
1993–94	39.6	57.5	55.3	54.7	47.8
1994–95[b]	41.1	58.3	57.1	57.5	48.9

Notes:
[a] Current and capital expenditure
[b] Revised estimates
Source: Based on data from Ministry of Finance, India.

Table 3.4. *Vertical fiscal imbalance in selected countries*

| Country | Year ending | Coefficient of vertical imbalance | | |
		1988	1989	1990
Australia	June 30	0.51	0.46	0.47
Brazil	December 31	0.24	0.20	0.31
Canada	March 31	0.24	0.23	0.21
West Germany	December 31	0.20	0.17	0.20
India	March 31	0.54	0.55	0.55
United States	September 30	0.14	0.14	0.15

Note: The degree of vertical imbalance refers to only state/
provincial/regional governments and has been computed as
$(1 - R/E)$, where
    R = total revenues including capital receipts of the states
        but excluding intergovernmental transfers
    E = total expenditures (current and capital) of the states.
Source: International Monetary Fund (1993), *Government Finance
Statistics.*

governments in 1994–95 collected only 41 percent of total revenues
(column 2), but their share in total current expenditure was 58 percent
(column 3). From the revenue sources assigned to them, they could finance
only about 57 percent of their current expenditure (column 4) and 49
percent of their total expenditure (column 6). Thus, although the states'
revenue collections were only about 40 percent, they had to depend on
transfers and loans amounting to over 26 percent of total revenues to meet
their spending requirements. It is also seen that for India, the states' dependence on the center for financing their expenditure, or the coefficient of
vertical fiscal imbalance, was the highest among the federations compared
in table 3.4. The revenue from own sources contributed only about 45
percent of expenditure and 55 percent of their expenditure was financed
through central transfers or borrowing.

The relative shares of the central and state governments in revenues and
expenditures presented in table 3.3 bring out the trends in fiscal centralization over the years from 1955–56. Interestingly, even when the states' revenues grew at a rate faster than those of the center, their fiscal dependence
on the latter showed an increase. The states' share in raising revenue has
increased marginally, particularly since the mid-1980s. However, their
share in total expenditure increased at a faster rate, by almost 10 percentage points since the mid-1970s (column 5 in table 3.3) indicating increasing fiscal dependency. Thus, the states' share in current expenditure
remained more or less at the same level, but the faster growth of current

expenditures than revenues resulted in a declining ratio of revenues to current expenditure. At the same time, even the broad constancy in the share of state government expenditure in the total indicates an increase in expenditure centralization. This is because the proportion of specific-purpose transfers for various central sector and centrally sponsored schemes in total transfers increased from 12 percent in the Fifth Plan (1969-74) to over 18 percent in the Seventh Plan (1985–90); presently, almost 15 percent of the states' expenditures are on these schemes over which the states have little control.

Horizontal fiscal imbalance

An important feature of Indian fiscal federalism is the wide interstate differences in revenue capacity and, consequently, per capita expenditures. There are fifteen relatively homogeneous general category states, but even these have wide differences in size, revenue-raising capacities, efforts, expenditure levels and fiscal dependence on the center. In addition, in terms of economic characteristics and endowments, the ten mountainous states of the north and the north-east differ markedly from the rest and therefore are considered "special category" states.

The differences in per capita revenue and expenditure among the states shown in table 3.5 brings out several important features. First, there are wide interstate variations in revenues both in per capita terms and in the ratio of revenue to state domestic product (SDP). Second, the variations indicate differences in revenue capacity and, partly, differences in states' revenue efforts. Third, the tax–SDP ratios in the special category states are lower than in the general category states even when their per capita SDP is higher. This is partly because in these states there is not much production activity and government administration is the major determinant of the SDP. Further, the size of the tax base is smaller than indicated by the SDP, because a significant proportion of government spending spills over the jurisdictions. Fourth, although the revenue bases in the special category states are low, their average per capita current expenditure is higher than not only the all-state average but also the average of high-income states.[9] Fifth, in the case of general category states, the fiscal dependence on the center is not only high but varies inversely with the per capita income. Per capita expenditures in high-income states are higher than the all-state average by 45 percent and those in low-income states are lower by 16 percent. Nevertheless, the system has led to significant equalization as may be seen from the fact that while the per capita taxes in low-income states are about a third of those in high-income ones, per capita expenditure in the former is close to 60 percent.

Major states	Per capita SDP (rupees)[a]	Per capita own revenue (rupees)	Own revenue as percentage of SDP[a]	Per capita current expenditure (rupees)	Own revenue as percentage of current expenditure
High-income states	*10 211*	*1 278.63*	*12.5*	*1 680.87*	*76.1*
Gujarat	7 600	1 233.82	16.2	1 601.92	77.0
Goa	11 658	2 632.4	22.6	3 499.84	75.2
Haryana	10 359	1 680.61	16.2	1 951.10	86.1
Maharashtra	10 984	1 213.82	11.1	1 578.65	76.8
Punjab	12 319	1 214.61	9.9	1 915.74	63.4
Middle-income states	*6 661*	*765.59*	*11.5*	*1 238.84*	*61.8*
Andhra Pradesh	6 651	744.43	11.2	1 151.37	64.7
Karnataka	7 029	970.42	13.9	1 325.3	73.2
Kerala	6 242	884.13	14.2	1 422.7	62.1
Tamil Nadu	7 352	960.32	13.1	1 527.72	62.9
West Bengal	6 055	447.78	7.4	959.89	46.7
Low-income states	*4 674*	*438.97*	*9.4*	*969.79*	*45.3*
Bihar	3 650	288.13	7.9	800.22	36.0
Madhya Pradesh	5 485	585.01	10.7	1 077.75	54.3
Orissa	4 726	384.07	8.1	1 048.61	36.6
Rajasthan	5 220	673.13	12.9	1 267.67	53.1
Uttar Pradesh	4 744	401.48	8.5	911.47	44.1
Special category states	*5 607*	*437.56*	*7.8*	*1 939.48*	*22.6*
Arunachal Pradesh	7 904	964.11	12.2	4 330.91	22.3
Assam	5 916	530.94	6.9	1 223.0	33.2
Himachal Pradesh	6 519	693.16	10.6	2 489.53	27.8
Jammu and Kashmir	4 244	439.81	10.4	2 162.23	20.3
Manipur	5 362	238.37	4.5	2 243.74	10.6
Meghalaya	5 519	399.53	7.2	2 528.58	15.8
Mizoram	6 599	462.84	6.7	5 399.42	8.6
Nagaland	5 870[b]	311.42	4.8	5 015.25	6.2
Sikkim	5 416[b]	868.70	15.6	3 916.40	22.2
Tripura	3 781	202.16	5.1	2 089.88	9.7
All states	6 287	653.5	10.4	1 158.24	56.4

Notes:
[a] SDP=State Domestic Product.
[b] Estimated.
Sources: Reserve Bank of India Bulletin (December 1995) based on data from Ministry of Finance, India.

Table 3.6. *Coefficients of variation in per capita state government expenditures (percentages)*

Expenditure/SDP items	1975–76	1980–81	1985–86	1990–91	1993–94
General administration	23.4	21.9	25.0	29.3	31.1
Education	32.9	31.7	26.4	20.3	26.9
Health	28.8	24.3	27.6	25.8	22.6
Total social services	35.2	29.6	31.1	26.0	24.7
Total economic services	37.4	34.0	41.0	36.7	31.6
Total current expenditure	26.0	23.5	24.8	23.2	27.1
Total capital expenditure	38.7	28.1	54.3	40.2	43.1
Total expenditure	26.6	23.0	28.3	24.2	28.1
Total per capita net state domestic product	29.9	31.7	31.7	34.1	36.2

Sources: Calculated from budget documents of state governments, various years.

Interstate disparities in India, even among the relatively more homogeneous general category states, are not only high but have also shown an increasing trend. In 1980–81, the per capita SDP in the richest state, Punjab (Rs 2,674), was about 2.9 times that of the poorest, Bihar (Rs 919). By 1993–94, this difference had increased to 3.4 times, with per capita SDPs in the two states of Rs 12,319 and Rs 3,650 respectively. The coefficients of variation in states' per capita own revenue as well as in per capita SDP increased over the period 1975–76 to 1990–91 (table 3.6). As interstate differences in the ability to raise revenues increased over the years, and as federal transfers did not entirely offset the fiscal disabilities of the poorer states, the coefficient of variation in expenditures also increased over the time period.

Intergovernmental transfers in India

Economic rationale for transfers

Intergovernmental transfers have been employed to fulfill a variety of objectives, and the design of a transfer scheme depends on the purpose for which transfers are given. In the literature, federal transfers are recommended for:

closing the fiscal gap
equalization
spillovers and to foster the provision of "merit" goods

Sometimes, the center also gives transfers to allow agency functions to be performed.

Closing the fiscal gap

An important reason for making transfers is to enable sub-central governments to undertake their functions satisfactorily when the revenues assigned to them are found to be inadequate. This is because the center has a comparative advantage in raising revenues, while the States have one in spending. The resulting vertical fiscal imbalance would have to be offset through a system of transfers from the center to states.[10]

Equalization

The imbalance between revenue capacity and expenditure need varies across states depending on the size of their tax base, the size and the composition of their population, and other factors affecting the cost of providing public services. The richer states, owing to their higher revenue capacity, can provide better standards of public services. To offset this fiscal disadvantage, equalizing transfers are required.

The argument for equalizing transfers is based on the horizontal equity grounds initially advanced by Buchanan (1950) and later developed by Boadway and Flatters (1982). With comprehensive income as the index of well-being, it has been argued that the federal income tax as presently structured cannot ensure horizontal equity as its base does not take into account the redistributive effect of states' fiscal operations. The states' fiscal operations cannot be distributionally neutral except in the unlikely case of their levying benefit taxes. When the quasi-public services provided by them are financed by resource rents or source-based taxes as against residence-based taxes, the net fiscal benefits (NFBs) will systematically vary. The residents in the resource-rich (high-income) regions will have higher NFBs and their higher public consumption will not be included in determining the tax base of the central government.

Boadway and Flatters (1982) define horizontal equity in two alternative ways. According to the broad view, the fiscal system should be equitable nationwide *vis-à-vis* the actions of all governments. Two persons equally well off before central and state actions must also be so afterwards. To fulfill this concept of horizontal equity, it is necessary to give transfers so that each province is enabled to provide the same level of public services at a given tax rate (as in a unitary state). In contrast, the narrow view of horizontal equity takes the level of real incomes attained by the individuals after a state's budgetary operation as the starting point and the central fiscal action will be directed to ensuring horizontal equity after the state's fiscal system has been established. The central budget need not offset the inequalities introduced by the operation of the state budgets *per se*, but takes the income-distributional effects of the states' fiscal operations as a given.

Transfers to correct spillovers

When there is no perfect "mapping," the provision of public services by subcentral governments may spill over the jurisdictions and such externalities may result in the non-optimal provision of public services. A Pigovian subsidy is required to "set the prices right." To be cost-effective, specific-purpose transfers made to the states to ensure optimal provision of public services require matching contributions from them.

The design of intergovernmental transfers

General-purpose transfers, as mentioned earlier, are given to ensure horizontal equity. As the objective of these transfers is to enable the subcentral governments to provide a given level of public services at a given tax rate, the transfers should offset the fiscal disadvantages arising from lower revenue capacity and higher unit cost of providing public services. This is achieved by giving unconditional transfers equivalent to the "need–revenue" gap (Bradbury *et al.*, 1984). The "need–revenue" gap measures the difference between what a state ought to spend to provide specified levels of public services and the revenue it can raise at a given standard level of tax effort.

Specific-purpose transfers, on the other hand, are intended to compensate spillovers or are given for merit good reasons to ensure optimal provision of public services by the states. The transfer system, therefore, should be specific-purpose and open-ended with matching ratios varying with the size of spillovers. As the responsiveness of the states to a given matching rate could vary with their level of income, equalizing matching ratios are also recommended (Feldstein, 1975).

Thus, in an ideal system, there should be an optimal combination of general- and specific-purpose transfers. General-purpose transfers would *enable* all the states to provide a given normative standard of public services for a given tax effort. The specific-purpose transfers would *ensure* a given standard of outlay on the aided services.

The Indian experience

Interregional transfer of resources is achieved through a number of policy interventions, both explicit and implicit. This is particularly true in a planned economy like India. The important interstate resource transfer mechanisms besides intergovernmental fiscal transfers include targeting investments in specific locations by the central government (regional policies), lending to the states at below market rates of interest, allocating a certain proportion of the resources of the banking system and financial institutions to different states,[11] lending to the states at below-market interest rates and making subsidized "priority sector" loan allocations. Resource transfers may result from interstate tax exportation as well.

We have already referred to the inequitable transfer of resources due to interstate tax exportation (Rao and Vaillancourt, 1994). The analysis of regional policies and loan allocations to the state governments and the private sector similarly indicates that the implicit transfer of resources through these means are sizable and inequitable. Table 3.7 presents population shares as well as the interstate distribution of outstanding loans from the government and the market, the priority sector credit allocations by the banking system, assistance by All India Financial Institutions (AFIs), and investments in central government enterprises in different states. The rates of interest on these loans are subsidized and there has also been a periodic rescheduling and write-off of central loans as well. The analysis shows that with respect to each of these sources the low-income states have received allocations much lower than their population percentages. The high-income states with a population share of about 19 percent received 24 percent of the outstanding loans and their share of central government loans alone was about 27 percent. They also received 35 percent of the priority sector credit allocations and 43 percent of the assistance given by AFIs; even the share of investments in central enterprises was 24 percent. The allocation from these sources to the low-income states, in contrast, was significantly lower than their share of population. Thus, the horizontal fiscal imbalance is exacerbated by inequitable financial flows on account of other policies.

A notable feature of intergovernmental transfers in India is the existence of multiple channels of transfer from the central government to the states. The Finance Commission every five years makes an assessment of the fiscal resources and needs of the center and individual states and recommends the shares of personal income tax and Union excise duty and grants-in-aid to the states. However, with development planning gaining emphasis, the Planning Commission became a major dispenser of funds to the states by way of grants and loans to meet their plan requirements. In addition to these two channels, various central ministries give specific-purpose transfers with or without matching requirements.

The trends in the relative shares of the three channels of central transfers[12] to states since the Fourth Five-Year Plan, as shown in table 3.8, show some interesting features. First, the share of statutory transfers in the total declined from 65 percent during the Fourth Plan (1969–74) to a little over 60 percent during the Seventh Plan. Second, the proportion of formula-

Table 3.7. *Interstate redistribution through regional, loan, and credit policies (percentages)*

States	Population share (1995)	States' share of outstanding liabilities, March 31, 1994				Share in bank credit, March 31, 1994		Share in AFIs assistance[a] (1994–95)	Share in capital stock of central enterprises (1990–91)
		Internal debt	Central loans	Other debt	Total	Priority sector	Total		
High-income states	18.7	14.4	27.7	18.8	23.6	35.4	29.4	42.8	24.1
Goa	0.1	0.3	0.8	0.3	0.6	0.3	0.3	0.7	negl.
Gujarat	4.9	3.4	6.2	3.4	5.2	4.9	5.4	13.2	5.0
Haryana	2.0	2.5	2.2	4.2	2.6	1.5	2.8	2.6	0.8
Maharashtra	9.4	5.4	10.3	6.3	8.7	25.3	15.8	23.5	17.6
Punjab	2.4	2.9	8.2	4.6	6.6	3.3	5.1	2.8	0.7
Middle-income states	30.9	34.4	28.9	26.2	29.5	33.4	37.3	29.7	25.3
Andhra Pradesh	7.8	9.3	7.2	4.1	7.1	6.8	8.9	7.5	10.1
Karnataka	5.3	4.9	4.6	4.8	4.7	6.0	6.8	6.1	2.3
Kerala	3.4	5.8	3.2	8.4	4.6	3.4	4.3	2.0	1.5
Tamil Nadu	6.4	7.1	5.6	5.4	5.9	10.3	11.1	9.3	5.2
West Bengal	8.0	7.2	8.3	3.4	7.2	6.9	6.2	4.8	6.3
Low-income states	43.6	43.1	34.5	46.9	38.3	14.4	24.2	21.9	34.1
Bihar	10.3	8.7	7.3	10.5	8.1	2.3	4.1	2.1	8.5
Madhya Pradesh	7.9	4.7	4.6	11.4	5.8	3.2	4.9	5.2	11.1
Orissa	3.7	6.3	3.3	5.8	4.3	1.3	2.2	2.3	5.3
Rajasthan	5.3	6.2	4.7	7.9	5.5	2.1	3.3	4.4	1.5
Uttar Pradesh	16.4	17.3	14.6	11.3	14.5	5.5	9.7	7.9	7.8
Special category states	5.4	8.1	8.2	8.1	8.1	1.9	2.8	2.2	7.5
Union territories	1.4	0.0	0.7	0.0	0.5	14.9	6.4	3.4	9.0[b]
All states	100.0	100.0	100.0	100.0	100.0	100.0	100.0	100.0	100.0

Notes:
negl.=negligible.
[a] All-India Financial Institutions
[b] Unallocated 4.9 percent
Sources: Report on Currency and Finance, 1994–95, Reserve Bank of India; Public Enterprise Survey, Ministry of Industry, Government of India.

Table 3.8. *Current transfers from the center to the states (Rs. billion)*

Plan periods/years	Finance Commission transfers			Plan grants			Other grants	Total
	Tax devolution	Grants	Total	State plan schemes	Central schemes	Total		
Fourth Plan (1969–74)	45.6 (54.2)	8.6 (10.2)	54.2 (64.6)	10.8 (12.8)	9.7 (11.6)	20.5 (24.4)	9.3 (11.0)	83.9 (100.0)
Fifth Plan (1974–79)	82.7 (50.2)	28.2 (17.1)	110.9 (67.3)	29.1 (17.7)	19.3 (11.7)	48.4 (29.4)	5.4 (3.3)	164.7 (100.0)
Sixth Plan (1980–85)	237.3 (57.0)	21.4 (5.1)	258.7 (62.1)	73.8 (17.7)	69.0 (16.6)	142.8 (34.3)	15.1 (3.6)	416.5 (100.0)
Seventh Plan (1985–90)	494.6 (54.2)	62.7 (6.9)	557.4 (61.0)	155.2 (17.1)	165.1 (18.0)	320.3 (35.1)	35.2 (3.9)	913.1 (100.0)
Eighth Plan								
1991–92	172.0 (52.2)	34.5 (10.5)	206.4 (62.7)	57.2 (14.2)	55.4 (16.8)	112.5 (34.4)	10.2 (3.1)	329.4 (100.0)
1992–93	205.2 (53.5)	26.4 (6.9)	231.7 (60.4)	78.4 (20.4)	65.2 (17.0)	143.9 (37.5)	7.2 (1.9)	383.4 (100.0)
1993–94	223.9 (51.4)	20.7 (4.8)	244.6 (56.1)	107.7 (24.7)	74.1 (17.0)	181.8 (41.7)	9.3 (2.1)	435.7 (100.0)
1994–95	248.5 (52.6)	24.3 (5.2)	272.8 (57.8)	99.0 (21.0)	94.5 (20.0)	193.5 (41.0)	5.3 (1.1)	471.6 (100.0)

Note: Figures in parentheses are percentages of total transfers.
Source: Based on data from Ministry of Finance, India.

based transfers given by the Finance Commission and the Planning Commission has declined and that of discretionary transfers has increased over the years. Third, within the Finance Commission transfer, the proportion of tax devolution has increased.

Finance Commission transfers

The Constitution specifies that the Finance Commission is required to

- distribute the shares of personal income tax and Union excise duty between the center and the states and among the states,
- recommend grants to the states in need of additional assistance, and
- address any other matter referred to them.

Although the Constitution does not place any restriction on the scope of the Commission, with the Planning Commission dispensing a significant share of transfers, the scope of the Finance Commission was restricted in practice to meeting the non-plan current requirements of the states.[13]

The Finance Commission's approach to making federal transfers consists of:

- assessment of overall budgetary requirements of the center and states to determine the volume of resources that can be transferred during the period of its recommendations;
- forecasting states' own current revenues and non-plan current expenditures;
- distributing assigned taxes, broadly on the basis of origin;
- distributing sharable taxes – the personal income tax and Union excise duties – between the center and the states and among the states; and
- filling the post-devolution projected gaps between non-plan current expenditures and revenues with the grants.

This is known as the "gap-filling" approach. The relative shares of the center and the individual states and the criteria adopted for their distribution among the States according to the recommendations of the Tenth Finance Commission are summarized in table 3.9.

An important feature of the tax devolutions recommended by the Finance Commissions is that, while the criteria adopted for distributing them are different from the principles of grants-in-aid, nowhere is it made clear that the economic objectives of the two instruments are different (Rao, 1987). The tax devolution is recommended mainly on the basis of general economic indicators, and grants are given to offset the residual fiscal disadvantages of the states as quantified by the Commissions. Even

Table 3.9. *Criteria for tax devolution: Tenth Finance Commission, 1990–95 (percentage)*

	Income tax	Excise duty
States' share	77.5	$40 + 7.5^a$
Criteria for distribution		
Tax effort	10.0	10.0
Population	20	20
Per capita SDP		
Distance formula^c	60	60
Area^b	5.0	5.0
Index of infrastructure	5.0	5.0

Notes:
[a] 7.5 percent is given only to the states with post-tax devolution deficits.
[b] subject to each state receiving the minimum of 2 percent and the maximum of 10 percent of the sharable taxes.
[c] Distance formula $= (Y_h - Y_i)P_i / \Sigma(Y_h - Y_i)P_i$ where Y_i and Y_h represent per capita SDP of the ith and the richest state, P_i is the population of the ith state, $(Y_h - Y_i)$ for the state h is taken to be equivalent to the value of the second highest per capita SDP state.
Source: India, Report of the Tenth Finance Commission, 1994.

in the case of tax devolution, until recently, the criteria adopted for the distribution of personal income tax and excise duties have been different. The Tenth Finance Commission also assigned 10 percent weight to the tax effort factor, but the measurement of tax effort itself is based on the assumption that the SDP is the sole determinant of taxable capacity and taxable capacity increases with increases in the SDP by an exponential of 2.[14] Further, assigning weights to contradictory factors like "contribution" and "backwardness" in the same formula for distribution has rendered the achievement of the overall objective of transfers difficult.

Over the years, attempts have been made by the successive Commissions to improve the redistributive element in the transfer scheme by assigning higher weight to per capita SDP, in either the "inverse" or "distance" forms.[15] Yet population has continued to receive the largest implicit and explicit weight. The redistributive effect has been further blunted by the terms of reference which require the Commission to use the 1971 population figures wherever population is used in the transfer formula. The purpose of this is to penalize the states with higher population growth rates. The important questions are, first, whether the federal transfer mechanism should be employed as an instrument of population policy and, second, even if it is, why those states with high population growth due to migration should be penalized.

The "gap-filling" approach outlined above has been subjected to criticisms. First, none of the Finance Commissions assessed the overall resource position of the center and the amount of resources required to meet its commitments on any objective basis. Second, the transfers made by the Finance Commissions were not designed specifically to offset fiscal disadvantages of the states arising from lower revenue-raising capacity and the higher unit cost of public services. While the tax devolution is determined on the basis of general economic indicators, grants are given on the basis of projected post-devolution budgetary gaps. Third, the design of the grants has serious disincentive effects on fiscal management of the states. Nor are the fiscally disadvantaged enabled to provide a given level of public service at a given tax-price.

The more recent Commissions tried to reduce the post-devolution gaps by substantially enhancing the share of tax devolution in total transfers.[16] At the same time, they tried to target the transfers by including different elements of backwardness, besides the "inverse" and "distance" variants of per capita income, thereby complicating the tax devolution formula. Also, the more recent Commissions introduced selective norms for the center and the states by targeting the rates of growth of revenues and expenditures and by assuming certain rates of return on their loans and investments. The Ninth Finance Commission actually estimated the revenue capacities and expenditure needs of the states. However, the practice of having different approaches for making tax devolution and grants has reduced the relevance of such exercises.

Plan transfers

The Planning Commission gives both grants and loans to the states to finance their plans. In earlier years, both the volume and the loan and grant components were project based, but since 1969 the assistance has been allocated on the basis of a formula (the Gadgil formula).[17] At present, 30 percent of the funds available for distribution is kept apart for the special category states and distributed among them on the basis of plan projects formulated by them, with 90 percent of the assistance given by way of grants and the remainder as loans. The 70 percent of the funds available to the major states is distributed with 60 percent weight assigned to population, 25 percent to per capita SDP, 7.5 percent to fiscal management, and

Table 3.10. *Formula for distributing state Plan assistance*

Variable	Weight
Population (1971)	60.0
Per capita SDP, *of which*	25.0
Deviation from the average to the states below average per capita SDP	20.0
Distance from the highest per capita SDP for all the general category states	5.0
Fiscal performance, *of which*	7.5
Tax effort	2.5
Fiscal management	2.5
National objectives	2.5
Special problems	7.5
Total	100.0

Note: The formula is applied to general category states. They receive 70 percent of the total Plan assistance, of which 30 percent is given as grants and the remainder as loans. The special category states receive 30 percent of total Plan assistance and 90 percent of the assistance is given as grants and the remaining 10 percent as loans. The distribution among them is based on the plans approved.
Source: Planning Commission, Government of India.

the remaining 7.5 percent to special problems of these states (table 3.10). In these states, 30 percent of the resources is given by way of grants and the remainder as loans. Thus, plan transfers and their grant and loan components are determined independently of the required plan investments, their sectoral composition, the resources available to the states, or their fiscal performances.

The tenuous relationship between the required plan investments and plan transfers becomes abundantly clear when we examine per capita plan outlays during the Seventh Plan (table 3.11). In all the major states except Maharashtra, the resources available for plan investments from the states' resources, before any central transfers were given, were negative. It is also seen that the deficits were higher in the poorer states. As the richer states had access to larger non-plan loans and as they could get greater central plan assistance, per capita plan outlays in high-income states were almost twice as much as in middle- and low-income states.

Assistance to the central sector and centrally sponsored schemes

This is the third component of transfer and is given for specified purposes with or without matching provisions. Grants for the central sector schemes are given to the states to execute central projects and are entirely funded by the center. Centrally sponsored schemes, on the other hand, are shared-

Table 3.11. *Per capita federal fiscal transfers and Plan outlay in the states during the Seventh Plan (1981–82 rupees)*

States (1)	Per capita annual SDP, 1982–85 (current prices) (2)	Index of taxable capacity, 1984–85 (3)	States' plan resources before statutory transfers (4) = (7)−(6+5)	Finance Commission transfers (5)	Non-plan loans (6)	States' plan resources after statutory transfers (7)	Plan assistance (including central schemes) (8)	Total plan outlay (9)
High-income states	*3 340*	*146.30*	*−134.24*	*321.43*	*534.83*	*722.02*	*533.18*	*1 255.20*
Punjab	4 013	169.18	−459.28	280.45	318.05	139.23	1 131.83	1 271.06
Maharashtra	3 384	142.75	229.72	316.24	509.77	1 055.73	233.52	1 289.25
Haryana	3 043	151.11	−175.07	344.39	570.99	740.31	463.18	1 203.49
Gujarat	2 929	122.16	132.35	344.62	740.53	952.79	304.20	1 256.99
Middle-income states	*2 206*	*112.82*	*−271.46*	*439.65*	*255.78*	*423.96*	*227.88*	*651.84*
Karnataka	2 461	117.68	−49.98	389.70	112.04	451.76	213.36	665.12
West Bengal	2 230	76.09	−421.11	483.04	278.40	340.34	140.56	480.90
Kerala	2 144	117.60	−521.60	440.26	380.98	299.65	308.19	607.84
Tamil Nadu	2 142	138.64	−186.56	439.21	316.60	569.25	229.51	798.76
Andhra Pradesh	2 053	114.04	−178.07	446.02	190.87	458.82	247.77	706.59
Low-income states	*1 689*	*50.06*	*−265.69*	*472.19*	*171.11*	*377.60*	*287.94*	*665.55*
Madhya Pradesh	1 860	58.14	−139.69	422.13	227.32	509.75	200.00	700.76
Rajasthan	1 820	67.46	−380.23	389.99	291.74	301.50	421.77	723.27
Orissa	1 728	37.72	−250.75	582.07	126.54	458.07	310.56	768.63
Uttar Pradesh	1 713	54.14	−256.19	440.86	143.54	328.21	272.18	600.39
Bihar	1 323	32.85	−301.61	525.89	66.20	290.49	235.21	525.70
Average of 14 states	2 345	99.97	−211.92	428.94	261.35	478.36	276.90	755.27

Sources: Columns 1 and 2: Second Report of the Ninth Finance Commission, Ministry of Finance, Government of India, 1990; other columns: finance and planning departments of the state governments

cost programs falling within the states' ambit with matching ratios which are uniform across the states, but which vary with the projects. There were 262 such schemes in 1985, and more were added in subsequent years. These transfers have attracted the sharpest criticism owing to their discretionary nature and the conditions attached to them. They accounted for about 36 percent of the total plan assistance, and about 20 percent of total current transfers was given to these schemes in 1994–95 (table 3.7).

In summary, the design and implementation of intergovernmental transfer schemes in India suffer from a number of shortcomings. First, multiple agencies with overlapping jurisdictions have blurred the overall objectives of transfers. Second, accommodating different interests has unduly complicated the transfer formula. Third, the design of the transfer system is not well targeted to achieve equalization and to ensure minimum service levels in the states. Fourth, transfers have disincentive effects on the fiscal management in the states. While there is certainly a role for specific-purpose transfers in the Indian federation, the design and implementation of the centrally sponsored schemes have not served the need. They have tended to multiply state-level bureaucracy and distort states' own allocations in unintended ways.

Equalizing effects of intergovernmental transfers

The correlation of central transfers with per capita SDP and their elasticities with respect to SDP clearly show that the transfers recommended by the Finance and Planning Commissions were equalizing (table 3.12). It is also seen that the equalizing effect was the highest under the award of the Ninth Finance Commission (1989–92). This finding is also confirmed by the analysis of interstate inequalities in per capita revenue collections and per capita revenue accruals shown in table 3.13. It is seen that:

- the aggregate transfers tend to equalize but the degree of equalization as measured by the reduction in the Gini coefficient during the period, 1989–92, was only about 0.107;
- the equalization achieved by the Finance Commission transfers was about twice as much as that of Plan transfers;
- equalization of transfers by both the Finance and Planning Commissions marginally increased over time;
- within the former, tax devolution has shown the highest degree of equalization.

In spite of the fact that the transfer system as a whole has appreciable equalizing impact, per capita revenue accruals, and hence per capita

Table 3.12. *Equalizing effect of transfers*

	Correlation coefficients with per capita SDP				Income elasticities			
Transfers	VI F.C. (1974–79)	VII F.C. (1979–84)	VIII F.C. (1984–89)	IX F.C. (1989–94)	VI F.C. (1974–79)	VII F.C. (1979–84)	VIII F.C. (1984–89)	IX F.C. (1989–94)
Shared taxes	−0.167	−0.706**	−0.849**	−0.809**	−0.024	−0.195*	−0.507*	−0.564*
Non-plan grants	−0.240	−0.289	−0.110	−0.286	−0.716	−0.070	0.302	−0.054
Total finance Commission transfers	−0.272	−0.551*	−0.664**	−0.765*	−0.201	−0.280*	−0.403*	−0.514*
Plan grants: state plan schemes	−0.263	−0.524*	−0.010	−0.425**	−0.243	−0.426**	−0.029	−0.557**
Plan grants: central schemes	0.342	−0.101	−0.162	−0.278	0.460	−0.066	−0.095	0.070
Total plan grants	0.091	−0.327	−0.092	−0.417	0.072	−0.236	−0.060	−0.282
Gross current transfers	−0.194	−0.519*	−0.663**	−0.716**	−0.115	−0.268**	−0.277**	−0.408**

Note: * Significant at 1 percent level. ** Significant at 5 percent level.
Elasticity coefficients relate to cross-section of 14 major states.
F.C.=Finance Commission.
Source: Estimated from data taken from the budget documents of the state governments.

Table 3.13. *Effect of federal transfers: Gini coefficients of fiscal variables*

Variable (per capita)	Sixth Finance Commission (1974–79)	Seventh Finance Commission (1979–84)	Eighth Finance Commission (1984–89)	Ninth Finance Commission (1989–94)
(1) Own revenue	0.2262	0.2355	0.2329	0.2575
(2) Own revenue + shared taxes	0.1805	0.1718	0.1640	0.1842
(3) Own revenue + Finance Commission transfers	0.1599	0.1615	0.1576	0.1742
(4) Own revenue + state plan transfers	0.2092	0.2138	0.2167	0.2350
(5) Own revenue + transfers for central schemes	0.2186	0.2184	0.2126	0.2350
(6) Own revenue + plan transfers	0.2030	0.1994	0.1993	0.2154
(7) Own revenue + total current transfers	0.1490	0.1417	0.1394	0.1508
(8) Degree of equalization: shared taxes (1–2)	−0.0457	−0.0637	−0.0689	−0.0732
(9) Degree of equalization: Finance Commission transfers (1–3)	−0.0662	−0.0740	−0.0753	−0.0832
(10) Degree of equalization: state plan grants (1–4)	−0.0170	−0.0217	−0.0162	−0.0224
(11) Degree of equalization: central scheme transfers (1–5)	−0.0076	−0.0170	−0.0203	−0.0225
(12) Degree of equalization: total plan transfers (1–6)	−0.0232	−0.0361	−0.0336	−0.0421
(13) Degree of equalization: total current transfers (1–7)	−0.0772	−0.0938	−0.0935	−0.1067

Note: Interstate Gini coefficients correspond to 14 major states only.
Source: Financial accounts of the state governments, various issues.

Table 3.14. *Regression results*

Dependent variable	Independent variable		$\bar{R}^2$
	Constant	Per capita SDP	
Per capita own revenue	−296.3650*	0.1760*	0.8524
	(2.4714)	(8.7200)	
Per capita total revenues	165.2228	0.1500*	0.7965
	(1.3369)	(7.2019)	
Per capita revenue expenditure	208.520	0.1580*	0.6500
	(1.100)	(5.0146)	
Per capita total expenditure	341.4971	0.1801*	0.6395
	(1.5679)	(4.9050)	

Notes:
The regressions have been estimated by employing the log–linear
model; $N = 14$. Figures in parentheses are t-statistics of the regression
coefficients.
* Significant at 1 percent level.
Source: Author's estimates.

expenditures, have a significant and positive relationship with per capita
SDP. As may be seen from table 3.14, the elasticity of revenue accruals, as
well as of per capita current expenditures, with respect to per capita SDP
is 0.15, which is only marginally lower than that of the states' own revenues (0.18).

Federal fiscal arrangements in India: major issues

The preceding analysis brings out the important features of federal fiscal
arrangements in India. The analysis highlights a number of shortcomings
which are due not merely to constitutional arrangements, but also to the
conventions, methods, and workings of institutions. To an extent, these
have been shaped by the developmental strategy, and economic liberalization would call for a review of the arrangements. Therefore, in reorienting
the federal fiscal arrangements to complement the needs of a market
economy, reforms are needed in both policies and institutions.

Federal fiscal arrangements in a market economy should aim at the efficient delivery of public services, ensure a nationwide market unfettered by
impediments, and activate welfare-improving competition among the
governmental units. Unlike in a planned economy where economic power
is centralized, fiscal functions in a market economy call for decentralization. Further, be it from a dynamic developmental perspective or from the
viewpoint of merely exercising preferences for public services through

"exit" and "voice," human resource development plays a critical role in a developing country. This primarily belongs to the domain of subcentral governments, and in the new environment, their relative role is likely to increase. The recent initiative to empower the urban and rural local bodies below the state level through the 73rd and 74th Amendments to the Constitution is likely to give a further thrust to fiscal decentralization.

Giving a larger role to the market in allocating resources would affect inter-regional equity as well. This is not to say that the planning process in the past succeeded in promoting balanced regional development. We have referred to the inequitable resource transfers due to financial policies, the center's own investment decisions, and interstate tax exportation. These, and the inability of the federal transfer system to adequately offset the fiscal disabilities of the poorer states, have led to inequitable distribution of plan outlay and, consequently, levels of infrastructure. Thus, in the liberalized environment, the richer states with better physical and social infrastructures, proximity to the markets, and responsive bureaucracy would attract a larger share of private investments than the poorer states unless corrective steps were taken to improve the relative competitive ability of the poorer states.

The reform of the federal fiscal system should begin with the re-examination of assignments. It is necessary to review whether the distinction between income and wealth from agricultural and non-agricultural sources serves any useful purpose. Again, assigning power to levy sales tax only on goods and the exclusion of taxation of services altogether from the purview of the states is clearly anomalous and has denied the states access to this growing tax base. Further, given that, in any case, concurrency in the commodity tax base of the center and the states exists, there is no reason why concurrent consumption tax powers cannot be given in the legal sense along with the institution of a mechanism to ensure coordinated levies by the center and the states. This, in fact, would give the states access to a wider tax base and reduce vertical fiscal imbalance. Of course, this could also accentuate horizontal imbalance, but the solution to this would lie in better targeting of the transfers to offset the fiscal disabilities of poorer states.

It must be admitted that the intergovernmental transfer system has, over the years, achieved a significant degree of equalization in the levels of public services across the states. Equally notable is the attempt to reduce discretion in the transfer system by increasingly resorting to formula-based transfers. Of course, the formulas used to distribute transfers still leave a lot of room for improvement in terms of both equity and incentives. It is therefore necessary to redesign the transfer system to improve accountability, incentives, and equity. In a more liberalized environment, inter-state inequality in the standards of public services is likely to increase. The general-purpose transfers should, therefore, be better targeted. Similarly, the centrally sponsored schemes must be designed to ensure minimum outlay on specified services throughout the federation. The states might perhaps be allowed to choose from among a number of priority schemes instead of establishing specific conditions for each scheme. Further, consolidation of the large number of centrally sponsored schemes and the introduction of broad conditionalities could improve flexibility for the states and reduce resource distortions.

Reforms are needed in the institutional mechanism as well. First, overlapping in the functions of different institutions should be avoided. The Finance Commission can assess and recommend transfers to cover the entire current needs of the states, and the Planning Commission can assess the requirements for physical infrastructure and give the required loans. The working of the Finance Commission, and the methodology adopted by it, should be changed so that disincentives to fiscal management are avoided. This requires them to function on professional lines. The appointment of professionals to the Finance Commission, the strengthening of its research capacity, a permanent secretariat undertaking continuous research, enabling greater interaction between governmental units, and imparting a greater degree of transparency to the functioning of the Commission are some of the other reforms urgently required.

Notwithstanding the weaknesses, it must be noted that the system of intergovernmental fiscal arrangements in India has served reasonably well for over fifty years. It has achieved significant equalization over the years, instituted a workable system of resolving the outstanding issues between the center and the states and among the states, and adjusted to the changing requirements. It has thus contributed to achieving a degree of cohesiveness in a large and diverse country. Nonetheless this analysis has brought out several areas of reform; and it is important to be aware that it is eminently possible to reform the system.

Notes

1 The recent (73rd and 74th) Amendments to the Constitution have sought to specify the domain of the governmental units below the state level (rural and urban local bodies) as well. However, they exercise their functions concurrently with the state governments, with the latter enjoying overriding powers. For an analysis of the rationale, achievements, and challenges in regard to local governments, see Singh (1996).
2 There are, however, some disagreements with such a functional allocation.

Gramlich (1987) and, more recently, Inman and Rubinfeld (1992) have argued that the subcentral units can make effective contributions to counter-cyclical policy. Similarly, Pauly (1973) has argued that redistribution should be considered a local public good and subnational units do have an important role to play in poverty alleviation; see Rao and Das-Gupta (1995).

3 "Competitive federalism" views governmental systems as competing entities analogous to firms. It combines the results of electoral competition in a democratic polity with the federal form of government. The competition analyzed in this context is not restricted price competition, but Schumpeterian entrepreneurial competition; see Breton (1987).

4 Bundling of public services on a "take it or leave it" basis increases welfare costs; see Breton (1987).

5 A possible exception is that of China and the former socialist countries of Europe where the local taxes are higher than their expenditures, thus requiring upward rather than downward transfers. However, the locally collected taxes are not really local taxes because their base and/or rates are decided at the central level; see Prud'homme (1995: ch. 2).

6 There are, of course, administrative difficulties in taxing agricultural incomes, and the expert committee that went into this issue actually recommended a presumptive method of taxation based on land holdings classified broadly according to productivity differentials (India, Ministry of Finance, 1972). However, the point made here is that in the prevailing situation, even in principle, it is impossible to have a comprehensive concept of income as the tax base, and differential treatment of income from agricultural and non-agricultural sources has formally opened up an easy avenue for evasion of the tax through misclassification.

7 Recently, increase in the prices of petroleum products led to reduction in the sales taxes on these products by a number of states.

8 See Breton (1987). Prud'homme (1995), however, asserts that decentralization could cause a downward shift in the production frontier owing to lower administrative efficiency. His argument ignores the fact that administrative efficiency of subnational governments itself is a function of assigning the responsibilities and resources to them.

9 Of course, the higher than average per capita expenditures in special category states cannot be entirely attributed to their inherent cost disability. It may also be due to bad fiscal management.

10 It is also possible to restore the balance through the unbalanced level cutting expenditures or raising more revenues, or by changing the assignment itself. However, if the imbalance has occurred even after efficient assignment, these methods of correcting the balance have an additional welfare cost.

11 In India, the statutory liquidity ratio stipulated for the commercial banks requires them to keep 35 percent of their resources in the form of government securities.

12 There is a considerable amount of confusion over the term "transfers." In Indian federal finance literature, central loans to states are also characterized as transfers. Such transactions involve transfers only to the extent of any interest subsidy or write-off of loans. Sometimes, on the recommendation of

the Finance Commissions, the central loans to the states are rescheduled, the rate of interest reduced, or even a portion of the loan itself is written off. A proper estimate of the transfers should include the implicit transfers arising from interest subsidy and loan write-off, which calls for a separate study. Here, we have taken only tax devolution and grants as transfers. Transfers arising from interest subsidy guarantees and loan write-off are not taken into account.

13 The grants (G_i) receivable by the ith state are given by:

$$G_i = E_i - (R_{oi} + R_{ai} + R_{si})$$
$$G_i \geq 0.$$

where E_i denotes projected non-plan current expenditures of the ith state, R_{oi} denotes projected own revenues of the ith state, R_{ai} denotes projected share of assigned revenues of the ith state, and R_{si} denotes shared taxes of the ith state.

14 Tax effort $(\eta) = T_i/Y_i^2$, where T_i is the per capita tax revenue collected by the ith state and Y_i is the per capita state domestic product of the ith state.

15 The "inverse" formula is given by:

$$(P_i/Y_i)/\Sigma_i P_i Y_i$$

and the "distance" formula is given by:

$$(Y_h - Y_i)P_i/\Sigma Y_h - Y_i)P_i$$

where Y_i and Y_h represent per capita SDP of the ith and the highest income state respectively and P_i is the population of the ith state.

16 The Seventh Finance Commission, for example, increased the states' share of Union excise duty from 20 to 40 percent.

17 The formula and its modifications from time to time are evolved on the basis of consensus within the National Development Council (NDC). The NDC comprises the cabinet ministers at the center, chief ministers of the states, and the members of the Planning Commission, and is chaired by the prime minister.

References

Boadway, R. W. and Flatters, F. (1982), *Equalization in a Federal State: An Economic Analysis*, Ottawa: Canadian Government Publishing Center.

Bradbury, K. L., Ladd, H. F., Perrault, M., Reschovsky, A., and Yinger, J. (1984), "State aid to offset fiscal disparities among counties," *National Tax Journal*, 37: 151–70.

Brennan, G. and Buchanan, J. M. (1980), *The Power to Tax*, Cambridge: Cambridge University Press.

Breton, Albert (1987), "Towards the theory of competitive federalism," *European Journal of Political Economy*, 3(1&2): 263–328.

Breton, Albert, and Fraschini, Angela (1992), "Free-riding and intergovernmental grants," *Kyklos*, 45: 347–62.

Buchanan, J. M. (1950) "Federalism and fiscal equity," *American Economic Review*, 40: 421–32.

Chelliah, R. J. (1991), *Towards a Decentralized Polity* (Fourth L. K. Jha Memorial Lecture), New Delhi: Fiscal Research Foundation.

(1993) "Agenda for comprehensive tax reform," C. N. Vakil Memorial Lecture at the Indian Economic Association Conference, Bombay.

Feldstein, Martin S. (1975), "Wealth neutrality and local choice in public education," *American Economic Review*, 65: 75–89.

Gramlich, Edward (1987), "Subnational fiscal policy," *Perspectives on Local Public Finance and Public Policy*, 3: 3–27.

Hunter, J. S. H. (1977), *Federalism and Fiscal Balance*, Canberra: Australian National University Press.

India, Ministry of Finance (1972), *Report of the Committee on Taxation of Agricultural Wealth and Income* (Chairman: K. N. Raj), New Delhi.

Inman, R. P. and Rubinfeld, D. L. (1992), "Can we decentralize our unemployment policies? Evidence from the United States," paper presented at the International Seminar in Public Economics, Tokyo (August 31-September 1).

King, David (1984). *Fiscal Tiers: The Economics of Multilevel Government*, London: Allen & Unwin.

Musgrave, R. A. (1983), "Who should tax, when and what?" in Charles E. McLure, Jr. (ed.), *Tax Assignment in Federal Countries*, Canberra: Australian National University Press.

Netzer, Dick (1991), "An evaluation of interjurisdictional competition through economic development incentives," in D. A. Kenyon and J. Kincard (eds.), *Competition Among States and Local Governments: Efficiency and Equity in American Federalism*, Washington DC: The Urban Institute.

Oates, W. E. (1972), *Fiscal Federalism*, New York: Harcourt, Brace, Jovanovich.

(1977a) (ed.), *Political Economy of Fiscal Federalism*, Lexington, MA: Lexington Books.

(1977b) "An economist's perspective of fiscal federalism," in Oates (1977a).

Oates, W. E. and Schwab, R. M. (1988), "Economic competition among jurisdictions: efficiency enhancing or distortion inducing?" *Journal of Public Economics*, 35: 333–54.

Pauly, M. V. (1973) "Income redistribution as a local public good," *Journal of Public Economics*, 2: 35–58.

Perloff, Harvey (1985), "Fiscal policy at the state and local level," in L. S. Burns and J. Friedman (ed.), *The Art of Planning: Selected Essays of Harvey S. Perloff*, New York: Plenum Press.

Prud'homme, Remy (1995), "On the dangers of decentralization," *World Bank Economic Review*, 10: 201–20.

Rao, M. G. (1987), "Fiscal imbalances in Indian federalism: trends and issues," Working Paper No. 30, National Institute of Public Finance and Policy, New Delhi.

(1993), "Indian fiscal federalism from a comparative perspective," paper presented at the Conference on Federalism in Diverse Societies, Center for Advanced Study on India, University of Pennsylvania, Philadelphia (November).

Rao, M. G. and Das-Gupta, A. (1995), "Intergovernmental transfers and poverty alleviation," *Environment and Planning C: Government and Policy*, 13: 1–23.

Rao, M. G. and Vaillancourt, F. (1994), "Inter-state tax disharmony in India: a comparative perspective," *Publius: The Journal of Federalism*, 24: 99–114.

Singh, Nirvikar (1996), "Governance and reform in India," Working Paper No. 356, Department of Economics, University of California, Santa Cruz.

Tiebout, C. M. (1956), "A pure theory of local government expenditures," *Journal of Political Economy*, 64: 416–24.

4

Indonesia and Pakistan: fiscal decentralization – an elusive goal?

ANWAR SHAH

Responding to a wide variety of concerns ranging from citizen disenchantment with national government failures to globalization, a large and growing number of developing countries (seventy at last count) have expressed a commitment or a desire to achieve a greater degree of decentralization. While there has been reasonable agreement on an economic framework to guide such reform efforts (see Shah, 1994) and often a reasonable national consensus on directions for reform, progress on such reform efforts has proceeded at a frustratingly slow pace in the majority of these countries. This chapter reviews the experiences of two large and diverse countries in reforming their fiscal systems, with a view to developing a better understanding of the potentials and perils of such efforts in developing countries. First, reasons are stated for our selection of the countries to be discussed. This is followed by discussions of their fiscal systems. A subsequent section reflects upon why the road to reform has been so difficult in the two countries. A final section draws some lessons of general interest to other reforming countries.

Indonesia and Pakistan represent interesting case studies in federalism for two reasons. First, the reform of fiscal systems is high on the policy agenda in both countries and innovative approaches to the design of intergovernmental fiscal relations have been followed. Second, in both countries, impediments to reform are arising less from a lack of institutional capacity at the local level and more from "rent-seeking" (the pursuit of enlightened self-interest) by bureaucratic and political elites. A study of these countries thus uncovers both the potentials and perils of federalism in developing countries.

Indonesia and Pakistan have many similarities. Both countries support large populations. At the end of 1996, Indonesia had an estimated population of 203 million and Pakistan 137 million. Both countries have pre-

The views expressed in this chapter are those of the author alone and should not be attributed to the World Bank. The author is grateful to Richard Bird and François Vaillancourt for helpful comments.

dominantly Muslim populations. Both countries share a colonial heritage: the former gained independence from Dutch rule in 1945 and the latter from British rule in 1947. Both countries inherited well-trained bureaucratic regimes from their colonial rulers. Both have shown a remarkable growth performance over the last two decades. Both countries have well-articulated systems of intergovernmental relations. While, by constitutional intent, Indonesia is a unitary country and Pakistan a decentralized federation, in practice, both countries have highly centralized governance structures. Political systems remain fragile in both countries and military interventions, political unrest, and threats of secession are facts of life in both countries. Political and bureaucratic corruption and red tape are rampant. Both countries are ranked low ("poor governance") on an index of quality of governance developed by Huther and Shah (1996) which embodies political participation, bureaucratic efficiency, social development, and economic management considerations.

In other respects, Indonesia and Pakistan are dissimilar. Indonesia is far more diverse in terms of its geography and the ethnic origins of its population. Political power in Indonesia is concentrated at the centre, whereas in Pakistan, in recent years, there has been a recentralization of power at the provincial level with feudal lords reigning supreme both at the centre and in the provinces. Private sector participation in the provision of public services is much greater in Pakistan than in Indonesia. Such participation in Pakistan has been a local response to the dysfunctional public sector. In contrast, Indonesian public services are reasonably well administered and the main potential improvement would be simply to match these services with local preferences. Indonesia faces a greater internal, but a far lower external, security threat than Pakistan. Indonesia has achieved greater economic maturity than Pakistan. End-1996 per capita GDP in Indonesia was US$ 1,210 compared to US$ 520 in Pakistan (table 4.1).

Given their differing backgrounds, the two countries have developed systems of intergovernmental fiscal relations to suit their specific circumstances. In the following, we review these approaches.

The fiscal system in Indonesia

Indonesia is an archipelago of nearly 14,000 islands, of which 930 are inhabited; it covers 1.9 million square kilometers and has an ethnically diverse end-1996 estimated population of 203 million. Since 1954, it has organized itself as a multi-tier unitary state, with its provinces as the second tier and local government as the third tier. There are 27 provinces (Level [*Dati*] I), 25 cities and towns (Level II – *Kotamadya*), 241 districts

Table 4.1. *A comparative impressionistic review of selected aspects of the fiscal system in Indonesia and Pakistan*

Selected Indicators	Indonesia	Pakistan
Population (end-1996)	203 million	137 million
Area	1.9 million square kilometers	0.8 million square kilometers
Per capita GDP (1996)	US$ 1,210	US$ 520
Fiscal constitution (*de jure*)	Unitary	Decentralized federation
Fiscal constitution (*de facto*)	Multi-tiered centralized unitary	Multi-tiered centralized federation
Subnational governments	27 provinces, 297 districts, 3,837 subdistricts, 5,000 villages	4 provinces, 15 municipal corporations, 156 municipal committees, 301 town committees, 40 cantonment boards, 118 district councils, 4,565 union councils
Provincial government constitutional status	Weak	Strong
Local government constitutional status	Weak	Weak
Actual provincial control of local governments	Moderate	Strong
Range of local government responsibilities	Limited	Limited
Citizen participation	Low to moderate	Low (rural) to moderate (urban)
Bureaucratic orientation	Improved service delivery	Command and control
Political and bureaucratic corruption	Moderate	High
Red tape	Moderate	High
Private provision of public services	Limited	Extensive
Provincial fiscal autonomy	Weak	Strong
Local fiscal autonomy	Weak	Weak
Local administrative autonomy	Weak	Weak
Local government role in public service provision	Moderate	Constrained
Transparency and predictability of the system of central–provincial transfers	Excellent	Good
Design of provincial–local transfers	Excellent	Non-existent
Quality and quantity of public services	Very good and extensive	Poor/unreliable or non-existent

(*Dati* II – *Kabupaten*), and 65,544 villages (*Desas* – ranging in population size from 200 to 55,000). The military and the civil service are represented in the national parliament. As the head of the central government, the President appoints provincial governors. Mayors are elected by local councils from candidates pre-screened by the center (the President) or the provinces (the governors). Provincial governors also appoint chief administrative officers of local governments. Appointment of most public officials at all levels is a responsibility of the center. Thus the center holds real and effective power in most public matters and provincial–local governments act primarily on behalf of the center in functions that are delegated to them by the center. Indonesia is also exceptional in the degree of dependence of its subnational governments on central revenues. In 1994–95, subnational governments were responsible for about 20 percent of the consolidated general government expenditures but raised only 7 percent of consolidated government revenues. This level of fiscal deficiency for subnational governments is large by international standards. It should also be noted that large regional disparities exist in Indonesia. For example, the per capita GDP of the poorest province (Nusa Tenggara Timur) is only 6 percent of the per capita GDP of the richest province (Kalimantan Timur).

The centralization of authority in Indonesia has traditionally been viewed as a means of preserving national unity and promoting economic growth. But there is now an emerging perception that a highly centralized fiscal structure may be imposing large political and economic costs on the country. This awareness has resulted in the adoption of a policy permitting gradual decentralization of decision-making. Government Regulation No. PP 45/1992 (on the implementation of regional autonomy with emphasis on second-level regions) represents the most serious attempt in recent years to define a specific course of decentralization. This regulation seeks to transfer some central and provincial responsibilities to the local level. State policy guidelines issued in 1994 reaffirm this commitment by establishing a framework guiding policy formulation over the Sixth Plan period, 1993–94 to 1998–99.

Expenditure assignment issues: a new strategy for weakening provincialization and strengthening localization

In Indonesia, nearly three-quarters of expenditure is directly undertaken by the center, and another 10 percent is effectively controlled by the center through the conditionality of its transfers to local governments. Even for the remaining 15 percent of expenditure, the center exercises some influence through its planning and budget approval process. Thus, overall, the distribution of responsibilities remains highly centralized.

In Indonesia, Law No. 5 of 1974 provides the overall legal framework guiding the distribution of responsibilities between levels of government. Specific regulations to implement this legislation have been slow in coming. Regulation No. PP45/1992 represented a major attempt to chart a more clearly defined course for the process of decentralization, and to accelerate this process. In this regulation, the focus of further devolution of responsibilities is Level II governments (districts), and the devolution envisaged is from both central and Level I (provincial) governments. The following functions are reserved for the center: defense and security affairs; judicial affairs; foreign affairs; part of general administrative affairs concerning heads of regions; and other administrative affairs that can be more effectively and efficiently managed by the central government. All other functions are to be considered for transfer to lower-level governments. The same regulation also specifies the following functions for Level I governments: inter-municipal (Level II) affairs; affairs that are not central to Level II development; and affairs that are implemented more effectively and efficiently at Level I. All other affairs of Level I governments are to be transferred to Level II governments in a gradual and continuous manner. All transfers are to be accompanied by the transfer of associated budgetary resources. The transfer of responsibilities will be linked to the capacities of Level II governments. The assessment of the readiness of these governments to assume additional responsibilities, and of their capacity-building needs, will be based on a rating of their existing institutional capacities. It is envisaged that some functions could in part be transferred initially for a four-year period, with the transfer completed and made permanent upon assessment of the Level II government performance during that period.

Indonesia is fast approaching a stage in its economic evolution where the present degree of centralization in the responsibility for the provision of public services will become increasingly untenable because of both its implications for efficiency and the strain imposed on the financial and institutional capacities of the center. Regulation No. PP45/1992, accordingly, represents a timely initiative. The broad framework it sets out for the transfer of responsibilities to local governments is consistent with general economic principles for intergovernmental assignment of expenditures. Within this framework, the actual allocation of responsibilities for individual services will need to be carefully determined. This process is to be guided by an interministerial body on regional autonomy, and will be supported by studies, some of which are already underway. For local public services, the following may serve as general criteria for the assignment of responsibilities: policy development, standards of service, and performance evaluation (center); oversight (provincial level); provision (local/regional level); and production (public or private, depending on the service). For some services that in principle can be assigned to the local level but require a minimum scale for cost-effective provision, for example, sanitation systems, a voluntary association of small contiguous municipalities divided into special-purpose regional bodies, is an option that can be considered. For most local public services, this would not be necessary for large, metropolitan municipalities. The assignment of responsibility for the provision of a public service to a particular level of government does not mean that government must be directly engaged in its production. In areas where private production and delivery of a public service would be feasible and more efficient, and would be consistent with ensuring an equitable access to the service, the responsible government needs to promote private participation. Examples of this are services that can be provided within a competitive framework, such as transport services and refuse collection.

Tax base assignment issues

In Indonesia, the major, most productive direct and indirect taxes are all assigned to the center. Personal and corporate (including oil and gas) income taxes, the main indirect taxes (namely, VAT, excises, and duties on foreign trade), and the local property tax are all centrally administered, with revenues from the last of these being shared with lower-level governments (16 percent to provinces and 65 percent to districts). Natural resource royalties for petroleum, mines, and forests are also collected by the center, but shared with lower-level governments. There are no supplementary ("piggyback") taxes levied by local governments on the tax bases administered by the center. Tax assignment in Indonesia emphasizes efficiency of tax administration and uniformity of the tax regime across the country. The centralization of taxes is also motivated by concerns for reducing regional disparities in the availability of public resources. While these objectives are legitimate and important, consideration needs to be given to how tax options at the subnational level can be broadened, consistent with these objectives. The present high degree of centralization of tax authority is an important reason why local governments are unable to self-finance but a small proportion of their spending.

Within the present broad framework of tax assignment in Indonesia, several possibilities for augmenting local tax authority could be considered. First, local governments could be given a greater role in the administration (including rate-setting) of the property tax. Levied on immobile assets, this tax is suitable for administration at the local level. A greater local role in its administration would likely improve incentives for collection. The central government could retain the assessment function for smaller towns but assume a supervisory role for the same in larger urbanized jurisdictions (which are already playing a significant role in the administration of the tax under central direction). Second, excises, which in Indonesia are used as special single-stage sales taxes (mainly on luxury items) alongside a general VAT, being residence-based taxes, can in principle be assigned to the subnational (provincial) level. Administrative reasons may necessitate keeping these taxes at the central level in the short term, but possibilities for instituting revenue-sharing could be considered in the interim. Third, subnational governments could be allowed to levy a tax on fuel consumption. At a moderate rate, such a tax could raise sizable revenues, besides supporting environmental objectives. At present levels of consumption, a 5 percent sales tax on gasoline and diesel could raise local own-source revenues by about 25 percent if assigned to provincial governments, or by 65 percent if assigned to district governments. Fourth, local revenues from the property tax could be augmented by the institution of frontage/development charges (tax per front foot of the property in new developments to pay for development of basic infrastructure). In industrial countries, frontage charges normally amount to about 5 percent of property tax revenues. Fifth, possibilities for local taxation of some non-basic public services, such as the telephone, could be explored.

Increasing revenues from existing regional or shared taxes
Subnational governments in Indonesia can levy a multiplicity of taxes, around fifty, but only a few of them are significant sources of revenue. About 90 percent of provincial tax revenue comes from just two taxes (motor vehicle registration and transfer taxes) and about 85 percent of district-level tax revenue comes from only six taxes (hotels and restaurants tax, street lights tax, entertainment tax, advertisement tax, business registration tax, and slaughterhouse tax). One desirable local tax reform is to eliminate a large number of levies that are unproductive, which would lower the costs of collection and free scarce administrative capacity to focus on the more productive levies, while also reducing tax-induced distortions. These "nuisance taxes" remain on municipal books as municipalities try to augment their revenues from all possible sources historically made available to them. There remains much scope for increasing yields from the more important taxes through better administration. Overall, it is estimated that stronger mobilization of revenues from existing and new

subnational taxes and from shared taxes and fees could roughly double subnational government own revenues. Even then, however, the share of such revenues in total government revenues will rise to only about 13 percent.

Making more effective use of local user charges
Appropriately charging for public services serves both to raise revenues and improve efficiency. User charges are especially important at the local level because, being closer to beneficiaries, local public services are more amenable to such charges than services provided by higher levels of government. In Indonesia, user charges contribute a sizable proportion of regional government revenues (about 15 percent at the provincial and 50 percent at the district level). However, the utilization of these charges remains well below potential. At the district level, fees and charges cover less than 10 percent of the outlay on public services. Heavy dependence on central transfers has created weak incentives for local cost recovery. Many public services are subsidized to make them affordable to the poor, but the subsidies are inefficiently targeted, tending to benefit those who are better off, for example, urban water supply. The equity objectives of subsidization could be met more effectively, and at a smaller cost in terms of foregone revenue, by better targeting the poor, for example, through the adoption of "lifeline" charges whereby the service is charged at full marginal cost or higher beyond a level of service use associated with the poor. Better central guidance to local governments on service pricing policies would be helpful, as the responsible local authorities often lack adequate understanding of the concepts of cost recovery. This should be supported by improved accounting practices at the local level to allow a clearer determination of the costs of service provision. Within central guidance on service pricing principles, local governments could be allowed greater authority in adjusting the level of charges. The present requirement for all adjustments in local charges to be sanctioned by the higher-level government acts as a disincentive to frequent revisions and often creates considerable delays. Appropriately designed schemes to allow retention by the agencies responsible for service delivery of part of the receipts from user charges, for direct use on the service, could provide a useful incentive to more vigorous cost recovery, for example, as currently allowed for some local health services. Finally, reducing the present proliferation of small charges would facilitate collection. In some cases, duplication of collection efforts could be avoided through consolidating charges, for example, a consolidated water tariff including charges for related sanitation and drainage services.

Table 4.2. *Indonesia: fiscal transfers to subnational governments, 1995–96*

Grant program	Allocation basis
General-purpose transfers	
Provincial Development Grant	Equal per province (85 percent); area (15 percent)
District Development Grant	Per capita with a floor
Village Development Grant	Equal per village
Less-developed Village Grant	Per capita
Specific-purpose transfers to provinces	
SDO: Subsidy for Autonomous Regions	Public sector wages
Provincial Road Improvement Grant	Length of road; condition of road; unit cost of construction and maintenance
Reforestation and regreening	Project review
Specific-purpose transfers to local governments	
SDO: Subsidy for Autonomous Regions	Public sector wages
District/Town Road Improvement Grant	Length of road; condition of road; density; unit cost of construction and maintenance
Primary School Grant	School-age children (ages 7–12); need for facilities
Health Grant	Need for medicine, health centers, and personnel
Reforestation grant	Project review

Intergovernmental transfers and loan finance

Even with feasible increases in local revenues, the gap between local expenditures and revenues is likely to remain large for some time to come. This underlines the importance of appropriately designing the system of financial support to local governments, in the form of transfers from the central government and loan finance.

Design of intergovernmental transfers

Central grants currently finance about 65 percent of expenditure at the provincial level and 70 percent at the district level. These transfers are of two kinds: block grants, for general-purpose local spending subject to some broad central guidelines; and specific grants, for expenditure on uses specified by the center and subject to relatively detailed central controls (table 4.2). The former include INPRES (*Instruksi Presiden*, or project funds authorized by the President) block transfers to each of the three main levels of local government – provinces, districts and villages. The latter include

SDO, a transfer that covers virtually all local government personnel expenses, and INPRES sectoral transfers for specific development expenditures on roads, primary schools, public health centers, and reforestation. As part of its policy of gradual decentralization, the government has incrementally raised the share of block grants in total transfers (from 16 percent in 1986–87 to 22.5 percent in 1995–96) and has also allowed local governments somewhat greater flexibility in the use of some of the specific grants.

There are several positive features of the design of the Indonesian intergovernmental grant system: the distribution of grants is transparent, determined by formulas utilizing objective criteria; the structure of grants is simple, as both the grants and the criteria used for distribution are few in number; and the grants achieve an overall equalizing effect on regional revenue availabilities. In its transparency and simplicity, the Indonesian grant system compares favorably with the grant systems typically found in developing countries.

There are, nonetheless, several improvements that could be considered in the design of the Indonesian grant system that would allow it to achieve its efficiency and equity objectives more effectively. First, the recent trend toward increasing the share of block grants in total grants should continue. Second, regional disparities in overall fiscal capacities (revenue-raising potential) could be better reflected in the distribution formulas for block grants, by including a fiscal capacity equalization factor. The criteria currently used for distribution – area, population and equal shares – are all focused primarily on capturing the differential needs of regional administrations. A better capturing of differential fiscal capacities to meet those needs would contribute to making the distribution of grants more equitable.

A third possible improvement is that the SDO grant could be consolidated with the general-purpose block grants to the respective levels of government. As presently designed, this grant creates strong incentives for higher government employment, and hence a higher wage bill, at the local level. The center tries to circumvent this perverse incentive by retaining major control over government employment at all levels, but this undermines local autonomy and flexibility in the allocation of budgetary resources between personnel and other recurrent (operations and maintenance) expenditures.

Fourth, the main improvement that can be made in the specific sectoral grants is to continue the shift toward using broad guidelines rather than detailed controls and physical targets in influencing the use of these grants. The allocation criteria for these grants are broadly appropriate, as they adequately serve their main objective (ensuring minimum standards of the targeted basic services across regions). One improvement would be to change the allocation of the reforestation grant from a project to a formula basis, as is the case with the other specific sectoral grants. For the health grant, a possible option is to redesign it as a per capita block transfer subject to central guidelines on standards of access and service levels.

A fifth, and final, possible improvement is that consideration could be given to assigning provinces a role in the allocation of central grants to the lower levels, by making some of the grants pass through them. The rationale for doing so is that provinces are better placed than the center, especially in a large and diverse country, to assess the needs and fiscal capacities of individual lower-level jurisdictions. A provincial role in grant administration could also contribute to closer monitoring of the use of the funds.

The Government has recently introduced (with effect from 1994–95), a new per capita block transfer to villages identified as lagging behind in development (INPRES *Desa Tertinggal*). The proposed grant program, focused on poverty reduction in targeted concentrations of poverty, is well structured overall. At the completion of its initial three-year period of operation, consideration could be given to making block transfers to villages part of a fiscal capacity equalization program.

Framework for local borrowing

Borrowing currently plays a very small part in financing regional government expenditures in Indonesia (less than 5 percent). The bulk of central financial support to regional governments takes the form of grants, as noted above. Whatever local borrowing does take place is predominantly from the central government, including the on-lending of foreign loans, much of it to finance urban water supply projects. The limited scale of local borrowing, and the negligible local use of loans from commercial sources, is a reflection of the local governments' weak revenue base. A strengthening of the local revenue position is a prerequisite for greater local use of loan finance. As progress is made in that direction, an increasing proportion of central support for local capital projects could, and should, be provided in the form of loans. This would allow central grants to be focused increasingly on poorer areas. A shift from grant to loan financing of capital projects would induce the adoption of stronger cost recovery policies by the local governments. As local financial capacities grow, non-government sources of loan finance could also be gradually tapped, for example, through the issue of municipal bonds, at least by the financially stronger municipalities. For the near future, however, the use of commercial borrowing by local governments must remain limited.

Framework for planning, budgeting, and monitoring

Indonesia has an elaborate planning process which integrates "bottom-up" and "top-down" feedbacks. The same process, however, currently undermines fiscal autonomy granted to subnational governments through general-purpose fiscal transfers. As a result, local governments have insufficient control over budgetary allocations for decentralized functions and funding for these programs also becomes fragmented. In addition, local inputs into the central planning process are quite limited and central planning dominates local priorities. Reform of central–local fiscal relations, therefore, needs to be underpinned by complementary adaptations in the institutional arrangements for planning, budgeting, implementation, and monitoring. An important general need is for greater clarity in the distribution of responsibilities among the different levels of government. To support efficient operations and proper account-ability, regulations should comprehensively define the responsibilities of each level of local government in terms of the decentralized functions, as distinct from the deconcentrated and co-administered functions. A related need is to reduce the fragmentation in the sources of funds for the decentralized functions (for example, there are as many as ten sources of funds for health service delivery at the district level, with one of them – health INPRES grant – further split into nine separately specified ele-ments). All central financial support to regional governments for the pro-vision of decentralized services should be in the form of grants, or loans, administered through their respective budgets. One implication of this is that direct and separate higher-level government budgetary interventions in the provision of decentralized services can be phased out. Some initia-tives toward this end have been taken, under donor-assisted projects, for the decentralized urban and health services. Improved systems for moni-toring and auditing regional government performance would facilitate reduced central reliance on direct, detailed controls on the local use of funds.

Federalism in Pakistan: charting a treacherous course toward provincialization

Pakistan has a total land area of 796,095 square kilometers and an esti-mated end-1996 total population of 137 million. It is a federation with four provinces, Punjab (56 percent of the population), Sindh (23 percent), Northwest Frontier Province (13 percent) and Balochistan (5 percent). In addition to the four provinces, parts of Kashmir which were included in

Pakistan are organized as the State of Azad Kashmir and enjoy self-government. Federally administered northern areas include the administrative districts of Daiamir, Ghanche, Ghizer, Gilgit, and Skardu. There are also seven self-governing federally administered tribal areas where the laws of Pakistan do not apply, a situation which is consistent with the tradition fostered under the British Empire. For administrative purposes, the provinces are divided and each division is subdivided into districts. Again, each district is divided into *tehsils*. At the district and *tehsil* levels, elected councils and provincial civil administrations have overlapping responsibilities.

Local governments in Pakistan do not have any distinct constitutional status; they are established by provincial governments and powers are determined by provincial statutes. At the present time, there are 5,195 local government units in Pakistan of which only 512 units are in urban areas. For local government purposes, urban areas are organized according to population into metropolitan corporations, municipal corporations, municipal committees, town committees, and cantonment boards. Metropolitan corporations have some deconcentration of metro functions by means of zonal offices. Karachi Metropolitan Corporation has in the past experimented with a zonal lower tier of local government called municipal committees. Land development and water and sewerage functions in large urban areas are the responsibility of provincial agencies called Development Authorities (DAs) and Water and Sanitation Agencies (WASAs) respectively, and for smaller municipalities development expenditures are undertaken directly by provincial line departments. Karachi Metropolitan Corporation represents the exception in water and sewerage with its own Karachi Water and Sewerage Board (KWSB). Rural areas are organized into a two-tier local government structure with the lower-tier union council representing several villages, and a larger rural area, called a district, having a district council comprising several union councils. Provincial statutes regarding local government organization are fairly uniform and provide for elected local councils to have broad powers over a wide range of local public services. In practice, however, for reasons to be discussed later, the existing system of local government has become dysfunctional.

In terms of program spending, the federal government dominates in defense, debt servicing, general administration, fuel and power, transportation and communications, industrial development, population planning, manpower management, water supply and sanitation, and subsidies. Provincial government spending dominates in law and order, food and agriculture, rural development, education, and health. Local government spending is pre-eminent in social welfare, parks and recreation, and animal care. Overall in 1994–95, federal government spending accounted for 67.2 percent of the consolidated program total, with provincial government spending at 28.8 percent, and local government spending representing only 4.1 percent. It is also interesting to note that federal and provincial governments accounted for 73.3 percent of total spending on local public services in the same year. At the same time, the federal government collects 90.7 percent of the total tax revenue, with the remaining 9.3 percent collected in roughly equal proportions by the provinces and local governments.

The 1973 constitution delineates the responsibilities of federal government (Federal Legislative List) and the areas of shared responsibilities (Concurrent Legislative List). All remaining functions are the domain of provincial governments. Local government functions are defined under provincial laws through the use of Local Government Ordinances. The federal government is responsible for such key areas as defense, foreign affairs, international trade, macroeconomic management, and industrial development, among others. The provinces and the federal government share responsibility for population planning, curriculum and syllabus planning, and social welfare, and the provinces are solely responsible for roads, highways, police protection and justice, agriculture, and post-primary education. Local governments are given responsibility for local public services such as basic education and health, fire protection, parks and recreation, and water and sewerage.

Despite the extent of decentralization of legislative responsibilities as set out in the constitution and provincial statutes, the actual assumption of responsibilities is more centralized. For example, though education is a subnational responsibility in Pakistan, the federal government nevertheless takes responsibility in national policy formulation, planning, curriculum, and managing centers of excellence. Similarly, although health care in Pakistan is a subnational responsibility and much of it is assigned to the local level, in practice, it is more centralized. The federal government is responsible for drug regulation and quality control, regulating the standard of professional education, undertaking measures for containing communicable disease, and interacting with external organizations.

Implications of the existing structure

A quick review of the federal structure in Pakistan suggests that the legislative division of powers in Pakistan as set out by the Constitution and provincial statutes compares favorably to the assignment based on fiscal federalism principles. However, the actual assumption of responsibilities by various levels of government during the past two decades has consistently departed from the *de jure* assignment. Higher level governments have increasingly encroached not only upon lower-level government responsibilities, but also upon traditional private sector functions. There appears to be a trend towards centralization of responsibilities, with the federal government assuming either an exclusive role (for example, in population planning, electricity, curriculum development, syllabus planning, and centers of excellence) or a dominant role (for example, in social welfare, vocational/technical training, employment exchanges, and historic sites and museums) for some of the functions on the concurrent list, and even for some specified to be purely provincial. It should be noted that while the major proportion of social welfare expenditure (87.7 percent in 1994–95) is carried out by local governments/religious institutions/community groups, these entities simply administer federally defined and financed programs. Similarly, provincial governments have gradually assumed a large number of functions previously carried out, and intended to be carried out, by local governments (for example, curative health, land development, primary education, farm-to-market roads, rural development, preventive health, water supply, drainage, and sewerage) and/or by the private sector (table 4.3). Superior institutional capacity at higher levels of government and the attendant efficiency in service delivery were cited by the federal and provincial governments as the main reasons for the centralization of responsibility for public services. The reason given for higher-level governments in Pakistan having assumed increased responsibility for direct provision of private goods and services has been market failures. Such involvement is quite widespread, and encompasses key economic areas including manufacturing, wholesaling, retailing, banking, and financial intermediary functions.

In general, wider interpretations of constitutional mandates by federal and provincial governments have had the following implications for public sector management in Pakistan.

The private sector is crowded out

Federal and provincial governments during the 1970s acted aggressively to curtail private sector participation in education and health services and in industry, banking, and finance. This resulted in limiting citizens' choices and lowering the quality and quantity of private and quasi-private goods and services. It is useful to note here that recent survey results indicate that the public sector in Pakistan is less efficient than the private sector in the provision of education and health services.

Table 4.3. *Pakistan: legislative responsibility and actual provision of services by different levels of government*

Legislative responsibility	Service	Actual allocation of functions
Federal government[a]	Defense	Federal government
	External affairs	
	Posts and telegraphs	
	Telephones	
	Radio and T.V.	
	Currency	
	Foreign exchange	
	Foreign aid	
	Institutes for research	
	Nuclear energy	
	Ports and aerodromes	
	Shipping	
	Air service	
	Stock Exchange	
	National highway	
	Geological surveys	
	Meteorological surveys	
	Censuses	
	Railways	
	Mineral oil and natural gas	
	Industries	
Federal provincial governments[b]	Population planning	
	Curriculum development	
	Syllabus planning	
	Centers of excellence	
	Tourism	
	Social welfare	
	Vocational technical training	Federal provincial
	Employment exchange	governments
Provincial governments	Historical sites and monuments	
	Law and order	
	Justice	
	Tertiary health care and hospitals	
	Highways	Provincial governments
	Urban transport	
	Secondary and higher education[d]	
	Agricultural extension	
	Fertilizer and seed distribution	
	Irrigation[e]	
	Land reclamation[e]	
Local governments[c]	Primary education	
	Curative health	Primarily provincial
	Preventive health	with minor local
	Water supply, drainage and sewage	government
	Farm-to-market roads	involvement
	Land development	
	Rural developments	Local governments
	Link roads	
	Intra-urban roads	

Table 4.3 (*cont.*)

Legislative responsibility	Service	Actual allocation of functions
	Street lighting Garbage collection Fire fighting Parks and playgrounds	

Notes:
[a] According to Federal Legislative List.
[b] According to Concurrent Legislative List.
[c] According to Local Government Ordinances.
[d] University education is funded by the federal government through the University Grants Commission (UGC), but is administratively controlled by the provincial governments.
[e] Development of irrigation and SCARP projects is a federal subject.

Decision-making is highly centralized

In areas of concurrent responsibility, the higher level of government has often adopted a dominant position. Decisions on most large capital projects require federal approval. And, as most local functions are being assumed by the provincial government, local participation in major public policy decisions that affect local people is by and large non-existent.

Efficiency and equity in public service provision are undermined

Since decision-making is significantly divorced from the people on whose behalf decisions are being made, there is a greater likelihood of imperfect matching of local public services with local preferences, and of inadequate levels of response to local needs. These problems are particularly acute in primary education and basic health. In primary education, enrollment rates are low (42 percent), dropout rates are high (50 percent between Grades 1 and 2) and female literacy rates are low (22 percent). In rural areas, fewer than 15 percent of girls complete five years of education, and only 1 percent of girls remain in school by age 14. Absenteeism by teachers goes unreported. Teachers are not accountable to local communities or parents or even to school heads, but are transferable at will by provincial departments of education. Centralization of primary education has also worked to create "ghost" schools which either exist on paper but cannot be located or have a presence in the form of school buildings but cannot find students. In basic health, performance under provincial administration is no better. Most health centers lack medicines and supplies and, in many instances, proper sanitary conditions. In rural areas, health centers often lack both medical personnel and supplies. Medical personnel are frequently transferred against their will. There are no channels for local participation and input in the provision of health care. While no welfare cost estimates on centralization are available for Pakistan, for industrialized countries such losses on account of simply misjudging preferences are expected to range over 9–20 percent of expenditures. Once one considers the lack of local accountability and participation, and the delinking of benefits and costs, welfare losses may be expected to be of a much greater magnitude in Pakistan.

Public sector accountability is impaired

Separation of taxing and spending decisions at the provincial and local levels compromises accountability as citizens do not know exactly who is responsible for which services. The level of government raising most of the revenues, that is, the federal government, may be blamed for provincial–local service delivery problems. Accountability is also impaired because of a lack of clarity regarding the roles of various levels of government in areas of shared responsibility.

The local public sector is weakened

In its early stages, Pakistan had a well-planned and well-developed local government organization structure. During the 1950s and 1960s, local governments were a vibrant part of the public sector and delivered most of the local public services. However, in the 1970s and 1980s, some of the more important local functions, such as primary education and basic health, were shifted upward to provincial governments. Currently, the federal and provincial governments dominate the provision of local public services. As an example, the federal and provincial governments collectively account for 95 percent of total public sector expenditures for water and sewerage. This centralization of local service responsibilities has led to deterioration in service quality, as accountability has been significantly impaired.

The implication of all these points is that the current degree of centralization of expenditure responsibilities has not served the country well and may not be sustainable in the long run.

The federal–provincial allocation of taxing powers

The allocation of taxing powers to various levels of government has an important bearing on the character of federalism and also accountability. For example, if the ability of subnational jurisdictions to raise their own tax revenues were restricted, this could impose significant constraints on the ability of these jurisdictions to fulfill their proper expenditure responsibilities, and could therefore compromise the potential benefits to be had from decentralization. The allocation of taxing powers is determined jointly by the constitutional assignment of tax sources by level of government, and by the extent to which each level, especially the federal, has chosen to exploit the major tax bases. The higher the tax rates chosen by the federal government, the less room there will be for raising revenues at subnational levels, and the more dependent will the latter be on the federal government for their revenues.

The 1973 constitution specifies the following as areas of taxing responsibility for the federal government:

- customs duties including export duties
- excise duties including duties on salt, but excluding duties on alcoholic liquors, opium, and other narcotics
- duties in respect to succession of property
- estate duty in respect of property
- income taxes other than on agricultural income
- corporation tax
- tax on sales and purchase of goods imported, exported, produced, manufactured, or consumed
- taxes on the capital value of assets, not including taxes on capital gains on immovable property
- taxes on mineral oil, natural gas, and minerals for use in generation of nuclear energy
- taxes and duties on production capacity of any plant, machinery, undertaking, establishment, or installation
- terminal taxes on goods and passengers carried by railway, sea, or air and taxes on their fares and freights tariffs.

All other forms of taxation not specified in the above list fall under the purview of provincial governments. The provincial governments then allocate some of these to local governments on the basis of Local Government Ordinances. The major sources of revenue for provincial governments are, in fact, transfers from the federal government in the form of revenue-sharing from several major federal revenue sources. In particular, the provinces have transferred to them predetermined shares of revenues. These are raised by federally administered taxes on incomes, the sales of goods and excise duties on sugar and tobacco, federally administered royalties on oil and gas, and hydroelectricity profits earned by federal government enterprises. The President indicates the federal taxes that would be subject to sharing when convening the National Finance Commission (NFC). This commission is an intergovernmental body with representation from federal and provincial governments and legislatures and is chaired by the federal finance minister. The NFC develops consensus recommendations regarding the federal and provincial shares, and formulas for provincial allocation. These recommendations are not binding on the federal government, yet when a consensus decision is reached, it is almost always followed since federal and all provincial governments are directly represented on the NFC. The major own-sources of provincial revenues are stamp duties, motor vehicle registration taxes, and entertainment taxes. Local governments rely heavily on provincially administered real property and motor vehicle registration taxes and on self-administered import/export (*octroi*) taxes. The use of these assigned taxing powers by the various levels of government in Pakistan results in actual revenue-raising being heavily concentrated at the federal level, much more so than is required to finance its expenditure responsibilities. The federal government collects 90.7 percent of consolidated current revenues and retains only 59.3 percent for own use. It is also interesting to note that while the federal government collects income and sales taxes primarily for transfers to provincial governments, which account for 85.7 percent of the provincial revenues, the latter governments also reciprocate by collecting capital values tax and the religious taxes, *zakat* and *ushr*, at rates determined by the federal government, and turning the proceeds over to the federal government. Such an arrangement whereby revenues are passed upward is unusual in federations, the notable exceptions being China (a unitary country) and Russia, where for historical and institutional reasons the major revenues are collected by subnational governments and shares are transferred to the central government. In Pakistan, the aforementioned are relatively minor revenue sources, and the reason for provincial administration, at least for the *zakat* and *ushr* – taxes which do not form part of the budget – is their religious nature.

One important and distinguishing feature of the constitutional assignment of taxing powers to the federal government and the provinces in Pakistan is the tendency to assign major tax bases exclusively to one level of government or the other. Moreover, those bases that are often the largest revenue sources, such as sales and excise taxes and income taxes, are assigned to the federal government. In many federations, such taxes are co-occupied by the two levels of government so both are able to obtain revenues from them independently, though preferably in a harmonized fashion. This tendency to exclusive assignment has been a factor leading to the highly centralized revenue-raising system observed in Pakistan, as well as possibly to the fact that revenue-sharing is resorted to as a means of transferring funds to the provinces. As noted later, revenue-sharing has the disadvantage of not fostering accountability at the provincial level. This feature of exclusive assignment is not present at the provincial/local level. Entertainment taxes and taxes on cinemas, hotels, and professions are co-occupied by provincial and local governments, usually with independent collection.

Tax assignment in Pakistan emphasizes efficiency in tax administration and uniformity of the tax regime across the nation, but as a result, neglects provincial and local autonomy and accountability considerations. Thus, provincial governments are almost completely dependent upon revenue transfers from the higher level of government to finance their own expenditures. This degree of separation of taxing and spending responsibilities may not be in the interest of either the federal or the provincial level of government. The federal government has been advised by the NFC award for 1991 to transfer 80 percent of the proceeds from the more dynamic revenue sources such as VAT and income taxes, and 98 percent of the proceeds from natural resource royalties, to the provinces. To raise revenues for its own purposes, the federal government must first look for greater effort on non-shared revenue sources such as excise taxes. Thus, its incentives to exploit the major broad-based revenue sources are considerably weakened. Provincial governments, on the other hand, have no control over their major sources of revenue, and may not have any incentive for cost efficiency or for raising revenues from own sources, as additional efforts may not be worth the political costs.

A possible option for reform would have the federal government retain exclusive responsibility for taxation of international trade, corporate income, and for value-added taxation of sales of goods and services. The federal government would maintain primary responsibility for taxing personal income, though with the ability of the provinces to piggyback at flat rates. The current practice of the federal government levying excises on production and royalties on natural resource exploitation and turning over the proceeds to the provinces could be reviewed. Provinces could have control over most excise taxes and over wage taxes, and could levy a broad-based single sales tax that is parallel to the federal VAT, with its base harmonized with the federal VAT at retail level. Furthermore, local governments could have a role in setting property tax rates, and access to electricity duties, school fees, water and sewerage rates, and taxes on cinemas, hotels, and entertainment services. This tax assignment should be consistent with the fixed constitutional arrangements for sharing fiscal powers.

It is interesting to note that in Pakistan in 1994–95, over 90 percent of all taxes were realized through withholding and voluntary payments, and 100 major corporations account for 75 percent of income, 80 percent of excises and 60 percent of sales taxes. Further, the record of the federal tax administrative bureaucracy in tax enforcement is not enviable. Surveys of businesses have indicated that the agency appears to be more zealous in collecting bribes than taxes (Stone, 1995). Therefore, institutional capacity for tax administration should not be considered to be a serious impediment to any changes in tax assignment.

These suggestions in aggregate would lead to a significant change in own revenues generated at various levels of government in Pakistan and would result in greater conformity of revenue means with expenditure needs for these governments.

Federal–provincial fiscal transfers

Matching revenue means as closely as possible to the expenditure needs of various levels of government serves to strengthen accountability in a federal system. Stronger tax performance and better cost recovery policies at the subnational level will help in this task. It is, however, desirable in federal systems for higher-level governments to have access to more revenues than those dictated by their direct program responsibilities alone. These additional revenues can be used to further national or provincial economic objectives such as setting national standards, securing economic union, and ensuring interregional and intermunicipal fiscal equity. The design of these transfers, however, is critical to achieving the objectives sought. The issues pertaining to the design of these transfers are the focus of this subsection. Federal fiscal transfers to the provinces are the dominant source of financing operating expenditures for provincial governments in Pakistan, accounting for 87.5 percent of such expenditures in 1994–95 (table 4.4). They financed nearly 99 percent of operating expenditure for the two smaller provinces. The design of these transfers has important implications for the fiscal behavior of provincial governments and for the efficiency and equity of public service provision in Pakistan. Provincial transfers to local governments, on the other hand, are of minor significance in local finances as the provinces have provincialized major local public services such as basic health, education, water, and sanitation. The existing structure of federal–provincial transfers is described in the following paragraphs. Subsequently, the structure is evaluated for consistency of its design with the objectives sought.

Federal government transfers to the provinces have both unconditional and conditional components. These are discussed in turn.

Table 4.4. *Pakistan: federal transfers to provinces, 1994–95: summary indicators*

	Punjab	Sindh	NWFP	Balochistan	All
Operating transfers (as % of gross operating expenditure)	82	84	99	99	87
Capital transfers (as % of gross capital expenditure)	15	12	9	8	12
Total transfers (as % of total expenditure)	71	72	75	72	72
Development loans (as % of gross capital expenditure)	31	26	18	17	25

Source: Shah, 1995.

Unconditional transfers

These transfers are advised by an intergovernmental body, the National Finance Commission, that is appointed every five years to conduct a review of federal transfers. Federal and provincial finance ministers, the federal finance secretary, and one additional member from each of the provinces are represented on the Commission. The NFC has a chequered history, with many instances of either not meeting, or meeting and not achieving a consensus view. Over the past two decades, only the 1991 and 1997 NFC recommendations have been made public and implemented. As a result of the 1997 award, the following federal unconditional transfers are currently available to the provinces.

The constitutionally mandated revenue-sharing program has three elements: revenue-sharing by origin, revenue-sharing by population, and special grants. Table 4.5 shows the details of the first two of these. For the second element, the NFC defined a divisible pool to be shared on a 62.5: 37.5 basis between federal and provincial governments. The divisible pool consists of the following taxes: taxes on income including corporation tax, but excluding taxes on income consisting of remuneration paid out of the federal Consolidated Fund; wealth tax; capital value tax; taxes on the sales and purchases of goods imported, exported, manufactured, or consumed; export duties on cotton; customs duties; federal excise duties, excluding the excise duty on gas charged at well-head; any other tax by the federal government. The 1997 NFC award recommended the following special transfers:

- To Northwest Frontier Province: Rs. 3.3 billion in 1997–98 escalated by changes in the consumer price index (projected annual rate of 11 percent) for a period of five years.

Table 4.5. *Pakistan: constitutionally mandated revenue-sharing program, 1997–98 (percentages to be shared)*

Tax	%
Revenues shared on the basis of collection	14.2 (22 billion rupees)
Excise duty and royalty on gas	3.6
Surcharge on gas	4.3
Royalty on crude oil	1.0
Profits on hydroelectricity	5.5
Revenue shared on the basis of population	81.5 (171.4 billion rupees)
Income taxes	21.1
Sales tax	19.5
Export duty on cotton	0.8
Excise duty on sugar	26.8
Excise duty on tobacco products	13.2

- To Balochistan Province: Rs. 4.1 billion in 1997–98 escalated by changes in the consumer price index (projected annual rate of 11 percent) for a period of five years.

Conditional transfers

These transfers are relatively smaller. Nevertheless, about a dozen large grant programs in excess of Rs. 100 million (1994–95) exist.

Matching grants for provincial resource mobilization: this program provides federal matching assistance at a 50 percent rate, up to a limit, for provincial revenue effort in excess of the historical average growth rate of 14.2 percent. The limits on these grants are Rs. 500 million each in the cases of Punjab and Sindh and Rs. 100 million each for Northwest Frontier Province and Balochistan. The program recognizes only fiscal effort resulting from increases in tax rates, withdrawal of exemptions, imposition of new taxes, and revision in rates of user charges. Development Grants are based on approval of provincial annual development plans (ADPs) by the federal government. Federal Contribution for Social Action Program provides matching transfers on a 75:25 basis to finance provincial development expenditures in education, health, water supply, and sanitation associated with the Social Action Program. Flood and Disaster Relief grants are by their very nature *ad hoc* in character, and are usually given to the provinces for emergency relief and repair and renovations to basic infrastructure following damage arising from natural disasters. Physical Planning and Housing Project Assistance transfers finance to federally approved provincial projects to upgrade urban infrastructure and housing projects. Federal assistance is given in the form of conditional non-matching grants. The Tameer-e-Watan Program provides block fund allocations to federal legislators (in 1994–95, Rs. 6 million each for members of the National Assembly and Rs. 5 million each for senators) to be used for development projects of their choice through provincial Ministries of Local Government and Rural Development. The Tameer-e-Sindh Program provides federal financing on an *ad hoc* non-matching basis for rural development initiatives in the province of Sindh. Federal line ministries also fund various provincial projects, usually in the areas of social welfare, population planning, health, irrigation, and drainage. The Prime Minister occasionally uses discretionary allocation to provide provincial/local governments with funds for special programs. Finally, while higher education in Pakistan is a provincial responsibility, the federal government through the University Grants Commission (UGC) has traditionally provided financing for university education. The funding mechanism used by the UGC is *ad hoc* and is primarily guided by budgetary needs for salary expenditures.

Almost all of these conditional grants programs are discretionary in nature rather than being formula-driven. This has the disadvantage of requiring that the grants be allocated by administrative decision, which can both be costly and detract from provincial decision-making autonomy. Also, available funds may be unpredictable, thereby hampering long-term planning.

An economic evaluation of federal transfers in Pakistan

Revenue-sharing and unconditional transfers
The revenue-sharing program suggested by the 1997 NFC award allocates selected revenue sources on the basis of collection, whereas others are distributed to the provinces on the basis of population.

The revenue-sharing by collection component, which distributes roughly 25 percent of total revenues, returns resource revenues (oil and gas excises, royalties, and hydroelectricity profits) by point of collection. Hydroelectricity profits of federal public enterprises are also returned to the province where the plant is located. The formula used to determine these profits makes no provision for capital consumption allowances. The existing program of resource revenue-sharing by origin seems difficult to justify as the federal government collects revenues at centrally determined rates and then returns them to provinces on the basis of the point of collection. The reason for doing so may be partly to give resource-rich provinces feelings of entitlement, and partly to provide political accommodation needed to maintain national unity. This treatment remains contentious as

Table 4.6. *Vertical imbalances in Pakistan, 1994–95 (percent)*

Tax collection level	Revenue share	Expenditure share	Surplus/deficit
National	90.2	67.1	23.2
Subnational	9.7	32.9	−23.2
Provincial	4.9	28.8	−23.6
Local	4.8	4.1	0.7
All levels	100.0	100.0	0.0

Source: Calculated from federal and provincial budget data.

the largest province is now seeking the same treatment for federal royal-ties/excises on cotton (see *The Dawn* [Pakistan], Internet edition, January 12, 1997). There seems to be neither an efficiency nor an equity argument for doing so, unlike the case of population, or needs-based revenue-sharing. Thus, asymmetric treatment of resource-based revenues is diffi-cult to justify and could be considered for inclusion in a general revenue-sharing pool to be distributed on a per capita and/or needs basis. Better still, such revenues could go to the federal general revenues pool for financing fiscal equalization transfers to the provinces. Furthermore, the assignment of hydroelectric profits to the province of location of the facil-ities could be reassessed as it undermines the financial ability and auton-omy of the national power enterprise (WAPDA).

About 85 percent of revenue-sharing funds are distributed by popula-tion. This program is to be commended for its simplicity, objectivity, and success in transferring a large pool of resources in a predictable fashion to bridge vertical fiscal imbalances. Moreover, the use of population implies that the funds are distributed in an equalizing manner. Although population is the sole criterion used to achieve regional equity, it is a rea-sonable approximation of the need for funds since many provincial expenditures increase in proportion to population. Overall, the transfers are strongly equalizing with respect to own-tax collections (the rank correlation is −1.0), and mildly redistributive with respect to provincial GDP (rank correlation is −0.4). The program, nevertheless, is subject to a number of limitations which are discussed in the following para-graphs.

Limitations of the existing revenue-sharing program
Large transfers to reduce vertical fiscal gaps have the potential of intro-ducing unintended adverse incentives (table 4.6). It is desirable to examine first the possible sources for this imbalance, and alternative means of dealing with these issues, before agreeing on the best system of inter-

governmental transfers. Vertical fiscal imbalance in Pakistan can be attributed to a number of causes.

Mismatch of revenue means and expenditure needs is an important source of the problem, especially the overcentralization of taxing responsibility. We earlier noted that centralization of expenditures has been used as a response to correct fiscal imbalances arising at the subnational levels. Tax decentralization on the other hand has remained an unexplored option. Such an option needs to be seriously examined to deal with this issue. While significant untapped potential exists that could raise provincial revenues from own-sources, these efforts alone may not be sufficient for meeting provincial expenditure needs given the set of tax bases currently assigned to the provinces. Therefore, both tax decentralization (for example, excises) and joint occupancy of some tax fields (for example, personal income taxation) could be looked at to reduce provincial fiscal imbalances. Existing tax assignments are inadequately used partly due to excessive dependence on federal transfers, which reduces collection incentives, and to weak tax administration.

Thus, in dealing with vertical fiscal imbalances, reassignment of some responsibilities, tax decentralization, tax base sharing, and tax abatement are options which could take precedence over unconditional grants or general revenue-sharing. The latter options impair accountability by separating taxing and spending responsibilities, and should be relied on only to the extent that decentralization of fiscal responsibility is not appropriate. This is clearly not the case in Pakistan. Here, there has been a trend to centralize both taxing and expenditure responsibilities and then rely on revenue-sharing to deal with the fiscal gap. These revenue-sharing transfers finance up to 95 percent of provincial expenditures. Such an overwhelming dependence of provincial governments on federal transfers has tended to undermine federal budgetary flexibility as well as impairing subnational public sector accountability. Furthermore, these transfers may discourage the provinces from realizing the full potential of own tax bases. Citizens do not see a link between taxes paid to a particular level of government and public services offered by that same level.

The program ignores fiscal capacity in addressing regional equity issues. In doing so, it lacks an explicit equalization standard against which program achievements can be measured. Adoption of a formal fiscal capacity equalization program, on the other hand, has the potential to determine total amounts of transfers, and their allocation among provinces by a formula that sets a specific standard of equalization to be achieved.

Finally, special fiscal need grants are intended to compensate the two fiscally disadvantaged provinces for their weak fiscal capacities but higher expenditure needs. In the absence of significant tax decentralization and a formal equalization program, such grants represent a pragmatic approach to dealing with expenditure need differentials.

Conditional transfers: an evaluation
Conditional transfers to subnational governments are advocated to ensure certain minimum standards of services across jurisdictions (conditional block grants); to pursue higher-level government objectives (could be conditional matching or non-matching); or to address interjurisdictional spillovers of benefits (conditional matching transfers). With the exception of a few selected programs discussed below, federal–provincial specific-purpose transfers in Pakistan are, in general, *ad hoc* and primarily used for agency functions or to advance political objectives. Moreover, they are awarded on a discretionary basis rather than being determined by objective formulas.

The program of matching transfers for resource mobilization was ill conceived. It rewards provinces for higher tax effort due to any changes in structure and rates of taxation but provides no incentives for revenue increases due to improvement in efficiency in tax collection and administration. Thus, it potentially opens up the possibility for a province to shift a significant burden of its taxation to non-residents by being lax in collection of existing taxes while introducing newer (possibly nuisance) taxes. The program also shows the federal government's lack of concern with the additional burden of taxation and the deteriorating quality and quantity of provincial public services. This is particularly worrisome as the effective burden of the public sector (taxation inclusive of bribes) in Pakistan is considered very high and the net (fiscal benefit of public spending minus the burden of taxation) of the public sector as a whole may be negative. The limits now set to this program are welcome as they limit potential abuses and also restore the credibility of federal commitment that had been tarnished by the unfilled open-ended commitment of a similar program under the 1991 NFC award.

The federal programs of matching transfers for the Social Action Program could be reassessed. Consideration may be given to instituting conditional block (per capita) transfers for primary education and basic health, whose magnitudes are determined by formula (for example, equal per capita) rather than by discretion. These transfers may be made directly from the federal government to metropolitan corporations. For other local governments, these grants would pass through provincial governments. The primary school grant could be made conditional on provinces meeting targets on decentralization of primary education and basic health, ensuring private sector financing on a par with the public sector (based on the number of graduating students) and overall targets on access to such education.

The basic health grant could be linked to standards of access to such services. Similarly, federal transfers to universities through the University Grants Commission could be eliminated and replaced by per capita transfers to provinces for post-secondary education. Provinces in turn may be encouraged to substitute own-transfer programs to both public and private universities and colleges, utilizing the number of graduates by program type as criterion. Various programs could be weighted differently but financing of public and private education would be on an equal footing.

Subnational government access to capital markets

The 1973 constitution (Article 167) allows unfettered capital market access to provincial governments guaranteed by provincial Consolidated Fund revenues (which include federal transfers) and subject only to any limits imposed by the provincial assembly, provided that provinces do not owe any debt to the federal government. All the provinces are heavily indebted to the federal government, so access to capital markets for financing provincial–local capital projects is not available to subnational governments in Pakistan. In 1994–95, debt charges accounted for 23 percent of provincial current expenditures. This amounts to 165.8 percent of own-source revenues. Most of this debt arises from capital investment in social sectors and, therefore, accumulation of assets results in little increase in debt-carrying capacity. Currently, the federal government does not encourage any additional borrowing power by subnational governments until they have stabilized their budgets. It is important to ensure, however, that the federal government neither supplies debt, subsidizes debt nor guarantees debt. Beyond this, credit market discipline is the key to responsible subnational borrowing.

The 1997 NFC provision which allows provincial borrowing to finance operating deficits could inadvertently encourage fiscal mismanagement. Subnational borrowing to finance current expenditures should be prohibited. On the other hand, if the provinces and, quite possibly, large metropolitan area governments meet quantitative guidelines on fiscal discipline, they could be permitted in the very long run to have access to private capital markets at their own risk with a clear understanding that the federal government would not guarantee such debt. To ensure that the provinces do face market discipline and that their borrowing strategies do not run counter to the federal government's macroeconomic stabilization objectives, the federal government might use the National Economic Council or another intergovernmental forum as a consultative panel on macroeconomic policy coordination and, more importantly, to disseminate information on provincial and metropolitan finances and capital-spending strategies to the private sector. This body could also catalyze the private sector's development of credit ratings of provincial and metropolitan governments to facilitate bond and loan finance. Needless to say, unless the creditworthiness of provincial governments is substantially enhanced with a strong own-resource mobilization effort, provincial access to capital markets would remain largely closed. Therefore, strengthening provincial–local revenue sources should receive priority attention. Access to private capital finance by smaller municipalities does not appear feasible in the near future. For such governments, provincially directed access, either through special funds or special arrangements like the FINDETER experiment in Colombia, might be examined.

Why the road to reform remains a field of dreams

Fiscal systems in Indonesia and, especially, Pakistan require significant restructuring. Indonesia has made slow and steady progress on such reform efforts. In Pakistan such efforts are stalled and even in a state of reversal in some areas. A number of factors impede the progress of reform in both countries to varying degrees.

Political factors

In Indonesia, the authors of the Constitution contemplated a centralized unitary country and dictated against the establishment of "states within the state." These concerns for political unity have dominated the design of institutions. Well-entrenched roles of the military and the civil service in political affairs, with a strong belief in command and control from the center, have sustained centralization of responsibility. Appointment of governors and mayors has also strengthened centralization and limited local autonomy. Social development, economic prosperity, and concern for improving the delivery of public services continue to bring a degree of accommodation for decentralized institutions.

In Pakistan, political instability and feudal interests have contributed to setting aside constitutional dictums and the introduction of a system of centralized governance. Pakistan has been under military rule for most of its existence and past military regimes did not accommodate decentralized decision-making. During the periods that political activities have been permitted, feudal influences have dominated the political system and favored either a centralization or a provincialization of authority. This is because, while Pakistan has experienced increased urbanization in recent years, with over 40 percent of the total population urbanized, the electoral system still operates on the 1981 distribution of population (17 percent urbanized). In rural areas of Sindh and Balochistan, and to a more limited extent in Punjab and Northwest Frontier province, feudal lords do not allow effective political participation. The use of the outdated distribution of population allows feudal lords to dominate politics at the federal and provincial levels. A centralized system allows these lords to have more effective control than would be possible under a decentralized system, with which the urban sector would have a more significant voice. To further entrench feudal powers, local governments are currently disbanded in all metropolitan areas even though the Supreme Court found this practice to be in contravention of the law. Grants to members of national and provincial legislatures for development projects also work against the development of local governments as these members enjoy a greater degree of autonomy in project execution in the absence of a well-functioning system of local government.

Bureaucratic factors

Both Indonesia and Pakistan have colonial legacies. The Dutch in Indonesia and the British in Pakistan instituted systems of bureaucratic control to achieve, with maximum efficiency, the colonial objectives of a predatory state. These systems created a civil service elite who were highly educated and dedicated to serving the colonial rulers. Their loyalty to rulers and detachment from the common man were duly rewarded by allowing them preferential access to all public services through elite institutions and by ensuring their financial security through a system of cash rewards and land grants. Thus, both countries inherited civil service regimes that were highly centralized, efficient, accountable, professional, and completely detached from the local population.

After independence in Indonesia, the civil service over time became an active political partner with the military in governing the country. Both partners viewed central control as a key element in holding this country of 14,000 islands together. A centralized regime was also conducive to capturing rents from private sector development. Over time, nevertheless, they also discovered that the initial degree of centralization was not sustainable. Therefore, allowing a substantial degree of autonomy to local governments while keeping a weak structure of provincial governments, was a necessary step to improving the delivery of local services. A gradual shift towards local control (localization) is thus seen as posing no threat to a command-and-control oriented bureaucratic regime.

In Pakistan, after independence, the civil service retained its "professional" orientation for a while. It continued benefiting from an increasing array of perks such as almost costless acquisition of prime real estate, free membership in sports and entertainment complexes financed by public funds, and privileged access to elite educational institutions for children. However, political purges of the civil service in the late sixties and early seventies set it on the road to administrative decline (see Haque, 1996). With insecurity over the lack of tenure, areas of public intervention expanded limitlessly, and perks and bribes mushroomed. Corruption enabled officials to insure their careers against political risks. Thus the structure became a highly centralized yet dysfunctional system of administration. A key feature of this system has a special bearing on local governance. Key positions in provincial (provincial secretaries) and district governance (divisional and district commissioners) are held on assignment by officers of the elite administrative corps (officially, the "Central Superior Services – Civil Service of Pakistan"). Although performing duties at subnational levels, these officials remain primarily accountable to the federal government only. This system negates federalism and reinforces federal control over local decision-making. For local governments, a particularly worrisome aspect of this system of governance is that if the local governments function well, the district commissioner's powers are considerably curtailed. On the other hand, if the local government is not operative, the district commissioner becomes the sole discharger of judicial and executive functions at the district level. No wonder it appears that local governments are not allowed to succeed in Pakistan.

Institutional factors

Institutional factors also impede effective decentralization. Traditional institutions, the mechanism of governance, and accountability over time have withered away but have not been replaced by newer institutions. Instead, the all-pervasive role of the state has retarded the critical observation of public policies and institutions. There is almost a complete monopoly by the government of institutions of critical thought and the media in both countries. Any critical review of government policies and programs invites a government backlash. In Pakistan, rural self-government worked well in earlier days of its independence. This system was abandoned in favor of a more centralized system, which has resulted in the denial of access to basic services for the rural population. While a lack of institutional capacity was cited as a reason for the disbandment of the participatory system, the newer system left a majority of citizens with no political voice and no access to basic public services. Indonesia, on the other hand, is now nurturing self-government in rural areas through its village development grants.

External participants

External participants may also unwittingly impede development of a decentralized public sector in developing countries. A multitude of factors contribute to this development. First, a centralized system lowers transaction costs for external assistance and enlarges the "comfort zone" for external participants in terms of monitoring the utilization of their funds for intended purposes. Second, some external participants have concerned themselves with the revenue performance ("resource mobilization") of developing countries. Such concerns may lead to larger centralized bureaucracies that pay little attention to the efficient delivery of public services. For example, in Pakistan, the improved revenue performance of governments has been accompanied by the deteriorating quality and quantity of public services. Third, centralized systems are more prone to suffer from an absence of an internal policy agenda owing to a lack of citizen participation and to be more dependent on external advice on policy reform. Typically this leads to quick policy fixes with little sustained reform. For example, in Pakistan, the 1956 constitution stated the achievement of universal literacy as a goal for the ensuing decade; forty years later, there has been little change in literacy levels. In population planning, with US assistance, Pakistan established a goal to reduce the population growth rate to 2 percent by 1975. Twenty years later, the growth rate has increased to 3.5 percent. Similarly, public deficit reduction has been an elusive goal for several decades. External assistance, contrary to its intentions, may have helped Pakistan to avoid facing difficult choices in reducing public sector interventions in the marketplace. The availability of generous external assistance may have played a part in motivating the federal government to assume some provincial responsibilities and the provincial governments to take over local government mandates.

Some lessons for developing countries

The experiences of Indonesia and Pakistan offer important lessons for reform of fiscal systems in developing countries.

(1) Institutions of citizen participation and accountability must be addressed in any serious reform of fiscal systems. Even in primitive societies, such as pre-British India, systems of local governance worked effectively to deliver local services and collect local charges because of the well-understood mechanisms of citizen participation and accountability. More modern systems of local governance, such as those run by elite Pakistani bureaucrats with training in management, including financial management, have failed owing to an absence of citizen voices and accountability checks. The reform effort must embody appropriate provisions for holding to account elected officials for negligence or misconduct. Independence of the judiciary and free media can play an important part in political and bureaucratic accountability. These elements have not been addressed in the Indonesian and Pakistani reform efforts.

(2) Civil service reform is also critical to the success of a decentralization program. Bureaucratic ownership of a reform program is critical, but such ownership is not forthcoming in most developing countries, where decentralization is seen as an attempt to weaken the power of the central bureaucracy. To overcome this, the reform of fiscal systems must include the reform of the central bureaucracy. Such reform must ensure that the center has no say in the recruitment and promotion of civil servants at the subnational levels, and that the remuneration of subnational services is competitive with that at the central government level. Further, incentive structures in the civil service should reward service orientation and performance and discourage command-and-control and rent-seeking. This can be accomplished through performance contracts and the recognition of specialized skills.

(3) Institutional capacity matters are of secondary importance and should receive lower priority in reform effort. Institutional capacity to develop and maintain modern organizational practices such as budgeting, auditing, and accounting systems is important but should not be considered as a barrier to decentralization, provided citizen participation and transparency in decision-making are ensured. Technical capacity can be borrowed from supportive higher-level governments, amongst other places.

(4) Asymmetric decentralization as provided under the Indonesian decentralization program and under provincial local government ordinances in Pakistan offers a thoughtful approach to decentralization. Regardless of the availability of help from higher-level governments, lack of institutional capacity should never be considered as an excuse not to decentralize. Instead, an objective program of decentralization which recognizes the nature and type of local government, its clientele, and its fiscal capacity can be developed. Moreover, various local governments can be assigned differential powers by taking into account the aforementioned factors, as was done in Pakistan in the past, and is being done more systematically in Indonesia by rating each local government.

(5) A major separation of spending and taxing decisions leads to lack of accountability in the public sector. In Pakistan, federal revenue-sharing transfers finance up to 99 percent of expenditures in some provinces. This delinking of taxing and spending responsibilities has led to accountability problems at the provincial levels. In the event of such delinking, the role of conditional (conditional on standards of services and access to such services but not on expenditures) block transfers is worth examining in order to enhance accountability.

(6) Sharing of revenue on a tax-by-tax basis distorts incentives for efficient tax collection. In Pakistan, tax-by-tax sharing of income and sales taxes has impeded reform of trade taxes which are not shared with the provinces.

(7) Successful decentralization cannot be achieved in the absence of a well-designed fiscal transfers program. The design of these transfers must be simple, transparent, and consistent with their objectives (table 4.7). The experiences of Indonesia and Pakistan offer important insights on grant design. For example, Indonesia's education and health grants use simple and objectively quantifiable indicators in the allocation of funds, and conditions for the continued eligibility for these grants emphasize objective standards for access to these services. Indonesian grants for public sector wages, on the other hand, represent an example of not so thoughtful design as they introduce incentives for higher public employment at subnational levels. Pakistan's matching grant for resource mobilization similarly rewards relatively rich provinces for additional tax effort. It also calls into question the credibility of federal commitment, as the federal government has not been able to meet the commitment arising from this grant program.

Table 4.7. *Principles and best practices in grant design*

Grant objective	Grant design	Best practices	Practices to avoid
To bridge fiscal gap	Reassign responsibilities; tax abatement; tax base sharing	Tax abatement in Canada and tax base sharing in Canada, Brazil, and Pakistan	Deficit grants; tax-by-tax sharing as in India and Pakistan
To reduce regional fiscal disparities	General non-matching fiscal capacity equalization transfers	Fiscal equalization programs of Australia, Canada, and Germany	General revenue-sharing with multiple factors
To compensate for benefit spillovers	Open-ended matching transfers with matching rate consistent with spillover of benefits	South Africa grant for teaching hospitals	—
Setting national minimum standards	Conditional non-matching block transfers with conditions on standards of service and access	Indonesia: roads and primary education grants; Colombia, Chile, and South Africa: education transfers	Conditional transfers with conditions on spending alone; *ad hoc* grants
Influencing local priorities in areas of high national but low local priority	Open-ended matching transfers (preferably with matching rate varying inversely with fiscal capacity)	Matching transfers for social assistance, as in Canada	*Ad hoc* grants
Stabilization	Capital grants provided; maintenance possible	Limit use of capital grants and encourage private sector participation by providing political and policy risk guarantee	Stabilization grants with no future upkeep requirements

Source: Shah, 1994.

(8) Finally, contrary to a common misconception, a developing country's institutional environment calls for a greater degree of decentralization than is needed for an industrialized country. For the efficient working of a centralized bureaucracy, advanced information-gathering and transmittal networks, an efficient and dedicated civil service, and well-developed institutions of citizen participation and accountability are needed. This is possible in the environment of an industrialized country. A more primitive public sector environment is better suited by a decentralized form of governance because information requirements and transaction costs are minimized by moving the decision-making closer to people who are affected by those decisions. Closeness also serves to enhance participation and to promote preference matching for public services, transparency, and greater accountability. The experience of Pakistan demonstrates that public sector performance is significantly improved by decentralized decision-making even when the enabling environment is quite weak.

References

Haque, Nadeem-ul (1996), *Appropriate Reform Strategies in Pakistan*, Washington, DC: International Monetary Fund.

Huther, Jeff, and Shah, Anwar (1996), *A Simple Measure of Good Governance and its Application to the Debate on the Appropriate Level of Fiscal Decentralization*, Washington, DC: World Bank.

Indonesia, Government of (1996), *Monitoring Indicators of Repelita VI*, Jakarta.

Manor, James (1996), "Political economy of decentralization," unpublished paper.

Shah, Anwar (1994), *The Reform of Intergovernmental Fiscal Relations in Developing and Emerging Market Economies*, Washington, DC: World Bank.

(1995), "Fiscal federalism in Pakistan: challenges and opportunities," World Bank, Washington, DC.

Shah, Anwar, Zia Qureshi *et al.* (1994) "Intergovernmental fiscal relations in Indonesia: issues and reform options," Discussion Paper No. 239, World Bank, Washington, DC (October).

Stone, Andrew (1995), "The climate for private sector development in Pakistan: results of enterprise survey," Private Sector Development Department, World Bank, Washington, DC.

5

Morocco and Tunisia: financing local governments – the impact on infrastructure finance

FRANÇOIS VAILLANCOURT

The purpose of this chapter is to present intergovernmental finance arrangements in both Morocco and Tunisia, focusing particularly on the financing of local sector investment. These two countries are of interest in a book of comparative studies since they can be seen as reasonably representative of the French tradition in this field, as perpetuated in Africa. Yet, there are significant differences between them. The chapter has four sections. The first presents the relevant institutional setting; the second describes the main characteristics of intergovernmental finance, which in Morocco requires a presentation of the pre- and post- (1996) reform systems; the third examines the financing of local investment; the final section then evaluates this system in comparison to an ideal system of responsibilities, taxes, transfers, and borrowing mechanisms.

The institutional setting

In this section, the main sociodemographic characteristics of Morocco and Tunisia are introduced. This is followed by a description of the organization of subnational governments in both countries. Finally, there is a commentary on key institutional features.

Sociodemographic characteristics

Table 5.1 summarizes the key sociodemographic characteristics of both countries. Morocco's territory encompasses a coastal plain, mainly on the Atlantic, the Atlas mountain ranges, and a desert region, while Tunisia has a coastal plain and a desertic region. Both countries depend on seasonal rain for their agricultural output and substantial parts of their populations reside on the coast.

I thank participants in the PARADI/ICTS conference and, in particular, Richard Bird and David Sewell for useful comments on a first draft.

Table 5.1. *Morocco and Tunisia:*
sociodemographic characteristics

	Morocco	Tunisia
Area (km²)	710 850	163 610
Population (1994) (thousands)	26 074	8 785
Density (pop./km²)	36.7	53.7
Literacy rate (1990) (percent)	49	65
GDP[a] (millions)	245 570	15 869
GDP per capita[a]	9 418	1 806
GDP per capita (US$)	1 041	1 822
Urbanization (1992) (percent)	47	57

Note: [a] GDP is for 1992 in Morocco and 1994 in Tunisia,
expressed respectively in Moroccan dirhams and
Tunisian dinars.
Sources: World Bank, *World Development Report 1994,*
tables 1 and 31; IMF, *International Financial Statistics
1996,* country tables.

There are two major ethnic groups in Morocco, the Berbers and the
Arabs, who speak the common official language – Arabic – and practice a
common religion – Islam. French is the most widely used European language. Morocco has a monarchy whose ruling family can trace its roots to
the prophet Muhammad thus providing it with both a civil and a religious
role. Since independence, the role of the monarchy has been evolving
slowly from a traditional to a constitutional one.

In Tunisia, there is one ethnic group, the Arabs, whose members speak
Arabic, and practice Islam. French is again the most widely used European
language. Tunisia is a republic with a dominant party.

The organization of subnational governments

Table 5.2 shows the organization of subnational governments in the two
countries.

In Morocco, the sixty-five provinces created in 1963 are each headed by
a governor appointed by the central government. Each province has a local
assembly which is elected by members of municipal and city councils.
Provinces are mainly responsible for rural investment and deliver few services to citizens.

Municipalities, of which there are 1,544, were created in 1960 and saw
their autonomy and powers increase in 1976 with the Communal
Charter (*Charte communale*). Some of these duties, listed in table 5.2, such
as urban transit and water, are carried out in some cases by autonomous

Table 5.2. *Morocco and Tunisia: subnational governments*

Main characteristics	Morocco	Tunisia
First level	Provinces: 65	Regions: 23
	(*Provinces and préfectures*)	(*Conseils régionaux*)
Second level	Municipalities: 1 544	Municipalities: 257
	Urban (cities): 247	Urban (cities): 257
	Rural: 1 297	Rural: none
Urban groupings	Urban communities: 14	Tunis district: 1
	(*Communautés urbaines*)	
Responsibilities of municipalities		
Roads and sidewalks	Yes	Yes
Street lighting	Yes	Yes
Garbage collection and treatment	Yes	Yes
Markets	Yes	Yes
Slaughterhouses	Yes	Yes
Urban transit	Yes (R)	No: national government
Water	Yes (R)	No: SONED
Sewers	Yes (R)	No: ONAS

Notes: R: Local or regional *régies* in some cases.
SONED and ONAS are national agencies.
Source: Table ronde sur le financement des investissements municipaux dans des pays du Maghreb (1995), Washington, DC: World Bank.

establishments (*régies*). Municipalities are administered by elected municipal councils (the last elections were in 1997). Each municipality, in turn, elects a mayor from amongst its members. Municipalities, while subject to the direction of governors, or the Ministry of the Interior, have become more independent in recent years. This is a result of various factors such as the increase in the quality of their personnel and the difficulty of supervising a larger number of local governments.

The number of municipalities reflects changes in 1992 that increased the number of cities from 97 to 247 by dividing some existing cities and by transforming urbanizing rural areas into cities, thus eliminating an intermediate category known as "autonomous centers" (*centres autonomies*). At the same time, the number of rural municipalities increased from 760 to 1,297 and the number of urban communities from 2 (Casablanca and Rabat) to 14, as a result of the growth in urban agglomerations.

Finally, one should note that a 1992 constitutional amendment gave regions the status of local governments but did not specify their numbers, powers, or budget. This was clarified in 1996 along with the change in the legislative system discussed later.

In Tunisia, most regions are made up of both urbanized (communalized) and non-urbanized (non-communalized) territories: only two are fully urbanized. In 1994, cities, of which there were 257, included 61 percent of the population. Regions are headed by a governor named by the central government and have a regional assembly made up of regional members of the national parliament, mayors, and appointed members. Populations in non-urbanized territories are often defined with respect to villages (agglomerations). Villages have consultative councils used as sounding boards by the region, but they have no formal recognition as local governments.

Cities are governed by elected municipal councils that elect a mayor within their ranks. The number of municipalities has been increasing through time owing to the decisions made by the central government. In addition to the responsibilities listed in table 5.2, some Tunisian cities are involved in the field of welfare through spending on day-care or allowances to the poor. Following the 1995 municipal elections, there has been a movement toward decentralization.

Some observations

While the Moroccan and Tunisian communal systems are both inspired by the French model, there are differences that are worth noting. First, Tunisia is more centralized than Morocco, and both countries are more centralized than a North American state or province, or than some European countries. The greater degree of centralization in Tunisia than in Morocco is perhaps explained by the following factors: a smaller territory (table 5.1), making it easier to exercise central control; a greater concentration of population that yields economies of scale from national programs; and a stronger tradition of central planning that persists today with the Ninth Plan, to be implemented in 1997–2001 – whereas planning has been abandoned in Morocco. The greater degree of centralization in both countries than in North America or parts of Europe is explained, in part, by the fact that lower overall levels of education and fewer amenities in smaller centers make it difficult to recruit competent municipal staff. Other factors such as the impact of colonization may also matter. In both countries, primary and secondary education and local police services are the responsibility of the national government as in the European (particularly the French) tradition.

A second noteworthy difference is that Tunisia's territory is not fully divided into municipalities whereas Morocco's is so divided. This is both a plus and a minus in fostering decentralization. A positive aspect is that the more homogeneous municipalities in Tunisia are implementing decentralization policies, since the managerial capabilities of the less well-endowed municipalities are still fairly good. This matters since the formal equality of the urban and rural municipalities in Morocco prevents the urban ones being treated differently by giving them more power commensurate with the greater sophistication of their staff, elected leadership, and better-informed electorate.

On the negative side, the absence of rural municipalities or counties as a result of the legal framework means that, even if the central government wished to devolve some powers to the rural areas, it could not do so at the present time. As a result, Tunisians living in similar-sized small agglomerations (less than 5,000 inhabitants) are faced with different degrees of control and different tax burdens, depending on whether their agglomeration is a commune or not. If it is a commune, they elect a communal council that collects local taxes, receives subsidies, borrows, carries out investments, and provides local services. If it is not a commune, there is no council; therefore, no local taxes, subsidies, or loans are received, and the region provides local services and carries out investment.

Intergovernmental finance

In this section, we present first, for the two countries in turn, the local tax system and the intergovernmental transfer scheme. In the case of Morocco, we also consider the reform of intergovernmental transfers. We then turn to the relative importance of these sources of funds and finally comment on both countries.

The funding mechanism: Morocco

Tax revenues

Own revenues in Morocco are collected from three sources:

(1) two national taxes assessed and collected by the central government, the receipts of which are transferred (less a 10 percent collection fee) to local governments; these are the urban tax (*taxe urbaine*) and the business tax (*patente*);

(2) one local tax assessed and collected by the central government, the supplementary urban tax (*taxe d'édilité*);

(3) thirty-six local taxes and fees assessed and collected by the local authorities.

The rates for centrally collected taxes are set by the central government. The rates for local taxes are set either centrally, locally within a centrally set rate band, or, in a few cases, just locally.

Table 5.3. *Morocco: parameters of urban tax and supplementary urban tax*

	Urban tax	Supplementary urban tax
Rates	0 to 30 percent, depending on value	6 or 10 percent depending on location (periphery/center)
Taxable value	Owner-occupied: 25 percent of assessed value	Owner-occupied: 25 percent of assessed value
	Rented: not taxable	Rented: 100 percent of assessed value
Empty units	Not taxable	Not taxable
New buildings	Exempt for five years	Not exempt

Source: Information provided by Moroccan officials.

Two taxes (*taxe urbaine* and *taxe d'édilité*) are assessed on the rental value (*valeur locative*) of taxable units. Leases are used to establish rental values directly or through comparisons between owner-occupied and leased units.

For housing units, the parameters listed in table 5.3 are used. For non-housing units, the urban tax rate is 13.5 percent and the supplementary urban tax rate, 6 or 10 percent. In addition, these commercial or industrial units must pay a business tax set according to the rental value, the type of business, and the nature and quantity of inputs used. As a result, several hundred categories are used in assigning one of six business tax rates. Note that business tax revenues collected in urban communities are distributed between cities on the basis of their populations.

The three main local taxes and fees are:

(1) market fees (wholesale, fish, souks, and slaughterhouses) that account for 28 percent of revenues;
(2) forestry income (rural municipalities) (19 percent of revenues);
(3) construction fees (14 percent).

One notes the variety of tax bases used, for example, sales and opening hours (beverage houses), number of students (private schools), and so on.

Transfers
Since the 1984 tax reform, Moroccan local governments have been entitled to at least 30 percent of national value-added tax (VAT) receipts. This entitlement replaced an entitlement to other indirect taxes which themselves replaced gate fees (*droits de porte*). Since the implementation of VAT

in 1986 and of the transfers in 1988, this 30 percent has been both the minimum and maximum share of VAT receipts transferred.

From 1988 to 1995, VAT transfers were divided into current and capital transfers. Current transfers were calculated as budget-balancing grants (*subvention d'équilibre*). Local governments submitted their forecast revenues, expenditures, and deficits to a joint Ministry of the Interior/ Ministry of Finance committee that examined them, modified them, and set the subsidy. Not surprisingly, such a system led to ever-increasing deficits. In particular, expenses included both principal and interest payments on loans (*annuités*) leading to costless borrowing with budgetary priority (*inscription d'office*) given to repaying the lending agency (*Fonds d'équipement communal* [FEC]).

Capital transfers were granted once current transfers had been set. Since budgets were often approved only toward mid-year, capital spending often lagged behind receipts by one year. In addition, the promise of 30 percent of VAT revenues quickly proved a strenuous one for the central government. As a result, some central government capital expenditures, such as primary school buildings and rural electrification, were designated (transferred) as local investment (*charges transferées*) along with some national expenditures deemed to benefit local governments (*charges communes*). As a result of this shifting from central to local government of the central deficit, investment funds available to local governments have dwindled in recent years.

The disincentives associated with deficit financing quickly became apparent to the Moroccan government, which decided in 1992 to replace it with a formula-based apportionment system. The introduction of the formula, originally planned for 1994, was delayed by the following factors. First, the creation in 1992 of several hundred new municipalities meant that 1992 data could not be used to calculate the various parameters used in the new formula. Since 1993 data would not be available until mid-1994, a decision was taken in early 1993 to move implementation from January 1, 1994 to January 1, 1995. Second, it was considered appropriate to update population figures using the 1994 census rather than rely on data from the previous census in 1982. This made implementation in 1995 difficult, but not impossible. Third, there was a debate within the Moroccan administration as to the advisability of this change. Within the Ministry of the Interior, some officials resisted this change since it reduced the discretionary power of the government, while others defended it for precisely that reason as well as with arguments of predictability and simplicity. Within the government, there was some resistance from the Ministry of Finance since this would have an impact on its ability to relabel central expenditures as local ones. The formula was put in place for an eighteen-month budgetary year (January 1996–June 1997) made up of the 1996 (transitional six-month period) and 1996–97 budget years. This change in the dates of the budgetary year applies to both central and local governments. It was introduced to provide better forecasting of economic conditions since the budgetary year now starts after the rainy season. This allows the Moroccan government to make decisions based on good information gathered on expected crop yield.

The transfer formula in place in 1996 can be summarized in the following steps.

(1) Establish the predicted amount of VAT for the fiscal year and multiply it by 0.3. This yields the amount estimated to be available for local governments.

(2) Reserve 30 percent of this 30 percent local share of VAT (9 percent of VAT revenues) for transferred charges (15 percent), common charges (10 percent) and the adjustment fund (5 percent), that is, unexpected expenditures on items like natural disasters. This 30 percent reserve and its composition can vary in the future. For example, transferred charges are expected to drop in 1997–98. However, one may see a need to fund a new order of local government as regions appear. Regions were created by a constitutional amendment in 1992, but their powers were defined only by a second set of amendments in September 1996. They number sixteen and are entitled to a share of the VAT revenues and to shares of the PIT and CIT that remain to be set.

(3) Allocate the remaining 70 percent as follows: urban municipalities and communities (UMC), 30 percent; rural municipalities (RM) 20 percent; and provinces and prefectures (PP) 20 percent.

(4a) Provinces and prefectures (PP). Each PP receives its 1995 wage bill. The sum of these wage bills is subtracted from the 20 percent, and the remainder (of the 20 percent) is allocated using three weighted criteria: identical fixed amounts for each PP (one-sixth); the area of the PP (one-sixth with minimum and maximum); and the population of the PP (two-thirds with a minimum).

(4b) UMC and RM funds are allocated according to the weighted sum of three criteria: lump sum (UMC: 15 percent; RM: 30 percent), equalization (UMC: 70 percent; RM: 55 percent), and tax effort (15 percent for both). Equalization targets are 1.25 times the average tax potential and payment is capped at a maximum of 2.5 times the average population. UMC tax potential is measured by the *patente, taxe urbaine*, and *taxe d'édilité*, while for RM, incomes from the tax on the sale of forest products (a half) and market fees are also used. In the case of UMC, this is reasonable since the assessed taxes are calculated using national tax rates and tax rolls prepared using national norms and rules. In the case of RM, the use of taxes on forest product sales and market fees poses a problem because, in both cases, these are realized rather than assessed amounts that thus depend on forest resources and on the decision to sell forest products and on the tax and market fee collection effort. Equalization may reduce these amounts.

Tax effort is measured using other taxes. Municipalities with a tax effort greater than 0.65 times the average tax effort receive an amount depending on their share of these extra tax revenues (half per capita, half gross amount).

(4c) The actual amount of transfers depends on actual VAT revenues.

(5) In 1996–97, transition rules yielded a subsidy at least equal to that of 1995. A three- or four-year transition is planned for the progressive replacement of the old subsidy by the new one.

The funding mechanism: Tunisia

There are two main sources of own revenues

(1) direct taxes made up mainly of the rental tax (*taxe locative* or TL), the business tax (TCL), the hotel tax (*taxe hôtelière* or TH), and the tax on unbuilt land (TTNB);

(2) indirect taxes and fees including an electricity tax and market fees.

Direct taxes

The two main taxes (about 40 percent each of direct tax revenue) are TL and TCL.

The TL (now superseded by the TIB, see below) is set nationally at 20 percent of rental value and is collected by the Ministry of Finance on housing units (industrial, commercial, and professional buildings are exempt), with the tax roll prepared by the municipality or commune (CU) through a triennial or quinquennial census. The law prescribes using rent as the tax base for rental property, while comparable values are set for owner-occupied housing. Rental information is to be obtained from the occupant. It is sometimes checked against information in registered leases, which itself may be inaccurate. New buildings are exempt for five years. In practice, communes use either the number of rooms or the surface floor area of the housing unit along with values per room or per square meter that vary according to the neighborhood to set the tax base for non-rental units.

The business tax is payable by individuals who pay income tax on profits or professional income, partnerships, and corporations. It is usually collected as one-fifth of 1 percent on local gross business income, subject to a maximum of 20,000 D per business and to a minimum of the notional TL that would have been collected if these establishments had been subject to the TL. Such a minimum requires the establishment of a business TL roll, something that is done in only a few communes. The main issue with the TCL is that businesses do not provide a proper breakdown of their activities by communes. As a result, communes like Tunis, where head offices are located, benefit unduly from it.

Indirect taxes
Other taxes include the electricity surtax collected centrally with a rate of 2 millièmes (1000 millièmes = 1 D) per kilowatt-hour and justified as financing street lighting. It also allows the electricity board to cover some of the expenses of municipal governments. Other taxes include the entertainment tax (the rate varies between 3 and 18 percent depending on the type of entertainment) and the tax on beverage houses with more than ninety tax rates.

In early 1997, the Tunisian parliament adopted modifications to local taxes to be implemented from January 1, 1997. The main changes were:

- Introduction of the TIB (*taxe sur les immeubles bâtis*). It requires communes to use notional values per square meter of floor area to establish the rental tax roll. The proposed values, to be set by presidential decree, will vary from 2 to 8 dinars per square meter, depending on the size of the housing unit and the neighbourhood. The TIB replaced the 20 percent tax rate by four tax rates of 8, 10, 12, and 14 percent. These tax rates will be applied by the communes on an area basis. Areas will be classified according to the availability of six services: garbage collection, street lighting, covered roadway, covered sidewalk, sanitary sewers, and rainwater sewers. The tax rates will be set as follows: one to two services: 8 percent; three to four services: 10 percent; five to six services: 12 percent; five to six services and other or better quality services: 14 percent.
- Raise the maximum TCL payable from 20,000 to 50,000 D and distribute the TCL (and the TH) more accurately, using square meters if necessary for multi-establishment enterprises.

- Simplify the entertainment and beverage house taxes.
- Introduce a contribution for new public parking to be paid by builders of new housing units with insufficient private parking.

Transfers

Current transfers are paid out by the *Fonds commun des collectivités locales* (FCCL). The budget of the FCCL is set by the central government and is not linked to any specific tax source. It is reviewed annually and is allocated as follows.

- A central reserve receives 25 percent while the communes (CU) and regional councils (CR) combined receive 75 percent.
- The 75 percent is allocated by decree between CUs (86 percent) and CRs (14 percent).

The total amount for communes is allocated according to three criteria: their population (45 percent), their tax effort measured by a three-year average of collections of the TL (45 percent), and a flat-rate amount for each (10 percent). Similarly, the total amount for regional councils is allocated according to their population (85 percent) and with a flat-rate amount for each (15 percent).

The central reserve is allocated to Tunis (*Ville, District,* CR), to regional capitals (*chef lieu*), to civil protection, to ONAS (*Office National de l'Assainissement,* responsible for sewers), and to the *Caisse des prêts et subventions aux collectivités locales* (CPSCL), the lending agency for local governments.

Sources of funds for local governments

Tables 5.4 and 5.6 present, for Morocco and Tunisia respectively, the relative importance of own revenues (two kinds) and transfers in current revenues for two years for all local governments, while tables 5.5 and 5.7 present, again for the two countries, own revenues and transfers by type of local government for one year. These tables show that by 1993, both in Morocco and Tunisia, transfers accounted for 35–40 percent of local government revenues. However, they also show different trends in Morocco (growing) and Tunisia (decreasing) in the importance of transfers. Again, in both countries, municipalities get a greater share of their revenues from their own sources than from transfers, while provinces and regional councils depend more heavily on transfers, especially so in Morocco. More recent data (not shown) indicate that this situation has not changed in recent years.

Table 5.4. *Morocco: sources of funds, local governments, 1991 and 1993*

		1991		1993	
		DH millions	%	DH millions	%
Tax revenues	(1)	3 810.3	72.2	3 713.1	60.7
Major taxes	(2)	2 112.4	40	1 775.9	28.7
Local taxes and fees	(3)	1 697.9	32.2	1 957.1	32.0
VAT deficit subsidy	(4)	1 467.2	27.8	2 403.1	39.3
Total current revenues	(5)	5 277.6	100	6 116.2	100

Note: (1)=(2)+(3); (5)=(1)+(4).
Sources: "L'équipement local et son financement: cas du Maroc," in *Table ronde sur le financement des investissements municipaux dans les pays du Maghreb* (1995), Washington, DC: World Bank; information provided by Moroccan officials.

Table 5.5. *Morocco: sources of funds by type of local government, 1993*

Sources of funds		Provinces	Rural municipalities	Urban municipalities
Total (DH millions)	(1)	832.5	1 131.3	4 152.4
Tax revenue (% of total)	(2)	12.7	71.6	56.2
VAT deficit subsidy (% of total)	(3)	87.3	28.4	43.8
% of local sector	(4)	13.6	18.5	67.9

Note: (1)=(4)×(5) in table 5.4.
Source: Information provided by Moroccan officials.

Table 5.6. *Tunisia: sources of funds, local governments, 1992 and 1993*

		1992		1993	
		DI millions	%	DI	%
Tax revenues	(1)	116.0	61.6	128.6	63.1
Major taxes	(2)	46.2	24.5	51.8	25.4
Local taxes and fees	(3)	69.8	37.1	76.8	37.7
FCCL subsidy	(4)	72.3	38.4	75.3	36.9
Total current revenues	(5)	188.3	100	203.9	100

Note: (1)=(2)+(3); (5)=(1)+(4).
Source: Information provided by Tunisian officials.

Table 5.7. *Tunisia: sources of funds by type of local government, 1993*

Sources of funds		Municipalities	Regional councils
Total (DI millions)	(1)	183.5	201.4
Own revenues (% of total)	(2)	65.1	45.8
Transfers (% of total)	(3)	34.9	54.2
% of local sector	(4)	90	10

Note: (1)=(4)×(5) in table 5.6.
Source: Information provided by Tunisian officials.

The size of the envelope

In Morocco, the legal size of the envelope is predetermined at 30 percent of VAT revenues, with the actual size depending on the state of the economy, which impacts on VAT revenues and on mandated expenditures (*charges transferées, charges communes*) by the central government. In Tunisia, the amount is set as part of the annual budget process. Both approaches have the weakness of single-year budgeting, with uncertainty as to a major source of revenue for local governments. The Moroccan system has the additional difficulty of requiring the central government to claw back resources to achieve budgetary equilibrium. The Tunisian system allows, at least in principle, for changes in overall funding commensurate with both changes in responsibilities and in autonomous revenue potentials, regardless of the evolution of a given revenue source. Before 1987, the Tunisian system was similar to the Moroccan one with the funding of the FCCL, created in 1975, depending mainly on the revenues from tax on gross business income.

In both countries, the responsibilities and funding of local governments are set centrally by a combination of laws enacted by parliament and decrees issued by the government. Since local governments are not seen as being a level of government in their own right, they do not formally negotiate these matters with the central government. That said, one should note that in Morocco one-third of the members of parliament are not elected by the population, but by various groups including local authorities. As a result, some members have special expertise and interest in local matters. In a reform implemented in 1997, the unicameral system was replaced by a bicameral system. All members of the lower chamber of parliament are directly elected, but two-thirds of the members of the upper chamber are elected by local and regional bodies.

The allocation formulas

The criteria used to allocate amounts between the rural and urban municipalities or between regional/provincial and local authorities are not clearly spelt out in either country. This leads to disparities on a per capita basis that may be justified by needs.

With respect to allocation among municipalities, the relevant comparison is between the post-1996 Moroccan formula and the Tunisian one, since, before 1996, the Moroccan allocations were settled on a case-by-case basis. The key difference is that the Moroccan formula now uses both deficiencies in fiscal potential (equalization) and tax effort, while the Tunisian one uses population (as a needs indicator) and tax effort. The Moroccan formula partially corrects differences in fiscal potential and thus favors the poor, while the Tunisian formula amplifies differences in fiscal potential as measured by collections and favors the rich.

These differences raise two questions. First, why do they exist and second, which approach is preferable? The answer to the first question is not obvious. One part of the explanation is that the Moroccan formula was put in place *ab novo*, drawing on foreign experiences as a source of inspiration, while the Tunisian one evolved from a situation where tax efforts (roll preparation and collection) were felt to be insufficient and thus in need of encouragement. Another part is that in Morocco's national assessment, norms for major sources of revenues provided the tax potential information required to introduce an equalization formula, whereas in Tunisia there are no national norms. The local tax reform of 1997 in Tunisia will generate such a national tax base, thereby allowing the use of fiscal potential. In 1998, such use was being considered to assist the poorer CUs. As for which approach is preferable, there is no reason for transfers to replicate local revenue patterns. If these patterns are deemed appropriate from a distributional perspective, then central government revenues should be lowered to allow local authorities to increase their tax effort so as to collect these additional revenues themselves.

The nature of own revenues

There are several factors worth noting here. First, in both Morocco and Tunisia, local governments have very little freedom in setting tax rates or user fees and are not legally responsible for tax collection, although they may encourage it and provide resources to facilitate it. They also play a more limited (Morocco), or small (Tunisia), role in establishing their tax rolls. Taking into account national and local taxes, we estimate that in Morocco local governments receive 70 percent of their own revenue from taxes with centrally set tax rates, while in Tunisia this share is 65 percent. As a result, they do not control their own revenue and cannot therefore increase or decrease their provision of local services freely in accordance with the wishes of their electorate (they can neglect to collect taxes and to provide services, but this will create tax arrears and unmet needs).

Second, there are similar taxes levied on a single residential tax roll that could be amalgamated to simplify collection, but which remain separate because of tradition or small differences in the tax statutes. One reason for this lack of reform is that these taxes are relatively unimportant in the national perspective and thus do not attract the attention of key policy-makers in the Ministry of Finance, where the rate and base setting authority resides.

Third, the two business taxes have shortcomings. The Moroccan *patente* tax roll is constructed by acquiring information on the types of goods sold and on the nature and amount of input used. Each establishment is then assigned to one of six classes of businesses with tax rates varying from class to class. To give an example, a dentist's office will see its tax rate vary between 15 and 30 percent of rental value according to the number of chairs and the availability or not of prosthesis-making facilities. This creates micro-economic distortions in the choice of input mixes but does not take into account the environmental impact of industrial and commercial activities.

As for the Tunisian TCL, it is levied on gross business income. It does not take into account the use of land or public infrastructure. As a result, high-yield square meters in luxury shops generate more TCL than low-yield square meters in a trucking/warehousing complex, even if the nuisance and impact of the latter are higher.

Financing local investment

In the third part of this chapter, we present the various sources of funds available to local governments in both countries and then examine them in turn.

Sources of funds

The funding mechanisms are summarized in table 5.8. In general, Moroccan municipalities have more freedom in their investment and borrowing decisions than their Tunisian counterparts and bear a greater share of the cost. However, the fit between national and local priorities is stronger in Tunisia. This is achieved, in part, by the subsidy scheme described in table 5.9.

Table 5.8. *Morocco and Tunisia: main characteristics of local government investment finance, 1995–96*

	Morocco	Tunisia
Own funds available	Yes. Excess of current revenues over expenditures + sales of assets	Yes. Excess of current revenues over expenditures + sales of assets
Alternative use	Held by government treasury Low-yield deposit	Held by government treasury Low-yield deposit
Loans agency	FEC – monopoly	CPSCL – monopoly
Interest rate	Market 12–13% (inflation ≈ 6%)	Non-market 6.5% (inflation ≈ 5%)
Subsidy	Before 1995: yes (VAT share) Since 1996 : no	Yes. By CPSCL or ministry with various rates depending on project (see table 5.9)
Take up condition	None	Twinned with loan for a planned project
Project selection	By local government on an annual basis. Loan-financed projects must meet repayment capability test.	By consensual process to prepare a five-year plan (PIC). Projects not in the plan can be financed by own resources.

Source: Table ronde sur le financement des investissements municipaux dans les pays du Maghreb (1995), Washington, DC: World Bank.

Table 5.9. *Tunisia: sources of funds for investments by local governments, 1995*

	Sources of funds (%)		
		CPSCL Funds	
Type of investment	Own resources	Loans	Subsidies
Roads, streets, lighting, sewers	30	37	33
Waterworks, garbage collection centers	20	35	45
Cultural and sporting equipment	18	18	64[a]
Rehabilitating low-income areas	— 30[b] —		70
Economic investment (slaughterhouses, markets, etc.)	40	60	0
Buildings	50	50	0
Equipment	28	72	—
Green spaces	37	41	22
Technical studies of investment projects	0	100	0

Notes:
[a] Not by CPSCL but by the relevant ministries.
[b] The exact percentage of own resources depends on the commune concerned.
Source: Table ronde sur le financement des investissements municipaux dans les pays du Maghreb (1995), Washington, DC: World Bank.

Table 5.10. *Morocco and Tunisia: sources of investment financing, five-year periods (percent)*

	Morocco (1990–94)	Tunisia (1992–96)
Savings	29.3	22.9
Subsidies	45.7[a]	39.1[b]
Borrowed funds	25.1	38

Notes:
[a] These VAT investment subsidies (ended January 1, 1996) include some transferred investments.
[b] 22.4 percent of the funds are from the CPSCL and 16.7 percent from various agencies and departments (mainly ONAS and Youth Ministry).
Source: "L'équipement local et son financement: cas du Maroc" and "Financement des communes," in *Table ronde sur la financement des investissements municipaux dans les pays du Maghreb* (1995), Washington, DC: World Bank.

In both countries, the lending agency – FEC or CPSCL – has recently been the subject of reforms that increased its administrative and funding capabilities and, in Morocco, its autonomy. Given that, and the changes in the VAT transfer in Morocco and in local taxation in Tunisia, one may expect that the share of subsidies reported in table 5.10 will decrease through time.

Some observations

Insofar as cash balances yield low or even negative real returns, there is an incentive for local governments to invest in low-yielding projects that pay a slightly higher rate of return. Cash balances should yield the market rate of interest, preferably in a competitive market for deposits.

The rate of interest on borrowed funds should also be the market rate of interest in order to face localities with the real cost of funds. Subsidies should be paid up front in a lump sum (Pechon, 1995).

The use of a variable subsidy rate to reflect the degree of national priority, which in turn depends on various factors including externalities, is a good signaling technique. There is no reason, however, to link the receipt of a grant to that of a loan for local governments with own funds available. To do so requires them to borrow at a rate higher than the yield on these funds.

Overall assessment

In the first three sections, various aspects of the local government systems in Morocco and Tunisia are presented and examined. In this section, an overall assessment is provided. Responsibilities and revenues are examined first, by putting forward three questions, examining what theory and best practice indicate are sensible answers, and confronting Moroccan and Tunisian institutions and practice with these answers. A checklist provided by Bird (1994) is then used to examine the financing of infrastructure.

Have the appropriate functions been devolved to local governments?

There is by now a well-accepted body of guiding principles on what criteria should be used to assess the level of decentralization. They can be summarized as follows for any function:

- the more important the economies of scale in production, the more centralized production should be;
- the greater the geographically based heterogeneity in tastes for a publicly provided service, the more decentralized production should be;
- the greater the area of impact associated with the production of a service, the more centralized it should be so as to avoid unwarranted spillovers between small jurisdictions;
- the greater the diversity in possible production processes and the larger the number of varieties of local services, the more decentralized production should be to encourage emulation.

These criteria justify the provision of all the services listed in table 5.2 by local governments. Yet, as shown there, this is not the case in Tunisia. One can thus state that the appropriate functions have been formally devolved in Morocco but not in Tunisia. If one takes into account that local governments remain, in both countries, under the supervision of the Ministry of the Interior, usually through provincial/regional governors, that their key staff are named by either the Ministry of the Interior (secretary-general) or the Ministry of Finance (tax collector) and that staffing levels and wages are subject to central approach, then effective decentralization is less than formal decentralization and inadequate in both countries.

Do local governments have appropriate tax revenues?

The taxation literature shows that local governments should finance themselves first by user fees for local services, and second, for services which are not easily priced, by local taxes, such as a property tax, borne by local users and not exported to residents of other jurisdictions (as business taxes can be).

Both Moroccan and Tunisian municipal governments receive about 60 percent of their revenues from taxes and fees and 40 percent from current transfers. This own-revenue share is low by North American standards, such as the 90 percent observed in Quebec (Vaillancourt, 1995), but not unusual when compared with various European countries in 1990 (France 65 percent, United Kingdom 40 percent, Germany 55 percent) (Costa, 1996). The fact that, in both cases, most tax rates and fees are not set autonomously is of greater concern, since it seriously limits local freedom in establishing the appropriate prices for services.

Are transfer mechanisms appropriate?

Transfers from national to subnational governments have two main roles. First, they can be used to increase the provision of a service that is under-supplied by the local governments, usually because they do not take into account geographical or intergovernmental spillovers. Second, they can be used to equalize tax potentials between local governments, thus allowing poor local governments to offer comparable levels of services to those of the richer ones.

In the case of Morocco, transfers have had an explicit equalization goal since 1996, although specific spending has not been targeted. In the case of Tunisia, current transfers increase or at least maintain disparities between local governments, hence are non-equalizing, while capital transfers are used to encourage certain kinds of investments that do not, however, have large spillovers, since drinking water and sewers are nationally provided. Overall, the Moroccan system is more appropriate than the Tunisian one.

Having examined decentralization in general, let us now turn to the more specific issue of infrastructure and decentralization. Bird (1994) argues that decentralization is not necessarily bad for the provision of infrastructure and that what matters are the incentives. They will be appropriate if they make "those who make the decision bear the financial (and political) consequences" (Bird, 1994:30). Thus, politicians should bear the costs of their mistakes, local citizens should pay for local services and local decision-makers should be accountable for the use of revenues. This requires an appropriate framework of reporting mechanisms.

Using these criteria, one concludes that the Moroccan institutions are more appropriate, since Moroccan local authorities must bear the full cost of their freely chosen investment, while Tunisian local authorities must negotiate their investment with the central government but benefit from both upfront and interest rate subsidies.

Conclusion

This chapter has presented and discussed intergovernmental finance arrangements in Morocco and Tunisia. While both countries have been influenced by the French system, there are important differences in their institutions. First, the local sector is less important in Tunisia than in Morocco (2.5 versus 3.5 percent of GDP: Vaillancourt, 1995) but is less dependent on transfers for current revenues. Second, the new Moroccan transfer system is more redistributive than the Tunisian one which is under review. Third, Moroccan local authorities have more freedom than the Tunisian ones in choosing investment projects but face market interest rates.

In some cases, institutional differences are accounted for by these differences in finance arrangements, while in others, they are hard to justify.

References

Bird, R. (1994), "Decentralizing infrastructure for good or for ill," Policy Research Working Paper 1258, World Bank, Washington, DC.

Costa, A. (1996), "Finances locales, une comparaison européenne," *Problèmes économiques* 2481 (August 7 1996): 20–1.

Pechon, F. (1995), "Le rôle du crédit et ses perspectives d'évolution," in *Table ronde sur le financement des investissements municipaux dans les pays du Maghreb*, Washington, DC: World Bank.

Vaillancourt, F. (1995), "Les collectivités locales dans l'économie: analyse et comparaisons internationales," in *Table ronde sur le financement des investissements municipaux dans les pays du Maghreb*, Washington, DC: World Bank.

6

Colombia: the central role of the central government in fiscal decentralization

RICHARD M. BIRD AND ARIEL FISZBEIN

As in a number of other countries in Latin America, prolonged and some-times violent conflict between "centralists" and "federalists" occurred in Colombia during the latter part of the nineteenth century. As in most of the continent, the centralists won.[1] Despite marked regional differences and persistent strong regional identities fostered by the difficulties of travel in a country broken up by mountainous terrain, Colombia's governing struc-ture remained highly centralized until very recently. The central govern-ment (and its many "decentralized" agencies) not only controlled almost all public revenues and expenditures but also, outside of the largest cities, virtually supplanted the traditional territorially based governments, the departments and municipalities, in providing even the most local of ser-vices. Little scope and little reward existed for local initiative, and the most successful local politicians were those who could best exploit the labyrinthine central government system for the benefit of their constitu-ents.

By the late 1970s, however, this system had begun to break down, for two reasons. First, and most importantly, central government finances were increasingly strained by the task of financing the expansion of local public services to an increasingly urbanized population. This strain was perhaps felt earlier and more strongly in Colombia than in other Latin American countries owing to the country's long tradition of maintaining a relatively stable and conservative central government fiscal policy.[2] Second, the highly centralized system was also contributing to political unrest, as such critical services as water, education, and health were failing to reach large segments of Colombian society. In the eyes of some reform-ers, elected local authorities with resources adequate to meet local needs appeared increasingly necessary. Whether as a response to these pressures,

Much of this chapter is based on a recent report prepared for the World Bank by the authors with the assistance of several colleagues (World Bank, 1996a), but it should be emphasized that the views expressed here are the personal opinions of the authors and are not to be attrib-uted to any other person or organization.

its own fiscal needs, or a desire to implement its own policies more effectively, the central government looked to decentralization as one way to deal with its fiscal difficulties, as indicated by its appointment in 1980 of a Commission on Intergovernmental Finance to study ways in which to increase reliance on local resources for local purposes.[3]

The report of this Commission turned out to be only the first of a series of important measures of fiscal decentralization which have gone on to this day, especially as one part of a major constitutional reform in 1991.[4] Following the continuing and commendably rational path the process of decentralization has taken to date in Colombia, the law implementing the fiscal decentralization mandated by this reform (Law 60) contained a "sunset" clause requiring formal evaluation and, if necessary, revision in 1996. This chapter reflects our participation in this process of evaluation.

Reforming the decentralization law means very different things to different people in Colombia. The core economic ministries of the central government – Finance and Planning – are concerned mainly with the loss of control as a result of the decentralization of revenues to subnational governments. In their view, these increased transfers lie at the root of the fiscal difficulties recently experienced by the central government, so their inclination is clearly to reduce the size of these transfers as well as to increase central government control of transferred resources. Sector ministries such as those in charge of health and education would like to use the opportunity to reform the law both to increase the amount of resources available for their sectors and to pursue their own reform agendas.[5] Although municipalities and departments do not appear to have a clear agenda, they would of course like to increase local control over resources without any reduction in the size of the transfers. Congress, which is in charge of the reform, similarly does not appear to have a clear agenda and would rather avoid changes if possible.

In these circumstances, our evaluation of the situation is that no major overhaul of the existing system is needed. Instead, what is required is a judicious combination of (1) fine-tuning to eliminate some problems arising from the present system of transfers, (2) considerable simplification of the existing rules governing intergovernmental relations, and (3) more, not less, decentralization. As we argue in this chapter, however, the central problems relating to decentralization in Colombia require more, not less, attention by the central government to improve its own performance in a variety of ways. Once this is done, preferably along the lines sketched here, the present system of fiscal decentralization as set out in Law 60 should, we argue, produce broadly acceptable results.

The next three sections of this chapter briefly outline the current system of intergovernmental finance in Colombia and our suggestions for change. The remainder of the chapter then considers several aspects of fiscal decentralization that have given rise to much concern in recent years in Colombia – as in other countries – with respect to its effects on the pattern of local expenditures, the level of local taxes, and, more broadly, macroeconomic policy.[6] A brief concluding section considers what lessons Colombia's on-going experience with fiscal decentralization may have for other countries.[7]

The system of intergovernmental finance

Although far from complete – and even further from perfect – the process of fiscal decentralization has gone a long way in Colombia, and seems likely to go further, in part at least because of the strongly regional character of the Colombian economy and a series of recent political and constitutional reforms that have made this regionalism fiscally real in a way that has not been true for a century. Unlike many other countries in Latin America, Colombia has never been dominated economically by its capital, Bogotá. Four cities have over a million inhabitants, and there are thirty cities with populations over 100,000. With the election of municipal mayors and, more recently, departmental governors, regions such as those centered around the other major metropolitan areas (Medellín, Cali, and Barranquilla) are no longer as politically subordinate to Bogotá as in the past.

In total, Colombia has 33 intermediate-level general governments (32 departments and the special district of the capital city), several national territories, and over 1,000 municipal governments. The assignment of expenditure responsibilities is by no means sharp: cities, departments, and the national government, for example, all have sections in charge of areas such as education, health, and transport and there are often other public decentralized agencies involved in the provision of the same services. In practice, however, municipal governments are responsible for local services (streets, water, and garbage removal), and share responsibility for health and education with the regional (departmental) governments.[8]

Variations from place to place in population density and most relevant economic and fiscal variables are considerable. Although there are over 700 municipalities with less than 15,000 inhabitants, over 70 percent of the population is classified as "urban."[9] About 30 percent of the population of about 35 million is concentrated in the three most prosperous and urbanized areas of Bogotá, Antioquia (Medellín), and Valle (Cali). Since these three areas also account for close to half of Colombia's gross domestic product (GDP), it is not surprising that there are wide differences in regional incomes, with ten departments having average per capita GDP of less than half the national average (which is about US$1,400). In contrast, per capita GDP in the sparsely populated area of Arauca is well over US$5,000 as a result of oil production. Generally, however, the ratio of per capita incomes in rich and poor regions is closer to two, or at most three, to one. *Within* each region, however, income dispersion between urban and rural and within each category is considerably greater. The very poorest people in Colombia are found in rural areas, but close to half the poor are in large urban areas.[10]

Although most of the statistics just cited come in the form of "departmental" numbers, the role of departmental governments, as table 6.1 indicates, is much less important than that of municipal governments, for two reasons. First, the general departmental governments have few and inelastic resources at their disposal (mostly from beer, liquor, and tobacco taxes) – in 1994, for example, departments accounted for less than 9 percent of total government revenues, compared to over 12 percent for municipalities – and few functions on which to spend them. Superficially, this may not seem to be true in view of the important role of departments in providing health and education services: the same source, for example, shows departmental expenditures as 19 percent of the total (compared to 21 percent for municipalities).[11] As noted below, however, departmental governments as such have until now played little real role with respect to these important functions, despite their formal responsibilities.

This situation is in the process of change, however, in part because the second reason why departmental governments have been unimportant, namely, that governors were appointed by the central government, changed in 1991 with the first regional elections of governors. The election of municipal mayors since 1986 has undoubtedly been a principal reason for the growing importance of municipalities in the Colombian fiscal and political scene. Similarly, the future for departmental governments may be different from the recent past. Nonetheless, for the most part the remainder of this chapter will focus on the municipal level, which is where the major decentralization to date has occurred and where the effects are most marked.

The importance of subnational governments

Table 6.1 shows the structure of the Colombian public sector in 1985, 1990, and 1994.[12] Somewhat surprisingly, these data suggest that the subnational sector as a whole has not become more important over this period as a

Table 6.1. *Colombia: the structure of the public sector (percentages)*

	1985	1990	1994
National			
Revenue	73.9	75.1	79.2
Expenditure	63.8	56.4	59.8
Departmental			
Revenue	13.6	13.1	8.4
Expenditure	19.9	20.5	19.2
Municipal			
Revenue	12.4	11.8	12.4
Expenditure	16.3	23.0	20.9

Source: Colombia, Departamento Nacional de Planeación.

share of total public sector activity. In terms of GDP, however, there has indeed been a marked growth in the importance of the subnational sector. In 1994, total expenditure at the departmental and municipal levels came to about 12.6 percent of GDP, compared to 9.2 percent in 1985.[13] Combined departmental and municipal own-source current revenue in the same years (based on the data underlying table 6.1) was only 6.7 and 5.5 percent respectively. The conclusion seems obvious: most of the substantial recent increase in subnational expenditures must have been financed by national transfers. National transfers rose significantly over this period, from about 2.5 to 5.0 percent of GDP, so that about 60 percent of the expansion of the subnational sector was accounted for by additional transfer financing. Another 10 percent was financed by expanded borrowing, with the balance being accounted for by increased own-source revenues.

From 1988 to 1994, according to the more detailed data in World Bank (1996a), total municipal government expenditures approximately doubled, from 2 to 4 percent of GDP, with most of the increase taking place in 1993–94. Current expenditures rose significantly, from 1.2 to 2.2 percent of GDP, but capital expenditures increased even more, from 0.7 to 1.8 percent over the period. In real per capita terms, Colombian municipal governments were spending over three times more on investment in 1994 than in 1988, compared to a doubling of current expenditures (excluding debt service) over the period.

Over this period, only 37 percent of the expansion of municipal expenditure was accounted for by increased national transfers, with another 21 percent being accounted for by increased borrowing, especially in 1994.

The single most important source of finance for the expanded municipal sector was thus increased own-source revenues. Municipal governments have access to potentially lucrative revenues of their own in the form of property taxes and (at least in the case of the larger urban areas) a tax on local business (the "industry and commerce tax," which is mainly levied on estimated gross receipts).

An important aspect of the municipal government universe in Colombia, however, is that the big cities are both very important and very different from the rest. In 1994, for example, the five largest cities accounted for 69 percent of total local current revenues, 49 percent of current expenditures, and 34 percent of local investment. They also accounted for 58 percent of all local borrowing in that year, but they received only 17 percent of national transfers. In contrast, the 582 municipalities with less than 20,000 inhabitants accounted for only 5 percent of own revenue and less than 4 percent of debt, but they received 30 percent of national transfers and accounted for 12 percent of local current expenditures and almost 20 percent of local investment. Colombia's smaller municipalities have always been very heavily dependent on transfers to sustain their level of activities. The recent constitutional reform definitely increased this dependence on transfers, but the dependence itself has long been a feature of Colombian local finance.[14]

Finally, it should be noted that the numbers set out above may be interpreted rather differently. It is true that from 1988 to 1994, subnational current spending (including transfers) increased by about 2.5 percent of GDP. However, 60 percent of this apparent increase resulted from accounting changes in the education expenditure financed by national transfers and did not reflect increased subnational control over expenditure allocation.[15] For the subnational sector as a whole, increased own revenues over the period essentially financed the balance of increased current expenditure. In other words, all the remaining increase in national transfers during the period, like the additional borrowing, went to finance the very substantial increase that took place in subnational investment (amounting to 1.4 percent of GDP).[16] As noted later, this is precisely the result the national government appears to have wanted.

Intergovernmental transfers

The key to understanding intergovernmental fiscal relations in Colombia is the system of intergovernmental transfers. This system has three basic elements: the *situado fiscal* (SF), the *participaciones municipales* (PM), and the *sistema nacional de cofinanciación* (SNC). The SF consists of 24.5 percent of national current revenues (2.7 percent of GDP in 1995); it is transferred to departments (and districts) to finance education and health in part in equal (per unit) shares and in part on a population basis. The PM also consists of a percentage of national current revenues, increasing annually to a scheduled maximum of 22 percent in 2002 (and amounting to 1.7 percent of GDP in 1995); it is transferred to municipalities for "social investment," on the basis of a complex formula which on the whole clearly favors the smaller and poorer municipalities. Finally, the SNC, which finances specified subnational projects on a "matching" basis amounted to a further 0.8 percent of GDP in 1995.[17] The principal characteristics of these three transfer programs may be set out briefly.

The *situado fiscal* in 1995 was 23.5 percent of national current revenues (increasing to 24.5 percent in 1996). These revenues are supposed to be divided as follows: 15 percent of the total is divided in equal parts among the departments, the Capital District (Bogotá) and the Special Districts of Cartagena and Santa Marta, and the remaining 85 percent largely in accordance with an estimate of "user" population (of public education and health facilities). The actual formula is quite complex, including, in principle, small components for "fiscal efficiency" and "administrative efficiency," although these elements appear to have little effect on the actual distribution. (The detailed formulas for both SF and PM [below] take two pages to set out in World Bank (1994).) Indeed, several departments receive amounts in excess of those given by the formula in order to cover actual expenditures – something which is legally possible because the departments in question are not "certified" to manage the SF. At least 60 percent of SF must be spent on pre-school, primary, and secondary education and 20 percent on health, with the remaining 20 percent on either (in practice, it almost always all goes to pay teachers' salaries).

The *participaciones municipales* in 1995 were 15 percent of national current revenues, increasing by 1 percentage point a year to 22 percent in 2001. These revenues are supposed to be distributed to municipalities (and *resguardos indígenas*) as follows. First, 5 percent of the total is distributed to municipalities with less than 50,000 inhabitants (in accordance with the formula set out next) and an additional 1.5 percent goes to municipalities along the Magdalena River, in proportion to the length of river frontage. Next, of the remainder, 40 percent is distributed on the basis of the number of inhabitants with "unsatisfied basic needs" (as measured by an index of *necesidades básicas insatisfechas*, or NBI), 20 percent in proportion to the degree of relative poverty of the municipality, 22 percent in proportion to population, 6 percent in proportion to "fiscal efficiency," 6 percent in proportion to "administrative efficiency," and 6 percent in proportion to the change in the NBI. PM transfers must be spent on "social investment," with at least 30 percent to education, 25 percent to health, 20 percent to water and sewerage (if less than 70 percent of population currently covered), and 5 percent to recreation, sport, and culture. The remaining 20 percent is *de libre asignación* but must still be spent on social investment. In all cases, rural areas must receive a share of expenditure at least equal to their proportion of population (and if the rural share is greater than 40 percent, they must get an extra 10 percent).

The *sistema nacional de confinanciación* consists of four funds: the Social Investment Fund (FIS), the Rural Development Fund (DRI), the Fund for Urban Infrastructure (FIU), and the Fund for Road Infrastructure (FIV). These funds help to finance projects by subnational governments through matching grants, with different matching rates applied for different types of projects.

The design and functioning of these three transfer programs is clearly of critical importance in determining the outcome of fiscal decentralization in Colombia. Each of these transfers generates incentives that may be more or less conducive to the maintenance and expansion of the coverage and quality of such critical services as education, health, or water. In addition, some have argued that the cumulative impact of these extensive central transfers – amounting to about 40 percent of total central government expenditure – has been to weaken macroeconomic policy by discouraging local efforts to raise own revenues and encouraging frivolous and irresponsible spending by transfer recipients. These points are discussed later in the chapter.

Policy objectives and transfer design

At present, five distinct policy objectives are addressed with the three transfer instruments outlined above (table 6.2). The first two objectives involve the provision of minimum service levels in education and health, respectively. These objectives are being pursued to varying degrees by all three transfer programs. A third important objective is to finance, at least in part, the cost of building the physical infrastructure necessary to expand the coverage of key services (water, education, and health); this objective is addressed through both the PM and the SNC. Apart from these specific "output" objectives, the system of intergovernmental transfers pursues two additional objectives. First, it attempts to increase the fiscal capacity of territorial entities to finance a variety of other decentralized or local services (for example, roads and recreation). The main instrument employed for this purpose is a percentage (20 percent) of the PM that in principle can

Table 6.2. *The system of intergovernmental transfers*

Objectives	Instruments		
	Situado fiscal	*Participaciones municipales*	*Sistema nacional de confinanciación*
Finance education	X	X	X
Finance health	X	X	X
Finance infrastructure		X	X
Increase local capacity to finance other services		X	
Interregional redistribution	X	X	X

be allocated freely (*transferencias de libre asignación*). At the same time, the system tries to compensate for differences in fiscal capacity or needs by the use of distribution formulas for both the SF and the PM that transfer proportionally more resources to the poorest entities.[18]

Using the same instruments both to finance the provision of education and health services and to redistribute resources with the purpose of increasing fiscal capacity and compensating for interregional differences may generate important cost inefficiencies because costs are not directly associated with differences in income or wealth. For example, in the case of the PM, the per capita transfers received by any municipality are strongly influenced by a poverty indicator, with the result that some local governments receive a transfer that, in per capita terms, is three to four times higher than that received by others in the same department.[19] An important part of these transfers is used to cover the recurrent costs of providing education and health services.[20] Since these costs are mainly established by national policies, they do not vary between municipalities by such large factors, and the variations that do exist cannot logically be linked directly to a poverty indicator.

Similarly, using the SNC to finance such recurrent costs of providing health and education services as teachers' salaries limits the administrative capacity of subnational governments, creates dependency on the national level, and thus likely reduces the efficacy with which services are provided. In 1995, for example, we estimate that two-thirds of the SNC funds directed to education corresponded to recurrent costs and only one-third to capital expenditures.[21]

Finally, assigning the function of financing infrastructure (new water systems, roads, schools, or hospitals) to an automatic and permanent transfer such as the PM (whose value is not linked to coverage needs) generates two types of problems. First, the national government loses a potentially important tool to implement the goals of its development plan and to direct resources to those regions with the most important coverage gaps. Second, even if one does not worry too much about this, given the way the role of central planning is commonly downplayed these days, the present system does not recognize the obvious fact that construction of infrastructure is a discrete event. Since, as noted below, other national policies virtually guarantee that local governments will lack the flexibility to allocate these resources to other uses, this rigidity in funding could lead to even more allocative distortions.

The basic principle that should guide the design of a system of inter-governmental transfers is that the purpose of transfers is *not* to finance particular governmental entities but rather to contribute to an effective provision of services to the population. To the extent that services are provided by subnational governments without the fiscal capacity to finance them fully, that there are externalities associated with the services in question, and that interregional differences in needs are important, transfers may be needed. But it is important to ensure that those responsible for the provision of a service have a clear mandate, resources to finance it (including, whenever needed, own resources), and flexibility to make decisions, and are held accountable for results. In addition to providing incentives for agents (recipient governments) to act as the principal (the central government) wishes, other critical elements of transfer design are simplicity, objectivity, and transparency.[22]

Financing education and health

In Colombia, arguably the principal objective of the transfer system is to guarantee the provision of minimum service levels of education and health to the population. Given the important externalities associated with those services and their special status (in accordance with the Constitution and economic development policy), the central government has assumed, in effect, the responsibility of financing the provision of these services. The magnitude of the minimum service level and the extent of its coverage among the population, however, constitute variables to be determined by policy considerations and resource availability. Education and health are by far the most important sectors affected by the system of intergovernmental finance in Colombia. The amount and design of all major transfers are dominated by concern for these two sectors.[23]

To put this another way, Colombia has initiated a process of decentralization in the education and health sectors at least in part because it considers that subnational governments are more effective in providing these services. Nonetheless, to date, there has been considerable confusion arising from the unclear allocation of expenditure responsibilities. In the case of education, for example, it is not at all clear who is in charge of what. The relative roles and responsibilities of the national, departmental, municipal, and school-level authorities need to be disentangled and clarified. Nonetheless, it is clear that both levels of subnational government will require resources from the national level in order to finance this service adequately. In the case of health, the concurrent implementation of social security reform makes the process of decentralization even more complex. It is not just subnational governments that receive transfers from the national level for health but also quasi-public enterprises (that is, hospitals) and companies offering health insurance packages to the poor. The complexity of this scheme precludes further discussion here.[24]

In general, however, the main guiding principle with respect to financing these basic services should clearly be that money should flow to the entities (even if they are not part of the public sector) that are actually responsible for the provision of these minimum service levels. The magnitude of the funds needed to finance the proposed new system of capitation grants for education and health is a function of unit costs (which could vary according to geographic and demographic conditions) and coverage. The main change needed in the existing system is to establish a direct link between the guaranteed service and its financing that is not a function of either current revenues or complex formulas attempting to measure poverty, effort, or other variables that do not represent the cost of providing the service.[25]

A problem of particular importance concerns the transition from the existing to a new system: how do we get there from here? More policy proposals probably founder on the rock of inadequate consideration of the transitional problem than any other. The major transitional problem with the revised transfer for education proposed in World Bank (1996a), for example, is that it implies a shift of teachers away from those localities with an "excess" of teachers towards those with a "deficit" (in terms of the standard per student allocation). As with all transitions, three dimensions need to be taken into account: (1) the pace at which deficits are rectified; (2) the pace at which excesses are corrected; and (3) the resolution of the imbalance if (1) does not equal (2). As a rule, it is easier to build up than to run down (although it is important not to dump too much new money too quickly into any governmental unit since it will always be spent, but not necessarily efficiently). Reducing government expenditures is never politically easy, particularly when, as in this case, it may involve moving personnel from more desirable locations to less desirable ones.

The reality is thus likely to be that it will be difficult to move from the present inappropriate distribution of official teachers to one more in accord with needs without putting additional funding into the system to finance the slower pace of reducing the excess. In other words, it may be that the only way to get "there" from "here" is by putting more money into the system – an ironic outcome, if true, given that one of the principal factors motivating decentralization has clearly been the desire to "off-load" some social expenditures from the hard-pressed central budget. Change to a better decentralized system may save funds in the long run, and should certainly produce more services for the same money, but the transition process itself is likely to cause considerable friction and to require that additional resources flow into the system, at least for some period.[26]

Financing infrastructure

The national government has two reasons for being interested in what local governments do in financing infrastructure. First, some local infrastructure projects may involve significant externalities. Second, some such projects may constitute essential elements of national development programs. National support of infrastructure related to the provision of basic education and health services, for example, may qualify for both reasons, as may national support of projects improving the level and quality of water supply and sewerage. Support of local roads and some rural development projects may be justified as part of the national effort to improve the economic productivity of poor rural areas.

Whatever the rationale for national interest in local investment in physical infrastructure, concern for the provision of services and the creation of new infrastructure is inappropriately mixed in the present transfer system. The amounts allocated through the existing transfer mechanisms bear no relation to any rational investment policy in critical areas such as education and health. Moreover, many of the investment projects currently supported (for example, with respect to sports and recreation) should likely not be eligible for national support in any case.

In a decentralized system, in principle, subnational governments should identify infrastructure needs and execute projects. Financing large infrastructure projects from local resources alone may of course not always be possible, given the scanty current revenues of most local governments. Moreover, small localities seldom have much access to private capital markets. If small local governments are to carry out costly public works, they must as a rule rely heavily on grants from higher-level governments.[27]

In theory, a matching grant, in which the central government pays part of an expenditure made by a local government, is the best way to finance projects in which some of the benefits from the local activity in question spill over to other localities. The share paid by the central government (the matching rate) should be related to the size of the spillover and may also depend in part upon the financial position of the local government (that is, by altering the matching rate in accordance with local capacities one can, in principle, stimulate similar responses in different localities).[28] Properly designed matching grants also have the political advantage of introducing an element of local involvement, commitment, accountability, and responsibility for the aided activities.

Money alone will not do the job, however; it must be provided in the right framework, in the right amounts, and to the right recipients under the right conditions. Revising the present SNC drastically along the lines sketched above and removing the requirement to spend most of the PM on investment are needed reforms. For such a system to work, however, the national government must have both clear objectives and an operational system that can work efficiently with subnational governments interested in having access to these resources. It is not clear that either condition is adequately satisfied at present, although some of the agencies now involved in the SNC appear to have operated quite successfully in some respects (World Bank, 1995).

General-purpose grant

As noted earlier, it appears at present that every transfer program in Colombia is intended to achieve every objective. In no area is this problem more obvious than with regard to the redistributive aspect of transfers. Although every transfer program seems to be intended primarily to give more to those who have less, the result can hardly be said to be a pattern of redistribution that makes much sense in terms of either efficiency or equity.[29] Essentially, the argument to this point has been that the two major growth-related programs with strong interpersonal redistributive elements – education and health – should be separated out and funded by a system of national capitation grants, thus emphasizing that the central distributional issue relating to these programs relates to redistribution among *persons* rather than *regions*. Similarly, the other main direct national interest in what subnational governments do (the provision of infrastructure related to these two programs and other projects with significant spillovers to broader regions) should be separated out more clearly and financed on a matching grant basis.

Such a system will not work properly, however, unless a final critical component of the system of intergovernmental transfers, which may be called a "general-purpose grant" (GPG), is put into place. A GPG has two important, and distinct, rationales. The first, and the most important rationale from a systemic perspective, is to provide the necessary underpinning for decentralization in general, and for the other transfers proposed above in particular, by equalizing (to some level) the fiscal capacity of territorial entities, thus putting all on the same footing with respect to incentives. The second rationale is to provide sufficient resources to enable all local governments, even the smallest and poorest, to provide a basic package of local services other than health, education, or construction of infrastructure.[30]

From a purely economic point of view, the second of these may appear to make little sense in some respects. However, in Colombia at present, and no doubt for years to come, most smaller rural areas will not be able to provide any significant local services solely from their own resources. This lack of local resources should not be confused with a lack of local capacity to make and implement suitable expenditure decisions, since there is strong evidence that even the poorest areas in Colombia have managed surprisingly well once they have been enabled and encouraged to do so.[31] In any case, a critical question in transfer design is often how to provide the basic resources such municipal governments need to survive while maintaining adequate incentives for them to do what they can in terms of raising their own revenues. Fortunately, it turns out that the transfer design needed to make the capitation systems for education and health and the matching grant system for infrastructure function properly will also accomplish the politically necessary task of ensuring the survival of even the fiscally weak.[32] And, as just mentioned, preliminary indications in Colombia suggest that such localities seem, on the whole, to spend the money as well, or better, than would occur under a more centralized system (World Bank, 1995).

Any sound design for intergovernmental transfers requires explicit incorporation in some way not only of an appropriate measure of "need" but also of "revenue capacity."[33] At one extreme, the aim might be to provide each local government with sufficient funds (own-source revenues plus transfers) to deliver a (centrally) predetermined level of services. Because such capacity-based transfers are in principle based on measures of *potential* revenue-raising capacity (not on actual revenues), no disincentive to fiscal effort is created by this approach. Differentials in the cost of providing services (for example, in rural or less densely populated areas) may or may not be taken into account.[34] Of course, transfers based solely on capacity measures do nothing to ensure that the recipient governments will in fact use the funds they receive as the central government might wish – unless receipt is conditioned on performance, and compliance is monitored in some way.

Although it is difficult to measure either "capacity" or "need" in any fully satisfactory way, some general-purpose grant along these lines is clearly needed to replace the confusing use of redistributive measures in the SF and PM transfers. Such a grant will enable all local governments to operate at some minimum level and provide other services besides health and education. At the same time, and more importantly, it will partially compensate for the large differences in fiscal capacity that exist and hence place all on a more level playing-field with respect to the (essentially) equal (per service unit) capitation grants proposed above for basic education and health. The key aspects of the GPG are that the use of the funds thus provided are at the discretion of the recipient (no earmarking – see next section) and, especially, that they are distributed according to need and fiscal capacity.[35]

Earmarking and expenditure mandates

As Colombian central officials see matters, the main problem with the present system of intergovernmental transfers is not, as we have argued, that its design provides inappropriate incentives but rather that its sheer size gives rise to three main problems: (1) the recipient governments do not spend the money correctly; (2) they have also slackened off in terms of collecting their own taxes; and (3) the growing burden of transfers on the central budget is a major obstacle to restoring macroeconomic balance. This and the next two sections discuss each of these problems in turn. We find little evidence in support of any of these arguments.

Owing to the perceived profligacy of local governments with the "easy money" flowing in from transfers, Congress has attempted to control local spending in three ways: first, by requiring almost all the PM to be spent on "social investment"; second, through such administrative controls as establishing fixed percentages of transfers that must be spent on certain sectors; and, finally, by limiting even the so-called "free" allocation of 20 percent of PM transfers. Unfortunately, such measures have created additional inefficiencies. The use of fixed percentages may easily lead to overspending in certain sectors. For example, it is unlikely that 15 percent of the PM can possibly be the optimal amount to be spent on health subsidies in all municipalities, as the current system implies. Moreover, the general restriction against using PM resources for recurrent expenditures[36] not only precludes some gains in allocative efficiency that may theoretically be expected with decentralization, but may even lead to an increase in the volume of current expenditures financed through credit, as this is one of the few means local governments have to escape such limits. Finally, the emphasis on administrative controls distracts the national government from its responsibility to monitor and evaluate the effectiveness with which subnational governments implement programs and provide the services for which they became responsible.[37]

The inefficiencies and distortions generated by the rigidity implicit in the transfer system itself, with its various rules as to how the funds may be spent, are further exacerbated by a proliferation of norms and mandates imposed on local governments. Laws such as those on public services, environment, and sports earmark local resources or impose significant costs on local finances. For many municipalities earmarking and unfunded mandates imply costs that surpass the 20 percent of the PM that is not already earmarked (table 6.3). Local governments now clearly have more resources than they did before Law 60; but in at least some cases they may now have even *less* freedom than before in terms of deciding how much should be spent on what.

Colombian public finances have long been characterized by extensive earmarking, that is, the assigning of revenues from specific sources to particular expenditures. Earlier studies found such earmarking to be particularly important at the municipal and, especially, departmental levels.[38] Although earmarking at the national level has been reduced in recent years, no similar changes have been made at the subnational level: most departmental own-source revenues, and a substantial fraction of municipal own-source revenues are still required by *national* legislation to be spent on particular activities. In addition to such revenue earmarking, and increasingly in recent years, almost all national transfers to subnational entities are earmarked in the sense that they must be spent on specific activities in amounts (or proportions) designated by national legislation. Finally, Colombia, like many other countries, offers many examples of unfunded legislative "mandates," that is, expenditure obligations imposed on subnational governments with no additional funding being attached.[39]

The importance of the earmarking and mandating of local own revenues may be indicated by reference to a recent detailed examination of a small number of specific municipalities.[40] As shown in table 6.3, all three of the municipalities examined, which varied widely in location, size, and sophistication, appeared to be spending as much as, or in some cases more than, required by Law 60 on the various areas of "social investment" designated there. Moreover, although some of the transfers received from the

Table 6.3. *Earmarking and mandates in specific*
municipalities (million pesos)

	Zipaquirá 1995 budget	Cajicá 1994	Polícarpo 1994
Law 142/93	73.0	12.9	0.1
Law 99/93	20.9	19.7	4.7
Law 3/91; Law 9/89	96.6	73.3	23.8
Law 136/94	53.8	31.9	9.2
SISBEN	20.0	17.0	10.0
Anticorruption	6.0	2.0[a]	0.0
Stratification	12.0	4.0[a]	0.0
Internal control	2.0	1.0[a]	0.0
Contraloría	69.0	23.0[a]	0.0
Personería	54.5	18.0[a]	0.0
UMATA	11.9	1.0	0.0
Total	419.7	203.8	47.8
As percentage of transfers	15.6	23.7	14.0

Note: [a] Estimated, based on actual expenditure on Zipaquirá,
assuming that cost is proportional to population.
The items identified in this table are (some of) those for which
national laws require municipal governments to spend either
specific percentages of their own resources (including the 20
percent *de libre asignación* of the PM transfer). Some of these items
– contraloría, personería – relate to nationally mandated increases
in the salaries of local officials. Others relate to major reforms in
other areas, such as the SISBEN requirement to register citizens
for purposes of health insurance. Still others simply reflect the
desire of national legislators to control municipal expenditures by
designating specific percentages or amounts to be spent on such
items as agricultural extension (UMATA), and the funds to be
spent on housing (Law 3/91 and Law 9/89), water and sewerage
(Law 142/93), environmental protection (Law 99/93), and the
training of municipal officials (Law 136/94).
Source: World Bank, 1996a, vol. II, p. 57.

national government were supposedly *de libre asignación* (that is, could be
spent as the municipalities wished), in fact most of the transfers, and in
some cases some own-source revenue in addition, were at least in principle also supposedly budgeted as specified by national laws.[41]

For the municipal sector as a whole, the evidence suggests that as a rule
total expenditures on "social investment" substantially exceeded the mandated requirements. That is, not only were the designated proportions of
the transfers spent on the designated activities but some additional local
resources were also spent. For example, in 1994 50 percent of transfers were
to be spent on designated activities, with 30 percent of the 50 percent, or 15
percent in total, going to education: the actual proportion of transfers spent

on education in 1994 was over 28 percent, or almost twice the required amount.[42] In short, if local governments are spending transfer funds incorrectly in some sense, the responsibility seems to lie with those who set the rules, namely, the central government.

Fiscal effort and fiscal flexibility

A recurrent theme in Colombia has been concern with the effort, or lack of effort, demonstrated by departmental and municipal governments in mobilizing local fiscal resources. This theme was, for example, emphasized in varying degrees by two major reviews of fiscal decentralization undertaken in 1981 and 1992 respectively.[43] More recently, the effect on local fiscal effort of the increased fiscal transfers to municipal governments resulting from Law 60 of 1993 has given rise to much concern and to a series of relatively inconclusive empirical studies in Colombia.[44]

Despite all the fuss, there is little or no evidence to support the apparently widespread belief in Colombia that the expansion of national transfers to date has significantly reduced local fiscal effort. The studies that support this conclusion, like those that do not, are far from robust,[45] and the available data on the whole suggest that the major sources of departmental and municipal own revenue have in recent years continued to expand at, or above, the rates observed in earlier years when transfers were lower.[46] Local governments on the whole appear both to have maintained their own efforts to collect revenues (as discussed below) and to spend the money sensibly and in accord with the wishes of local people (World Bank, 1995).

In any case, the constant focus on "fiscal effort" in recent Colombian discussion seems misguided conceptually, empirically, and in policy terms. Conceptually, while it is not easy to define fiscal effort, it is probably most meaningfully understood as the ratio of actual taxes collected to "potential" taxes estimated on the basis of some standard measure of fiscal capacity and some standard (for example, national average) tax rate.[47] Even when so defined, the general absence of reliable empirical estimates of fiscal capacity renders the concept non-operational. Moreover, given the very limited flexibility Colombian departments and municipalities have to alter their revenues through their own actions in any case, it is far from clear to what extent it is meaningful to interpret the behavior of revenues as reflecting their "effort."

With respect to most major departmental and municipal taxes, for example, both the tax base and the tax rate (or, in some cases, a maximum rate) are determined by national legislation. In the case of the local property tax, the single most important source of local own-source revenues, in most of the country the tax base can be increased only by the action of a national agency (the Instituto Geográfico "Agustín Codazzi" for periodic reassessments and the central government for annual inflation indexing). The provision for automatic adjustment of cadastral values in Law 14 of 1983, for instance, has been consistently determined by the central government to mean that such values should be increased by less than the increase in the consumer price index (CPI).[48] When combined with the fact that regular reassessments in much of the country occur at much longer intervals than the recommended three years, the result is that the only way that local governments which levy the maximum allowed rate can increase property tax collections is by collecting the taxes assessed more rapidly.[49]

It is common to note the very low level of property taxes in countries such as Colombia and to argue that there is obviously much room for increased local "fiscal effort" in this respect. Again, there is of course some truth in this, although experience everywhere suggests that it is neither quick nor easy to obtain additional revenues from property taxes (Dillinger, 1991). In Colombia most local governments have little possibility of doing so anyway because they control neither the tax rate nor the tax base. In the larger cities the most "flexible" local tax is a tax on business – the (not particularly desirable) industry and commerce tax.[50] However, there is little scope for this tax in the smaller municipalities, many of which have little of either industry or commerce. Indeed, in the smaller communities it is hard to see any way in which local governments could increase revenues quickly other than by borrowing – a fact which may explain at least some of the increase in recourse to this source that has occurred in recent years.

On the whole, the evidence to date in Colombia appears to support more the so-called "flypaper effect" – that is, that transfers tend to increase total expenditures by about the same amount as the transfers because local taxes are not reduced – than the "fiscal effort hypothesis" that increased transfers result in reduced local taxes. If so, this casts doubt on the good sense of following the frequent advice to place still greater weight on rewarding fiscal effort by increased transfers – unless, for some reason that is far from clear in the context of Colombia today, a larger public sector is in itself assumed to be a major policy objective.

The correct focus of attention with respect to subnational revenues in Colombia is thus not the arguable and, it appears, so far unimportant deterrent effect of increased transfers on local revenues but rather the more important questions of the effects of these transfers on local expenditures and the inadequate design of both the major transfers and of most local revenue sources. It would seem advisable for the central government to focus on problems which are entirely within its own policy domain rather than on what seems to be the non-problem of inadequate fiscal effort by the local governments – a problem which, even if it exists, cannot readily be dealt with by national government policy, and which arguably should not be even if it could be.

On the other hand, it should perhaps be noted that there is an alternative and more meaningful way in which to interpret the strong emphasis in the work of such authors as Wiesner (1992, 1995) on the importance of taking "fiscal effort" more explicitly into account in designing transfer programs. From this perspective, the reason for the concern with fiscal effort is not some technical worry about the substitutability of national transfers for local resources. Rather, it arises from the importance of requiring local citizens to pay, in some meaningful sense, for what they get so that those who make local expenditure decisions will be held accountable (through local political institutions) for their actions. So long as local governments spend "other people's money," according to this plausible argument, they are unlikely to be under much local pressure to spend this money efficiently.

While studies such as World Bank (1995) suggest that this may be an unduly pessimistic reading of Colombian experience to date, it is surely correct to say that experience everywhere indicates that people are more careful in spending money they have to earn (pay themselves) both because they are aware of the pain of taxation as well as the pleasure of expenditure and because they will feel more "ownership" of the activity as a result. From this perspective, careful attention should indeed be paid to local resource mobilization as an essential component of any successful decentralization exercise. Unless increased transfers are matched by some local contribution, however small it may be in the poorest communities, it is unlikely that the full efficiency benefits of decentralization can be realized. People do not, it seems, take ownership of what is given to them in the same way as they do of things they have to pay for themselves, at least in part. And without local ownership, expenditure efficiency seems unlikely to be enhanced by decentralization.

Transfers and deficits

An interesting aspect of the recent move to decentralize public sector activities in many countries around the world has been the revival of an old worry – that subnational governments, left to their own devices, will act in a macroeconomically "perverse" fashion.[51] In the case of Colombia, as in other Latin American countries such as Argentina and Brazil, the basic worry is that increased national transfers will induce subnational governments to cut their own taxes while expanding expenditures both through increased transfers and through "leveraging" increased borrowing of their new (transfer) revenue base. Subnational deficits, and hence total public sector spending and the overall public sector deficit, will hence expand. Although little or no evidence of such destabilizing effects in Colombia is visible to date, even those whose studies produce such reassuring news are quick to point out that the future may be worse in this respect, as transfers continue to expand and local governments become more irresponsible.[52]

When the national government transfers revenues to subnational governments, it also, as a rule, transfers expenditures. This has certainly been the case in Colombia over the last few years: the entire increase in the SF, for example, and (as discussed above) the entire transfer to municipalities has been explicitly earmarked, in effect, for specific expenditures. In other words, subnational expenditures in principle should, in the absence of behavioral reactions, increase by exactly the same amount as subnational revenues. That is, revenues available for expenditure at the national level decline and those available at the subnational level rise by the same amount as subnational expenditures. In this framework, the overall effect of this accounting change obviously depends *not* on the amount of the transfers but rather on two other factors: what happens to national expenditures and what happens to non-transfer (own) subnational revenues.

Consider the latter first. One of three things may happen to subnational revenues as a result of increased transfers: they may decline ("fiscal laziness," decrease in fiscal effort, or "substitution effect" of transfers); they may remain the same as in the absence of transfers ("flypaper effect"); or they may – as some seem to desire – actually increase local own revenues ("stimulative effect" of grants). As discussed above the evidence, such as it is, suggests that, at least up to now, there is no evidence of a decrease in fiscal effort. In other words, the local reaction to transfers suggests that there has been no change in the size of public spending and deficits ("flypaper") or even an increase in the size of local spending but not in the deficit ("stimulation").

Now consider national spending. Unless national spending falls by at least the amount of the transfer, the result will definitely be an increase in both the total size of the public sector and the size of the public sector deficit. Table 6.4 illustrates the various possible outcomes. In this table, national expenditures and subnational revenues are the critical exogenous variables, national revenues are assumed to be given, and subnational expenditures are assumed to increase by the amount of national transfers.

Table 6.4. *Macroeconomic effects of increased transfers*

G_n	−	−	−	0	0	0	+	+	+
G_s	+	+	+	+	+	+	+	+	+
G_t	?	?	?	+	+	+	++	++	++
T_s	−	0	+	−	0	+	−	0	+
D_n	−	−	−	0	0	0	+	+	+
D_s	+	0	−	+	0	−	+	0	−
D_t	?	−	−−	+	0	−	++	+	?

Key:

G_n National government expenditure (excluding transfers)
G_s Subnational government expenditure (including transfers)
G_t Total public sector expenditure $(G_n + G_s)$
T_s Subnational own revenues
D_s Subnational deficit including transfers $(G_s - T_s)$
D_n National deficit excluding transfers $(G_n - T_n)$; T_n assumed constant
D_t Total public sector deficit (since T_n constant, varies as $G_t - T_s$)

+ =increase; − =decrease; 0=no change; + + =strong increase; − − =strong decrease;
? =unknown "depends on relative magnitudes of offsetting changes".

Under these circumstances, total spending – the size of the public sector – will increase as a result of increased transfers unless national spending declines by the same amount (or, most improbably, subnational taxes and hence own-revenue financed subnational spending fall by *more* than transfers!). Similarly, the total public sector deficit will increase with increased transfers unless national spending declines proportionately, unless (again most improbably) offset by a large enough increase in local taxes. In short, given that on the whole the evidence suggests that local taxes will remain steady or increase a little, rather than decline (or increase a lot), the key to the impact of increased transfers on macro stability lies in the behavior of *national* (non-transfer) spending.

How does this analysis work out in Colombia? One view is that most of the marked adverse swing in public sector current saving in recent years is attributable to increased transfers, and some have interpreted this to mean that increased transfers to regions are the villain on the macro scene. This seems unwarranted. In the first place, the total magnitude of the real increase in *regional* transfers is much smaller than the swing in the deficit. Most of the apparent increase in central government transfers is attributable to (1) the reform of the social security system, which involves a transitional increase in (non-regional) transfers in order to make explicit a deficit that was always there but not previously accounted for explicitly, and (2) the redefinition of the SF to encompass a wider range of educational expenditures. These expenditures were previously shown as national expenditures; they are now shown as national transfers and subnational expenditures. In reality, however, they are still national expenditures (to pay nationally set wages of teachers).[53]

Even apart from these accounting factors, there has clearly been an increase (about 1 percent of GDP) in national transfers to municipalities – and as mentioned earlier this amount is scheduled to increase steadily in the future. Until now, all of these increased transfers have effectively flowed to nationally mandated expenditures. In effect all that is happening is that a portion of national revenues is being indirectly spent on national objectives through the agency of subnational governments. But there has been no corresponding reduction in direct national expenditures. In short, if there is a villain in this picture it would appear to be the national government which has failed to reduce its own program expenditures in proportion to the extent such expenditures are now being carried on at the local level.[54]

On the whole, given their relatively inflexible tax base, Colombian local governments have probably done as well as could be expected in raising real resources in the last few years. Of course, some have done better than others; and all could no doubt do better, but that is not the point. Given the basically unpromising subnational revenue base, unless expenditure is actually to decline (in relative terms) *either* transfers must be increased, *or* borrowing must be expanded.[55] Is it surprising that some local governments have chosen the latter path? Of course, from the point of view of strict fiscal virtue they should have bitten the bullet and reduced expenditures at once, but even local politicians, like central politicians, are human and tend to take the easy way out, if there is one.[56]

Indeed, a final comment on this general area is that national fiscal virtue in budgetary matters may in part have been achieved by creating local villains by pretending that the downward shift of revenues to local governments that has clearly taken place in Colombia has not been accompanied by an equally strong downward shift of expenditures. Matters may get worse in this respect in the future. Local governments in Colombia are now responsible for virtually all the expenditure functions (for example, health and education) which account for expenditure growth in countries all around the world. At the same time, they are primarily restricted to an antiquated and unresponsive revenue basis, which even at its best – and of course it is very far from its best, particularly in the less advanced areas – probably could not provide adequate resources to maintain the required local share of funding. Intergovernmental finance seems likely to be a controversial subject in Colombia for years to come.

Lessons from Colombian experience

Decentralizing the public sector in any country is, as some recent authors have emphasized,[57] a process that is not without danger. As yet, however, the alleged "dangers" of decentralization are not very visible in Colombia. Indeed, even under the distorted system of incentives facing local government in Colombia, the early evidence in support of the developmental benefits of decentralization in terms of public sector efficiency is surprisingly positive (World Bank, 1995). With a better-designed incentive structure, there seems good reason to hope that even more favorable outcomes may emerge over time. What is needed to improve efficiency is not so much a radical redirection of Colombia's policy of decentralization as some redesign of transfers combined with better-informed and more consistent implementation on the part of the national government than has been evident to date.

Of course, improving the incentives for effective and efficient provision of services in a decentralized environment in any country is likely to require reforms in addition to those affecting the transfer system. In the case of Colombia, for instance, it is necessary to clarify the distribution of responsibilities between levels of government and address institutional bottlenecks in several sectors (for example, education; see World Bank, 1996a). Second, changes are needed to ensure that subnational governments have sufficient flexibility to use resources, eliminating earmarking (and mandates) that do not respond to very clearly established needs. Third, changes are needed to give subnational governments more flexibility in altering tax rates to mobilize resources.[58] Finally, changes are needed to promote responsibility and accountability in public sector performance at all levels of government. Many of these points seem much more widely applicable than just in Colombia.

Whatever is done on the revenue side, many of the constraints currently imposed on local government finance by the extensive use of earmarking and expenditure mandating should clearly be removed in Colombia. The constant extension, and frequent change, of these various attempts by the national level to direct subnational expenditure patterns in detail is not only basically inconsistent with the stated general intent of decentralization but is also likely to guarantee that decentralization in the sense of developing effective and efficient subnational governments will fail. An essential ingredient of strengthening local fiscal capacity therefore seems to be some weakening of national control over what local governments do with the money.[59]

Moreover, if decentralization is to work, those charged with providing local infrastructure and services must be accountable both to those who pay for them and to those who benefit from them. Enforcing accountability at the local level requires not only clear incentives from above but also the provision of adequate information to local constituents and the opportunity for them to exercise some real influence or control over the service delivery system. Informal community organizations almost by definition must be structured like this or they cannot exist, but it can be a real challenge to introduce a similar degree of responsiveness into formal governmental organizations.

Accountability is the key to improved public sector performance, and information is the key to accountability. The systematic collection, analysis, and reporting of information that can be used to verify compliance with goals and to assist future decisions is a critical element in any decentralization program. Information is needed not only on financial aspects (budgeting and expenditure reporting) but also on inputs, outputs, and, where possible, outcomes to ensure accountability. Such information is essential both to inform public participation through the local political process and for the monitoring of local activity by central agencies responsible for supervising and (usually) partially financing such activity. Unless local "publics" are made aware of what is done, how well it is done, how much it costs, and who paid for it, no local constituency for effective government can be created. As a recent study of local government capacity in Colombia makes clear, a stronger community voice is often an essential ingredient for improved government performance, both through making it easier to identify local preferences and through strengthening accountability.[60]

Since the election of mayors was introduced in 1986, a reduction in clientelism and more transparent and fair electoral practices have conferred more legitimacy on the leadership role of mayors and made the position more attractive. A renovation in municipal leadership has resulted. Many current mayors are political outsiders with backgrounds either in the private sector or in civic movements independent of political parties.[61] With decentralization, municipal political life has become more clearly local in nature, increasing demands on new local leaders to respond to their communities.

In addition to devolving some degree of real political responsibility to local residents, a sound decentralization program must also be accompanied by an improvement in the evaluation capacity of the central government. Decentralization and evaluation are not substitutes; they are complements. An essential element of the "hard budget constraint" system needed to induce efficient local decisions is thus adequate central enforcement capacity in the shape of credible information-gathering and evaluation. The "carrot" of central financial support of local efforts must be accompanied by the "stick" of withdrawn support if performance is inadequate, which of course requires both some standard of adequacy and some way of knowing how performance measures up. To mention perhaps the most obvious and simple example: if a recipient of transfer funds does not submit an adequate financial report, it should not receive such funds.[62]

In sum, Colombia's ongoing experience with fiscal decentralization suggests that success requires the central government to pay more attention to its own actions and to worry less about what local governments are doing, or not doing. Specifically, the central government should: (1) decide more clearly what it is trying to do; (2) redesign its policy instruments to achieve its objectives more efficiently; (3) free local governments from many of the present restrictions on both revenues and expenditures that hamper them from operating efficiently; (4) ensure that it has sufficiently accurate and timely information to know what is going on with respect to subnational finance; and (5) alter its policies if, and only if, a change is necessary to achieve some important national policy objective. Once it has got its own act together, the central government can and should let decentralization take its course without constant changes in direction and policy.

If the rules of the game are set up properly so that local governments account properly for funds they are expending on behalf of the national government, and there is at least a modicum of local political accountability for what they do with their own funds, there should be no need for the present cumbersome system of interventionist measures – many of which in effect attempt to compensate for the lack of clear national policies but fail in this task and instead succeed mainly in making it impossible for anyone to run a subnational government efficiently. Getting the rules right does not, of course, guarantee success, certainly not in every locality, but it is clearly an essential first step to realizing the potentials (and avoiding the dangers) of decentralization in any country.

From this perspective, Colombian experience over the last few decades suggests at least three important lessons for other countries. First, there is much to be said for proceeding down the path of decentralization with deliberation and care. To illustrate: the provision in Law 60 requiring a thorough, public examination of the effects of decentralization after an initial five-year period is commendable and deserves emulation elsewhere. Second, democracy matters: local elections have proved particularly important in improving local capacity and "ownership" of public sector programs and hence accountability. Third, whether there is democracy or not, to a large extent central governments get the local governments they deserve by virtue of the incentives their policies create for local governments. The central role of central governments in determining the outcome of fiscal decentralization is clearly evidenced by recent Colombian experience.

Notes

1 A brief account of this history and the situation at end of the 1970s described in the rest of this paragraph may be found in Bird (1984). The next two paragraphs closely follow portions of a previous update in Bird (1990a).

2 For an account of fiscal policy in the early postwar years, see Bird (1970); a comparative analysis of more recent years may be found in Perry (1992).

3 The Commission report was published as DNP (1981); Bird (1984) is an English version of this report.

4 For an outline and discussion of the relevant constitutional changes, see Wiesner (1992).

5 For example, the Ministry of Health wants to adjust the decentralization law to help implement a reform of the social insurance system.

6 The last of these problems is, for example, at the centre of recent critical papers on fiscal decentralization by Prud'homme (1995), and Tanzi (1995); our own views on the pros and cons of decentralization are on the whole closer to those in two subsequent papers responding to Prud'homme – McLure (1995) and Sewell (1996).

7 Unfortunately, it sometimes seems that all anyone outside Colombia knows about the country is its problems with drugs and political violence. Both of these problems exist, and are important, but since neither of them affects the issues discussed in this chapter in any fundamental way, they are not further discussed here.

8 See the discussion of the institutional structure for providing these services in World Bank (1996a: annexes 1 and 2), as well as the earlier discussion in Bird (1984).

9 Most of the figures in this paragraph are taken from Ferreira and Valenzuela (1993). It should perhaps be noted that, as is common in Latin America, a *municipio* includes both any urban area (*cabecera*) and the surrounding rural territory, so some counted as "urban" may live in very small communities indeed. Nonetheless, there is no question that the bulk of the Colombian people now live in urban areas, rather than in rural areas as was the case only thirty years ago.

10 See World Bank (1994) for a detailed study of poverty in Colombia.

11 Data from Wiesner (1995). The difference between the revenue and expenditure figures cited reflects the importance of central government transfers, as discussed below.

12 A word of caution seems warranted with respect to these (and most other) public sector figures in Colombia, namely, that it is not difficult to find different figures that seem to refer to the same concepts for the same years. To illus-

trate: the figures in table 6.1 were obtained from the Departamento Nacional de Planeación in September 1996 as a result of a request to duplicate and update the similar figures in Wiesner (1995: 128). Nonetheless, the figures in table 6.1 for 1985 (the only year of overlap) are significantly different from those in Wiesner, and no clear trends are shown in the table. Still, one has to work with what one has, and these were the latest authoritative data available at the time of writing this chapter.

13 However, on the basis of data in World Bank (1996a: annex 3), which net out transfers within the subnational sector, the 1994 figure for the subnational sector is only 10.6 percent of GDP; again, it is difficult to reconcile figures from different sources. Unless otherwise indicated, the remaining data in this section come from the source just cited.

14 This is, for example, one of the major themes in Bird (1984).

15 See the discussion in DNP (1995a).

16 The excess of transfers plus borrowing over investment is accounted for by various "balancing" items that have not been explicitly discussed here.

17 All these figures are as estimated in World Bank (1996a). For discussion of these transfers, see also Wiesner (1995).

18 Through the use of quotas (*cupos*) and differential matching rates, SNC is also used as a redistributive instrument, but this aspect is not further discussed here.

19 The poverty indicator used – the NBI (*necesidades básicas insatisfechas*) index – has been shown to be quite deficient (World Bank, 1994).

20 For example, 30 percent of the PM spent on education was used to pay teachers' salaries (DNP, 1995a).

21 This estimate is based on unpublished data kindly made available to the authors by DNP.

22 These guiding principles are widely accepted in the international literature, for example, Shah (1994) and Bird (1990b). Note that we are not discussing the arguably quite distinct case of "truly federal" countries; on this, see Bird (1995) and Bird and Chen (1996).

23 Unfortunately, it is not possible within the limits of this chapter to describe the complex present arrangements for financing education and health or the equally complex current proposals for reform in these areas, so readers may have to take some of the following in faith; for detailed analysis, see World Bank (1996a): annexes 1 [on education] and 2 [on health].

24 See World Bank (1996a: annexes 1 and 2), for further discussion.

25 Specific ways of implementing such a system are discussed in detail in World Bank (1996a), which considers such questions as the unit cost of provision, the number of units provided, the rate of extension of coverage, adjustments to unit cost over time, the division of transfers between departmental and municipal levels of government, the rate of transition, and the monitoring and enforcement of the system.

26 More positively, it should be noted that this cost is already being paid since the current system is not conducive to expenditure rationalization and cost control. Under the proposed system, this additional cost would have not only a purpose but also, more importantly, a termination date.

27 Subsidized loans could be used instead, but this common practice is undesirable. Rather than (in effect) mixing grants and loans in this way, it is better to keep them separate: give a grant where warranted, but otherwise require all lending to be done on commercial terms, with no explicit or implicit national subsidies or guarantees.

28 This is the concept of "wealth neutrality" popularized by Feldstein (1975).

29 See, for example, the discussion in Wiesner (1995), Sánchez and Gutiérrez (1995), and World Bank (1996a: annex 3).

30 The economic case for such equalization transfers is often confused with questions more properly related to interpersonal redistribution. The basic argument is that since it has been decided, for whatever reason, to charge local governments with the delivery of an adequate "minimum bundle" of local public services to citizens, and all citizens of Colombia should be entitled to some basic level of such services regardless of where they happen to live, equalizing transfers to localities (not persons) are needed to achieve this goal.

It should perhaps be noted that this objective of providing similar public services regardless of location may conflict with the desirability of migration from less (privately) productive to more productive locations. Although this subject has been discussed extensively (if not very conclusively) in the literature, it is not further considered here on the assumption that in Colombian conditions, the relatively small differences in location-specific public service bundles (excluding education and health, which are assumed to be portable) that might result in different locations from an equalization program are unlikely to be significant factors in migration decisions.

31 See the extensive analysis of the surprising degree of local "capacity" to manage efficiently in World Bank (1995).

32 For a related argument, see Bird (1993).

33 See, for example, Shah (1994) and Ahmad (1997).

34 Caution is necessary in introducing such differentials because it is easy to turn a simple, transparent formula into an obscure and manipulable one by introducing too many refinements in the definition of the elements of the formula.

35 Those interested in the details of how the general scheme sketched in this section would work in Colombia are referred to World Bank (1996a), especially annex 5.

36 In a clever bit of wordplay "social investment" has been interpreted to cover the salaries of education and health workers. But one cannot get the streets cleaned this way.

37 The tendency to "over-regulate" expenditure in advance, in a futile attempt to make up for the failure to monitor adequately what is actually done is an old and pervasive problem in Colombia; see, for example, the discussion in Bird (1992).

38 McCleary and Uribe (1990), for example, estimated that two-thirds of municipal, and four-fifths of departmental, current income were earmarked if net public enterprise profits were included. This ratio fell to only about 20 percent of current revenues for municipal governments if net profits of their enterprises

were excluded; the similar figure for departments was over 75 percent. For a similar analysis for earlier years, see Bird (1984).

39 A particularly egregious recent example is the requirement in a recent "anti-corruption" law that all local governments, no matter how small, must establish and maintain a free "800" number for citizen complaints. The cost of complying with this provision in some of the more remote localities which do not even have telephone service could easily exceed the entire PM transfer!

40 For details, see World Bank (1996a: annex 4).

41 Note that this is in addition to any earmarking that may have been imposed by the local governments themselves; the practice seems as popular at the local level as elsewhere in Colombia, but of course the implications of local councils voluntarily choosing to limit their expenditure choices are quite different from those of having such limits imposed upon them.

42 Although based on data from DNP (1995d), our conclusion differs because the DNP analysis considers only the amount of the *inversión forzosa* portion of the transfer that is so spent rather than the total amount of the transfer that is spent on education.

43 See Bird (1984), as subsequently updated in part in World Bank (1987) and World Bank (1989), and Wiesner (1992); see also Wiesner (1995).

44 See, for example, Wiesner (1995), Steiner and Correa (1994), Ferreira and Valenzuela (1993), Fainboim, Acosta, and Cadena (1994), Vargas *et al.* (1994), Junguito, Melo, and Misa (1995), Maldonado (1995), Sánchez and Gutiérrez (1994, 1995), CGR (1995), and DNP (1995b).

45 The empirical evidence of an adverse effect on effort in studies such as those cited in note 44 is mixed – some studies find such an effect and some do not. Moreover, many studies appear to be flawed either in terms of data (few studies seem to have taken much care in assembling or understanding the data used) or methodologically. To cite only two examples from the "effort" literature: Slack and Bird (1983), in an early econometric study, found an adverse effect on fiscal effort, but this study relates the SF to departmental own revenues even though the SF is not received by the departmental governments and there was therefore no reason to expect their fiscal behavior to react to changes in it. More recently, Steiner and Correa (1994) contended that they found "fiscal apathy" at the subnational level, but this conclusion rests on regressing local tax revenues on national transfers, and it is hard to see how one could expect any other result, given the inelasticity of most local taxes and the rapid increases in national transfers as a result of the constitutional reform. To interpret such results as telling us anything meaningful about local fiscal effort seems hardly legitimate.

46 See above and World Bank (1996a: annex 3).

47 See Bird (1976) and Bird and Slack (1990), and sources cited therein, for earlier discussions of this issue.

48 See the discussion in World Bank (1989); matters have not changed in this respect since this report was written.

49 To put this point another way, as Linn (1980) shows, the effective rate of property tax is a function of the collection ratio, the statutory rate, exemptions, and the assessment ratio. Let TC = taxes collected, TL = taxes assessed,

AVT = taxable base, AV = assessed base (including exempt property), and MV = market value. Then the effective tax rate, TC/MV = TC/TL*TL/ AVT*AVT/AV*AV/MV. Of these ratios, only the first is clearly under municipal control, so any assessment of "effort" with respect to property taxes should focus on changes in this ratio only. Unfortunately, no information is available on this subject.

50 For a critical discussion of this tax, see Bird (1984).

51 The literature on the alleged "fiscal perversity" of subnational governments from the point of view of macro stabilization dates back to the early Keynesian era, when it was argued that subnational governments would tend to accentuate recessions by cutting back on their expenditures exactly when the economy needed stimulus; see the review and appraisal of this argument in Rafuse (1965) and Oates (1972).

52 See, for example, the studies by Sánchez and Gutiérrez (1995) and Junguito, Melo, and Misa (1995).

53 For a detailed discussion of how education is financed and controlled, see World Bank (1996a).

54 Of course, some of the increased national expenditures in the last few years have arisen for other, quite legitimate, reasons such as increased security costs; but in the present context what this means is that other national expenditures should have been reduced still further if expansionary effects were to be avoided.

55 There is of course no direct correlation between the amount of money spent on a function and the services delivered, so that considerable care must be used in asserting that local expenditures are too important to be cut.

56 Given the very limited taxing powers available to local governments in Colombia and the impossibility of widespread local government bankruptcy, the only way to reduce the "moral hazard" of subnational borrowing resulting in central government bail-outs may be to institute a credible review/control system for debt work-outs along the lines discussed for Argentina in World Bank (1996b), but this subject cannot be further developed here.

57 See Prud'homme (1995) and Tanzi (1995).

58 Specifically, localities should be able to set tax rates on residential property and perhaps determine certain other tax rates as well, although their freedom to tax non-residents (for example, through taxes on exporting sectors) should be restricted. For further discussion, see Bird (1993).

59 This recommendation assumes that, as mentioned in note 56, localities will have no recourse to national funding on a discretionary basis – no bail-outs.

60 The following paragraph is based on World Bank (1995).

61 In the 1988 and 1990 municipal elections, the two major political parties controlled almost 90 percent of the municipalities (Gaitán and Moreno, 1992). In the 1992 elections, however, candidates from non-traditional parties gained control of about one-third of the 1,000 municipalities.

62 Interestingly, this is not now done in Colombia, where over 100 small municipalities apparently never submit any information to the central government but nonetheless regularly receive transfer payments. The apparent explanation is a political one: for the most part, these municipalities are those

in which the writ of the central government does not run because they are largely controlled by various guerilla movements (and/or drug dealers).

References

Ahmad, Ehtisham, ed. (1997), *Financing Decentralized Expenditures*, Cheltenham: Edward Elgar.

Bird, Richard M. (1970), *Taxation and Development: Lessons from Colombian Experience*, Cambridge, MA.: Harvard University Press.

—— (1976), "Assessing tax performance in developing countries," *Finanzarchiv*, 34: 234–65.

—— (1984), *Intergovernmental Finance in Colombia: Final Report of the Mission on Intergovernmental Finance*, Cambridge, MA.: Harvard Law School, International Tax Program.

—— (1990a), "Fiscal decentralization in Colombia," in R. Bennett (ed.), *Decentralization, Governments and Market*, Oxford: Clarendon Press.

—— (1990b), "Intergovernmental finance and local taxation in developing countries: some basic considerations for reformers," *Public Administration and Development*, 10: 277–88.

—— (1992), "Budgeting and expenditure control in Colombia," *Public Budgeting and Finance*, 2: 87–99.

—— (1993), "Threading the fiscal labyrinth: some issues in fiscal decentralization," *National Tax Journal*, 46: 207–27.

—— (1995), "Fiscal federalism and federal finance," *Anales de las 28 Jornadas de Finanzas Públicas*, Facultad de Ciencias Económicas, Universidad Nacional de Córdoba, Argentina.

Bird, Richard M. and Chen, Duanjie (1996), "Federal finance and fiscal federalism: the two worlds of Canadian public finance," in D. Perry *et al.*, "Essays on fiscal federalism and federal finance in Canada," Discussion Paper No. 6, International Centre for Tax Studies, University of Toronto.

Bird, Richard M. and Slack, Enid (1990), "Equalization: the representative tax system revisited," *Canadian Tax Journal*, 38: 913–27.

CGR (Contraloría General de la República) (1995), *La situación de las finanzas del estado 1994: Informe del Contralor General de la República*, Bogotá.

DNP (Departamento Nacional de Planeación) (1981), *Finanzas intergubernamentales en Colombia*, Bogotá.

—— (1995a), "Política de consolidación de la descentralización," CONPES 2788 (June 15).

—— (1995b), "Impacto de las transferencias sobre los recursos propios de los municipios: una contribución a la discusión" (October 7).

—— (1995c), "Estudio de casos municipales" (October 5).

—— (1995d), "Evaluación de la destinación de la participación de los municipios y de los resguardos indígenas en los ingresos corrientes de la nación para la vigencia 1994" (September 20).

Dillinger, William (1991), *Urban Property Taxation in Developing Countries*, Washington, DC: World Bank.

Fainboim Yaker, Israel, Acosta Navarro, Olga Lucia, and Cadena Clavijo, Hector José (1994), "El proceso reciente de descentralización fiscal en Colombia y sus perspectivas," *Coyuntura Económica*.

Feldstein, Martin (1975), "Wealth neutrality and local choice in public education," *American Economic Review*, 65: 75–89.

Ferreira, Ana Maria, and Valenzuela, Luis Carlos (1993), *Decentralización fiscal: el caso colombiano*, Santiago, Chile: CEPAL.

Gaitan Pavia, Pilar, and Moreno Ospina, Carlos (1992), *Poder local. Realidad y utopia de_la descentralización en Colombia*, Bogotá: Tercer Mundo.

Junguito, B. Roberto, Melo, B. Ligia, and Misa, A. Martha (1995), "La descentralización fiscal y la política macroeconómica," Banco de la República, Bogotá.

Linn, Johannes F. (1980), "Property taxation in Bogota, Colombia: an analysis of poor revenue performance," *Public Finance Quarterly*, 8.

Maldonado Copello, Alberto (1995), "Estudio sobre transferencias y esfuerzo fiscal municipal," Departamento de Investigaciones Colciencias, Fundación Universidad Central Bogotá (August 31).

McCleary, William A. and Uribe Tobon, Evamaria (1990), "Earmarking government revenues in Colombia," WPS 425, Country Economics Department, World Bank, Washington, DC (September).

McLure, Jr., Charles E. (1995), "Comments on Prud'homme," *World Bank Research Observer*, August 10: 221–26.

Oates, Wallace E. (1972), *Fiscal Federalism*, New York: Harcourt, Brace, Jovanovich.

Perry, Guillermo (1992), *Finanzas públicas, estabilización y reformas estructurales en América Latina*, Washington, DC: Inter-American Development Bank.

Prud'homme, Remy (1995), "The dangers of decentralization," *World Bank Research Observer*, August 10: 201–20.

Rafuse, Robert (1965), "Cyclical behavior of state–local finances," in R. A. Musgrave (ed.) *Essays in Fiscal Federalism*, Washington, DC: Brookings Institution.

Sánchez Torres, Fabio, and Gutiérrez Sourdis, Catalina (1994), "Descentralización fiscal y transferencias intergubernamentales en Colombia," *Coyuntura Económica*.

(1995) "Colombia," in Ricardo Lopez Murphy, (ed.), *Fiscal Decentralization in Latin America*, Washington, DC: Inter-American Development Bank.

Sewell, David (1996), "The dangers of decentralization according to Prud'homme: some further aspects," *World Bank Research Observer*, February 11: 143–50.

Shah, Anwar (1994), *Perspectives on the Design of Intergovernmental Fiscal Relations*, Policy Research Paper, Washington, DC: World Bank.

Slack, N. Enid, and Bird, Richard M. (1983), "Local response to intergovernmental fiscal transfers: the case of Colombia," *Public Finance/finances publiques*, 38: 429–39.

Steiner, Roberto, and Correa, Patricia (1994), "Decentralization in Colombia: recent changes and main challenges," Lehigh University, Lehigh, PA.

Tanzi, Vito (1995), "Fiscal federalism and decentralization: a review of some efficiency and macroeconomic aspects," in Michael Bruno and Boris Pleskovic (eds.), *Annual Bank Conference on Development Economics*, Washington, DC: World Bank.

Vargas, Cesar, *et al.* (1994), "Financiamiento del desarrollo regional: situación actual y perspectivas," *Planeación & Desarrollo.*

Wiesner Duran, Eduardo (1992), *Colombia: Descentralización y federalism fiscal: Informe final de la Misión para la Descentralización*, Bogotá: DNP.

———(1995), *La descentralización, el gasto social y la gobernabilidad en Colombia*, Bogotá: DNP and Asociación de Instituciones Financieras.

World Bank, (1987), "Colombia: a review of recent fiscal decentralization measures," Report No. 6631-CO (April).

———(1989), "Colombia: decentralizing revenues and the provision of services: a review of recent experience," Report No. 7870-CO (October).

———(1994), *Poverty in Colombia*, Washington, DC.

———(1995), *Local Government Capacity in Colombia: Beyond Technical Assistance*, Washington, DC.

———(1996a), "Colombia: reforming the decentralization law: incentives for an effective delivery of services," Report No. 15298-CO (April).

———(1996b), "Argentina: provincial finances study: selected issues in fiscal federalism", 2 vols., Report No. 15487-AR (July).

7

Argentina: fiscal federalism and decentralization

ERNESTO REZK

From a fiscal viewpoint, Argentina must still be regarded as a formal federation, rather than a truly federal country, in so far as the experience of the last sixty years shows that the provinces shifted the responsibility for the main taxes (income, sales, excise and fuel taxes) into the central government's hands, despite their constitutionally ample independent taxing and spending powers. The resulting revenue concentration (at the national level) was matched by a spending decentralization process whereby the responsibility for key areas, such as education, health, and housing, was transferred to the provinces.

In relation to the above-mentioned features, this chapter, after some brief theoretical considerations, examines the analytic aspects of decentralization in Argentina. Both macro and micro issues of intergovernmental fiscal relations are reviewed and scrutinized. The chapter also sheds light on the likely evolution of federal fiscal arrangements; in particular, whether the situation will evolve in the direction of delegation (strengthening of the principal–agent relationship) or, on the contrary, toward devolution, in which mechanisms of collective decision-making closer to the public choice approach can be expected to prevail.

An outline is also given of the key elements of the institutional setting in Argentina, as well as a description of changes over time of assignments of expenditures and taxes between the central and the subnational governments. The relevant quantitative aspects of Argentine federal finances and intergovernmental fiscal arrangements are shown with statistical data for the period 1983–95.

Understanding fiscal decentralization

Theoretical and policy-oriented interest in fiscal decentralization rose during the eighties as a result of various unprecedented situations faced by countries all over the world.

Bird (1993: 207) based the revival and new strength of decentralizing processes on developing countries' *ad hoc* policies purposively aimed at escaping from ineffective and inefficient governance, macroeconomic instability, and inadequate economic growth. Tanzi (1995: 296), in turn, mentioned the role played by developments in the European Union which are in favor of decentralization.[1] He assigned a similar influence to the growing disenchantment with powerful central governments (especially in industrial countries), which have proved to be incapable of stabilizing their economies or of improving the distribution of income, and have created a presumption toward giving more power to both the market and subnational and local governments.

Fiscal decentralization is also found in countries like Argentina and Brazil, where the major macroeconomic problems of the eighties (mainly inflation and fiscal deficits) required important fiscal adjustment programs to be implemented at the central level, subject to constraints imposed by subnational governments' own constitutional fiscal powers and the existing arrangements among different government levels.[2]

Even though the growth in importance of decentralizing processes can be explained at least in part on allocative and efficiency grounds,[3] the notion of decentralization is far from being a simple one. This is demonstrated in the three categories[4] distinguished by Bird (1995):

- *deconcentration*: this is where decentralization occurs within the national level and limits itself to simply scattering fiscal responsibilities among regionally established branch offices;
- *delegation*: this is the situation typically depicted by the principal–agent model, the rationale being that the higher government level chooses to achieve its allocative goals more efficiently by transferring spending functions and funds to subnational and local governments on the understanding that the latter will carry out their spending commitments in line with the central government's policy objectives;
- *devolution*: in this case, fiscal decentralization means not only lower levels' legal authority to carry out expenditure assignments (which they also have under *delegation*) but also, and far more importantly, their control of decisions concerning their spending functions.

As Bird (1995) emphasizes, devolution not only stresses allocative efficiency but also political values such as enhanced governance (local responsiveness) and political participation.[5] The concepts of administrative and fiscal decentralization, used in the existing literature, imply similar notions according to Tanzi (1995: 297). The former embodies situations in which most taxes are levied by the central government, although funds are transferred to subnational governments to carry out their spending activities as agents, following the guidelines and controls imposed by the national level (delegation). The latter is more akin to the situation in most federations where the subnational levels have constitutional or legal powers to raise taxes and perform spending functions in which they have complete decision-making authority, that is, local autonomy.

Delegation and devolution variants of fiscal decentralization can also be analyzed in terms of the theoretical approach underlying collective decision mechanisms, as well as in terms of the scope for independent decision-making at different government levels. As mentioned above, delegation entails the use of the principal–agent relationship to constitute contracts whereby the principal (the central government) appoints agents (subnational governments) to act on its behalf. Within this approach, the central government transfers funds to lower levels (either conditional grants or conditional matching grants), expecting them to deliver public goods or services according to predetermined standards and quantities, while, on the other side, local governments accept this delegation, expecting to maximize their own economic and equity goals.[6] As Wiesner (1994: 181) and others make clear, given that local governments are expected to satisfy presumed central government priorities and national policy objectives, the notion of fiscal responsibility means here that subnational and local governments are accountable to their principal and not to local taxpayers or residents.

The well-known public choice approach[7] relates to devolution by requiring that the different government levels finance most of their spending functions out of their own taxes and revenues (the principle of financial autonomy). It also shows that the accountability of subnational governments is to their taxpayers and not to the central level; the acknowledged link between taxing and spending ensures, in turn, what Bird (1995) defined as "the maintenance of a legitimate system of governance in terms of public support of government." Public choice fiscal models and devolution raise another interesting issue, stressed by Wiesner (1994), that is the fact that subnational and local governments' ample autonomy for spending must be exercised subject to a budget-constrained choice which induces efficient resource allocation; in this respect, taxpayers' demands for goods and services resemble those of efficiency-maximizing buyers.

The setting in Argentina

Argentina is constitutionally a three-tiered federation composed of the national government, twenty-three provinces and the autonomous government of the city of Buenos Aires[8] (which houses the federal capital), and over a thousand municipalities. In all cases, elected officials exercise executive powers (president, governors, and mayors), whereas legislative powers are in the hands of elected senators and representatives[9] (at the national and provincial level) and of elected municipal councillors (in the case of local governments). All elected executive and legislative members remain in office for four years, except for national senators whose mandate lasts six years. The members of the national and provincial Courts of Justice are nominated by the Executive Powers and respectively appointed by the Congress and the provincial legislatures. The Senate is, at least in theory, the main and most important federal body. Not only does each province, regardless of its population, have three senators but the Constitution rules that the Senate must be the chamber of origin for certain laws involving relations among jurisdictions (for example, those setting up revenue-sharing systems) or policies checking economic disparities among provinces or regions.

As Argentina is a federal country, besides political powers, subnational and local governments constitutionally have ample independent fiscal and spending functions. Hence, the validity of the argument that the country has behaved more like a "formal" rather than a "true" federation (following Bird's [1995: 295] definition of both terms) stems from the subnational and local governments falling short of properly implementing their autonomous broad powers for taxing and expenditure. In this respect, the national constitution dictates that provincial constitutions must ensure the administration of justice and primary education in their jurisdictions. At the same time, provinces are recognized in their precedence in that they are entitled to have their own political institutions and may keep all powers not expressly delegated to the central government. Municipal autonomy and regimes are also constitutionally guaranteed, provinces being responsible for establishing the institutional, political, administrative, economic, and financial content and scope.

With regard to the assignment of spending functions, except for defense (a central government commitment) and law and order (the central and subnational governments have exclusive authority), there are practically no fields for which responsibility is constitutionally limited to a single level.[10] Thus, for most types of expenditure all three levels exhibit concurrent competencies, although in practice certain fields are in the domain of a single government level (social security services, predominantly in central government's hands, illustrate this assertion).

The tax assignment issue, as dealt with by the Constitution, reveals another feature of the highly federal-like fiscal setting in Argentina. Only export and import duties can be exclusively imposed by the central government; both the central and subnational levels share the faculty to raise indirect taxes whereas the former can levy direct taxes only for limited time periods and on grounds of defense, common security, and general welfare.[11] Put plainly, however, the implementation of the main direct tax in Argentina (income tax) amounts in practice to provinces yielding their control of this tax to the national government.[12] Local governments' fiscal powers, as described by provincial constitutions, normally apply to user charges for services rendered to residents; municipalities are, however, empowered to collect taxes on property, business, and consumption,[13] and contributions for improvements.

The actual tax assignment in Argentina, as shown in table 7.1, shows that the assignment of revenue sources to various government levels is broadly consistent with the widely accepted Musgravian economic criteria.

Fiscal instruments are more efficiently and equitably administered by the central government in the case of:

- tax bases unevenly distributed among jurisdictions
- taxes on mobile production factors
- taxes aimed at stabilization and redistribution goals

Fiscal instruments fare better at the subnational and local levels in the case of:

- taxes on totally immobile factors and assets
- residence-based taxes on consumption

Fiscal instruments such as benefit contributions and user charges are suited to all levels.

Table 7.1 already hints at what will become clear in the quantitative overview of the following section; that is, that overlapping tax systems (rather than separate revenue sources)[14] founded on jurisdictions' fiscal faculties led to revenue-sharing as the preferred method of tax coordination in Argentina. Starting in 1935, revenue-sharing has thus become the main intergovernmental fiscal arrangement, whereby the central government and the provinces intended to achieve the goal of avoiding tax competition among jurisdictions. They also aimed to ensure that both levels had direct access to tax revenues that were sufficient to close the fiscal gap. In other words, the rationale for the system was that transfers from shared taxes, plus their own revenues, should in principle permit provinces to finance their spending functions.[15]

Table 7.1 shows that the primary distribution[16] of shared national taxes involves not only the central and subnational levels but also national and provincial[17] social security systems and diverse funds accruing to

Table 7.1. *Argentina: tax assignment – responsibility for administration, collection and disposition of revenues (percentage shares in tax revenues)*

A. Tax levied by the central (national) government

	Nation	Provinces and the city of Buenos Aires	National social security system	Provincial social security systems	Various provincial funds[a]
Personal and corporate income tax	22.82	35.04	29.60	—	12.54
Value-added tax	31.74	43.16	22.15	2.20	0.75
Excise taxes (internal taxes) and others	35.66	48.49	15.00	—	0.85
Tax on assets	17.83	24.25	7.50	—	50.42
Tax on personal goods	—	—	90.00	10.00	—
Tax on fuel sales	29.00	—	—	—	71.00
Energy tax	—	—	—	—	100.00
Tax on salaries	—	—	100.00	—	—
Stamp duty	100.00	—	—	—	—
Import duties	100.00	—	—	—	—
Export duties	100.00	—	—	—	—
Statistics tax	100.00	—	—	—	—

Note: [a] Existing funds are mainly conditional transfers to provinces for their use in the following fields: energy, infrastructure, roads, public works, housing, and education. There also exists a subsidiary fund for regional compensation and another for unconditional Treasury grants to provinces.

Table 7.1 (*cont.*)

B. Taxes levied by the provinces[b]

	Provinces	Municipalities	Provincial social security systems	Various municipal funds[a]
Turnover tax	80.00	16.10	—	3.90
Urban and rural property tax	80.00	16.10	—	3.90
National tax-shared revenues	80.00	16.10	—	3.90
Tax on provincial and municipal payrolls	—	—	100.00	—
Stamp duty	100.00	—	—	—
Tax on motor vehicles	—	100.00	—	—
Social infrastrucure tax	100.00	—	—	—
Tax on gambling	100.00	—	—	—
Tax on turf activities	100.00	—	—	—
Fees and user charges	100.00	—	—	—

Note: [b] Notwithstanding marked similarities, there are in Argentina twenty-three provincial tax-sharing systems. Revenue disposition has been illustrated here by the prevailing scheme in the province of Córdoba, which fairly represents the rest.

C. Municipalities fiscal revenues[c]

Property tax
Contribution on improvements
Business tax
Advertisement and publicity tax
Tax on raffles and other games of chance
Tax on energy sale
Tax on cemetries' occupancy
Various fees and user charges[d]

Notes:
[c] This fiscal revenue pattern belongs to the city of Cordoba's municipal government but, again, most local governments in Argentina share the same revenue structure.
[d] Fees received by municipalities are normally collected for streets, pavements, and public spaces' occupancy, and for applications or requests to the local government for an administrative action. User charges are normally linked to sanitary protection and inspections in public places, as well as to the approval, supervision, and inspection of gas networks, and the construction of houses and buildings within municipal boundaries.

provinces in the form of conditional transfers on a principal–agent basis. The percentages of the primary distribution have undergone continual changes since the system came into being in 1935, although each time a new intergovernmental arrangement was enacted (table 7.2), the resulting percentage pattern generally favored subnational governments as these were left with a bigger portion of shared taxes.[18] Thus, after the last modification occurred in 1990, the provinces retained 57.05 percent of the total net shared amount (that is to say, the balance remaining after funds for national and provincial social security systems and other special funds have been deducted) while the central government kept only the remainder (42.95 percent).[19]

Twenty-three independent revenue-sharing systems also exist at the subnational level, whereby each province and its municipalities participate in the distribution of the main provincial tax and of national shared taxes. As in the national case, primary distribution also entails the establishment of several (now municipal) funds for specific purposes.

Regarding secondary distribution, objective-devolving and equalizing parameters ceased to exist after 1988 (table 7.2) and revenue disposition among provinces has been thereafter performed on the basis of Law 23 548's fixed coefficients, agreed upon by means of political negotiations and whose value has remained constant ever since.[20] However, explicit distribution criteria exist in almost all provincial revenue-sharing schemes, partly based on devolution principles such as municipal population, area, own revenues, and efficiency in tax collection, and partly on equalizing principles that may allot part of the funds equally or relate distribution to local governments' social spending, expenditure budgets or theoretical salary needs for minimal public service levels.[21]

One point worth mentioning in this connection is that the widespread use of revenue-sharing (since 1935) for channeling intergovernmental fiscal relations has so far been based upon "contract laws" promulgated by Congress, so called because they require provincial legislatures' explicit ratification before their content becomes mandatory for both government levels. The 1994 Constituent Assembly changed this situation by giving constitutional status to revenue-sharing and dictating that a new system (entailing objective distribution criteria and built-in fund transfers to provinces and the city of Buenos Aires) be implemented from January 1, 1997, in which primary and secondary distribution is directly related to subnational jurisdictions' services, functions, and competencies.[22]

The Constituent Assembly also introduced a clause whose expected positive impact on decentralization is certain to occur since it favors better future decisions concerning delegation or devolution from the center to the

Table 7.2. *Tax-sharing systems (1935-95) – criteria for secondary distribution (percentage shares)*

		Equalizing criteria				
		Spending needs				Total for equalizing criteria
	Devolution criteria	Current spending	Minimum spending	Supply cost	Tax capacity	
Period (1935–53)						
Law 12139 (1935)						
Internal taxes on consumption	91	—	9	—	—	9
Internal taxes on production	100	—	—	—	—	0
Law 12143 (1935)	40	30	30	—	—	60
Law 12147 (1935)	40	30	30	—	—	60
Decree 14342 (1946)	40	30	30	—	—	60
Law 12956 (1947)	36	27	27	10	—	64
Law 14060 (1951)	100	—	—	—	—	0
Period (1954–72)						
Law 14390 (1954)	16	—	82	—	2	84
Law 14788 (1959)	25	25	25	25	—	75
Period (1973–84)						
Law 20221 (1973)	0	—	65	10	25	100
Period (1985–95)						
Law 23548 (1988)[a]	—	—	—	—	—	—

Note: [a] Existing laws, for this period, do not specify any method for the calculation of distribution indices.
Source: Own estimates based on mentioned legal regimes.

provinces. The clause states that no transfer of competencies, functions, or services is to be accomplished unless the previous revenue reassignment took place by means of a Congress law which was in turn ratified by the province concerned.

Performance of federal fiscal arrangements and of decentralization[23]

Despite the fact that constitutional provisions suggest that the federal finance[24] perspective characterizes intergovernmental fiscal relations, the empirical evidence that has been gathered clearly shows that Argentina is one of the more fiscally concentrated federations in the world, in which local governments are by far the political system's weakest link, and that interjurisdictional fiscal arrangements (apart from revenue-sharing) are

Table 7.3. *Distribution of tax revenue by source and level of government, 1995*

	Income tax	Social security contributions	Property tax	Indirect tax domestic	Indirect tax internation.	Other taxes	Total
Central government	100.00	89.30	11.70	73.80	100.00	53.00	77.30
Provinces	0.0	10.70	67.90	21.30	0.0	41.50	18.90
Municipalities	0.0	0.00	20.40	4.90	0.0	5.50	3.80
% of total	11.30	24.00	6.80	42.30	9.00	6.60	100.0

Source: Own estimates based on figures from the Informe Económico 1995, Secretary for Economic Programming, Argentina, April 1996.

better depicted by the delegation variant of decentralization and by an extensive use of the principal–agent analytical model. The above assertion on concentration finds empirical support not only in tables 7.3 and 7.4, which show each government level's actual tax-raising and spending assignments, but also in tables 7.5 and 7.6, for 1991 and 1993 respectively, indicating that the national government increased its participation in two of the four major spending groups.[25]

As previously noted, the marked tax centralization makes itself evident through the actual distribution of fiscal powers in Argentina (table 7.3). The central government was responsible in 1995 for more than 77 percent of tax yield, while provinces and municipalities respectively accounted for almost 19 percent and 4 percent of the total. This concentration results from taxes exclusively raised by the central government (like non-shared import and export duties, and taxes on salaries on personal goods) while the other important taxes in terms of GDP points (VAT 6.0 percent, income tax 2.34 percent, excise taxes 0.7 percent and liquid fuels tax 0.64 percent) are also collected by the central government and transferred to provinces both by the revenue-sharing system and through various conditional grants that reassert the federal government's preferences for delegation rather than devolving decentralization (table 7.1). Table 7.3 not only stresses the dominance of consumption taxes (42.3 percent)[26] but also the role they play in actual own provincial revenues (around 48 percent). At this level, indirect taxation is overwhelmingly represented by the turnover tax, whose replacement by a consumer tax at the retail level, owing to its cascading and pyramiding effects and to its negative impact upon exporting sectors,[27] is being discussed. This is despite its important contribution to provincial budgets and the relative ease of collection. Table 7.3 also shows that property taxes are mainly collected at subnational levels, where their yield of 24.4 percent makes them the second most important tax in terms

Table 7.4. *Vertical imbalance, 1995*

	Before transfers		After transfers[a]			
	Central governm.	Provincial governm.	Central governm.	Provincial governm.	Central governm.	Provincial governm.
Revenue share[b]	81.80	18.20	58.06	41.94	54.26[c]	39.20[c]
Expenditure share	64.30	35.70	56.39	43.61	56.39	43.61
Surplus/deficit	17.50	(17.50)	1.67	(1.67)	2.13	(4.41)

Notes:
[a] Includes transfers due to any existing interjurisdictional fiscal arrangement between the central government and the provinces.
[b] It includes revenues of all kinds (excludes borrowing).
[c] When the overall fiscal deficit is allowed for (see note 28).
Source: Own estimates based on figures from the "Informe Económico 1995," Secretary for Economic Programming, Argentina, April 1996 and on data from the Secretary for the Assistance to the Provincial Economic Reform.

of contribution to provinces' own revenues. As for Argentinian municipalities, this government level, contrary to other federations' experience, has so far played a minor role in consolidated tax collection (only 3.8 percent relative to 8 percent and 14 percent reached by German and Brazilian local governments respectively), the main part of which consisted of property and business taxes, diverse fees, and user charges which cover, on average, less than 50 percent of their spending needs.

Fiscal centralization is only partially reduced by intergovernmental transfers of all kinds (table 7.4), as almost 60 percent of total tax revenues are still retained by the central government. As will be noticed, the relatively greater decentralization observed on the expenditure side requires corrections in present intergovernmental arrangements for revenue assignment and distribution, if one wants the 1.67 percent computed subnational governments' deficit to disappear.[28]

Tables 7.5 and 7.6, showing spending data for 1991 and 1993 respectively, by function and by jurisdictions' percentage share, give empirical support to the assertion that the revenue centralization pattern did not hold in the case of some expenditures in which sustained decentralization processes occurred, although mainly in the form of delegation. Such were the cases of primary and secondary education and welfare and, to a minor extent, health, for the provision of which, provinces assumed exclusive or very important roles.[29] In support of this argument, table 7.7 shows that unconditional grants to provincial governments dwindled from around 80 percent of the total from 1983 through 1991 to 73 percent in the period 1991–95. At the same time, conditional grants grew from their traditional

Table 7.5. *Total spending by level of government, 1991 (percentage shares)*

	All government levels	National government	Provinces	Municipalities
Total expenditure	**100.00**	**55.64**	**35.67**	**8.68**
Administration and law and order	*100.00*	*47.12*	*35.39*	*17.49*
General services	100.00	31.95	32.78	35.27
Justice	100.00	43.59	56.41	0.00
Defense	100.00	100.00	0.00	0.00
Public order and safety	100.00	43.20	56.80	0.00
Social expenditure and spending on human resources	*100.00*	*53.37*	*38.37*	*8.26*
Education, science, and technology	100.00	33.63	63.99	2.38
Health	100.00	50.40	43.27	6.33
Housing	100.00	8.06	91.94	0.00
Welfare	100.00	10.91	63.64	24.45
Social security	100.00	76.04	23.96	0.00
Labor	100.00	100.00	0.00	0.00
Other expenditure	100.00	0.00	0.00	100.00
Infrastructure for economic affairs and services	*100.00*	*57.27*	*39.76*	*2.97*
Primary sectors	100.00	10.53	89.47	0.00
Fuel and energy	100.00	79.07	20.16	0.78
Manufacturing	100.00	71.43	14.29	14.29
Services	100.00	58.82	36.97	4.20
Other expenditure	100.00	18.92	75.68	5.41
Public debt	*100.00*	*93.75*	*6.25*	*0.00*

Source: Based on data provided by the Secretary for Economic Programming.

20 percent to 27 percent of overall transfers. Finally, funds for decentralized services (mainly education) increased to around 10 percent of total grants received by provinces and amounted to 34.5 percent of conditional transfers. Given that the responsibility for important social services (education and health) was transferred to provinces in the last four years, it is clear that agency relationships (and not mechanisms akin to public choice) underlie decentralization, to the detriment of both the principles of financial autonomy and fiscal responsibility (towards their residents) of subnational governments. It is, however, an encouraging feature concerning local decision-making, that automatic transfers (shared revenues, disequilibria funds, and royalties to oil-producing provinces) gradually became the almost exclusive components of unconditional grants while the non-automatic discretionary Treasury grants (ATN in table 7.7) saw their share reduced to 2.0 percent of overall transfers by 1995.

Table 7.6. *Total spending by level of government, 1993 (percentage shares)*

	All government levels	National government	Provinces	Municipalities
Total expenditure	**100.00**	**57.13**	**35.12**	**7.75**
Administration and law and order	*100.00*	*51.72*	*32.40*	*15.88*
General services	100.00	39.15	29.36	31.49
Justice	100.00	54.55	45.45	0.00
Defense	100.00	100.00	0.00	0.00
Public order and safety	100.00	45.13	54.87	0.00
Social expenditure and spending on human resources	*100.00*	*55.60*	*37.69*	*6.71*
Education, science, and technology	100.00	25.21	72.49	2.29
Health	100.00	48.03	45.79	6.18
Housing	100.00	12.50	87.50	0.00
Welfare	100.00	5.81	79.07	15.12
Social security	100.00	80.65	19.35	0.00
Labor	100.00	100.00	0.00	0.00
Other expenditure	100.00	0.00	0.00	100.00
Infrastructure for economic affairs and services	*100.00*	*54.62*	*40.16*	*5.22*
Primary sectors	100.00	26.47	73.53	0.00
Fuel and energy	100.00	78.13	20.83	1.04
Manufacturing	100.00	66.67	8.33	25.00
Services	100.00	53.01	39.76	7.23
Other expenditure	100.00	0.00	87.50	12.50
Public debt	*100.00*	*92.77*	*7.23*	*0.00*

Source: Based on data provided by the Secretary for Economic Programming.

In assessing whether spending functions (whether by delegation or devolution) fulfilled Oates' decentralization theorem,[30] aggregate figures in tables 7.5 and 7.6 permit conclusions that, although limited in scope, reveal the trend followed by expenditure assignment in Argentina. The percentages shown indicate a certain degree of overlapping of spending functions, which is undoubtedly attributable to concurrent powers constitutionally granted to government levels in almost all spending fields. A more careful inspection of tables 7.5 and 7.6 shows for administration and law and order, but not for defense spending (which is exclusively national), a relatively even participation of central and subnational governments, which can be explained by the typical duplication of executive, legislative, and judiciary powers, and police forces in a federation.

The massive social expenditure delegation to provincial governments which, except for social security payments and services, are now involved

Table 7.7. *Unconditional and conditional transfers to provinces and the city of Buenos Aires, 1983–95 (percentages)*

| | Unconditional transfers | | | | | | Conditional transfers | | | | | | | | | |
| | Automatic | | | Non-automatic | | | Automatic | | | | | | | | Non-aut. | Total |
	1	2	3	4	5	6	7	8	9	10	11	12	13	14	15	
1983	27.0	0.0	8.1	45.8	0.0	4.3	0.0	0.0	0.0	0.0	0.0	3.4	0.3	9.7	1.3	100
1984	28.9	0.0	8.8	40.4	0.0	4.4	0.0.	0.0	0.0	0.0	0.0	2.3	0.4	13.8	1.0	100
1985	65.3	0.0	10.9	1.7	0.0	6.4	0.0	0.0	0.0	0.0	0.0	3.7	0.8	9.7	1.5	100
1986	60.9	0.0	11.6	4.6	0.0	5.6	0.0	0.0	0.0	0.0	0.0	3.8	0.9	10.7	2.0	100
1987	55.5	1.9	8.9	5.7	0.0	4.6	0.0	0.0	0.0	0.0	0.0	6.2	0.7	15.2	1.3	100
1988	57.9	7.5	11.8	1.0	0.0	5.8	0.0	1.8	0.0	0.0	0.0	1.5	0.6	11.2	0.9	100
1989	60.3	8.8	7.6	1.7	9.4	2.1	0.0	1.2	0.0	0.0	0.0	1.3	0.0	7.4	0.3	100
1990	65.6	2.0	8.1	0.9	3.8	1.7	0.0	2.1	0.0	0.0	0.0	2.5	0.1	11.5	1.7	100
1991	73.8	2.2	4.9	1.2	1.7	0.7	0.0	0.6	0.0	2.9	0.3	1.9	0.2	8.6	1.1	100
1992	66.3	1.5	4.1	1.7	0.0	1.7	8.9	0.9	2.2	2.1	0.9	3.4	0.6	5.6	0.2	100
1993	62.7	3.8	3.8	2.5	0.0	1.9	9.0	1.4	4.2	1.1	1.0	1.6	0.7	5.8	0.6	100
1994	61.7	3.6	3.4	3.5	0.0	1.9	8.7	1.2	5.4	0.8	1.0	1.8	0.5	6.2	0.2	100
1995	63.5	3.8	3.8	2.0	0.3	2.0	9.2	0.8	6.1	0.4	0.8	1.2	0.6	5.2	0.4	100

Key to columns:
1. Tax-sharing system
2. Disequilibria fund
3. Royalties
4. National Treasury grants (ATN)
5. Anticipated taxes
6. Road construction
7. Decentralized services
8. Social security
9. Income tax (infrastructure)
10. Educational fund
11. Infrastructure transfer
12. Others
13. Energy fund (FEDEI)
14. National housing fund (FONAVI)
15. Regional Disequilibria fund
Source: Own estimates based on figures from the Secretary for the Assistance to the Provincial Economic Reform.

in 70 percent of spending in this field, may be taken as an indication that the subnational level is in a position to internalize geographically the costs and benefits of services and also to check possible spillover effects. In Argentina, the provinces and the city of Buenos Aires are practically responsible for primary and secondary education (post-secondary education is still a central government responsibility) as well as housing and welfare programs. Shared with the central government are health and social security services (in the latter case only for pension payments and other services to provincial and municipal personnel). Subnational governments receive various conditional revenues to finance these services, as detailed in table 7.7. Subnational governments are also active with respect to infrastructure and economic expenditure, and their share of 40 percent takes the form of direct social overhead capital provision and of sectoral services to productive activities.

In analyzing the rationale whereby most social and human resources expenditure is being decentralized to provinces in Argentina, Oates' theorem must be quoted again in that provinces are generally considered to be (save perhaps for the case of some provinces' exclusive provision of complex or specialized medical attention)[31] the political jurisdictions with respect to which spillover effects can be identified and controlled. Nevertheless, it must be borne in mind that for the main decentralized services (such as education and housing), what has been transferred is the provision or the respective program operation while policy objectives and design mostly remain in central government's hands. This confirms rather than denies the emphasis placed on the attainment of efficiency goals. The underlying rationale here is that subnational governments will be keener to identify communities' needs and preferences and, for this reason, decentralization will be conducive to allocative and productive efficiency.[32]

When decentralization is assessed in relation to municipalities, table 7.6 stresses not only that their importance is minor relative to other levels (7.75 percent of total public spending) but also that their role is mainly confined to performing general administrative functions (including diverse control and inspection services and supervision of land use). Additional roles are in providing traditional "community" services as well as some still incipient performance in social areas such as primary education, preventive health care, and social welfare. It is thus concluded that in Argentina, actual decentralization in relation to local governments still falls short of both constitutional powers and real economic possibilities, in part because localities have failed to take a more active role with respect to club-like local public goods.[33] Such provision by municipalities is consistent with economic principles, as these goods allow technical excludability and benefit and cost appropriation to local residents only.

The fiscal gap in Argentina

Existing tax and spending function assignments among the central and subnational governments have in part been the cause of the country's serious vertical fiscal imbalance. According to table 7.4, it appears that while revenues in 1995 reached 96 percent of spending at the national level, resources from all sources (after intergovernmental transfers have been accounted for) only made up, in the same year, 90 percent of total provincial expenditures.

The measurement of the fiscal gap was here performed by using alternative versions for the vertical fiscal imbalance coefficient[34] whose formulas and yields for the period 1983–95 are shown in table 7.8.

Notwithstanding criticisms raised by Bird (1986), this coefficient's values, and their evolution in the period considered, allow some interesting conclusions to be drawn. It is to be noted, in the first place, that provinces' own fiscal resources finance less than half of provincial spending (as measured by V_{ce} when shared revenue is regarded as a transfer). It is, however, worth pointing out that despite marked cyclical behavior, since the Stabilization Program started in 1991 values have been close to the traditional historic floor of 40 percent.[35] Nonetheless, this still leaves Argentinian provinces well behind the fiscal situation of subnational governments in other federations, like Brazil, in which states and municipalities levy on average more than 60 percent of total tax revenues. The extreme values shown in table 7.8[36] (31 percent and 49 percent) are explained by the effect of the 1989 hyperinflation upon tax revenues and the fact that revenues recovered more than expenditures in 1993.

The acute inflation endured by the country during the second half of the eighties,[37] the climax of which was reached with the 1989 and 1990 hyperinflations, also damaged provincial finances, as the calculated values of V show for the period 1986–89. This illustrates the uneven way in which national and subnational governments, linked by inter-jurisdictional tax arrangements, bore the fiscal revenue losses caused by inflation differently. In fact, whereas the yield of the formal tax system in 1988, 1989, and 1990 was respectively 17.3 percent, 18.1 percent, and 20.8 percent of GDP, the figures were 21.6 percent, 28.5 percent, and 25.1 percent when the inflation tax is included within the estimation of the tax yield.[38] In other words, the inflation tax (exclusively appropriated by the central government) reached, in these years, 19.7 percent, 36.7 percent, and 17.1 percent of total

Table 7.8. Vertical fiscal imbalance coefficients, 1983–95

	1983	1984	1985	1986	1987	1988	1989	1990	1991	1992	1993	1994	1995
						(millions of 1995 pesos)							
T_o	4090	5445	5637	6793	6092	5308	4359	5101	6081	8374	9443	9959	8999
T_s	3352	3070	6836	7652	7479	6639	6693	6471	8960	9871	9629	9807	9082
R_o	1067	1235	1007	1583	1381	1220	1256	985	1070	1604	4836	1989	1967
G_o	6688	5227	1321	2027	2226	2324	3047	1463	1210	1082	1553	1659	1422
G_c	2359	2323	2315	2895	3764	2495	1368	1925	1975	3939	4178	4421	3800
B	−605	2318	1003	1272	2718	3372	1172	3080	1774	639	−217	1947	3734
E	16951	19617	18120	22222	23660	21359	17895	19025	21070	25509	29422	29783	29004
V	0.47	0.62	0.80	0.78	0.75	0.77	0.75	0.82	0.85	0.80	0.81	0.80	0.82
V^e	0.50	0.50	0.74	0.72	0.63	0.62	0.69	0.66	0.76	0.78	0.81	0.73	0.69
V_{ce}	0.30	0.34	0.37	0.38	0.32	0.31	0.31	0.32	0.34	0.39	0.49	0.40	0.38

Key to rows:
$V = 1 - [(G_o + G_c)/E]$
$V^e = 1 - [(G_o + G_c + B)/E]$
$V_{ce} = 1 - [(T_s + G_o + G_c + B)/E]$

where:
G_o Unconditional national grants to provinces
G_c Conditional grants to provinces
B Net borrowing by provinces
T_s Provinces' revenue from shared national taxes
T_o Provinces' own tax revenue
R_o Provinces' other non-fiscal revenue
E Provincial expenditure
Source: Own estimates based on figures from the Secretary for the Assistance to the Provincial Economic Reform.

national tax revenues, which is in line with the enlargement of the fiscal gap (table 7.8) and with the trend followed by V in the second half of the decade.[39]

Values for the measures V (when shared revenue and net borrowing are both considered part of subnational governments' own revenue) also exhibited a cyclical pattern throughout the period considered, their respective maximum and minimum figures being 85 percent for 1991 and 47 percent for 1983. The 80 percent floor achieved since 1990 (in spite of important increases in overall provincial public expenditure) responded to improvements in the collection of national taxes (mainly VAT and income tax) and this was immediately reflected in revenue-sharing and in the other transfers to provinces (including the conditional ones for decentralized services).

In sum, while V_{ce} figures depict in general a poor provincial performance, as regards their own fiscal base[40] (excluding shared taxes), the coefficient's value approached the level of many federations (except Brazil) when shared revenues were included among the provinces' own fiscal resources, and even reflected a smaller fiscal gap than in Australia or Canada, where V reaches 70 percent on average. This positive feature points out that despite possible imperfections, revenue-sharing can still be regarded as the best available option for the system of federal finances in Argentina.[41]

Measures aimed at checking the problem of vertical fiscal imbalances entailed a mix of instruments on the part of the federal government: conditional and unconditional transfers summarized as follows, as already shown in table 7.7. Conditional transfers, amounting to 26.7 percent in 1995, included automatic grants for financing services decentralized to provinces and to the city of Buenos Aires (9.2 percent) and a further set of other automatic transfers for specific use, accruing from diverse funds, of which infrastructure (6.1 percent), house-building (5.2 percent), road construction (2 percent), social security (0.8 percent) and energy (0.6 percent) are particularly worth mentioning. The non-automatic conditional transfer was fed from a Regional Disequilibria Fund whose share (0.4 percent) was almost nominal and far from being decisive in any policy sense.

As for unconditional transfers, apart from the already mentioned dominant part taken by existing revenue-sharing arrangements (table 7.7), that made up 63.5 percent of a total of 73.4 percent in 1995, the remaining automatic grants consisted of royalties to oil-producing provinces (3.8 percent) and of payments from the Fiscal Disequilibria Fund (3.8 percent) set up in 1993 as a part of the Fiscal Agreement[42] between the central government and the provinces. Non-automatic unconditional transfers were in turn mostly represented by the so-called Treasury grants (ATN) (2 percent).[43]

The percentages reached in 1995 by conditional and unconditional grants support the argument that the central government was gradually exercising more control over recent provincial fiscal development. This feature was particularly noticeable in the provisions of the Fiscal Agreements, many of which were oriented toward achieving "tax base homogeneity" and "tax rate limits and uniformity," not to mention in the pressures exerted upon provinces aimed at setting budget spending limits and doing away with presumably economically inefficient taxes (turnover tax, stamp duties, and taxes on energy).[44]

Horizontal fiscal imbalances

Different Argentine provinces do not have comparable fiscal situations. They exhibit deep fiscal differences arising from existing socioeconomic disparities whose magnitude is stressed in table 7.9. The table shows that five jurisdictions (covering 27 percent of the total area of Argentina) embodied almost 70 percent of total population and 80 percent of GDP in 1995, and that maximum per capita income (for the city of Buenos Aires) was 8.5 times the minimum one (for the province of Formosa). The same feature occurs with regard to other indicators such as the unemployment and activity rates and the poverty indices for the different provinces.[45]

As expected, regional socioeconomic disparities affected tax collections in many subnational governments (table 7.10 for 1994) and only the High Revenue 1 provinces (and most of the High Revenue 2 group plus Entre Rios and San Luis) had per capita own tax revenues higher than the "all provinces average." This statistical conclusion is by no means surprising if one expects a positive functional relationship between income per capita (and tax potential) and actual tax yield in each province. On the expenditure side, per capita spending shows both the effect of population density (economies of scale) and the spending "floor" ensuring administration and public goods and services provision in each jurisdiction. In this connection, and contrary to what was noted earlier on the revenue side, the spending of almost all High Revenue 1 provinces fell short of the "all provinces average," while in the other groups it normally exceeded the average sum.[46] Obviously, the persistence of such a disparity between relative revenue and spending levels has been made possible because the redistributive feature of most national transfer arrangements (revenue-sharing inclusive) enables poorer provinces to maintain extremely high per capita spending levels. This assertion is illustrated by table 7.10, which shows that intergovernmental grants of all kinds financed more than 90 percent of per capita spending in Low Revenue 2 provinces (Catamarca and La Rioja) whereas such grants financed barely 45 percent of High Revenue 1 provinces' per capita outlays. Nevertheless, equalization is not being implemented on equity grounds in Argentina, i.e. with a view to financing a minimum provision of public goods and services in each jurisdiction. What really happens is that less favored provinces normally get resources to finance their disproportionate public employment, which rules out the possibility of efficiency and effectiveness objectives of public expenditure being achieved since more public employment does not necessarily mean more and better services. The latter assertion is proven with table 7.11 which shows that, with the exception of the special case of the two underpopulated Patagonian provinces of Santa Cruz and Tierra del Fuego, the Low Revenue 2 provinces (Catamarca and La Rioja) exhibit both the highest number of public employees per thousand inhabitants and the maximum per capita public spending in personnel. In spite of this their governments are permanently subject to criticism for their low standards of service provision and their poor administrative performance.[47]

Finally, the intended (though so far unsuccessful) policy to check horizontal fiscal disparities through secondary distribution of shared taxes is depicted in table 7.2. This shows that ever since revenue-sharing was implemented for the first time in 1935 a gradual replacement of devolution by equalizing criteria took place in favor of poorer provinces. This feature is seen more clearly in table 7.12. While richer and higher tax revenue producing provinces had small shares in secondary distribution, the share going to the poorer provinces followed a consistently rising trend in the revenue-sharing period 1935–94.[48]

Conclusions

This chapter has clearly shown that Argentina has not so far taken advantage of the possibilities arising from its federal institutional setting, despite existing constitutional provisions whereby subnational and local governments are given significant independent fiscal and spending functions. In particular, decentralization has been more marked in spending than in the tax field thus creating a situation of vertical fiscal imbalance, which in turn has entailed a resort to diverse conditional and unconditional federal grants.

In several important fields, spending decentralization took place mainly through delegation[49] which, together with the marked tax collection concentration at the national level, brought about a lesser degree of financial autonomy on the part of the subnational level and a gradual switch of

Table 7.9. Provincial social and economic indicators

	Provinces' share of GDP (%) (1)	Index of per capita provincial GDP (Average = 100) (2)	Population for 1995 (3)	Surface area (sq. km.) (4)	Population density for 1995 (5)	Unemployment rate for 1995 (%) (6)	Activity rate for 1995 (%) (7)	Poverty index for 1995 (%) (8)
High Revenue 1	78.3	114	23 671 686	754 926	31	15.7	44.17	15.8
MCBA[a]	22.9	265	2 998 006	200	14 940	13.3	49.00	8.1
Santa Fe	9.7	114	2 934 220	133 007	22	18.4	41.00	17.6
Mendoza	4.4	101	1 500 818	148 827	10	6.7	37.30	17.6
Buenos Aires	33.8	88	13 333 670	307 571	43	16.6	45.90	17.1
Cordoba	7.5	89	2 914 972	165 321	18	15.9	38.00	15.1
High Revenue 2	6.5	114	1 971 777	930 423	2	13.2	40.70	20.3
Tierra del Fuego	n.a.	n.a.	96 917	21 263	5	10.4	40.80	22.4
Santa Cruz	0.7	134	180 115	243 943	1	7.1	38.80	14.7
La Pampa	1.1	135	280 876	143 440	2	10.6	41.90	13.5
Chubut	1.5	131	396 800	224 686	2	14.5	39.00	21.9
Neuquen	1.5	113	460 395	94 078	5	16.5	40.10	21.4
Rio Negro	1.7	106	556 674	203 013	3	13.5	42.40	23.2
Medium Revenue	9.7	72	4 647 860	476 411	10	15.1	36.75	27.5
Tucuman	2.9	83	1 209 716	22 524	54	19.2	37.30	27.7
San Luis	0.7	76	320 109	76 748	4	10.4	38.50	21.5
Salta	1.9	69	952 174	155 488	6	15.7	38.00	37.1
Jujuy	1.1	69	551 804	53 219	10	12.4	33.80	35.5
Entre Rios	2.1	68	1 063 416	78 781	13	13.2	35.10	20.6
San Juan	1.0	63	550 641	89 651	6	14.0	38.50	19.8
Low Revenue 1	4.7	43	3 761 596	426 050	9	10.6	34.26	36.0
Corrientes	1.3	53	852 685	88 199	10	14.7	35.60	31.4
Santiago del Estero	0.9	45	696 092	136 351	5	8.6	32.70	38.2
Chaco	1.1	43	890 548	99 633	9	12.8	33.40	39.5

Misiones	1.0	39	877 904	29 801	29	7.8	35.70	33.6
Formosa	0.4	31	444 367	72 066	6	6.4	33.00	39.1
Low Revenue 2	*0.8*	*52*	*533 725*	*192 282*	*3*	*11.8*	*36.37*	*27.7*
Catamarca	0.5	60	287 567	102 602	3	12.2	36.60	28.2
La Rioja	0.3	42	246 158	89 680	3	11.3	36.10	27.0
All provinces	*100.0*	*100*	*34 586 644*	*2 780 092*	*12*	*15.0*	*41.77*	*19.9*
Maximum value	33.8	265	13 333 670	307 571	14 940	19.2	49.00	39.5
Minimum value	0.3	31	96 917	200	1	6.4	32.70	8.1
Average	4.2	84	1 441 110	1 158 837	634	12.6	38.30	24.7
Standard deviation	7.8	51	2 616 918	73 433	2 983	3.5	3.90	8.8
Max./min. value	112.7	9	138	1 538	20 234	3.0	1.50	4.9

Note: [a] Municipalidad de la Ciudad de Buenos Aires.

Sources:
(1) Fundación de Investigación Económica Latinoamericana, 1992
(2) Own estimates
(3) *Statistical Yearbook, Republic of Argentina,* 1995 (INDEC)
(4) *Statistical Yearbook, Republic of Argentina,* 1995 (INDEC)
(5) *Statistical Yearbook, Republic of Argentina,* 1995 (INDEC)
(6) Rate of open unemployment in urban areas (October 1995) (INDEC)
(7) Rate of activity in urban areas (May 1995) (INDEC)
(8) Percentage of households with Unsatisfied Basic Needs (NBI) (INDEC)

Table 7.10. *Per capita provincial revenue and spending, 1994 (1995 pesos)*

	Total rev. (1) = (2)+(5)	Own rev. (2) = (3)+(4)	Own tax rev. (3)	Other own rev. (4)	National revenue (5) = (6)+(7)+(8)	Shared tax rev. (6)	Royalties (7)	Other transfers (8)	Total spending (9) = (10)+(11)	Current spending (10)	Capital spending (11)
High Revenue 1	*702*	*407*	*360*	*47*	*295*	*188*	*2*	*105*	*726*	*636*	*90*
MCBA	976	903	837	65	73	55	0	18	969	888	80
Santa Fe	754	339	297	42	415	296	0	119	764	699	64
Mendoza	781	341	257	84	440	270	32	137	832	727	105
Buenos Aires	600	322	287	36	278	160	0	117	616	525	90
Cordoba	791	388	324	65	403	298	0	105	888	772	116
High Revenue 2	*1628*	*418*	*248*	*169*	*1210*	*498*	*234*	*478*	*1903*	*1489*	*414*
Tierra del Fuego	3626	723	587	147	2903	734	350	1819	4665	3886	779
Santa Cruz	2826	524	319	199	2302	866	479	957	2917	2079	843
La Pampa	1719	567	260	311	1152	650	22	480	1607	1195	408
Chubut	1106	205	110	92	901	390	144	367	1376	1183	195
Neuquen	1748	509	259	241	1239	376	527	336	2152	1555	597
Rio Negro	1150	337	252	87	813	441	71	301	1456	1227	230
Medium Revenue	*912*	*236*	*153*	*83*	*676*	*459*	*5*	*212*	*1033*	*875*	*158*
Tucuman	704	156	128	28	548	381	0	166	831	675	156
San Luis	1428	344	248	96	1084	704	0	379	1614	1132	482
Salta	805	209	94	115	596	394	16	186	942	810	132
Jujuy	1026	260	93	169	766	500	0	266	1140	982	158
Entre Rios	967	326	247	80	641	444	6	192	957	871	85
San Juan	1033	195	133	60	838	591	4	243	1341	1179	162
Low Revenue 1	*870*	*130*	*91*	*39*	*740*	*511*	*3*	*226*	*930*	*783*	*148*
Corrientes	726	99	79	20	627	422	0	205	747	654	93
Santiago del Estero	965	134	96	37	831	569	0	262	1036	916	121
Chaco	885	153	100	53	732	542	0	190	894	752	141
Misiones	695	117	102	16	578	370	11	197	804	665	139
Formosa	1312	161	67	95	1151	805	7	339	1435	1112	325

Low Revenue 2	1769	157	88	75	1606	885	0	721	1910	1738	172
Catamarca	1499	110	99	14	1386	933	0	452	1746	1647	99
La Rioja	2087	212	75	146	1866	829	0	1037	2104	1845	258
All provinces	817	341	292	58	466	288	16	163	874	749	125
Maximum value	3626	901	837	311	2903	933	527	1819	4665	3886	843
Minimum value	600	91	67	14	73	55	0	18	616	525	64
Average	1259	300	223	96	940	501	69	370	1410	1166	244
Standard deviation	709	201	175	73	635	222	150	383	866	688	216
Max./min. value	6	10	13	22	40	17	—	101	8	7	13

Source: Own estimates based on figures from the Secretary for the Assistance to the Provincial Economic Reform.

Table 7.11. *Provincial public employment and spending on personnel, 1995*

	Employees per thousand inhabitants	Wage spending per employee (US$)	Per capita spending in personnel (US$)
High Revenue 1			
MCBA	27	1 631	538
Santa Fe	31	1 080	400
Mendoza	28	1 307	435
Buenos Aires	22	1 003	260
Cordoba	28	1 281	427
High Revenue 2			
Tierra del Fuego	53	3 292	2 095
Santa Cruz	76	1 791	1 627
La Pampa	57	1 051	716
Chubut	47	1 317	749
Neuquen	62	1 321	986
Rio Negro	53	1 240	781
Medium Revenue			
Tucuman	45	786	427
San Luis	54	1 007	653
Salta	44	1 012	530
Jujuy	51	1 024	625
Entre Rios	41	1 068	529
San Juan	64	816	628
Low Revenue 1			
Corrientes	45	842	454
Santiago del Estero	56	826	552
Chaco	41	1 164	569
Misiones	39	897	420
Formosa	72	898	776
Low Revenue 2			
Catamarca	81	1 016	984
La Rioja	97	1 031	1 194
All provinces			
Maximum value	97	3 292	2 095
Minimum value	22	786	260
Average	51	1 196	723
Standard deviation	18	500	408
Max./min. value	4	4	4

Source: Own estimates based on figures from the Secretary for the Assistance to the Provincial Economic Reform.

the latter's fiscal responsibility as accountability followed the revenue source (that is, to the principal rather than to residents).[50] All in all, conditional transfers to provinces represented in 1995 a record figure of almost 30 percent of total transfers. In this connection, the use of principal–agent relations, rather than public choice-like mechanisms for collective deci-

Table 7.12. *Secondary participation by provinces, selected years (percent)*

	1935	1946	1958	1972	1973	1984	1994
High Revenue 1	*67.5*	*70.3*	*65.6*	*59.5*	*50.7*	*51.5*	*43.7*
MCBA	5.0	8.8	11.1	4.7	0.0	5.3	0.0
Santa Fe	12.6	12.6	10.3	8.7	9.1	8.4	8.9
Mendoza	19.9	9.7	5.3	5.2	4.7	4.2	4.2
Buenos Aires	20.7	29.7	31.0	32.9	28.0	25.4	21.9
Cordoba	9.3	9.5	7.9	8.0	8.9	8.2	8.8
High Revenue 2	*0.0*	*0.0*	*1.8*	*8.1*	*8.9*	*9.8*	*9.9*
Tierra del Fuego	0.0	0.0	0.0	0.3	0.0	0.3	0.7
Santa Cruz	0.0	0.0	0.0	1.6	1.4	1.5	1.6
La Pampa	0.0	0.0	0.0	1.5	1.8	1.4	1.9
Chubut	0.0	0.0	0.0	1.6	1.7	1.9	1.6
Neuquen	0.0	0.0	0.0	1.4	1.7	2.0	1.7
Rio Negro	0.0	0.0	1.8	1.7	2.3	2.6	2.5
Medium Revenue	*27.6*	*20.7*	*18.4*	*17.1*	*19.6*	*18.6*	*21.9*
Tucuman	9.6	6.2	4.1	3.7	4.6	5.0	4.7
San Luis	0.6	1.4	1.5	1.4	1.8	1.5	2.3
Salta	2.3	1.9	3.4	3.2	3.8	3.9	3.8
Jujuy	2.6	1.6	2.7	2.5	2.2	2.2	2.8
Entre Rios	3.8	5.4	4.3	3.9	4.7	3.5	4.9
San Juan	8.7	4.2	2.4	2.4	2.6	2.4	3.4
Low Revenue 1	*3.8*	*7.0*	*11.4*	*12.7*	*17.2*	*16.6*	*19.7*
Corrientes	1.9	4.0	3.6	3.9	3.8	3.5	3.7
Santiago del Estero	1.9	3.0	2.5	2.3	4.0	4.0	4.1
Chaco	0.0	0.0	3.0	2.7	4.1	4.0	5.0
Misiones	0.0	0.0	2.3	2.4	3.0	3.0	3.3
Formosa	0.0	0.0	0.0	1.4	2.3	2.2	3.6
Low Revenue 2	*1.1*	*2.0*	*2.8*	*2.6*	*3.7*	*3.5*	*4.8*
Catamarca	0.5	1.1	1.4	1.4	1.9	1.9	2.7
La Rioja	0.6	0.9	1.4	1.2	1.7	1.6	2.1
All provinces	*100.0*	*100.0*	*100.0*	*100.0*	*100.0*	*100.0*	*100.0*
Maximum value	20.7	29.7	31.0	32.9	28.0	25.4	21.9
Minimum value	0.5	0.9	1.4	0.3	1.4	0.3	0.7
Average	6.7	6.7	5.6	4.2	4.5	4.2	4.3
Standard deviation	6.5	7.1	6.8	6.3	5.5	4.8	4.2
Max./min. value	41	33	22	110	19	87	32

Source: Own estimates based on figures from the Secretary for the Assistance to the Provincial Economic Reform and from Nuñez Miñana and Porto (1983).

sions, was accentuated following the Convertibility Economic Program and particularly since 1993, when Fiscal Agreements were imposed on provinces to achieve national stabilization goals.[51]

The revenue-sharing system has been, for more than sixty years, the preferred mechanism for tax coordination in Argentina, not only among national and subnational governments but also among provinces and their municipalities. At the same time, the secondary distribution of revenue-sharing was one of the instruments resorted to for checking horizontal fiscal imbalances. This is sufficiently proven by the fact that devolution criteria were gradually and totally replaced by equalizing criteria in the successive revenue-sharing.[52]

The higher per capita transfers received by some backward provinces resulting from re-distributive policies aimed at favoring poorer provinces have, however, failed to check horizontal fiscal disparities, since national grants only permitted larger provincial expenditures whose efficiency and efficacy were dubious. In other words, the direction imposed on secondary distribution did not prove to be a successful policy for achieving redistribution goals (as the poverty index figures in table 7.9 show for low-income provinces) and, what is worse, curtailed incentives for fiscally backward provinces to develop their own tax potential,[53] thus perpetuating the almost complete dependence on transferred funds and the persistence of horizontal fiscal imbalances.

The 1994 Constituent Assembly introduced important changes in the fields of fiscal federalism and federal finance by giving, for the first time in the country's history, constitutional status to revenue-sharing as the key interjurisdictional fiscal arrangement and setting up the framework within which the new regime would supposedly come into being, from January 1, 1997.[54]

The 1994 constitutional reform also meant a step forward with respect to the devolution variant of decentralization, and in relation to the likelihood of a "true" rather than a "formal" federation, by mandating that no future transfer of services would be possible unless accepted by the concerned province and accompanied by a matching transfer of funds or revenue sources.

In sum, the present concern of subnational governments regarding federal finance issues shows increasing provincial awareness of their role in a federal context and their real desire to regain the exercise of taxing powers previously yielded. The Federal Congress is at the very root of this change, as for the first time in decades both senators and representatives are reluctant to endorse the national government's new fiscal faculties in so far as they may collide with provinces' constitutional faculties or shrink the proportion of national revenues shared with the provinces.

Notes

1 Tanzi (1995: 296) argued that the creation of a central entity transcending the European member states in some economic functions opened up a debate which was similar to those analyzed in discussions relating fiscal federalism and fiscal decentralization.

2 Argentina is, however, a good example for showing that fiscal decentralization is progressing but is subject to important setbacks: the central government, on the grounds of achieving macroeconomic stabilization goals, has
enforced since 1992 a Fiscal Agreement whereby provincial governments
have had to limit their total spending and to revise and adapt (following
national guidelines) their tax systems in exchange for a guaranteed shared
revenue floor.

3 Although a more precise concept would be that policies favoring decentralized
decision-making enable governments to perform their assigned tax and spending activities subject to efficiency and equity objectives.

4 Each depending on the degree of independent decision-making exercised at the
subnational and local level.

5 Bird (1994) argues that outcomes, in this variety of fiscal decentralization, are
presumed to be satisfactory simply because the process itself is intrinsically
desirable, insofar as it institutionalizes the participation of those affected by
local decisions.

6 By assuming a straight application of the approach, with implied symmetric
information and agents' fair behavior by agents, agency problems (adverse
selection and moral hazard) are here ruled out.

7 Public choice refers to the economic study of non-market decision-making
mechanisms and is also defined as the application of economics to political
science. This theory is embedded in the Wicksellian link between a public good
and the tax used for its financing and in the viewpoint that the collective choice
process amounts to voluntary exchanges among individuals from which every-
body benefits.

8 By the last constitutional reform, in 1994, the city of Buenos Aires changed its
political status. The designated mayor was replaced in 1996 by an elected head
of government, and a Chamber of Representatives replaced the former municipal council. However, the jurisdiction cannot totally be equated to a province
as the national government still retains responsibility for some functions and
services (for instance, the police force) while the Congress keeps some legislative faculties. Transfer of justice to the city is now favored by the national
government.

9 The Argentine Congress is bicameral: senators represent the provinces and the
city of Buenos Aires while representatives are chosen in proportion to population, taking the country as a single district; direct election applies in both cases.
Unicameral and bicameral legislatures coexist at the provincial level; again,
senators represent provincial departments (in provinces having this chamber)
while provinces also stand as single districts for the election of representatives.

10 As an interesting case, provinces can provide post-secondary education.
However, all non-public universities in Argentina are funded by budgetary
transfers from the central government.

11 This in turn implies that no restrictions exist for subnational governments to
raise direct contributions.

12 The income tax was created in Argentina in 1935, practically together with, and
included in, the first revenue-sharing system between the central government
and the provinces. In order to fulfill what the Constitution prescribed, the

income tax law was established for a limited time period and has since been permanently prorogued.

13 Municipalities have been applying taxes to the consumption of energy (levied on the basis of electricity and gas sales to households and firms). As from 1993, provinces signing the Fiscal Agreement agreed to ensure that local governments will do away with these contributions.

14 Separation of tax sources was actually the prevailing situation until 1935, when the first revenue-sharing scheme was implemented.

15 This balance seldom occurred in reality mainly because of provincial tax administrations' failure to reach even modest tax yield targets and because provinces partially bore the financial burden of transferred services as accompanying grants did not fully make up the cost of programs.

16 The terms primary and secondary distribution refer to the apportionment between the central and the provincial governments and among the provincial governments, respectively, of tax revenues included within the national revenue-sharing system.

17 Provincial social security systems only provide services and pay pensions to provincial and municipal employees.

18 The evolution of the primary distribution since 1935 clearly shows the share gained by provinces (figures are percentages):

Year	National government	Provinces	Others
1935	82.5	17.5	
1947	79.0	21.0	
1973	48.5	48.5	3.0
1988	54.7	42.3	3.0
1990	57.0	43.0	

19 Changes in percentages occurred not only because of political negotiations through which governors exerted pressures on the central government but also because of changes in the rates and in the taxes included in the revenue to be shared. Nevertheless, as table 7.1 shows, the percentages mentioned can be deceptive as they apply after the amount of revenue shared has been reduced by the amount destined to provincial social security systems and other specific funds which cannot be spent freely by the provinces.

20 As from 1992, the central government guarantees a "floor" revenue to provinces signing the Fiscal Agreements; that is to say, fixed distribution parameters apply over actual tax revenues or over an agreed amount, whichever is greater. The term Fiscal Agreements refers to fiscal instruments whereby provinces accept a curtailment in their tax and spending powers (elimination of some distorted duties, limits on rates, replacement of turnover tax, and limits on annual spending) for which they would be granted the above-mentioned "floor" shared revenue, the elimination of the tax on assets and effective reduction (to firms) of social security contributions (50 percent on average, but varying according to the region).

21 In some provinces the inverses of population and fiscal capacity are used as equalizing criteria, thus favoring low-density and poorer municipalities.

22 Equalizing criteria are not just included but, rather, emphasized, as the constitutional mandate literally states that the system "will be fair, solidarity-framed and will give priority to the achievement of similar degrees of development and quality of life, and of equal opportunities throughout the country."

23 This section is largely based on Rezk (1995) and Rezk, Capello, and Ponce (1996).

24 This situation of federal finances is taken to occur, in Bird's sense (1995: 294), when the relationship between the central and subnational governments (both having independent fiscal powers) is one of negotiation among equals; that is, between government levels that are each, within a sphere, coordinate and independent.

25 Figures for 1993 indicated that the spending for all government levels amounted to 26.9 percent of the Argentinian GDP, 18 percent of which belonged to social expenditure and spending on human resources, 4.7 to administration and law and order, 2.5 percent to infrastructure for economic affairs and services, and 1.7 percent to public debt.

26 One of the principal problems with fiscal decentralization in developing countries, in contrast to developed ones, arises because of the high degree of dependence of the former on consumption taxes and the apparent difficulty of working out adequate "two-level" consumption tax systems. This comment is also applicable to latent problems in the Argentinian national and provincial tax structure.

27 Despite successive postponements, this replacement is one of the main conditions imposed upon subnational governments signing Fiscal Agreements.

28 Percentages 1.76 and -1.67 come up when revenues and expenditures, respectively are consolidated for all government levels, assuming that no national deficit exists. Given that this assumption was not realistic for 1995, the last two columns of table 7.4 include a new vertical fiscal imbalance estimation where the national fiscal deficit is allowed for.

29 Suffice it here to point out that while provincial spending in elementary education went from 92.3 percent (in 1991) to 95 percent (in 1993) of the total consolidated spending for Argentina, total provincial figures for secondary education rose from 40.8 percent to almost 100 percent of the total in the same period.

30 Oates' classical argument (1972: 55) is that each public service should be provided by the jurisdiction which has control over the minimum geographic area that would internalize benefits and costs of such provision.

31 An example of this could be public hospitals in the city of Buenos Aires and in the provinces of Buenos Aires, Córdoba, Santa Fé and Mendoza.

32 Nevertheless, Prud'homme, in a recent article (1995), challenges the merits of decentralization for allocative efficiency on the following two grounds: for assuming hypotheses not easily defensible in developing countries and for placing emphasis mainly on demand efficiency instead of supply or productive efficiency.

33 The politico-institutional situation of Argentinian municipalities is similar to neither Brazilian local governments (direct central–municipal relations) nor Canadian ones (only provincial–municipal relations). However, it is closer to

the latter apart from strong revenue-sharing links with provinces and their dependence on certain provincial transfers. Local governments do not have in practice constitutionally legal impediments to seek aid at the central government level, for instance the financing of determined public works or the control and management of infrastructure (for example, the municipality of Córdoba's overt lobbying and pressure upon the national government as it sought to improve its own chances as an interested party in the airport privatization).

34 Despite its widespread use, the conceptual validity of the coefficient (due to Hunter [1977]) has been challenged by Bird (1986) on the grounds that, measured by a single number, balance is taken to be an "unequivocal good" (i.e. success will depend in any federal fiscal system on whether this balance is achieved). On the other hand, given that the coefficient is expected to measure subnational governments' degree of dependency on central governments, interjurisdictional fiscal arrangements in each country involve differing degrees of control not reflected in results obtained by the coefficient; this makes international comparisons difficult.

35 This is a consequence of both the success in checking high inflation and the pressure exerted from the central government upon provinces urging them to improve their tax administration systems.

36 The lowest percentage for the period (30 percent) was in 1983; this year was not included as it was when the military handed over political power to civilians. Until then, provinces did not have any real autonomy, as governors were appointed by the central government.

37 The following percentages are the inflation rates, measured by the consumer price index, experienced by the Argentinian economy from 1989 to 1994.

1989:	3 079
1990:	2 314
1991:	171
1992:	24.9
1993:	10.6
1994:	3.9

38 Including, of course, those taxes with revenue that was shared among the national government and the provinces.

39 As from 1991 (and coincidentally with the stabilization program initiated by the Argentina government), the incidence of inflation tax practically died out as figures for 1991-94 indicate that it reached 2.1 percent, 0.8 percent, 0.8 percent and 0.7 percent, respectively, of all fiscal revenues.

40 It is widely accepted that tax evasion in Argentina is higher at the provincial level (or at least in the majority of provinces) because of weaker fiscal compliance-inducing mechanisms.

41 The overwhelming politico-institutional acceptance of the revenue-sharing system in Argentina is certainly an important policy datum.

42 See the considerations on the concept of Fiscal Agreements in note 20 above.

43 These Treasury grants are highly criticized and resisted by most provincial

governments since they are allocated to provinces in a totally discretionary manner and following, in some cases, party lines.

44 It was pointed out (Rezk 1995: 8) that Fiscal Agreements reflect the tradeoff between national stabilization goals and provinces' financial autonomy.

45 To gain a better understanding of the figures and percentages in table 7.9, note that total GDP, per capita GDP, the unemployment rate and the activity rate for the period 1992-94 were:

	1992	1993	1994
GDP	$226.7 bill.	$257.6 bill.	$281.6 bill.
Per capita GDP	$6 786	$7 620	$8 235
Unemployment rate (May/Oct.)	6.9%/7.0%	9.9%/9.3%	10.7%/12.1%
Activity rate (May/Oct.)	37.6%/38.8%	37.6%/37.6%	38.0%/37.6%

46 The economically backward and sparsely populated western province of La Rioja provides one of the most interesting cases of horizontal fiscal imbalance, as per capita outlays were 3.4 times greater than in Buenos Aires whereas the latter had per capita own tax revenue 3.83 times larger than the former.

47 The problem of accountability (to the province's taxpayers or to the national government) is also raised here as in both cases national transfers of all kinds amount to 90–92 percent of their total revenues.

48 The good performance of provinces in the High Revenue 2 category is due to the royalties received by these oil-producing regions.

49 That is the case of fields of experience in which provinces have a dominant role relative to the national government (for instance, primary and secondary education, housing, welfare, and, increasingly, health, according to tables 7.5 and 7.6); as can be seen from table 7.7, conditional transfers include grants for decentralized services, for housing (FONAVI) and for unsatisfied basic needs in the conurbation of the city of Buenos Aires. With regard to provincial spending on infrastructure and economic services, there are also conditional transfers for energy (FEDEI), road construction and, since 1991, infrastructure projects.

50 This assertion should not, however, be taken in black and white terms as provincial governments are also accountable to their citizens for transferred services. A proof of this is that whenever people demonstrate in provinces (demanding a greater quantity or higher quality of services such as education) the national and provincial governments are both subject to criticisms.

51 The relative increase of conditional transfers was acknowledged by the World Bank report on Argentina (1996: 32) when it stated "since 1991, the primary distribution system (of shared tax revenues) changed several times, in line with the need of the central government to cut the overall fiscal deficit and to appropriate some funds from the 'coparticipable' pool." In practice, those changes amounted to reductions in the unconditional coparticipable pool and increases in the earmarked funds for provinces and social security systems.

52 This is in turn reflected by the percentages of the secondary distribution for the period 1935-94, in table 7.12.

53 One negative feature in the provinces, which is particularly severe in the "low-income" ones, is the extremely poor performance of their tax administrations.
54 Although there exist several versions of the new system, none has reached legislative status (even at the level of Senate committees) as the constitutionally imposed deadline of January 1, 1997 has proved impossible to meet. Therefore, the present percentages, for primary distribution, and the percentages of Law 23548 for the secondary distribution, will continue being used in the meantime.

References

Bird, R. M. (1986), "On measuring fiscal centralization and fiscal balance in federal states," *Environment and Planning C: Government and Policy*, 4: 389–404.
   (1993), "Threading the fiscal labyrinth: some issues in fiscal decentralization," *National Tax Journal*, 46: 207–27.
   (1994), "A comparative perspective on federal finance," in K. Banting, D. Brown, and T. Courchene, eds., *The Future of Fiscal Federalism*, Kingston, Ont.: Queen's University School of Public Policy.
   (1995), "Fiscal federalism and federal finance," *Anales de las 28 Jornadas de Finanzas Públicas*, Córdoba, Argentina.
Hunter, J. S. H. (1977), *Federalism and Fiscal Balance*, Canberra: Australian National University Press and Center for Research on Federal Financial Relations.
Nuñez Miñana, A. and Porto, A. (1983), *Distribución de la Coparticipación Federal de impuestos, Análisis y Alternativas*, Buenos Aires: Consejo Federal de Inversiones.
Oates W. (1972), *Fiscal Federalism*, New York: Harcourt, Brace, Jovanovich.
Prud'homme, R. (1995), "On the dangers of decentralization," Policy Research Working Paper 1252, The World Bank, Washington, DC.
Rezk, E. (1995), "Federal finance in the Argentine, Germany and Brazil," *Annals of the Arnoldshain Seminar* I, J. W. Goethe University, Frankfurt and *Anales de las Jornadas de Finanzas Públicas*, Córdoba, Argentina.
Rezk, E., Capello, M., and Ponce, C. (1996), "Arreglos fiscales interjurisdiccionales en Argentina," International Seminar on Fiscal Federalism and Federal Finances, Córdoba, Argentina.
Tanzi, V. (1995), "Fiscal federalism and decentralization: a review of some efficiency and macroeconomic aspects," in M. Bruno and B. Pleskovic, eds., *Annual World Bank Conference on Development Economics*, Washington DC.
Wiesner, E. (1994), "Fiscal decentralization of the public sector," in *Economic and Social Progress in Latin America 1994 Report*, Special Report: *Fiscal Decentralization*, ch. 1, Washington DC: Interamerican Development Bank.
World Bank (1996), *Argentina. Provincial Finances Study: Selected Issues in Fiscal Federalism*, Report No. 15487 AR, Washington, DC.

8

South Africa: an intergovernmental fiscal system in transition

JUNAID K. AHMAD

South Africa is addressing critical questions of intergovernmental fiscal relations as it undertakes the process of abolishing apartheid and redefining its system of governance. In the process, fundamental changes are being implemented in the structure of government: the constitution has been radically redesigned; new tiers of government are being created; decentralization has been initiated; electoral accountability has been extended to all irrespective of race; and, finally, the rapid delivery of basic public goods for the non-white community has commenced.

This chapter discusses how the intergovernmental fiscal system is being radically altered to support these fundamental changes.[1] In particular, it focuses on the restructuring of the provinces and the metropolitan areas of South Africa. The success and sustainability of the reform of the intergovernmental system will depend critically on the coordination of the change process for these two tiers of government. The first section of this chapter sets the stage by describing how apartheid laws influenced the intergovernmental fiscal system in South Africa. The following section of this chapter provides a discussion of how the new provinces have been constituted. A third section focuses on the structure of urban governance for the large cities of South Africa. In a final section, there is analysis of some of the tensions inherent in the changes being undertaken.[2]

Initial conditions: the consequences of apartheid

South Africa's policies of racial separation created dualism in intergovernmental fiscal relations, as in social and economic life. Overwhelming fiscal dependency in black areas coexisted with considerable self-sufficiency and autonomy in white areas.[3] This section describes how the spatial policies of apartheid affected the fiscal structures of regional and local governments in South Africa.

Table 8.1. *Shares of revenue, expenditure and transfers by tier of government,*
1990–91

	Revenue shares	Expenditure shares	Transfers as percentage of own revenue
Central	80.1	70.9	—
Province	2.0	9.7	83.6
SGT/TBVC	6.7	11.8	58.1
Local	10.6	7.6	17.8
Total	100.0	100.0	—

The national context: the apartheid structure

Before the historic elections of April 27, 1994 the structure of government
in South Africa comprised three tiers: the center, the regions and local
authorities. The regional tier included the Provinces, the Self-Governing
Territories (SGTs), and the TBVC (Transkei, Bophutaswana, Venda, and
Ciskei) group. Local authorities consisted of the Regional Service Councils
(RSCs),[4] the Black Local Authorities (BLAs) and the White Local
Authorities (WLAs). The national boundary was formed by the four
provinces and the SGT/TBVC states. Each province was served by several
RSCs. In turn, the RSCs spanned groupings of BLAs and WLAs.

Under apartheid, South Africa was a highly centralized state. According
to 1990–91 budgetary figures, for example, the central government
accounted for approximately 80 percent of the total revenues and 70
percent of the total government expenditures (table 8.1). Local governments, on the other hand, represented about 10 percent of revenues collected and about 8 percent of expenditures. Given that the provinces were
deconcentrated arms of the center, these figures actually understate the
extent of centralization.

This high level of centralization, however, masked a duality at the subnational level: nationwide about 80 percent of the revenues of white
municipalities originated from own-sources. By contrast, at the regional
level, the corresponding figures for the provinces and the SGI/TBVC states
were 16 percent and 42 percent respectively in 1990–91. The dependence
of BLAs on the center was equally high, with fiscal transfers from the
center accounting for over 75 percent of total revenues.

The system of apartheid thus fostered a dual intergovernmental structure. On one hand, the central government provided the bulk of the fiscal
resources of the TBVC, SGTs, and BLAs, and on the other, it allowed white
local authorities sufficient fiscal and regulatory autonomy to act as an inde-

pendent tier of government. The origin of this system can be traced directly to the spatial policies of apartheid (Bruckner, 1994).

Spatial policies and the structure of government

Regional governments

Apartheid reserved 87 percent of the country's land for the whites, who currently constitute only 13 percent of the population. The black community was physically herded into ten "homelands," artificial jurisdictions containing some of the most desolate territory in the country. Four of these – Transkei, Bophutaswana, Venda, and Ciskei (the TBVC states) – accepted the political fiction that they were separate nations, while the remaining six did not, preferring the status of "self-governing territories" (SGTs).

The economic conditions of the homelands resulted in weak fiscal capacities for most of these racially segregated regions. To ensure a modicum of services, the central government provided the homelands with large fiscal transfers and access to centrally guaranteed loans from capital markets and the public sector. In addition, to foster an economic base, central tax incentives were provided for economic activities to be located in the homelands. Even with the fiscal transfers from the center, the delivery of basic services was meager. This situation was in part due to the weak administrative capacities of the bureaucracies but primarily a result of the lack of political accountability of the homeland governments. With no threat of electoral change, the appointed leaders of the homelands had little incentive to serve their communities. Neither did the center provide any incentive: dedicated to sustaining apartheid, the central government remained willing to finance the growing fiscal deficits of the homelands.

Local governments

Nowhere is the impact of the spatial policies of apartheid more visible than in the cities of South Africa (Swilling, 1991). At first, influx control laws attempted to regulate the growth of the white cities by controlling the migration of blacks from the homelands. But with the need to ensure a steady stream of workers for the urban economy, and ultimately with the difficulty of regulating migration, the controls were replaced by residential laws. These permitted the blacks to remain in the white urban areas as long as they were restricted to residential settlements at the urban fringe – often one to two hours from the centers of employment. As a result of these policies, the shape and pattern of urbanized land in South African cities showed the following common characteristics:

- the physical separation of black and white cities
- an extreme dispersion and fragmentation of settlements, with high-density low-income areas located at the urban fringe
- a concentration of jobs and services centered in the white areas containing most of the retail and service activities.

Eventually, the growth of the black population in the urban areas forced the central government to give municipal status to the townships. By the mid-1980s, the metropolitan areas were characterized by municipalities divided along racial lines, called black and white local authorities (BLAs and WLAs).

Financing of BLAs

Apartheid policies forced the concentration of lower-income households in the townships and placed effective barriers to the growth of the formal manufacturing and commercial sector in the BLAs. These regulations deprived the black community of ownership of land and housing and stopped the growth of a property tax system. In the long run, the lack of property rights also prevented the black community from using land and housing as a form of collateral to generate both a growing economic and a taxable income base. User charges and rents from the delivery of services and housing by the public sector were expected to be the main sources of revenue for the BLAs. Rent and service charge boycotts were, however, used as an effective tool to protest at the lack of representative government structures, thus diminishing the already limited amount of revenue being collected by the BLAs. Together, these factors ultimately resulted in growing budget deficits. As in the case of the homelands, these were financed by fiscal transfers from central government.

The dependence on upper-tier financing is well reflected in the data for BLAs in the former Central Wits area, which was one of the richest regions in the country: as table 8.2 shows, own revenues accounted for only a small portion of total revenues. For central RSCs as a whole, own revenues of BLAs in 1991–92 were approximately 5 percent of total revenues. The rest were either central government transfers through provincial administrations, or grants for current expenditures from RSC levies (payroll and turn-over taxes).

The situation nationwide was similar, with grants from the central government accounting for over 80 percent of the revenues of the BLAs. Initially classified as bridging loans and intended for financing capital expenditure in black communities, the flows were eventually converted by the central government to explicit grants for financing current expendi-

Table 8.2. *Revenue structure of BLAs in Central Wits: 1991–92 budget (million rand, percentages in parentheses)*

	Alexandra	Diepmedow	Dobsonville	Soweto
Own revenue	0.3	3.5	0.9	9.9
	(0.86)	(6.45)	(8.11)	(5.46)
Health grant	0.7	0.6	0.0	10.1
	(2.02)	(1.10)	(0.0)	(5.57)
Provincial grant	16.8	28.2	7.4	103.4
	(48.41)	(51.93)	(66.67)	(57.03)
RSC grant for O&M	16.9	22.0	2.8	57.9
	(48.70)	(40.52)	(25.23)	(31.94)
Total	34.7	54.3	11.1	181.3
	(100)	(100)	(100)	(100)

Table 8.3. *Central Wits: contributions to net income (including interest and grants) (percentages)*

	1990–91[a]	1991–92[a]	1992–93[a]
Property taxes	40.10	52.67	51.38
of which			
Residential	12.10	15.80	15.40
Industrial/commercial	17.20	24.40	23.70
Government	10.70	12.50	12.30
Surpluses from services	23.22	11.19	13.81
Other	4.42	4.46	3.98
Interest	29.25	28.54	27.80
Grants	3.01	3.13	3.03
Total	100.00	100.00	100.00

Note: [a] Year ending June 30.

ture. In addition, as explained below, even the RSC revenues, intended to finance capital expenditures in the black communities, were increasingly diverted to finance the current deficits of BLAs.

Financing of WLAs

Relative to BLAs, the fiscal story of WLAs was one of sharp contrasts. As the data on Central Wits RSC in table 8.3 suggest, grants from other tier governments accounted, on average, for approximately 3 percent of the total income of WLAs; the corresponding figure for BLAs was close to 95 percent. Property taxes, implicit taxes on the consumption of electricity,

Table 8.4. *Shares of property taxes in total revenue: actual and required (for electricity and water surpluses to be generated from property taxes)*

		Actual share	Required share
1989–90	Johannesburg	17.5	32.4
	Roodeport	22.9	27.6
1990–91	Johannesburg	15.9	30.5
	Roodeport	23.0	27.0
1991–92	Johannesburg	22.3	30.4
	Roodeport	22.9	28.3

water, and other services (or the surpluses on trading services), and interest income provided the main sources of income for WLAs.

Several important features of the WLA finances should be noted. First, the implicit taxes on consumption of services represented an important source of income for WLAs. To ensure access to this source of revenue, local authorities were given the exclusive right to distribute services such as water and electricity. As a result, each white municipality had its own distribution network. In a relatively integrated urban setting such as Central Wits, for example, there were at least five separate local authority distribution utilities for water and electricity, and nationwide there were more than 700 at the local level. These distribution utilities purchased electricity and water in bulk and distributed it to users within their municipal boundaries. Consumers paid not only full user charges for capital, operating, and maintenance costs but also an implicit excise tax on water and electricity. Between 1990 and 1992 the tax on electricity in the various WLAs in Central Wits averaged around 20 percent. The average for water was 11 percent. There were large variations around these averages, with Johannesburg, for example, charging 45 percent implicit tax rate on electricity in 1991 and Randburg charging 22 percent for water.

The revenues from the high level of taxation of electricity and water were used to cross-subsidize other services and dampen the increases in property taxes. In fact, in the major WLAs, taxes on properties were set residually after the municipalities had decided on the level of profits to be generated from the distribution of services such as electricity and water. For example, table 8.4 shows for Johannesburg and Roodeport the required increases in the share of property taxes in total revenue if the combined amount of electricity and water surpluses were to be generated from taxes on property.

The cross-subsidy from trading accounts to property taxes, however, pointed to a second characteristic of the WLA finances: the role of cross-subsidy between businesses and residents. Overall, residents in WLAs in the Central Wits area received a rebate of the order of 35–60 percent of their property tax payment, which was not available to businesses or commercial property.

The final fiscal incidence and efficiency of this system of finance are not obvious. Clearly, by zoning businesses within white communities, WLAs have been able to cross-subsidize their residents by means of property tax rebates. However, to the extent that businesses were able to pass on the cost of these excess charges, especially in the case of non-tradables, the cross-subsidy was proportionately less. On the other hand, given the highly integrated nature of the labor market in the metropolitan areas, the potential for exporting part of this tax burden from WLAs to BLAs may have been high, thus further protecting the cross-subsidy to white residents. This latter issue has been one of the principal sources of social and political tensions generated by the policies of apartheid. By zoning businesses within their municipal boundaries, WLAs forced members of the black community to work and consume in white areas, thus indirectly financing part of the cross-subsidy to white residents.

Regional service councils

To supplement the central transfers for BLAs, the national government in 1987 also authorized the creation of RSCs/JSBs (Joint Services Boards). Given the authority to raise payroll and turnover taxes over a larger metropolitan area comprised of several WLAs and BLAs, the RSCs had the authority to finance, on a project-by-project basis, capital investments of a regional nature and also infrastructure in the black townships. Even though the mandate was to finance capital investments, the RSC budgets were progressively diverted to fund the current account deficits of BLAs – thus reducing the need for central government to continually increase fiscal transfers. For example, in the 1992–93 budget, the Central RSC allocated approximately 40 percent of its revenues to finance the current expenditures of BLAs in its jurisdictions. The remainder was used to finance capital investment in the townships.

By creating a fiscal arrangement over a group of WLAs and BLAs, RSCs formed a geographic boundary that had the potential of capturing some of the spillovers resulting from the fragmented nature of the conurbations. For example, by levying turnover and payroll taxes within the boundaries of WLAs and financing investments in the BLAs, the RSCs returned to the black community some of the share being captured by WLAs.

In sum, the policies of apartheid left a legacy of centralized government structures in South Africa. The centralization was a result, first, of spatial policies which forced the black community to be clustered in economically weak regions. Only large fiscal transfers could sustain these "homelands" and townships. Second, it was a direct result of the racial policies of segregation. It may be argued that given the economic consequences of apartheid, decentralized financing of racial policies would have created, over time, strong incentives for subnational governments to opt out of the racial system. Strong central control was therefore necessary to enforce a common system of segregation and distribute its costs across the regions.

Creating new provinces

The January 1994 interim constitution radically altered the fiscal landscape. The homelands were abolished, their territories reintegrated into South Africa, and nine new provinces were created. The provincial assignment of expenditure and taxation powers and the weak fiscal base of most new provinces have left them with significant vertical fiscal imbalances and horizontal fiscal disparities. Most provinces are, therefore, dependent on large central grants, creating potentially a significant mismatch between political and fiscal autonomy. The Financial and Fiscal Commission was established by the Constitution as an independent body to address, in effect, this tension. Its political and legislative ability to address the problem of disparities remains to be seen.

Elimination of racial jurisdictions

The elimination of racial jurisdictions – SGT/TBVC states at the regional level and BLAs at the urban level – has been central to the creation of a non-racial government in South Africa. It signaled an end to the spatial policies of apartheid and provided the geographical basis for holding elections. But more fundamentally, the new boundaries have shaped the fiscal capacities of the emerging jurisdictions and are influencing the evolution of the inter-governmental fiscal system.

The debate on drawing the boundaries of the new provinces has been influenced by several factors. Proponents of decentralization, and certainly those who feared the emergence of a Leviathan in an ANC-dominated central government, strongly advocated creating provinces of equal fiscal capacity. The proposed boundaries made little economic or political sense – giving rise to potential spillovers, where integrated urban agglomerations faced the threat of being divided, or possible community clashes, where the new jurisdictions ignored the historical and cultural roots of the different ethnic groups. In the final analysis, the idea of equalizing by reshaping boundaries rather than using fiscal transfers was rejected.

The level of urbanization in South Africa was also raised as a fundamental factor in drawing the provincial boundaries. Unlike the rest of Africa and more similar to the middle-income countries of Latin America, South Africa is a highly urbanized economy. Indeed, four metropolitan areas account for approximately 60 percent of the GDP and about 50 percent of the population.[5] In this context, it was argued that large provinces made little economic sense and proposals were put forward for the establishment of several – seventeen to twenty – smaller "regions," thus giving prominence to the urban nature of the country. It was also argued that if large provinces were to be established, the metropolitan areas should receive regional status.

The new interim constitution finally divided the country into nine provinces. The metropolitan areas were not given regional status and, according to the new constitution, are very much under the jurisdiction of the new provinces.[6] For the most part, the boundaries between provinces are based on the lines of the "development regions" established in the National Development Plan. These lines primarily reflect market forces in the private provision of goods and services. The provision of public services (the geographic scope of benefits, spillovers, and economies of scale) was rarely considered. Even so, these boundaries created fewer problems than those found in many federations, which often follow rivers, including navigable ones straddled by large metropolitan areas – a sure recipe for spillovers of costs and benefits.

Table 8.5 shows the correspondence between the nine new provinces and the fourteen former administrative entities (the four administrative provinces, the four TBVC homelands, and the six SGT homelands). Overall, nine new provincial capitals, nine new parliaments, and nine new executives ("premiers") were chosen, and nine new provincial administrative bodies were created. The problem, however, was not only one of subdivision of the four existing provinces into nine. Since the homelands had to be reabsorbed, their governments were eliminated and absorbed into the new provincial governments (in the case of civil servants). In each of these cases it was necessary to divide the fiscal affairs of the previous administrative entities among the new provinces. Only in KwaZulu/Natal did the mergers entail combining only two of the previous entities (Natal and KwaZulu), both of which fell entirely within the new province. Even now, several years after the creation of the new provinces, the practical problems of the merger of the previous jurisdictions continue to challenge the newly elected leaders.

Table 8.5. *Jurisdictional changes*

New province	Former administrative entity
Gauteng	Transvaal
Northern Province	Transvaal Venda Gazankulu Lebowa
Mpumalanga	Transvaal Bophuthatswana KaNgwane KwaNdebele
North West	Cape Transvaal Bophuthatswana
Free State	Orange Free State Bophuthatswana QwaQwa
KwaZulu/Natal	Natal KwaZulu
Eastern Cape	Cape Ciskei Transkei
Northern Cape	Cape
Western Cape	Cape

Source: Development Bank of South Africa, 1995, table 22, p. 88.

Expenditure assignment

In addition to the creation of a new regional tier with new political and administrative units, the restructuring of the intergovernmental system has led to a significant decentralization of expenditure assignments. In the previous system, the provinces were, in effect, administrative arms of the center and responsible for implementing the mandates of the center. In 1993–94 provincial governments accounted for approximately 22 percent of total public expenditure. By 1995–96, expenditure responsibilities of the provinces had increased to approximately 40 percent of all public expenditures and included major items such as health, education, and housing.

Tax assignment

Under the new constitution, the provinces can impose taxes, other than income tax, value-added tax (VAT), and other sales taxes, and they can impose surcharges. But exercise of this authority requires an Act of Parliament passed after consideration of recommendations by the Financial and Fiscal Commission. The provinces can share in revenues collected nationally from the individual income tax, the VAT, and the fuel tax.

Experience from other countries suggests that the prohibition of provincial income taxes, VAT, and other sales taxes is appropriate. Unless implemented as surcharges, provincial income taxes would entail costly duplication of administration and compliance procedures, and perhaps undesirable complexity and economic distortions. Brazilian experience shows that a provincial VAT is difficult to implement without investment in a significant administrative apparatus (McLure, 1994). Since the central government levies a VAT, provincial sales tax could impose unacceptable burdens of compliance and administration. As a result, provincial surcharges on the income tax base of the central government provide the only acceptable source of substantial amounts of own revenue for the provinces (provincial surcharge on excises was, technically, another possibility, but was barred under the new constitution). Such charges should be administered by the central fiscal authorities; in the case of the company income tax, uniform rules could be used to apportion the income of firms operating in more than one province. Surcharges would provide some provinces with substantial fiscal autonomy. By choosing higher or lower surcharge rates, they could have larger or smaller budgets and respond better to the preferences of the citizenry.

Government has, however, decided not to devolve any major tax instruments to the new provinces. As a result, in the new South Africa, while the provinces have achieved political autonomy and the new political and administrative leaderships have inherited increased expenditure responsibilities, their revenue autonomy remains curtailed. In the past, provinces' own revenues were approximately 5 percent of the revenues collected by all tiers of government. In the new intergovernmental system, they are approximately 2 percent. Central government thus continues to have access to the rate and base setting authority of the three main taxes – personal income tax, corporate income tax and VAT – leaving provinces to rely on grants from central government to overcome vertical fiscal imbalances. In this respect, the fiscal structure of South Africa resembles the highly centralized structure of Australia, rather than the relatively decentralized systems found in Canada and the United States.

Horizontal inequality
No matter which taxes are assigned to provincial governments, there are going to be substantial differences in the abilities of the various provinces

to finance public services from their own tax revenues. This is an inevitable result of the economic disparities among the provinces and the concentration of economic activities in a handful of metropolitan areas. Whereas the estimated GDP per capita for the country in 1991 was R5,042, it was as much as R10,949 for Gauteng region, but only R2,317 in Eastern Cape and R1,266 in Northern Province. The national average for personal income per capita for the same year was R2,566, compared to R4,993 for Gauteng, R1,358 in Eastern Cape, and R725 in Northern Province. These figures suggest that in addition to the need for grants to overcome the vertical imbalance, equalization transfers will be needed to reduce the fiscal disparities that currently exist.

The Financial and Fiscal Commission

The Constitution has established the Financial and Fiscal Commission (FFC) and entrusted it with a variety of powers related to intergovernmental fiscal relations. In a preliminary draft of its Framework Document (1995), the FFC defined itself as

> an independent and impartial statutory institution, accountable to the legislature, with the objective of contributing towards the creation and maintenance of an effective, equitable, and sustainable system of intergovernmental fiscal relations, rendering advice to legislatures regarding any financial and fiscal matter which has a bearing on intergovernmental fiscal relations.

The Constitution requires the national legislature to consider the recommendations of the FFC on a variety of issues, including

- the sharing of revenues with the provinces
- taxes, surcharges, and user charges to be imposed by provincial governments
- borrowing by provincial and local governments
- guarantees of loans to the provinces.

In addition, the FFC is supposed to make recommendations on taxes proposed by local governments, the sharing of provincial revenues with local governments, and provincial guarantees of loans to local governments. Thus, in principle, the FFC could be an extremely important part of the system of fiscal relationships in South Africa. Yet, it is an appointed body, with no independent power base. Its eventual role remains to be seen.

Under the Constitution, each province is entitled to "an equitable share of revenue collected nationally to enable it to provide services and to exercise and perform its powers and functions." The FFC has articulated three objectives of intergovernmental grants: efficient resource allocations; fiscal equity; and development of fiscally sound and democratically responsive provincial government. It proposes using an objective and relatively simple grant formula to achieve this, explicitly rejecting the use of *ad hoc* grants. The grant system explicitly addresses the issues of vertical and horizontal fiscal balance.

Vertical balance

Reflecting the constitutional allocation of functions of government and its beliefs that the most pressing service deficits are at the subnational level and that most activities of the central government do not grow with population, the FFC in 1996 proposed a freeze in real spending of the central government for the following three years; thus all public revenues made available by growth (conservatively estimated to increase from 2.5 percent per year to 3 percent over five years), except those needed to reduce the budget deficits from 5.8 percent to 4.5 percent of GDP, should be available to the provinces via grants. Under the FFC's proposals, the central government's share of financial resources would drop from 56.5 percent in the fiscal year 1995–96 to 53.1 percent in 2000–01.

Horizontal balance

The FFC has proposed a three-part grant formula. The unconditional "basic grant" is intended to provide for each province "the fiscal resources necessary to function as an efficient and accountable government for its people." This part is based on population figures; in recognition of the special problems of the rural areas (substantially greater poverty levels, higher unemployment, and the greater cost of providing services) each rural person has been counted as equal to 1.25 urban persons.

The second part is intended to allow provision of a "national standard" level of public services. This part comprises grants for primary and secondary education (a given amount per student aged 5–17) and primary health care (a given amount per qualifying member of the population).

The third part of the formula focuses on "fiscal capacity equalization" of the provinces. FFC has proposed a surcharge rate on the personal income tax base as a source of own revenues for the provinces. On the basis of this tax instrument the FFC has proposed an equalization formula. The formula equalizes around the national average level of tax capacity and ensures that the equalization component is self-financing without imposing any additional claim by the provincial governments on the private economy.

Funding

The FFC proposes to fund grants from a pool of revenues from the individual income tax, the VAT, and the fuel tax, instead of having different sharing rates for each. Besides being simpler, this avoids the risk of the central fiscal authorities concentrating resources on the taxes with the lowest sharing rates. Funding of "national standards" grants would be given first priority, with the pool of funding available for "basic grants" determined as a residual.

Phase-in

This grant structure would result in reductions in shares of grant funds (in real grants in two cases) going to four of the provinces (Western Cape, Eastern Cape, Northern Cape, and Free State) and increases in shares going to the other five. To allow for orderly retrenchment and efficient expansion, the FFC proposes to phase in its formula over a five-year period, with floors (a fall of 3–4 percent) and ceilings (a rise of 5–6 percent) on annual changes in real grants.

Structure of urban governance

As new provinces were being created, a similar process was unfolding at the urban level, with the creation of new metropolitan governments. In deciding the organization of the metropolitan systems, the urban political leadership faced several options. One was to maintain the status quo of jurisdictional fragmentation,[7] or a structure of urban governance under which the responsibility for the same functions lies with many local governments operating in the area. In the case of South Africa, the proposal was to merge adjacent BLAs and WLAs into new municipalities – a twinning of sorts – and allow several of these "twins" to operate as independent municipalities. A second option was to create a centralized metropolitan government with the BLAs and WLAs in each urban area being merged into a single local government. A third option, one that was not actively debated, was the model of functional fragmentation, under which the provision of services is area-wide and is shared between general-purpose local government and autonomous agencies. Applied to South Africa, this model implied that service utilities could serve several municipalities (the "twins") or a metropolitan government.

The process of urban restructuring is continuing. The optimal structure of urban governance in South Africa will eventually depend on how the political process in South Africa ranks the objectives of fiscal stability, income distribution, and efficiency as the dominating concerns of public policy. In practice, the political process has given equal importance to each of these factors and the emerging structure of the urban governance in the metropolitan areas reflects these tensions.[8] This section discusses some of the criteria that are influencing the structure of urban governance and uses the examples of Johannesburg and Cape Town to describe the process of change at the urban level.

The organizational structure of metropolitan areas in South Africa will be largely influenced by political considerations, different dimensions of efficiency in the delivery and financing of services, distributional objectives, and the concern of central government that financing of local services does not undermine the macroeconomic stability of the economy (Ahmad, 1997).

Political considerations

Abolishing the racial basis of the local government system is a fundamental political consideration in the reform of urban governance in South Africa. As in the case of the provinces, a redrawing of jurisdictional boundaries and a merger of BLAs and WLAs either into a metropolitan structure or as "twins" in a model of jurisdictional fragmentation is, therefore, inevitable.

Political considerations also include the creation of a system of local government through which local council members can be held accountable and responsible for their decisions. The primary instrument to achieve this objective is the electoral system. However, efficient markets, especially for land and capital, can complement the influence of the electoral process in holding in check the behavior of local officials. Similarly, accountability is enhanced through access to direct fiscal instruments by local authorities. Officials can be held responsible for their actions if, at the margin, decisions to alter the level of services are reflected in increases or decreases in tax rates directly under their control.

In considering the political dimensions of structuring urban governance, therefore, policy-makers have the difficult task of choosing an organization for financing and delivering services that is best able to strengthen the political institutions of democracy while enabling markets and fiscal instruments to hold local officials accountable. How this interplay between political institutions, markets, and fiscal instruments evolves will certainly influence the choice between jurisdictional and functional fragmentation and a centralized metropolitan form of government for the cities of South Africa.

Efficiency considerations

Efficiency can be defined along several dimensions. It includes the extent to which the preferences of the constituencies can be reflected in the local budgets and also the extent to which technical efficiency can be achieved by taking advantage of the economies of scale inherent in the delivery of services.

In the case of South African cities, locational efficiency is an equally important issue. With the end of apartheid's zoning policies, the distribution of population and business activity over the urban areas is in a state of flux. Already, in several of the major metropolitan areas, there has been a decentralization of employment from the core cities into the surrounding white municipalities. In addition, in some cities, there has been an outflow of white residents from the city center and an inflow of black residents from adjacent townships and regions. In this context, it will be crucial that any strategy for financing urban infrastructure does not distort the locational choices facing individuals and firms. In the case of South Africa's metropolitan areas, drawing of narrow municipal boundaries may result in unequal fiscal burdens in the financing of urban services. The potential for distorting locational decisions would therefore be high.

The different models of urban governance involve tradeoffs over the various dimensions of efficiency. Consumer preferences are best reflected in homogeneous and small local government structures but could lead to overall losses in consumer welfare if fragmented local authorities attempt to deliver and finance services whose benefits and costs are area-wide. On the other hand, locational distortions are minimized and technical efficiency is realized under a metropolitan structure.

Income redistribution

The mobility of factors at the local level is an important consideration in limiting the responsibility for income redistribution to upper-tier governments. Cognizant of this important constraint on implementing redistributive policies at the local level, South Africa has begun to manage the issue of income redistribution through the intergovernmental system by coordinating redistributive policies among different levels of government. Urban governments are therefore expected to play a part in this process.

In particular, to avoid the locational distortions that would be associated with redistributive measures, a more consolidated urban governmental structure such as a metropolitan system is being advocated. A metro-wide structure would not only minimize the locational impacts, but could also achieve efficiency objectives by accommodating wide variations in levels of urban service demand without imposing a uniform level of service provision. In other words, instead of completely passing on the responsibility for redistribution to the central government, centralization at the local level through some form of metropolitan governance structure provides local authorities with the flexibility to implement redistributive measures without significantly reducing efficiency.

Fiscal stability

Access to significant long-term finance will be required to improve the standard of municipal services for the black community. However, borrowing by city governments, indeed by any large local government, raises the potential problem of moral hazard. The sheer economic size of the metropolitan areas of South Africa suggests that central government would face considerable political and financial resistance to allowing such cities to default and face bankruptcy in a situation of financial duress. South Africa's cities may be "too big to be allowed to fail." In this context, capital markets would perceive the debt of urban governments in South Africa to be an implicit obligation of central government and, consequently, instead of acting as a disciplining device may, in fact, be "too generous" in financing their investments.

Central government in South Africa is debating alternative mechanisms for addressing this policy problem of enabling access to capital markets by local governments while avoiding the pitfalls of moral hazard. Two different mechanisms are being assessed. First, government is exploring the possibility of legislating clear rules of "bankruptcy" for local government. International examples being discussed include the US model of a financial control board and the New Zealand model of court-appointed receivership. Under both, a worsening fiscal situation of a local government is addressed by the imposition of a control process that takes away managerial autonomy from the elected officials and passes it to an independent board. A buffer is thus created between different tiers of government. To be credible the process will need to impose the cost of "bankruptcy" on both the elected officials (for example, loss of autonomy) and creditors (uncertainty about payment).

Second, government is looking at the possibility of centralizing the borrowing powers of local government whereby the center would either borrow directly and on-lend to the local governments or allow a public financial intermediary (PFI) to perform this on-lending operation. For several reasons, however, centralization of borrowing powers may fail to provide macroeconomic control over the fiscal affairs of government as a whole (Ahmad, 1997). International experience from several countries – and indeed the past history of South Africa – suggests that the allocation of credit through public institutions inevitably gets embroiled in a political process. Capital does not necessarily flow to the most productive but often to those who are politically the most astute. In such cases, government borrowing may be inefficient and the subsequent investments generally unproductive. This has the potential of contributing to a gradual loss of fiscal control as more and more borrowing is required to deliver a minimum level of public services. In addition, the institutional incentives of PFIs are such that they may not be immune to the moral hazard syndrome. In fact, more than in the case of subnational governments, which generally have access to tax bases and whose politicians have to face an electoral process and could, therefore, face the consequences of their myopic decisions, PFI employees are seen as responsible to central authorities and their debt perceived as an off-budget obligation of central government. In fact, by removing the direct relationship between capital markets and subnational governments, PFIs can undermine a potential instrument for ensuring the efficiency and accountability of local government.

An alternative, but also a complement, to the process of control boards described above is to structure urban governance in such a way as to minimize the problem of moral hazard. A possible solution would be to privatize public goods, or alternatively, as Baumol and Lee (1991) suggest, create "contestable markets" for the participation of the private sector in the financing and delivery of public goods. Simply put, changes in technology worldwide now permit the privatization of the delivery and financing of what are still considered public goods in many countries including South Africa. These include, for example, distribution of water and electricity at the retail level, transportation services, and garbage disposal. By placing these in the private domain, governments may avoid the problem of moral hazard: bankruptcy of these entities would enable other private sector parties to bid for their assets. This lack of competitive pressure and threat of takeover in the public delivery of municipal services leaves open the issue of the implicit financial obligation of central government and the assumption that one tier of government under financial duress would be supported by another tier.

The privatization route has the additional advantage of enabling service deliverers to access financial equity as well as borrow in the capital markets. Because equity-holders stand to lose in the case of bankruptcy, the participation of financial equity provides an incentive internal to the structure of the service provider to monitor debt, creating another layer of protection against moral hazard that is not present in a public system of delivery. In addition, the availability of private sector bond insurance provides an added mechanism for ensuring that central governments do not take on the role of "banker of last resort." In the event of an issuer default, the bond insurers guarantee the timely payment of interest and principal in accordance with the issuer's original payment schedule. The insurer will often work with the issuer to address the financial problems and, therefore, minimize its own losses. Generally, the guarantee is irrevocable and the bonds are guaranteed for their life regardless of what may happen to the issuer.

The model of private sector delivery and the availability of bond insurance agencies suggest that devolving financial and delivery responsibilities of governments, if possible, onto the private sector is an important component of ensuring macroeconomic stability. This implies that choosing the functional fragmentation model of metropolitan governance, with the area-wide delivery of services in the private sector, is an alternative tool for achieving the fiscal stability objective of central government.

Johannesburg and Cape Town: two examples

The metropolitan areas of Johannesburg and Cape Town epitomize the changes occurring at the city level in local government's fiscal affairs. The situation in both cities suggests that a hybrid structure of urban governance is a model that may be applicable for the large metropolitan areas. But different political processes in the two cities may lead to very different models being finally implemented.

A metropolitan government has been created in Johannesburg and Cape Town. Political considerations of ensuring a non-racial structure and the recognition that urban governments will have responsibility for implementing some measure of income redistribution were two important justifications for the creation of a metropolitan government. The merger of adjacent BLAs and WLAs – the twinning option – would have only partially fulfilled the political objectives of creating a non-racial local government structure. In all of the major urban centers, some fiscally strong WLAs were physically not close enough to any BLAs to justify a merger. In addition, in many cases there would be significant fiscal disparities between the newly merged BLAs and WLAs. A larger metropolitan boundary was necessary to avoid the potential locational distortions that might emerge from local financing of services within narrow administrative boundaries.

Fiscal autonomy and accountability were also important in the move towards a metropolitan structure. Intergovernmental transfers could, of course, be used to compensate for the fiscal disparities between the different "twinned structures" and support a more fragmented local government structure – the jurisdictional fragmentation model of urban governance. There was sufficient evidence from the past, however, to suggest that reliance on intergovernmental transfers might reduce the fiscal autonomy and accountability of local governments – two important elements in ensuring the benefits of fiscal decentralization. In addition, there was significant concern about the predictability of such transfers and the uncertainty it would create in local government planning. Finally, political leadership at the central government level was convinced that the fiscal base of the urban sector would be sufficient to support the expansion of municipal services into the black community while freeing central government fiscal resources to fund national public goods. Such horizontal cross-subsidy between municipalities could take place within a metropolitan system.

While a metropolitan tier was perceived as necessary for achieving fiscal autonomy and accountability of local government *vis-à-vis* the central government, it was nevertheless viewed as too far removed from the communities. To further enhance the accountability of officials, bring government closer to the constituencies and, therefore, improve economic efficiency, Johannesburg and Cape Town adopted a two-tier metropolitan structure: a first, metropolitan tier overseeing a group of "twinned" municipalities in the second tier. In addition, a second tier provides a political check on attempts by the metropolitan tier to engage in extensive redistribution. It offers, therefore, a level of protection for the former WLAs and may have been an important necessary concession to the white community to allow the formation of a metropolitan tier in the first place.

While the two-tier model was initially politically accepted and was in the process of being implemented, the issue of the allocation of fiscal responsibilities – expenditure and tax assignments – remains unresolved, and is still in a state of flux. If implemented, privatization of municipal services will significantly influence the assignment of expenditure between the metro and the municipal tier and, subsequently, the assignment of taxes.

Expenditure responsibilities

It was suggested that concerns about fiscal stability and operational efficiency favored the privatization of municipal services. The extent of the economies of scale in the delivery process will be an important determinant of whether the municipal service should be privatized at the metro-politan or municipal level and whether there will be one or multiple pro-viders in an urban jurisdiction. Where economies of scale do not exist (for example, in garbage removal) several private providers could operate in one metropolitan area, each serving a different municipality. In either case, private providers facing competitive pressures would have the incentive to respond to the willingness-to-pay of the customers and tailor the stan-dard of delivery to demand. For local public goods, on the other hand, eco-nomic efficiency suggests that the division of labor between the metropolitan tier and the municipalities would depend on which jurisdic-tion benefits from the expenditures. Street lighting, for example, could well be a municipal responsibility. Roads, to take another example, with met-ropolitan-wide spillovers in costs and benefits would be better financed by the metro tier.

If privatization of municipal services is accepted as part of the reform process, a critical element of urban governance will be the regulatory func-tion of government. This function is needed to ensure, in particular, that a private monopoly does not emerge in delivery of services, especially where direct competition in the market is not possible. The general issue of whether regulatory functions should be central or local or whether they are a concurrent responsibility of different tiers of government is beyond the scope of this chapter. However, given that most of the municipal ser-vices should be privatized at the metropolitan level, it is logical that the metro tier should have the regulatory responsibility of overseeing the per-formance of the privatized entities and managing the privatization process.

In addition to the role of regulator, a fundamental function of the metro tier would be in the area of income redistribution. Given the fiscal dispar-ities between the different municipalities, the metro tier could have the responsibility for equalizing their fiscal capacities.[9] However, if the model of functional fragmentation is accepted and municipal services are deliv-ered through the private sector, an additional component of the metro's distributional responsibility could be to target fiscal transfers directly to low-income households, for example, through vouchers, to ensure access to a basic minimum level of services.[10] Because this type of fiscal assistance would be to individual households, access to a minimum level of service within a metropolitan area would not be location-specific. Locational deci-sions of households would therefore be undertaken on the basis of eco-nomic costs and benefits rather than fiscal considerations. In addition, by allocating the responsibility for distributional objectives directly to the public sector, the service deliverer would have the flexibility of focusing on operational efficiency and pricing services according to economic criteria. This separation of distributional and efficiency objectives in the pricing and delivery of municipal services would also promote locational efficiency.

Tax assignments

The discussion on tax assignment takes as its starting point the expenditure assignments discussed above and that, in the short to medium run, the tax instruments originally assigned to the RSCs, WLAs, and BLAs will become available to the new urban governments.[11]

Assigning the payroll and turnover taxes

Zoning policies separated the residences of the blacks from their places of employment and purchase of consumption goods. In addition, for administrative convenience, payroll taxes were collected at the source of employment and turnover taxes in the jurisdiction in which the taxed transactions occurred. In both cases, this was primarily in the WLAs. To the extent that each metropolitan jurisdiction will include both BLAs and WLAs and, therefore, the residences and the places of employment and consumption of the black community, it would be more efficient and equitable to assign the turnover and payroll taxes to the metro tier.[12]

In addition, while the incidence of these taxes is on the residents of both the former WLAs and BLAs, most of the revenues will be used to fund expenditures for low-income black households. Given its potential redistributive function, the assignment of the payroll and turnover taxes to the metro tier is, therefore, appropriate. At the same time, given that low-income communities are part of these tax bases, there would be an incentive for metropolitan authorities not to be excessive in pursuing their redistributive objectives.

Central fiscal transfers

Central transfers have traditionally been used for redistributional purposes. It is expected that in the new fiscal system the transfers will continue to be directed to achieve distributional objectives. The metro tier would, therefore, be the appropriate tier at the local level to manage these transfers.

Property taxes

Property taxes are a mainstay of finance in urban areas and an efficient tax instrument for financing local public goods. In addition, autonomy in setting property rates can help establish the accountability of local officials. Residential property taxes should, therefore, remain at the level of the municipalities to ensure that local officials can respond to the preferences of their constituencies.

However, there is an important redistributive issue regarding the use of commercial property taxes. As in the case of payroll and turnover taxes, the issue arises from the location of residences and businesses. As discussed earlier, apartheid policies zoned economic activities in WLAs and provided these jurisdictions with exclusive access to commercial property taxes. Given that economic activities will remain "locked-in" in the former WLAs for some time to come, a case can be made on redistributive grounds for the sharing of revenues from commercial property between the municipalities and the metro tier.

Inman (1996) also provides an argument based on fiscal efficiency for transferring the non-residential property tax to the metropolitan tier. Based on the experience of several metropolitan areas in North America, Inman suggests the possibility of municipalities using the commercial property tax base to indulge in a "beggar-thy-neighbor" type of tax competition. To avoid this outcome, Inman suggests a Minneapolis-St. Paul model of sharing the commercial tax base at the metropolitan level. The objective would be to levy a common commercial property tax at the metropolitan level, pool the revenues, and transfer it back to the municipalities on a formula basis (e.g. capacity equalization or poverty targeting).

Surcharges on municipal services
If current municipal services are privatized, local authorities could preserve their access to revenues from water and electricity by converting the implicit surcharges into explicit excise taxes on utility services. To minimize locational effects and tax avoidance and given that the services will be delivered at the metropolitan level, such taxes should be assessed and collected on a uniform basis at the metropolitan level rather than at the municipal level. If fiscal transfers to low-income households are financed by explicit taxes on these services, it may be administratively easier to have the service providers act as the administrators of taxes and subsidies. Alternatively, the service provider could provide cross-subsidies between households at different income levels through the pricing of the services – a less preferable option given the potential for distorting prices and, once introduced, the tendency of the public sector to "tax" private entities through greater cross-subsidies.

In sum, in a two-tier metropolitan system it would be efficient and equitable to assign central fiscal transfers, payroll and turnover taxes, and excise taxes to the metropolitan tier. Residential property taxes would remain at the municipal level while taxes on commercial property could be shared between the two tiers. This tax assignment is based on the allocation of expenditure suggested earlier which included giving the metro tier the primary role in income redistribution while privatizing the basic municipal services. The assignment is also based on minimizing potential locational inefficiencies and providing a check on the extent to which metropolitan governments can undertake redistribution of income.

The structure of urban governance in the major metropolitan areas of South Africa is undergoing a dramatic transformation. The model of separate municipalities has given rise to a hybrid metropolitan system in Johannesburg and Cape Town. The abolition of the racial basis of the cities, distributional concerns, and the legacy of apartheid's spatial polices were major determinants of the choice of a metropolitan system. Establishing greater fiscal autonomy – for local authorities from central government and for municipalities from the metropolitan tier – was an important consideration in favoring a two-tier structure.

However, the two-tier system is being questioned. In the case of Johannesburg, metropolitan government has used an inefficient and *ad hoc* rule for implementing interjurisdictional equalization. It has imposed a uniform property tax rate across the metropolitan area and shifted any resulting fiscal surplus from one jurisdiction to another. Not only has this resulted in sharp increases in property taxes in many jurisdictions – of the order of 100–200 percent – but shifts in fiscal flows have also subsidized the deficits of municipalities whose credit control is weak. In addition, municipalities with surpluses now have an incentive to ensure their elimination. In the case of Cape Town, the RSC revenues have been used to expand the metropolitan bureaucracy and provide *ex post* budget relief for the municipalities. As a result, in both cities, the *ad hoc* fiscal system has produced inefficient redistribution and political fighting between municipalities over the use of funds. As a consequence, delivery of local goods to the black community has fallen far below expectation.

In the face of this crisis, central government has adopted the position of favoring the model of a centralized metropolitan government – the "mega-city model," as it has been named in South Africa – with municipalities being converted into administrative wards. The assumption is that a centralized model will facilitate more rational systems of redistribution and accelerate delivery of services. In the coming weeks and months, the political debate will decide whether the mega-city model will be implemented nationwide or whether cities will be given the local autonomy to go their own route. At this stage, Johannesburg seems to be moving toward a mega-city model. Cape Town, on the other hand, is debating the possibility of a two-tiered structure integrated through a fiscal system as described above.

Unresolved tensions: the evolution of intergovernmental fiscal relations

Four important issues are shaping the evolution of the intergovernmental system in South Africa: the extent of fiscal autonomy and accountability of provinces and cities, the level of capacity at different levels of government to manage decentralized responsibilities, the role of financial markets, and the relationship between provinces and the metropolitan areas. How these issues will be addressed will determine the extent of decentralization of the governmental tiers and the relative role provinces and metropolitan areas will play in the economic affairs of the country.

Accountability, fiscal control, and cooperative governance

A major tension that is emerging in the fiscal affairs of the different tiers of government is between accountability and fiscal stability. One perspective, perhaps that of central ministries, is that fiscal stability and control is best achieved, especially during a period of transition, by having central control of tax instruments and by limiting the borrowing powers of subnational governments. This approach assumes that the political process is in its infancy and markets sufficiently imperfect that control from the top is necessary to maintain fiscal discipline.

Another perspective, perhaps that of the Financial and Fiscal Commission, is that political accountability and fiscal control may be achieved simultaneously by providing subnational governments with own revenues and direct access to capital markets. In this model, the threat of having to raise own taxes and face capital market prices for wrong policy decisions is assumed to be more effective in limiting the potentially myopic behavior of politicians than the alternative of central controls. The latter would have to be through administrative and bureaucratic budgeting rules and monitoring systems for the flow of funds. The decentralized model of accountability and fiscal control would also suggest that there are alternative approaches to managing the risks of decentralization (for example, legislating a bankruptcy process for the public sector and managing implicit financial obligations explicitly) which do not require full centralization of fiscal powers. In fact, the current fiscal crisis of Johannesburg and some of the provinces and the center's insistence on no "bail-outs" will test whether the center will fall prey to the pressures of moral hazard or establish the framework for subnational fiscal discipline.[13]

South Africa has chosen, for the moment, not to provide provincial governments with a tax base, relying instead on central grants to fund provincial expenditures. It remains to be seen if this system will enable the twin objectives of political accountability and fiscal macro control to be achieved. It may be hypothesized that without the threat of having to use own taxes, provincial leadership may not have the incentive to spend efficiently. The potential political game that may be played is one of a provincial leadership's ability to shift the responsibility for a lack of delivery onto central authority in the hope of inducing additional funding *ex post*. In other words, the problem of moral hazard also exists on the fiscal side of funding governments.

Grant funding also raises the problem of explicit and implicit conditionality and unfunded mandates. Currently, the public sector wage structure and sectoral conditionality on spending (percentages for health and education, in particular) are set from above, leaving provinces with limited expenditure flexibility. In addition, with central ministries losing expenditure responsibilities but maintaining the ability to set national standards, there is a possibility that provinces may be saddled with unfunded mandates or the exact opposite may happen as central government policies end up being ignored. In combination with the lack of fiscal instruments, the conditionality of the grants may be creating a situation where the new provinces are, like their predecessors, deconcentrated arms of the center. Cognizant of the fact that elected political bodies will have difficulty in accepting administrative roles, there is a move towards a concept of "cooperative governance." This concept is not well defined but entails a joint approach, or cooperation, between provincial and central government in budgeting and delivery implementation.[14] What it entails in practice is still to be determined.

The issue of fiscal autonomy and accountability is also central to the mega-city debate. It is slowly being recognized that the issue of redistribution is not at the heart of the choice between a centralized metropolitan government and a two-tiered model. Policies of redistribution can be designed equally well under either model of metropolitan government. In the two-tiered system, for example, an intra-metropolitan fiscal transfer system can be designed to achieve intermunicipal fiscal equalization as well as interpersonal equalization through poverty-targeted grants to households. Instead, what is at issue is accountability and governance. A two-tier model, with municipalites having access to own taxes, may provide greater checks and balances than a centralized system. In sum, therefore, the fiscal instruments offered to provinces relative to the center and to municipalities in the intra-metropolitan fiscal system will be important determinants of the overall level of accountability of the intergovernmental system.

Capacity and decentralized responsibility

Limited capacity in public administration and political management is an important constraint in the delivery process in South Africa today. This lack of capacity is particularly evident at the provincial level and has been presented in policy debates as an important argument in favor of not giving fiscal responsibilities to provinces. Instead, it is argued that a program of capacity-building needs to be undertaken before a process of decentralization can be initiated.

The relationship between capacity constraints and the feasibility of decentralization is not clear cut. A unique study of decentralization experience in Colombia suggests that capacity-building actually increased with decentralization (Fiszbein, 1995). Expressed simply, giving responsibility to lower-tier governments and opening the electoral process put pressures on subnational governments to invest in a capacity-building process. This demand-driven approach seems to have elicited greater demand for capacity-building when compared to the traditional top-down, supply-driven system adopted in many countries. In addition, the experience of Colombia seems to suggest that a demand-driven system leads to a more diverse supply response. The private and public sectors and community organizations all have a role in enhancing the capacity of both the political and administrative leadership.

The issue of capacity also raises the possibility of adopting an asymmetric approach to decentralization. Not all provinces or local governments are equal in terms of fiscal and human capacity. These differences suggest that decentralization of fiscal responsibilities need not be implemented uniformly across the nation and across all levels of governments. For example, major cities may be candidates for inheriting greater fiscal responsibilities than smaller towns or rural local governments. Similarly, one or two provinces may have the capacity to better manage their own affairs. In these circumstances, the center could adopt a phased approach to decentralization.

Separating fiscal from financial issues: some general considerations

The role of governments in the financial sector has important implications for the design of an intergovernmental fiscal system. To begin with, the fiscal base of subnational governments, which is defined by both the vertical and the horizontal dimensions of fiscal decentralization, establishes, in effect, the "collateral" that will determine their access to financial markets. Policy uncertainties on the fiscal side, therefore, such as uncertainty in the allocation of tax bases or the unpredictability of intergovernmental transfers, will influence the extent to which different tiers of government can take advantage of financial markets. It may even be that the uncertainty will be read by capital markets as the national government's way of centralizing fiscal powers. Subnational debt may then be interpreted as being a direct obligation of central government. Defining the fiscal rules is therefore a necessary step in enabling access to capital markets and resolving the moral hazard problem.

More importantly, government's involvement in the financial sector dampens the economic role of capital markets in allocating credit and signaling creditworthiness. The financial sector's ability to promote economic efficiency and the accountability of local officials, important elements of a decentralized model of government, are adversely affected. Thus, promoting fiscal decentralization by only devolving tax and expenditure responsibilities will not allow local governments to take advantage of the efficiency gains that can be achieved through the interplay of political jurisdictions and capital markets in the financing and delivery of services at the local level. To draw an analogy, would a decentralized model of local government be effective if labor mobility between local jurisdictions was controlled?

In addition, if the centralization of borrowing powers facilitates access to finance by local authorities that are not creditworthy or makes capital more "affordable," central government will have provided, in effect, an implicit subsidy through the financial sector. If the objective is to provide such subsidies, a preferable alternative would be for central government to convert the implicit financial subsidy into an explicit fiscal grant and allow local authorities to pledge such transfer as collateral in accessing capital markets. Such lump-sum transfers would not distort the price of capital and would enable local authorities to establish a direct relationship with capital markets. Fiscal subsidies have the added advantage of being transparent and more easily monitored, and stand a greater chance of being held in check via the political process.

Centralization of borrowing powers may distort the economic incentives faced by local authorities in other ways. As von Hagen (1991) and Wildasin (1995) suggest, fiscal restraints on capital market activities are often circumvented and the resulting behavior – for example, dipping into pension funds and engaging in off-budget activities – may impact on the allocation of resources. Wildasin (1995) suggests that restricting the access to capital markets may also lead local authorities to reduce their investments in local goods. In the case of South Africa, the political pressure for the rapid delivery of local services is sufficiently high that central government may be forced to compensate local governments for the restriction on borrowing by eventually funding local services through intergovernmental transfers. In effect, this would mean that central tax bases would be funding local goods – bringing back centralization through the back door.

In sum, the discussion suggests that keeping the fiscal and financial roles of government separate and decentralizing borrowing powers may be fundamental in ensuring an efficient system of intergovernmental fiscal relations. In particular, such measures would provide the incentive for local governments to be more efficient in their delivery and financing of services. Equally important, the separation may be necessary to ensure that government intervention does not impede the functioning of the capital markets – a distinct possibility in the context of low-income countries where financial markets are thin and government is the predominant borrower in the economy.

Central government in South Africa has established several public financial intermediaries to assist in the financing of urban and rural infrastructure. The regulatory framework for determining the relationship between the public and private financial intermediaries and fiscal and financial dimensions of intergovernmental relations remains to be clarified.

Provinces and metropolitan governments

In most countries, boundaries between regions and the relationship between different tiers of government were created in a pre-urban setting. In such a setting, where the population was largely rural and the economic base linked to agriculture, it may have made economic sense to provide regional governments with substantial fiscal powers and to make local governments subordinate to them. In South Africa's urbanized setting, however, where most of the population lives in urban areas and local governments provide most subnational services, should all local governments be subordinate to regions? The question is specially relevant where cities are so large that it seems appropriate to establish some form of metropolitan government.

It may be argued that there is little reason to make all local governments – especially those of larger metropolitan areas – totally subordinate to regions. In a modern urban society many public services have either local or national significance, but not regional significance. This line of reasoning has important implications for the structure of intergovernmental fiscal relations. First, it suggests that some functions that are commonly assigned to regional governments may be best assigned to metropolitan governments or to the central government. Second, central government may consider giving some metropolitan governments the status of a region.

The South African constitution is, however, not clear on whether all local governments including the metropolitan governments are under the regulation of provinces or whether local governments are an independent sphere of government. As a result several tensions are emerging. First, provinces are politically reluctant to allow fiscal transfers to be sent directly to the cities. Second, central government has centralized the borrowing authorities of provinces on the correct premise that provinces do not have the fiscal capacity to enter into a direct relationship with capital markets and that permitting such a relationship to emerge would have been fraught with moral hazard. This has left the central government in a difficult political position for passing legislation enabling cities to go directly to the market. Third, the decision not to provide a tax base to the provinces has prevented central government from providing a surcharge on personal income tax to the metropolitan areas and eliminating the inefficient turnover tax. Fourth, by not providing provinces with a tax base, the center has left open the possibility of the provinces taking a share of metropolitan and local government revenues – a possibility not ruled out by the Constitution. Ultimately, in the case of Gauteng, which is primarily an urban complex, the province could have played the role of a metropolitan tier – the fiscal equalizer as described in the case of Johannesburg. The establishment of Gauteng province precluded this option.

The intergovernmental fiscal system in South Africa is still in a state of flux. It is truly a system in transition. The changes that are taking place are fundamental. A new constitution has been established which has catalyzed the process of restructuring the political, economic, and fiscal relations between different tiers of government. In doing so, the leaders of South Africa have attempted to create a democracy, begin the process of delivery of public goods to all irrespective of race, foster economic growth, and maintain fiscal stability. Few nations have attempted such a transformation in such a short period and few have achieved such a level of success as South Africa. Whether the success will persist will be determined by the changes in the intergovernmental system of the country.

Notes

1 The chapter draws on McLure (1994) and Ahmad (1997).

2 The process of reform in South Africa is a very dynamic one and one which is undergoing rapid changes. Therefore, the story outlined in this chapter is of necessity incomplete.

3 Differences between white and black areas were not the only ones; apartheid also imposed differences between the Indian and Colored population. For expositional economy, this chapter focuses on the differences between black and white.

4 In Province of Natal these were called Joint Service Boards (JSBs).

5 In fact, the urban sector accounts for over 80 percent of GDP and approximately 62 percent of the population. Agriculture and the rural economy accounts for only 5 percent of GDP. That approximately 40 percent of the population still resides in rural areas is due in large part to the spatial policies of apartheid.

6 In this sense, the new constitution adopts a regional approach inherent in constitutions written during a time when cities did not exist, urbanization was limited, and economies were predominantly rural. As argued later, it is not clear from a public finance perspective, whether, in the context of an urbanized society, externalities and spillovers have a regional basis or are defined on national and local levels only.

7 Albeit without the racial nomenclature.

8 In their international review of the structure of urban governance, Bahl and Linn (1992) conclude that while the centralized metropolitan model seems to dominate, the structure of urban governance in most countries is a hybrid.

9 The experience of Minneapolis-St. Paul in metropolitan tax base sharing provides an interesting case study of how fiscal disparities were reduced across 188 municipalities (Rusk, 1993).

10 It may be more appropriate for the national government to finance a voucher program but for a metropolitan government to implement it.

11 See Wildasin (1993) and McLure (1994) for an analysis of the efficiency of existing local taxes, alternate fiscal instruments for local governments, and the efficiency and equity implications of relying on central tax bases for financing local infrastructure investments.

12 The incidence of the payroll and turnover taxes will, in practice, be spread more widely than just the metro area, as in the case of Johannesburg. There may be a case, therefore, for sharing these revenues nationally, not just on a metropolitan basis. This might, however, reduce the fiscal autonomy of the metropolitan tier as the metros would, as a result, rely more on transfers from other tiers. This tradeoff between efficiency of tax instrument and autonomy of metropolitan governments is better addressed by replacing payroll and turnover taxes with alternate fiscal instruments. For a discussion of this point, see Wildasin (1993) and McLure (1994).

13 The management of subnational fiscal crises including addressing the "bankruptcy" of several provinces and local governments has been an important part of the evolution of the intergovernmental system during this period of

transition for South Africa. It is an issue that has not been discussed in this chapter. However, it should be stressed that the management of these crises while a regulatory framework is still being developed is one of the success stories of government in the field of fiscal management.

14 An important aspect of the intergovernmental system and at the heart of the concept of "cooperative governance" is the design and implementation of the budgeting system also known as the Medium Term Expenditure Framework. This chapter has not analyzed the evolution of this very important budgeting framework, which is also one of the success stories of government.

References

Ahmad, Junaid (1997), "Structure of urban governance in South Africa," in David E. Wildasin, ed., *Fiscal Aspects of Evolving Federations*, Cambridge: Cambridge University Press.

Bahl, Roy, and Linn, Johannes (1992), *Urban Public Finance in Developing Countries*, New York: Oxford University Press.

Baumol, William, and Lee, Kyu Sik (1991), "Contestable markets, trade and development," *World Bank Economic Observer*, 6: 110–23.

Bruckner, Jan K. (1994), "Welfare gains from removing regional land-use distortions," Working Paper, AF1EI, World Bank, Washington, DC.

Development Bank of South Africa (1995), *South Africa's Nine Provinces: A Human Development Profile*, Pretoria.

Fiszbein, Ariel (1995), *Local Government Capacity In Columbia*, Washington, DC: World Bank.

Inman, Robert (1996), "Provincial grants in South Africa," unpublished draft.

McLure, Charles (1994), "Intergovernmental fiscal relations in South Africa," Working Paper, AF1EI, World Bank, Washington, DC.

Rusk, David (1993), *Cities Without Suburbs*, Princeton, NJ: Woodrow Wilson Center Press.

Swilling, Mark, Humphries, Richard, and Subhane, Khehla (1991), *Apartheid City in Transition*, Cape Town: Oxford University Press.

von Hagen, Jurgen (1991), "A note on empirical effectiveness of formal fiscal restraints," *Journal of Public Economics*, 44: 199–210.

Wildasin, David E. (1993), "Local finance of urban infrastructure in South Africa," Working Paper, AF1EI, World Bank, Washington, DC.

(1995), "Financing local government outlays in South Africa," Working Paper, AF1EI, World Bank, Washington, DC.

9

Bosnia-Herzegovina: fiscal federalism – the Dayton challenge

WILLIAM FOX AND CHRISTINE WALLICH

The challenge of fiscal federalism in Bosnia is perhaps unique in the world: the Dayton talks held in October 1995, immediately after the ceasefire, began with a fully blank slate.

- How would the new nation that emerged as a result of the peace talks be structured from a fiscal perspective?
- What would be the role of the central state and what would be that of the two subnational units (the "entities") that constituted it?
- How would the three previously warring communities of Croats, Bosnian Muslims (Bosniacs), and Serbs work together to form a central government, what would the entity governments look like, and what would be the fiscal functions and rights of these entities?
- How would the entities, in turn, be structured internally, and what would be their fiscal governance?

All these questions were open in October 1995, when the international community worked together with experts and political leaders to forge, for Bosnia, a new constitution, and the new intergovernmental fiscal system that would be set out in it. The new system of fiscal federalism should, it was agreed, be able to withstand the stresses that would be a natural consequence of the centrifugal forces still present in the country, be economically sensible, and yet also obtain the consensus of the three parties who would live with it and implement it. The purpose of this chapter is to describe Bosnia's current arrangements in fiscal federalism, to outline the unique challenges that the Dayton system proposed, and to draw some lessons for the design of fiscal federal systems in ethnically diverse economies.

The findings, interpretations, and conclusions expressed in this chapter are entirely those of the authors, and do not necessarily represent the views of the World Bank, its executive directors, or the countries they represent. Very useful comments and assistance were provided by Wei Ding, Sweder van Wijnbergen, Sebnem Akkaya, Luis Alvaro Sánchez, Jennifer Keller, Richard Bird, François Vaillancourt, and Stanley Winer.

The Dayton fiscal and governance challenge

Under the Dayton accords, Bosnia-Herzegovina (hereafter, Bosnia) was established as a single sovereign state composed of two "entities," the Federation (comprising two major ethnic groups, and split between Croat-majority and Bosniac-majority areas) and the Serb Republic (*Republika Srpska*). The Federation has a three-tier fiscal system – the Federation, cantons, and municipalities. While most cantons in the Federation are mono-ethnic, there are two multi-ethnic cantons, and many multi-ethnic municipalities. The Serb Republic is a largely mono-ethnic entity as a result of the war. It has a two-tier structure, consisting of the Republic and the municipalities. Freedom of movement is intended to prevail and the right of return is to be respected under the Dayton agreements.

As a result of the war, the unified fiscal system of the old Republic of Bosnia-Herzegovina was broken up, and until recently there were three totally different fiscal systems in the country – one in the Croat-majority area of the Federation, one in the Bosniac-majority area, and one in the Serb Republic. While all three systems bore the imprint of their Yugoslav origins, the system in the Croat-majority area came, over the course of the four years following Bosnia-Herzegovina's declaration of independence, to be harmonized with that of Croatia, while that of the Serb Republic became harmonized with that of the current Federal Republic of Yugoslavia – Serbia-Montenegro. The Croat and Bosniac systems have now begun to be merged, as new Federation structures are put in place. Customs structures, the tax administration, customs levies, excises, and several other taxes are now largely harmonized. However, the divergence between the Federation and the Serb Republic systems remains significant.

Income and spending differences

There are significant income differences between ethnic groups in Bosnia, and these differences are reflected in income differentials between the different parts of the Federation and between the Federation and the Serb Republic. Recent (1995) estimates suggest per capita incomes of about US $500 in the Bosniac-majority area of the Federation (accounting for 2.5 million of Bosnia's total current population of 3.5 million),[1] about US$1,800 in the Croat areas of the Federation (some 400,000 population), and about US $1,000 in the Serb area – Serb Republic (700,000 population). This disparity in per capita incomes suggests major differences across these areas in terms of tax bases and taxable capacities, and in the absence of equalization policies, in terms of service provision levels.

Even prior to the war, there were differentials in public service levels across the regions in Bosnia. The war, which broke the fiscal structure into three separate systems, has significantly exacerbated spending differences. In the Bosniac-majority area, for example, the pension level was 11.4 Deutschmarks (DM) per month in 1995, while the scheme operating in the Croat-majority area paid pensions of about 65 DM per month. Estimates put the damage from the war at over US $20 billion (World Bank, 1996). However, the destruction of infrastructure and public utilities, as well as of the capital stock in the productive sectors, hit the Bosniac areas the hardest, since industry and most core infrastructure facilities had been strategically located in central Bosnia since the early days of Yugoslavia. The tax bases of the Bosniac-majority area and its ability to generate income have thus been significantly impaired.[2] By contrast, the Croat-majority area's strategic location near the coast enabled this region to control trade into the interior of the country during much of the war, and despite its limited resource endowment, to generate substantial revenues from customs and other trade-related levies. The Serb Republic's economy has been badly damaged by the embargo, and is expected to recover only slowly.

A role for equalizing policies?

These differences in taxable capacities and public service provision levels would suggest, other things being equal, that from both equity and efficiency perspectives, inter-entity (and intra-entity, in the case of the Federation) fiscal equalization policies could have a constructive role to play in the new fiscal system. Such policies would prevent the large differences in access to fiscal resources currently available to the subnational entities and the groups within them from being translated into large differentials in the supply of public services and infrastructure.[3] From both perspectives, one might be especially concerned about those public services with major externalities for the nation as a whole, such as health and education, which are the domain, under the Dayton constitution of the entities (or, in the Federation, the cantons).

Implicit in this view of equity and efficiency is that the relevant domain of concern (McLure, 1994) for efficiency- and equity-focused redistribution policies is the nation as a whole, that is, all of Bosnia. Under such a view, the population of Bosnia sees itself as "Bosnian," instead of as "Croat," "Bosniac," or "Serb," and supports policies that address interregional disparities. On the other hand, if people's primary allegiance is to the national groups within the entities, there will be a more limited view of the domain of concern, and differences in the average incomes of groups within an entity or between entities, or in the average level of public service provision, may not be the predominant concern of these groups.[4]

A strong role for the central state?

The vast challenge of recovering from the destruction of war would also suggest that a strong central government, capable of maintaining macroeconomic stability (see Prud'homme, 1994; Tanzi, 1995), that creates a "common economic area" throughout Bosnia and mobilizes resources for reconstruction through effective budgetary and foreign borrowing policies, could also bring substantial benefit. With the near-complete destruction of the productive sectors' capital stock and a major portion of the country's infrastructure destroyed, effective use of scarce domestic budgetary resources and foreign flows could not be more critical.

However, as this chapter will suggest, the legacy of war, and the legacy of the intergovernmental fiscal system in Yugoslavia, make the hope for a strong central government difficult. The state that has been created out of Dayton, far from being empowered and fiscally robust, is one with no taxing powers of its own, and therefore is dependent totally on the entities for resources via "contributions" to the state budget. Its spending authority is virtually nil. From a macro perspective, its ability to manage a stabilization policy using fiscal instruments is highly constrained. The state's discretionary macroeconomic management tools are limited further by the fact that the central bank is to be run initially as a currency board.[5] With a weak fiscal authority at the center, the potential for regional equalization is also limited. And, after the national elections, the state may not borrow abroad or indebt itself, without the consent of the entities. In a nutshell, Dayton set up a "bottom-heavy" system with most responsibilities and rights in the hands of the entities. Clearly, setting up an intergovernmental system that makes sense, especially in this fraught political context, is a major challenge.

The legacy of Yugoslavia

The legacy of Yugoslavia has significant relevance to the design of Bosnia's intergovernmental fiscal system; some would say that it is the specter that still hangs over the design of such policies. Yugoslavia was always the most decentralized of the socialist economies, both in terms of its economic and fiscal management and its political structures. The republics had significant autonomy from the very beginning, unlike the rest of the socialist world, and the power of the republics was further increased in the 1963 constitution, creating the basis for the emergence of centrifugal forces early on. Tax reforms in 1971 gave greater revenue-raising powers to the republics and local authorities, and the 1974 Constitution transferred many functions to the republics, with "areas of common interest" remaining the responsibility of the state. These included military expenditures, administration, and economic interventions, including support to enterprises.

Yugoslavia's six republics were highly differentiated in income level and culture. Slovenia was by far the most prosperous, with a per capita income in 1990 of US $6,500, with Croatia the next best-off. Bosnia-Herzegovina, Macedonia, and Montenegro were considered the least-developed republics. Bosnia's per capita income in 1990 was only 29 percent of that in Slovenia (and Macedonia's only 22 percent). Further, the level of per capita budget expenditures in these republics reflected these large income differences. In the social sectors, for example, Slovenia's per capita social spending was twice the Yugoslav average, while social spending in Bosnia and in Macedonia was 70 percent of the average (OECD, 1992). These spending differentials were the result, *inter alia*, of different initial endowments and incomes, but equally importantly, of the strong reliance, peculiar to the socialist world, on "derivation-based" systems of revenue-sharing. Most fiscal revenues were nationally "owned" and retained by the areas in which they were collected, so that the socialist revenue systems typically benefited those areas with the more robust tax bases.

Regional redistribution policies: who gained from cross-subsidies?

Addressing the huge regional imbalances in income and expenditures was an early objective of Yugoslav federal policy. Federal support to the republics came through two channels – fiscal and financial. The fiscal channel had several streams. The "Fund for the Development of the Least Developed Regions," established in 1965, introduced explicit support to the less-developed regions in Yugoslavia – Bosnia-Herzegovina, Montenegro, Macedonia, and Kosovo.[6] At its peak, this fund mobilized some 2 percent of Gross Social Product (GSP) from the better-off regions which contributed a fixed proportion of their GSP to the fund.[7] Federal budgetary resources were also directed to raising the level of social outlays in the poorer republics. The financial channel operated through the republic-level commercial banking systems and the central bank,[8] and contributed both to Yugoslavia's hyperinflation and to its external indebtedness.

Many attempts have been made to estimate the overall magnitude and net effects of these fiscal and financial transfers between republics. Vodopivec's (1991) empirical estimate of the net redistribution among republics of all the subsidies and taxes suggests that the three better-off republics (Slovenia, Croatia, and Serbia) were net "taxpayers" and the three less-developed republics (Bosnia-Herzegovina, Macedonia, and Montenegro) were net beneficiaries. Such estimates, however, can only be suggestive at best, given that – as in much of the socialist world – the inter-republic redistributions through the fiscal and financial systems were, in the end, a series of *ad hoc*, bargained, and very non-transparent agreements, whose effects and incentives were not at all well understood, and whose very murkiness gave rise to much dissatisfaction among the republics.

Structural vulnerabilities

The better-off republics' dissatisfaction with federal redistributive policies was compounded by another feature of Yugoslavia's intergovernmental fiscal system – the "bottom-up" system of intergovernmental revenue flows, which Yugoslavia had in common with most other socialist countries, and which still holds in Bosnia today (Bird, Ebel, and Wallich, 1995). This system conferred a very special vulnerability on the federal budget, since all tax revenues were collected at the republic level (or below) and transferred upwards to the federal budget in agreed shares (the federal government received all of the federal sales tax and all import duties). In addition, fiscal "contributions" from the republics, over and above those they made to the federal Fund for the Development of the Least Developed Regions, were negotiated annually, to balance the federal government budget.

The role of fiscal factors in the break-up

There were many reasons for the break-up of Yugoslavia, but it would be incorrect to suggest that fiscal, quasi-fiscal, and redistributional factors played no role. Redistribution policies of this scope were bound to nourish political separatism, as prosperous republics became more and more reluctant to release resources to poorer republics. The lack of transparency in the system made it possible for each republic to argue that it bore the costs of the intergovernmental system, while the benefits accrued to others, so that each thought the others gained at its expense. Woodward (1995) argues, compellingly, that the centralizing budgetary and financial policies designed to give the central government more control over stabilization policy, supported by the international community in the late 1980s, further exacerbated such tensions, since they reduced the budgetary autonomy of the better-off republics and empowered the central government, fiscally and financially, with greater command over resources. The vulnerability conferred by the design of the system itself finally surfaced, as the three most prosperous republics – Slovenia, Croatia, and Serbia – withheld federal tax revenues from the federal budget in 1991. It was with this history that the partners at Dayton began their work.

Some lessons?

What lessons can be drawn from Yugoslavia's break-up for the creation of fiscal federalism in Bosnia? And what lessons might one hope to incorporate into the new structure that emerged from Dayton? There would seem to be several.

First, because of the Yugoslav legacy, the designers at Dayton had to take into account the inherited suspicion of a strong central state and its perceived potential for abusing its power. This limited the role that could be given to national-level taxing powers or centralized spending. Second, the designers found that the notion of "ownership rights" over revenue collected on one's territory was hard to overcome – this was perhaps even more so in the ethnic regions of Bosnia, recently emerging from war, than in Yugoslavia, where territorial claims to revenues were very strong indeed. Third, and related, the designers had to contend with a *prima facie* need for, but apparent virtual intolerance of, fiscal transfers along the lines of the Federal Fund or other cross-subsidies between areas, and sometimes even within multi-ethnic municipalities.

But, even if no other fiscal lesson was learned from the demise of Yugoslavia, the vulnerability of the federal fisc to transfers from below was clear to the designers of the new structure. And yet, the state that emerged had no revenue powers of its own. The vulnerability of the federal fisc to a decentralized tax administration was similarly evident. And yet, the bottom-up system of revenue administration remained. This reflects the fact that the design of Bosnia's new system was driven very strongly by the interests of the entities, whose agreement had to be obtained to the new structure.

The Dayton rules

Under the Constitution, major government budgetary responsibilities are shared among the four levels of government – the state, the entities, the cantons and the municipalities (World Bank, 1996). The state government has exclusive responsibility for foreign and foreign trade policies, customs policies, monetary policy, immigration, refugee and asylum policies, air traffic control, payment of international financial obligations of Bosnia incurred with the consent of both entities, regulation of inter-entity transport, communications, and international and inter-entity law enforcement (but not the raising of an army, which is an entity-level responsibility). All government functions not explicitly assigned by the Constitution to the state are assigned to the entities (though the entities may agree to relinquish some of their responsibilities to the state). The state government has *no* independent tax sources under the Constitution (although the Constitution provides that with the approval of the state parliament, the state may levy its own taxes in the future), and is expected to finance its activities almost entirely from transfers from the two entities. Two-thirds of the state's revenues are to come from the Federation and one-third from the Serb Republic to cover the budget approved by the state parliament.

Under the Federation's constitution (June 1996) the entity governments have a wide range of expenditure responsibilities, including exclusive responsibility in their territories for defense (there are currently three armies: one in the Serb Republic and two in the Federation, one Bosniac and one Croat), internal affairs, police, environmental policies, economic and social sector policies, agriculture, industry, refugees and displaced persons, reconstruction programs, and justice, tax, and customs administration. This constitution provides that some of these functions may be exercised jointly with the cantons, or separately, or by the cantons with coordination by the Federation's government. Thus, the Federation and cantons exercise joint responsibility for health, environmental policy, infrastructure for communication and transport, social welfare, and interior affairs, among others.

The cantons (in the case of the Federation) are responsible for all other matters not granted expressly to the Federation. These include education, culture, housing, public services, local land use, and social transfer expenditures. Each canton is authorized by the Federation's constitution to delegate its responsibilities to the municipalities in its territory.

The municipal governments in the Federation are granted "self-rule on local matters," including all responsibilities delegated to them by the cantons. In the case of municipalities with a majority population that is different from that of the canton as a whole, the canton must delegate *all* responsibilities described in the preceding paragraph to the municipal government.

Municipal governments in the Serb Republic are responsible for all matters not explicitly the responsibility of the entity – and largely parallel the combined responsibility of cantons and municipalities in the Federation.

Can Dayton work?

More appropriately, is the Dayton structure the best for Bosnia, and if not, how should the structure be altered? These are complex questions, particularly since the equity implications associated with government structures, and the particular importance linked to cross-subsidies in Bosnia, make it very difficult to determine what is the best system.

The complicated, multi-level government structure arising from the peace arrangements reflects an ardent aversion to a strong state government that derives from the experience of being part of Yugoslavia. Better-off minority groups are particularly concerned that their rights will not be upheld, and as a result they envision being economically disadvantaged. The fear is that a strong central government would continue the Yugoslavian tradition of cross-subsidies providing greater benefits to the less well-off majority group. The war has further diminished the willingness of some nationalist groups to view Bosnia as a single country and to work for the better of the whole. Creating a government with most expenditure responsibilities and revenue-raising powers at the subnational level was expected to limit the opportunity for transfers to the majority. The paranoia is sufficiently strong that favoritism of the majority is seen behind every program. For example, apprehension exists within the Federation that government-run economic development programs will be designed to support industries that predominate in the majority areas.

The difficulty of creating governments in this environment can be seen in the relationship between the Bosniacs and Croats in structuring the Federation. Croat majority areas favor relatively strong canton governments, while the Bosniac areas favor a relatively strong Federation. The Croats, as the better-off, but minority population, want to continue decentralizing responsibilities to lower levels of government, where ethnicity and incomes are relatively more homogeneous, and therefore opportunities for cross-subsidies are lessened. The Bosniacs argue for service delivery and revenue collection concentrated in the Federation where they might better be able to effect cross-subsidies. Economies of scale seem to indicate that many functions would be better performed at the Federation level given the relatively small geographic area and population size of the cantons. However, the discussions are heavily driven by equity and not efficiency.

It is too early to judge fully the Dayton agreements on the basis of actual events. Still, some general problems can be seen. First, the tax and expenditure assignments are imprecise, leaving the potential for disagreements and requiring difficult political negotiations to reach accords. Even where there is greater precision in the rules, some of the assignments are inefficient and need to be reconsidered. Second, little room is allowed for cross-subsidies to exist anywhere in the structure. This means large inequities can be expected to develop since economic conditions differ widely across the country. Third, most of the government structures appear potentially sustainable, if not efficient. However, the state's roles are very limited, and its funding sources are precarious. As a result, the state's sustainability is in question. Finally, government's share in the economy after the many transitions is still to be determined. The remainder of this section provides a detailed examination of specific issues in the Dayton rules.

Imprecision of expenditure rules

Despite the appearance of clear guidelines on which government is responsible for delivering which services, the Dayton rules are confused and create overlapping responsibilities. Not surprisingly, very different perspectives exist on what the final outcome should be. Overlap occurs when the state is charged with one aspect of service delivery and the entities with another. For example, the state is to do "customs policy" and the entities "customs administration." These assignments leave in question which level is to set tariff rates, which is to determine exemptions, which gets control over the revenues, and a number of other practical issues. Similar overlap occurs at the Federation and canton levels, which are assigned joint responsibility for human rights, health, environmental policy, transportation and communication infrastructure, social welfare policy, immigration and asylum, tourism and natural resources.

Little is said about municipal responsibilities. The relatively centralized structure already in place will remain in the Serb Republic. In the Federation, the issue is which responsibilities are cantonal and which are municipal. Municipalities are granted self-rule and are also permitted to perform functions delegated by the cantons. The probable outcome is a different relative set of duties in each canton, given their geographic and demographic diversity. Differing patterns of responsibility will reflect varying sizes, ethnic compositions, and political strengths in the cantons. No problems should arise from assigning provision to different government levels as long as governments are creative in achieving efficiency in production and tax powers follow expenditure responsibilities.

A series of other specific problems with the expenditure rules can be identified. In some cases there is no clear assignment of functions. Pensions are such an example, though they might be categorized under one of the general functions listed in the Dayton agreements. In other cases, assignments are politically difficult, such as having defense delivered by the Federation. In a third set of cases, the assignments may be economically inefficient; higher education being set as a cantonal rather than a Federation responsibility is such an example.

Expenditure responsibilities being imprecise or being assigned to the wrong level of government does not necessarily mean the assignments will be inefficient, since governments could negotiate efficient arrangements, such as cooperative service delivery. However, the recent history of events in Bosnia make such negotiations particularly difficult, implying that there are likely to be economic inefficiencies over the short to medium term.

Expenditure policy

The war arrested the transition to a market economy and the corresponding relative reduction in the size of the public sector. The war years led to *ad hoc* and very distorted budgeting and expenditure practices in the Bosniac, Croat, and Serb areas. Expenditures were heavily focused on military purposes, with about 45 percent of each entity's budgeted expenditures going for military uses. Data are unavailable on the total extent of military expenditures because large off-budget military purchases and spending financed by foreign governments occurred as well. Budgets for non-military purposes were only provided as necessary and depending on available resources. Expenditures were made essentially on a cash basis. Governments made payments when resources were available, and suspended payments when they were not. Pensions and wages – for military and non-military workers – often went unpaid. Factor payments bore little relationship to market value.

Expenditure rationalization is an important area for reform. The size of the public sector needs to be limited to make room for private sector development, and the structure of public expenditure programs needs to be improved to facilitate growth, while maintaining an acceptable level of social protection. Public expenditures currently represent more than 40 percent of Bosnian GDP, and this is in the context of substantial public sector arrears in wages, pensions, military, and debt service. Reduction of overall public sector expenditures to sustainable levels as a percentage of GDP will require major cuts in many areas of public expense; key areas for reduction are defense, subsidization of the economy, and entitlement programs such as pensions. Pension payments cannot be based on prewar earnings and expectations, and must be scaled back to a level that is consistent with reasonable wage tax rates. (Tax rates are currently in excess of 90 percent on net wages.) A rationalization of public expenditure programs will be required to accompany this process of downsizing the government, as well as to provide better targeting of public expenditure. Highest priority must be given to public expenditures which provide a framework that will allow the private sector to flourish – appropriately selected infrastructure is essential. Subsidization of outdated, unproductive public enterprises must be given the lowest priority.

Great care must be taken to avoid building large administrative structures in the public sector – a potential problem that could be exacerbated by the large number of overlapping governments. Early experience evidences a propensity for cantons to overstaff their central offices with political appointees. For example, Tuzla canton already has over 300 employees performing administrative functions. These practices must be stopped at the canton level and avoided in all governments. Efforts to rationalize salaries for government employees resulted in large percentage salary increases during 1996, expanding the size of the budget for administrative staffs. The raises, mandated by central governments, have placed many cantons and municipalities in the difficult position of having insufficient resources to finance their expected salary payments. As a result, employees in some areas receive raises but do not in others.

Finance and tax administration

The Dayton agreements offer fewer specifics about financing arrangements after 1996 than about expenditures. Three general guidelines are given: the entities and their constituent governments are given responsibility for finance and tax administration; the state is to receive two-thirds of its funding from the Federation and one-third from the Serb Republic; and there is to be a Federation tax administration. All three create significant issues in practice.

Financing of the state

The Constitution indicates that the state is to adopt a budget for the expenditures necessary to finance its responsibilities. No explicit own-source revenues are provided for the state, but the state can generate revenues through charges such as passport fees. Two-thirds of the financing that remains is to be provided by the Federation and one-third by the Serb Republic, a bottom-up arrangement reminiscent of the former Yugoslavia.

The state's sustainability is a concern in this environment where a strong degree of distrust exists. No limitation is placed on state spending, other than that expenditures are to be the ones necessary to finance its responsibilities. The financing structure differs from a conventional grant system, since the recipient is telling the grantor how much to provide. Disagreement between the state and the entities over what are necessary expenditures should be expected, and the entities are likely to balk at times about paying their share. Difficulties with funding of the United Nations may be an appropriate parallel. Tax rates will need to be higher in the Serb Republic than in the Federation to generate the respective revenue contributions because of the greater aggregate population and income in the Federation. As a result, pleas of unfairness can be expected.

The state may be less accountable for spending revenues raised by the entities. Also, variability in revenue flows will be borne solely by the entities, which in principle are unable to reduce contributions to the state to help lessen the effects of unexpectedly low revenues. There are two sides to this coin, since entities do benefit if better than anticipated revenues result.

Federation finance and tax administration
Tax structures, emanating from the Yugoslav tradition, are similar in the two ethnic areas. The Bosnian structure as of November 1995 is given in table 9.1. Ownership of tax revenues, control over tax rates and bases, and tax administration are separable. Division of these, with, say, the Federation administering taxes that are owned by both the Federation and cantons, is normally based on conditions that may not be fully in place. A level of trust must exist, so that the government owning revenues is certain that the administering government will transfer the appropriate amounts in a timely fashion.[9] In some cases, local offices of the Russian State Tax Service are passing resources to the regions and municipalities and giving the Russian Federation government what remains, a pattern that is the Bosnian concern. Cantons fear Federation collection will be to their detriment and the Federation feels the same in reverse.

The owning government must also feel that the administering government will make a faithful effort to collect revenues. Pressures and incentives in the administering government may be such as to focus more of its limited resources on collecting revenues that it can keep, than on taxes going to other governments. Allowing the administering government to retain part of revenues as a collection fee can help, but it still gets more revenue benefits from collecting taxes that it totally retains.

In such a small country, administrative and compliance efficiencies

Table 9.1. *Bosnia-Herzegovina: tax structure, November 1995*

Tax	Type of tax (description)	Rate
Taxes on individuals and corporate profit		
Taxes on individuals	Schedular taxes on certain components of income are supplemented by a further tax on gross personal income exceeding a specified threshold	
Payroll tax	Withheld by employer	10%
Farming tax		5–10%
Self-employment tax		36%
Tax on income from property		Progressive rates depending on the type of income
Tax on total personal income		Progressive rates, scale from 5–50%
Republic reconstruction tax	Base is net wages; withheld by employer	10%
Tax on corporate profit	Tax is paid by enterprises and other legal entities realizing profit, whether or not domiciled in the Republic	36%
Tax on games of chance	Tax paid by individuals	15%
Social security contributions		
Employees		
Old age insurance		17%
Health insurance	The gross wage is the base for payment of the contribution	14%
Unemployment insurance		2%
Employer		
Old age insurance		17%
Health insurance	The gross wage is the base for payment of the contribution	14%
Unemployment insurance		2%
Tax on property		
Tax on real estate transactions	Tax paid by legal entities and individuals at the time of a real estate transaction	15%

Tax	Description	Rate
Gift and inheritance tax	Paid on real estate and personal property over a certain value	0–14.4%
Motor vehicle tax	Tax paid by individuals on vehicles less than five years old and engine size exceeding 1.6 liters	1,500 dinars per year
Boat tax	Paid by individuals on boats exceeding 5 meters in length	900 dinars per year
Sign tax	Paid by legal entities and individuals on a sign displayed	DM 50 to DM 250 annually
Tax on weekend cottages	Paid by individuals on the construction value of the structure	From 0.10–1% on the value of construction
Domestic taxes on goods and services		
Sales tax on products	Tax paid on final consumption, but on alcoholic and non-alcoholic beverages, tobacco products, coffee, petroleum and petroleum products, paid on first sale	5–20%
Sales tax on services	Paid by legal entities and individuals on services subject to the tax	10%
Sales tax surcharge	A general surcharge on goods, levied on the sales-tax inclusive price	10%
Excise taxes		
Tax on petroleum products	Paid by the producer or importer	DM 0.08–0.4 per liter depending on the product
Tobacco tax	Paid by the producer or importer	DM 0.22–2.3 per pack
Beer tax	Paid by the producer or importer	DM 20–30 per hectoliter
Alcoholic beverage tax	Paid by the producer or importer	DM 8–10 per liter of pure alcohol content
Non-alcoholic beverage tax	Paid by the producer or importer	From DM 1–20 per hectoliter
Tax on imported automobiles	Paid by the legal entity or individual on a new imported automobile with a power exceeding 75 kW	DM1 900–8000
Tax on imported coffee	Paid by the legal entity or individual who brings coffee into the Republic	From DM 1–4 per kg
Taxes on international trade		
Import duties		0–21%

Source: International Monetary Fund.

should arise from Federation (or state) control over most tax rates and bases, since uniform rates and bases will be more difficult to achieve with devolved control. However, political incentives can cause Federation officials to make concessions on tax bases where the revenues are owned by the cantons. Granting concessions against another level of government's tax bases offers all of the same political gains but fewer costs because the concession-granting government does not have to face the budgetary consequences of its actions. Tuzla canton has already complained that concessions given by the Federation to reduce the electric company's wage taxes have significantly reduced Tuzla's receipts. Again, willingness to give control to another level of government requires a strong degree of trust, despite the incentives and history creating a perception that the trust would be misplaced.

Separate tax administrations, with offices located in each municipality, are currently operating in the Bosniac and Croat areas. A significant next step in development of the Federation must be creation of a Federation tax administration, as called for in the Dayton agreement. Legislation was passed in 1996 establishing most tax collection at the Federation level, but the tax administration was not operating even in late 1997.

Structural conditions in Bosnia suggest that grants should be an important financing source for cantons and municipalities. One reason is that any assignment of revenue ownership is likely to lead to both vertical and horizontal imbalances because data for estimating expected tax collections are poor and the weak economies in some areas will leave them unable to provide minimum service levels. Some mechanism, presumably operating through a grant system, needs to be in place to smooth financing problems during the interim as assignments are finalized and regional economies rebound. Also, a system of grants could be used to exploit economies of scale in tax collection, enhance equity in revenue distribution, and account for geographic externalities in consumption. However, the very limited tolerance for cross-subsidies between geographic areas suggests that grants must play a small role in overall finance during the near term. Unlike transfers made during the Yugoslavian years, any grants that are introduced must be transparent and rely on objective indicators. A system of grants based on negotiated formulas or *ad hoc* procedures would be particularly inappropriate for Bosnia, given the lingering distrust still prevailing among different groups in society.

Debt policy

The IMF and World Bank require that their lending be to the internationally recognized government, which is the state, but no agreement has been reached on how external debt service is to be financed. The Constitution says that "Each Entity shall provide all necessary assistance to the government of Bosnia and Herzegovina in order to enable it to honor the international obligations."[10] Like many Dayton rules, implementation of this statement is unclear. One possible interpretation is that each entity is to make contributions according to the two-thirds Federation, one-third Serb Republic rule. However, blind adherence to this rule is likely to generate controversy that could lead to one entity refusing to pay its share. Even getting agreement from the entities to borrow through the state has been very difficult. Determining a means for financing debt service is more complicated.

The Dayton agreements allow little flexibility for macroeconomic policy, but the governments may seek to operate at a deficit, both to ease financing problems and to stimulate the economy. Some examples are already apparent. The original 1996 Serb Republic budget assumed a deficit equal to one-third of spending. The 1996 state budget included authorization for borrowing and for letters of guarantee. In practice, the ability to borrow is extremely limited. The *Republika Srpska* budget did not pass when it was recognized that there was no means of financing the deficit. Thus, with the central bank operating as a currency board and a weak banking sector, concerns about deficits may be unimportant in the short term.

Governance during 1996

The Dayton agreements were drafted with expectations that the complete, anticipated government structure would not be operative in 1996. In any event, a transitional period is necessary because time-lines in the agreements were impractical, a difficulty exacerbated by political problems in getting legislative approval for many facets of the agreements.

Revenue assignments in the Federation for 1996 were negotiated between the IMF, the World Bank, and the government. The state was to receive a share of customs tax revenues. The Federation was given access to excise taxes and the share of customs taxes not passed to the state. Other taxes in the Federation were to go to the cantons.

The state has performed minimal operations, in as much as broad-based acceptance of the state's role was hampered in the pre-election period. The presidency was elected on September 14, 1996, but the government was slow to be formed. The state budget was a relatively small DM 61.4 million for 1996, and is mostly used for wages to operate ministries and for the set-up costs of providing diplomatic functions and issuing documents. The state received about 30 percent of customs tax revenues from the

Federation, but there has been considerable controversy over how much it should get. The Serb Republic did not contribute to state finance in 1996.

The Serb Republic government structure was not altered by the agreements, so no transition was necessary. However, the initial budget proposed by the Ministry of Finance was 50 percent above expected revenues. The parliament sent the budget back for adjustment, and the government operated under an interim budget. Spending was limited to available funding during the first three quarters of 1996, and revenues are running about 15 percent below estimates. The Serb Republic had an explicit deficit equal to about 1 percent of GDP in 1995, and a payment to cover some of the 1995 shortfall was included in the 1996 budget. The majority of revenues are collected at the entity level, and shares of the revenue are transferred to finance municipal functions. The municipality of Banja Luka has argued strongly that for political reasons, it is receiving less than its legislated share of taxes.

The Federation has not begun to operate as a fully fledged government. Ministries have been formed and ministers and some staff appointed, but only the Federation's customs bureau is fully operative. A combined payments bureau just began to function at the end of 1996. Most functions are still being performed by the former governments in the Bosniac and Croat majority areas, or by cantons and municipalities. Tax revenues continue to be collected by the former Bosniac and Croat governments, with some of the revenues being transferred to the cantons and municipalities. The Federation began receiving customs and excise tax revenues in May 1996. By the end of September 1996, the Federation had received income of DM 183.9 million and had expended DM 173.4 million. Only DM 13.0 million has gone toward salaries and materials.

All ten cantons had been formed by the time a law establishing their geographic boundaries was passed in June 1996. However, most of the cantons have elected a legislature and president, and are establishing a working framework that includes constitutions. Only the cantons of Tuzla, Zenica, and Bihac can be described as functioning. Organization of these three was well under way before peace, in part because these regions were cut off from Sarajevo during the war and had, *de facto*, to set up their own institutions.

Options for the future

It is difficult to be fully prescriptive about the best government structure for a country where so much change is under way. The complexity of making such prescriptions is exacerbated by Bosnia's recent history, which includes being part of Yugoslavia and participating in the war, and by the various agreements that have already been made. Still, a series of recommendations that would enhance the public sector's operational efficiency can be made.

Shifting functions to the state

A number of functions could be managed much more effectively by the state than at the entity level. The entities would do well to identify where efficiency gains are likely, and to seek agreement to transfer the functions to the state. Examples are the administration of a value-added tax (should one be legislated), enterprise profits taxes, and customs. The entities could assign the functions to the state, but both entities would need to agree. Three conditions need to be in place for delegation to occur: significant efficiency gains must result; transfer must be Pareto-optimal; and there must be reasonable security that the agreements will not be violated.

Nonetheless, political discord, fears that agreements will not be adhered to, and envy could lead the entities to reject efficient delegation.

Coordination between the entities

Open borders that allow the free movement of goods and services and permit the economy to expand are a requirement of the Dayton agreements, but they oblige the entities to cooperate in setting tax administration and policy. For example, a value-added tax cannot be easily imposed at a subnational level without internal borders, but such borders would violate the Dayton agreements. Even a tax or boundary check between the Serb Republic and the Federation would be inconsistent with rapid economic growth, and would create ample opportunity for abuse. One form of abuse would be imposing a recording fee at the checkpoint that could quickly be escalated to become effectively a customs duty. The potential for abuse is equally large in customs administration. Close coordination must substitute for borders to ease administration of these taxes, unless administration is delegated to the state.

Given the open economy (even at the borders with Croatia and Yugoslavia), the tax policy of each entity must also be carefully coordinated with that of the other.[11] Differentials between areas in customs, consumption, and capital tax rates[12] provide significant opportunities for tax avoidance and evasion and will result in concentration of imports, production, and sales in the lowest tax areas.[13] The best way to limit tax competition and the resulting resource migration is for the entities to set tax rates on mobile factors, consumption, and customs which are close to each other. The coordination could be informal, based simply on observing the other entity's tax policies, or more explicit, through negotiations. More efficient tax policy is likely to result from explicit cooperation, but there is currently no mechanism in place through which the dialog can occur.

Size of government

Government must be reduced substantially to a size that is appropriate for facilitating the private sector's operation, providing a sustainable, reasonable safety net, and ensuring delivery of services that are essential to an acceptable quality of life. The multi-layer government structure raises the challenge of attaining a smaller size while achieving public sector goals, but emphasizes the importance of being vigilant in seeking efficiency in government.

In recent years, budget control has been exercised by limiting spending to available revenues, with no expectation that planned expenditures will actually be financed. Budgetary practices need to be rationalized so that expenditures are set to meet appropriate goals, with the expectation that all expenditures, including wages and pensions, normally will be met. Rationalization of spending will require that expenditures for defense, the safety net, and subsidization of the economy be reduced.

In addition, the budget cannot be expanded to accommodate arrears. A number of outstanding claims on Bosnia arise from frozen foreign exchange deposits and unpaid pensions and wages. The total value of these claims is more than DM 13 billion in the Federation, or about ten years of current own-source revenues. Recently, foreign exchange bank books worth nearly DM 5 billion were issued allowing former Republic of Bosnia-Herzegovina soldiers to make explicit claims against the Republic. The recognition of explicit claims on a case-by-case basis must be curtailed, and previous decrees and laws repudiated. It is essential that any settlement of these liabilities should occur using revenues from the sale of assets (such as could arise from housing and enterprise privatization) and that no mechanism for settling liabilities should have implications for the budgets of the state, entities, cantons, or municipalities. Political and equity-based concerns will be the key factors in deciding the relative compensation paid for these claims.[14]

Budgetary savings can be obtained through more efficient operations. First, better delivery mechanisms must be identified. Diseconomies of small scale must be overcome through creative means of consolidating certain functions. The state or inter-entity cooperation should be used wherever significant efficiency gains are possible. Similarly, cantonal or municipal cooperation could allow the scale necessary to deliver certain services efficiently. Healthcare, higher and secondary education, transportation, and environmental services are obvious areas for cooperation. Privatization of service delivery is an option that permits both the benefits of private sector incentives and the capacity to expand the geographic area for service provision.

Second, public sector employment must be scaled down to acceptable levels. In certain circumstances, public employment can be a stopgap for job shortages, but it cannot serve as a long-term strategy for job creation or as the safety net. Public sector employment should be determined by the number necessary to deliver services efficiently. It is essential that current administrative staffs be streamlined, and every service be examined for areas of potential reduction.

Assigning expenditure functions in the Federation

Four criteria are used for recommending the optimal assignment of public functions among the Federation, cantons, and municipalities:

- the potential for economies of scale
- the existence of interregional spillovers
- variation in preferences
- the desire for equalization and tolerance for cross-subsidies.

A recommended assignment of functions within the Federation (in some cases including the state) based on the tradeoffs among these criteria is shown in table 9.2. The Federation should be responsible for areas with mainly Federation-wide impacts. The Federation's constitution has already assigned several functions to the Federation, including defense, federal police, justice, and customs administration. It would be reasonable to assign additional functions to the Federation, including university education, some medical care, intercanton transport, environmental control, and part of social welfare. Cantons and municipalities will have responsibility for many functions including much of healthcare, education, housing, fire protection, and utility services. Despite the substantial responsibilities assigned to cantons and municipalities, Federation expenditures are a significant share of total (see table 9.5).

Agreements should be reached between cantons and their constituent municipalities regarding the specific sharing of responsibilities. The Federation's constitution requires that municipalities that are pre-

Table 9.2. *Recommended assignment of public functions*

Service category	Type of service	Level of government
Healthcare	Primary	Municipality
	Secondary (hospitals, curative)	Canton
	Tertiary (infectious disease, research)	Entity
Education	Primary	Municipality
	Secondary	Canton/municipality
	University	Entity
Transportation	Roads/highways (intracity)	Municipality
	Roads/highways (intercity)	Canton/entity/state
	Airports	Entity
	Public transportation: intracity	Municipality
	Public transportation: intercity	Entity
	Private transportation, taxis	Canton/municipality
	International	State
Environmental	Air/water pollution	Canton
	Water/forestry	Entity/state
Housing	All	Canton
Solid waste, water, sewer, fire	All	Municipality/canton
Land use/zoning	All	Municipality
Licensing/regulation	All	Canton
Cultural policy	All	Canton
Tourism	All	Canton
Social welfare	All	Canton/entity
Telecommunications	All	Entity/state

dominantly composed of a minority population in the canton be permitted to deliver services locally. A key problem is determining the revenues, that otherwise would go to the canton, that are to flow with the expenditures. Minority municipalities must receive a revenue allocation that legitimately allows them to meet their service responsibilities, without creating unreasonable fiscal strain on local citizens. Careful design of the revenue arrangements is important because ethnic problems often arise locally, yet can frequently be solved if much of the power for decision-making is local (Tishkov, 1993). Cantons could devise transfer schemes that would make it very difficult for minority municipalities to finance service delivery, which could lead to strong disagreements.

Tax assignment in the Federation

As a rule, canton and municipal revenues should be based on a combination of assigned revenue instruments and grants, with the goal of ensuring vertical balance. This means that each level of government would have sufficient revenue capacity to fund the services for which it is responsible. Furthermore, tax and grant assignments must be made with an eye not only on the funding of current service levels but also on future service needs. That is, revenue buoyancy must be carefully considered when assignments are made. Each level of government – the Federation, cantons, and municipalities – must have sufficiently buoyant revenue sources to provide the amounts needed to pay for the delivery of services over time.

As noted above, it is important to differentiate among the separate steps of the taxation process when making tax assignments. These steps include tax administration, definition of tax bases, setting of tax rates, and tax ownership. The level of government in charge of collecting a tax need not be the one that defined the tax base, set the tax rate, or owns the tax revenues. Locally owned taxes (cantonal or municipal taxes) need not be locally administered, and federally imposed and collected taxes can be – and in other countries often are – shared with other levels. Alternatively, taxes could be collected at the canton level and shared with the Federation. In fact, it is recommended that for the most important taxes, the definition of the tax base and possibly the setting of the tax rate be done at the Federation (and ultimately the state) level, while allowing cantons and municipalities some flexibility over revenue instruments. Economic integration, tax compliance, and tax administration would be greatly enhanced by nationally uniform bases and rates for customs, excise, corporate and personal income taxes, and sales or value-added taxes. However, cantons must be protected from the Federation exempting taxpayers or narrowing the base for taxes where the Federation has little or no revenues at stake. A proposed set of assignments for the Federation is in table 9.3.

Three criteria must be considered in determining the appropriate tax ownership assignments. First, tax assignment must bear a strong correspondence to the expenditure responsibilities of each government level to ensure that adequate financing is available to deliver required services. A perfect relationship between expenditure responsibilities and tax revenue ownership is not required (and probably is not desirable) because grants can be made from a government that owns revenues to assist another government in financing its expenditure responsibilities. Second, tax assignment must not violate the Constitution, the Dayton agreements, and other international agreements. Third, tax ownership must be consistent with the administrative ability to measure where the taxable activity occurs, if revenues are to be distributed on a sites-of-collection basis. For example, ownership of customs taxes based on

Table 9.3. *Summary of suggested tax assignments*

Tax type	Tax administration	Tax base	Tax rate	Revenue ownership
Customs	Federal or state	Federal or state	Federal or state	Federation and state
Excises	Federal	Federal legislation	Federal legislation; surcharges set by cantonal or municipal assemblies	Federation; cantons or municipalities may impose retail level taxes
Wage and personal income	Federal or canton	Federal legislation	Basic rate set by the Federal legislation; surcharges set at the cantonal level	Shared by the Federation, cantons, and municipalities
Corporate income	Federal	Federal legislation	Federal legislation	Federation
Sales tax (retail level)	Federal; feasible but complicated at the cantonal level	Federal legislation	Rates to be set by Federal legislation; surcharges can be set by cantons	Federation, cantons and municipalities
Property tax	Municipal	Federal legislative framework	Municipal level	Municipal level
Real estate transfers	Municipal	Federal legislative background	Municipal assemblies	Municipal level
Motor vehicles	Municipal	Federal legislative framework	Cantonal level	Cantons and municipalities
Social security contributions	Federal	Federal legislation	Federal legislation	Funds
User fees, social services	Service-providing agencies	Cantonal legislation	Cantonal or municipal providers	Service-providing agencies
User fees, utilities	Service supply companies	Regulatory frameworks	Service-providing companies subject to regulatory oversight	Service-providing companies
VAT	Federal	Federal legislation	Rates to be set by Federal legislation	Shared between the Federation and the cantons

Note: In this table, tax assignments are suggested between the state and the Federation's government. Similar tax assignments between the state and the Serb Republic entity could be suggested.

Table 9.4. *Tax revenue assignments for the Federation, 1997 (percentages)*

Revenues	State	Federation	Cantons	Total
Customs duties	7.4	92.6	0.0	100.0
Excise and special import duties	0.0	100.0	0.0	100.0
Wage and income taxes	0.0	50.0	50.0	100.0
Profits tax	0.0	50.0	50.0	100.0
Sales tax	0.0	0.0	100.0	100.0
Other taxes	0.0	0.0	100.0	100.0
Total revenues	1.3	40.0	58.7	100.0

Table 9.5. *Tax revenue distribution for Bosnia, 1997 (million DM)*

	State	Serb Republic	Federation	Cantons	Total
Revenues					
Customs duties	25.0	39.7	208.3	0.0	273.0
Excise and special import taxes	0.0	0.0	225.0	0.0	225.0
Wage and income taxes	0.0	60.0	20.0	20.0	100.0
Profits tax	0.0	0.0	70.0	70.0	140.0
Sales tax	0.0	78.0	0.0	500.0	578.0
Other taxes and fees	15.0	21.0	0.0	179.0	215.0
Total revenues	40.0	198.7	523.3	769.0	1 531.0
Expenditures					
Expenditures (except army, social programs and debt service)	40.0	116.7	163.3	769.0	1 089.0
Expenditures: army, social programs and debt service	0.0	82.0	360.0	0.0	442.0
Total expenditures	40.0	198.7	523.3	769.0	1 531.0

Note: The Federation and Serb Republic data do not include special funds for healthcare, unemployment, and pensions. The Serb Republic data do not include municipal revenues.

where the imports are consumed is administratively impractical at the municipal or canton level.

The Federation needs to take a number of important steps before tax ownership can be determined precisely and implemented effectively. Expenditure assignments must be structured before final tax assignments can be made. Also, the full set of Federation tax laws need to be enacted and enforced. A mix of laws from the Federation and the old Croat and Bosniac areas is currently being enforced on the Federation side.

Tax assignments that would result in vertical balance, given expected 1997 expenditure assignments, were estimated (tables 9.4 and 9.5).[15] The assignments assume that no intergovernmental transfers occur, other than those implicit in the assignments. The state needs to receive 7.4 percent of Federation and 17.3 percent of Serb Republic customs tax revenues to finance its expenditures. The difference in shares illustrates the effect of having one-third of the state financed by the Serb Republic and the other two-thirds financed by the Federation. No other detail was estimated for the Serb Republic.

In the Federation, the remainder of customs taxes, and excise, special import and enterprise profits taxes are assigned to the Federation. Wage, income, and profits taxes are assumed to be split evenly between the Federation and the cantons.[16] The cantons and municipalities receive the range of smaller taxes including the real estate, judicial and advertising taxes.

The revenue assignments were proposed in order to create vertical balance in the system, but several important cautions should be noted. First, the assignments will allow horizontal imbalances at the canton and municipal levels. Estimates suggest several cantons would have significant deficits, arising from both the expenditure and revenue sides. Revenues are constrained in some areas because of very weak economies and expenditure needs are larger in some places than others. Second, the expenditure assignments used here are similar to those in place for 1996, except most spending for health, education, and police services is passed to the cantons. Changes in the expenditure assignments will necessitate changes in revenue assignments. Third, very minimal grants from the Federation to the cantons are allowed for in the financing scheme. Own-source revenues should be the major financing source because of accountability, concerns about cross-subsidies, and differences in service demands, and for other reasons. Still, a greater role for grants exists, and development of a transfer system would require additional tax assignment to the Federation. Finally, the assignments fail to recognize differences in revenue buoyancy, and will have to be altered over time if expenditures grow at different rates from revenues. Subnational governments are often assigned taxes with low buoyancy. However, more than 60 percent of the revenues assigned here are from the relatively buoyant sales and wage taxes.

Most taxes, including the corporate and personal income, excise, customs, and value-added taxes would be best administered at the entity level, and in several cases at the state level. A limited number of revenue sources, such as the property tax and user fees, could be administered at the subentity level. Taxes are administered at the entity level in the Serb Republic and legislation has been passed for administration at the Federation level as well. Advantages in terms of lower operational costs, coordination of administration, and uniform practices all argue strongly in favor of the Federation. The key is to design an administrative and revenue distribution system that safeguards the cantons and municipalities so that they will be willing to accept Federation administration.

Conclusion

Progress in developing the governments in Bosnia has been slower than was envisioned when the Dayton agreements were penned. This is not surprising since there is little or no world experience of developing governments in the short period of time assumed in the agreements. There are positive signals in Bosnia, such as a number of government institutions becoming operative and revenues being passed to both the state and the Federation. Still, the challenge of achieving fully operational governments remains.

Traditional economic models of federalism, like that on which this chapter's analysis is based, suggest a government structure assuming there is an intent to achieve Pareto efficiency for the entire country. Current attitudes in Bosnia suggest that many people in each ethnic group see themselves as members of their group, rather than as Bosnians, and are not broadly concerned about the welfare of the whole country or access to public services outside their group. The motivation for the fiscal federalism structure proposed in the Dayton agreements is better interpreted as an effort to manage conflict between the ethnic groups. Federalism in a conflict management sense does not require that each group be given its own state, but does lead to the conclusion that institutions of power should be brought closer to people so that decision-making can be more sensitive to the different ethnic groups (Tishkov, 1993). Decentralization in this context is a means to lessen the points where disagreement exists, rather than a structure to obtain economic efficiency. Common institutions at the state, entity or canton levels are maintained, but only for functions that must be broader in scope. The fiscal (and other) interdependencies from common institutions at the state, entity, and canton levels provide opportunities to build relationships and trust over time.

The government structure included in Dayton is workable. However, unless governments negotiate other arrangements, the likely outcome in the short to medium term is diseconomies of scale in provision of certain services, as some that can be provided at lower unit costs at the state level are provided at the entity level, and some with lower unit costs at the entity level are delivered at the canton or municipal level. Services with geographic spillovers will be underprovided because governments will fail to account adequately for the benefits received by members of other ethnic groups. Further, little consideration will be afforded to equity among groups, resulting in widely different access to services across the country. Better service delivery mechanisms from a national, Pareto-efficient perspective will not be selected given the very strong distaste for cross-subsidies and the fear by minority groups that they will be dominated by a larger group. More efficient arrangements can be expected to evolve over time as confidence in the government structure grows.

Horizontal imbalances will be large in the Federation, and grants will be used to a very limited extent to offset these imbalances. The resulting problems will be lessened in the next several years to the extent that the former Bosniac or Croat governments are able to provide some resources to the more financially deprived areas, or the donors help fund infrastructure and other needs. But donors will not finance operating expenditures, and maintenance of new infrastructure investments will place greater demands on limited budgets, so financial problems in the places least able to pay could grow. Economic growth that increases revenue-raising capacities across Bosnia is one approach to offsetting imbalances. Also, differences in access to services could be lessened with a system that allocates more grants to places with the greatest expenditure needs and with the least revenue capacity.

Notes

1 Bosnia's prewar population was 4.5 million, of which some 3 million have had to leave their towns and villages, with 1 million estimated to be refugees abroad, mostly in Western Europe. Another 250,000 people are dead or missing.

2 It could be argued that the concentration of industrial conglomerates, made non-viable because of transition shocks in Bosniac-majority areas, would have led to some decline in the tax bases of this area even without the war.

3 In the short term, this is expected to be donor-financed, but as the economy recovers, a domestic contribution to infrastructure finance is anticipated.

4 McLure (1994) has made these observations about the service provision differentials in the Russian Federation and the issue of whether natural resource revenues "belong" to all Russians, or to the territories (*oblasts*) in which they are located. The same observations about preferences and tolerances for redistribution also apply to Bosnia.

5 There will be a one-time opportunity to issue currency when the currency board is established, from which the state may accumulate seignorage revenue. However, the revenue is expected to be limited, and cannot be relied upon as a continuing revenue source. While the possibility of seignorage revenue is removed by the establishment of a currency board, the state may earn some revenue through interest earnings on foreign exchange reserves. In the interim

and until a new currency is in place, the seignorage from the circulation of the Deutschmark in the country accrues to the Bundesbank in Germany (and of the kuna to the Croatian Central Bank).

6 Kosovo along with Voivodina, which is largely Hungarian-populated, is now a dependent province within Serbia-Montenegro.

7 78 percent of Federal Fund resources were mobilized from the three better-off republics in the 1970s, falling to 75 percent in the 1980s (Federal Statistical Office of Yugoslavia). Gross Social Product may be thought of, very roughly, as equivalent to the more familiar GDP or GNP measures.

8 The financial channel was effected in two ways. First, commercial banks in each republic could supplement their deposit resources by borrowing from their republic branch of the National Bank of Yugoslavia. Empirical studies suggest that the central bank did play a role in the regional allocation of credit through this mechanism, although it is difficult to get a consistent picture of who were the gainers and who were the losers (World Bank, 1989). Second, the commercial banks in each republic met the financial losses of enterprises which amounted to 5–6 percent of GSP in the latter part of the 1980s. The inflation this process gave rise to was felt by all, but the "benefits" of the system (financing of losses) were concentrated in Bosnia-Herzegovina, Croatia, and Serbia (World Bank, 1989).

9 The peculiar Yugoslav institution, the SDK, (the Social Accounting Office), which exists in a somewhat truncated form in Bosnia today, makes it possible to pinpoint closely where consumption, employment, and production take place and where taxes should be collected. So far this system has been inadequate for generating confidence in the governments getting their appropriate shares.

10 Constitution of Bosnia and Herzegovina, Annex 4, Article III, Section 2(b).

11 Coordination between the Serb Republic and Yugoslavia and between the Federation and Croatia is already well under way.

12 The Dayton agreements can be interpreted as requiring common customs tax rates, but the entities are free to set the other tax rates.

13 Labor migration in response to tax differentials is not a significant issue in the current environment, given the lack of freedom of movement between entities.

14 These claims do not include the international debt of Bosnia.

15 Revenues and expenditures were estimated separately. Expenditure requirements were based on budgeted and actual 1996 expenditures and assumed growth rates for the state and Federation. Additional transfers to the state are necessary if the state is to remit debt amortization payments. Canton and municipal expenditures were estimated using actual 1995 expenditures for the various services, and assumed growth rates. Revenue estimates for 1997 are based on actual collections in 1995, the first nine months of 1996, and assumed growth rates. No attempt is made to estimate the separate revenues of municipalities and cantons in the Federation. Defense, social programs, and debt service are used to balance expenditures and revenues and do not include off-budget expenditures.

16 The split wage tax could be designed as a piggybacked wage tax, as has been proposed by the IMF.

References

Bird, Richard M., Ebel, Robert D., and Wallich, Christine I., eds. (1995), *Decentralization of the Socialist State: Intergovernmental Finance in Transition Economies*, Washington, DC: World Bank.

Ding, Wei (1991), "Costs and benefits of union and interdependence of regional economies," Unpublished paper, World Bank, Washington, DC.

Farsad, Mansour (1991), "Yugoslavia: economic integration and viability of a breakup," draft Working Paper, Eastern Europe Department, World Bank, Washington, DC.

Federal Statistics Office of Yugoslavia, *Yugoslavia*, annual.

McLure, Charles E., Jr. (1994), "The sharing of taxes on natural resources and the future of the Russian Federation," in Christine I. Wallich, ed., *Russia and the Challenge of Fiscal Federalism*, Washington, DC: World Bank.

OECD (1992), "Regional developments and developments in the republics of Yugoslavia," March: 36.

Prud'homme, Rémy (1994), "On the dangers of decentralization," Policy Research Working Paper No. 1252, World Bank, Washington, DC.

Tanzi, Vito (1995), "Fiscal federalism and decentralization: a review of some efficiency and macroeconomic aspects," in Michael Bruno and Boris Pleskovic, eds., *Annual World Bank Conference on Development Economics*, Washington, DC: World Bank.

Tishkov, Valery A. (1993), "Nationalities and conflicting ethnicity in post-communist Russia," Working Paper series, Conflict Management Group, Harvard Law School, Cambridge, MA.

Vodopivec, Milan (1991), "Redistribution through the soft budget constraint," World Bank (October).

Woodward, Susan (1995), *Balkan Tragedy*, Washington DC: Brookings Institution.

World Bank (1989), "Yugoslavia: financial sector restructuring: policies and priorities," Report No. 7869-YU, World Bank, Washington, DC (November).

    (1996), *Bosnia and Herzegovina: Toward Economic Recovery*, World Bank Country Study, Washington, DC: World Bank.

Index